REGIS ST LOUIS

RIO DE JANEIRO

CITY GUIDE

INTRODUCING RIO DE JANEIRO

Pão de Açúcar (Sugarloaf; p79) is one of Rio's dazzling icons

JOHN PENNOCK

Rio de Janeiro stretches between beach and mountain, with colonial neighborhoods, modernist style and that addictive sound that ties it all together: samba. Welcome to the *Cidade Maravilhosa* (marvelous city).

Once the adopted home of the Portuguese crown, Rio has long entranced visitors. Magnificent festivals such as Carnaval and Reveillon (New Year's Eve) are renowned, but the city has plenty of other occasions for revelry – weekend samba parties in Lapa, celebrations at a Flamengo football match, and impromptu music jams at sidewalk cafés in Leblon, Centro or any other corner of town.

Music is the lifeblood of Rio, with a soundtrack that begins with samba and encompasses old-school bossa nova, hip-hop, funk and Brazil's many regional styles. Catch the beat at open-air bars, old-fashioned dance halls or hypermodern nightclubs and lounges.

The setting is another reason why visitors fall hard for Rio. Rain forest still covers large swaths of the metropolitan area, while the city's dramatic mountains and white-sand beaches weave together one of the world's most striking urban landscapes. On sunny days, Cariocas (residents of Rio) head outdoors to cycle the shoreline, surf the waves, sail on Baía de Guanabara, hike the forests of Tijuca or rock-climb the face of Pão de Açúcar.

The Rio experience is about many things, from watching the sunset over Arpoador to dancing to live samba at an antique-filled bar in Centro. It's people-watching in Ipanema, seafood feasts overlooking Lagoa, and coming face-to-face with that spirit of spontaneity and joy seemingly found around every corner of this dynamic tropical city.

RIO DE JANEIRO LIFE

Life happens out-of-doors in Rio. Drawn outside by sunshine (and cramped apartments), Cariocas find love, conflict and all the other varieties of human experience on the streets and beaches of town. Its big festivals are almost entirely outdoor events, while an afternoon at the beach, followed by a night of open-air eating, drinking and merry-making, are the preferred ways to spend a day.

Not surprisingly, gossip travels fast in this community. At cafés and juice bars, Cariocas swap the latest rumors. Political scandals often hog the headlines. Like many other countries, the media leans toward sensationalism, and splashy stories get much play. Celebrities tend to come crashing into the headlines. Hot topics here are who's cheating on whom, which Hollywood playboy was frolicking with you-know-who on Ipanema Beach and which Brazilian actress is doing nude magazine spreads this week. Occasionally, international stars – who tend to appear in small flocks during Carnaval – also become part of the talk of the town.

Crime, poverty and the gulf between rich and poor are other subjects that, if not mentioned, usually lurk in the subtext of news stories. Rio is a city divided into haves and have-nots. At one end are the million-odd Cariocas living at or below the poverty line, many in favelas (shanty towns), while at the other extreme are the rich living in luxury high-rises, with a maid and driver. The dividing line is often little more than a highway. While the chasm is wide, positive changes are underway. According to a report by the UN, more than 10 million Brazilians have risen above the poverty line since 2000. During the last decade, Rio (along with the federal government) has invested millions in infrastructure projects in the favelas, in attempts to raise living standards. The ongoing favela 'pacification' program has also made a handful of well-known favelas safer than they've been in years – decision-making and the future of the community belongs to local residents not to the drug lords who once called all the shots.

Whether they're rich or poor, there are some important ways in which the city comes together. The hundreds of roving Carnaval block parties often draw a diverse mix of folks who share nothing but the love of a wild celebration. The beaches of Rio, free and open to all, also host a democratic mix. Surfers, kids from the favelas, models, pensioners, hippies, yuppies, straights, gays, the slender and portly all share Ipanema Beach as the sun shines on the *Cidade Maravilhosa.*

RICARDO GOMES

Dancing in the streets at Carnaval (p50)

HIGHLIGHTS

RICARDO GOMES

IPANEMA & LEBLON

Ipanema and Leblon have it all: beautiful beaches, great restaurants and bars, and elegant boutiques that can quickly drain your wallet. Bossa nova was born here, and there's still plenty of soul in these vibrant, tree-lined streets.

RICARDO GOMES

JOHN MAIER JR

JOHN MAIER JR

❶ Ponta do Arpoador
This rocky outcropping is one of the best vantage points in Rio for watching the sunset (p63)

❷ Zazá Bistrô Tropical
Join the beautiful crowd over fusion fare at this handsome restaurant (p131)

❸ Ipanema Beach
Stroll, surf, sunbathe or simply people-watch (p63)

❹ Banda de Ipanema
Join the rabble-rousers at this colorful Carnaval parade (p52)

❺ Baretto-Londra
Rio's A-list bar since its opening in 2007, with an interior designed by Philippe Starck (p152)

❻ Osklen
Get an eyeful of the latest fashions at this stylish boutique (p113)

❼ Cafeína
A good place to take in the scene on this ever-lively street (p133)

JOHN MAIER JR

JOHN MAIER JR

JOHN MAIER JR

GÁVEA, JARDIM BOTÂNICO & LAGOA

Just inland from Rio's picturesque saltwater lagoon, these upscale neighborhoods have a great dining and drinking scene, plus botanical gardens and a planetarium. Lakeside attractions include outdoor restaurants along the shoreline and a running and cycling track.

JUDY BELLAH

JOHN MAIER JR

3

RICARDO GOMES

JOHN PENNOCK

❶ Helicopter Tour
Depart from the lake's helipad for a magnificent view over Rio (p226)

❷ Palaphita Kitch
A splendid Polynesian-style bar that's ideal for a sundowner (p153)

❸ Lagoa Rodrigo de Freitas
A great spot for a morning jog or cycle (p71)

❹ Jardim Botânico
The botanical garden is a verdant refuge from big-city bustle (p70)

❺ 00 (Zero Zero)
Inside the planetarium, this nightspot has one of Rio's best dance floors (p166)

❻ Baixo Gávea
Join the people parade at one of Rio's many bustling bars (p152)

JOHN MAIER JR

JOHN MAIER JR

MAURO SPEZIALE/GETTY

COPACABANA & LEME

Once a Brazilian icon, Copacabana is a diverse neighborhood with a marvelous beach and plenty of hidden gems among its high-rises, including live-music venues, edgy dance clubs and top-notch restaurants. Tiny Leme, with its quiet beaches and sleepy streets, feels more town than big-city suburb.

RICARDO GOMES

❶ Beachside Kiosks
Copacabana's sparkling new kiosks offer a fine setting for a drink or a bite without leaving the sands (p137)

❷ Morro do Leme
A peaceful vantage point for checking out divers and fishers (p74)

❸ Copacabana Beach
One of Rio's icons, this long, scalloped beach is truly magnificent (p75)

❹ Allegro Bistrô Musical
Browse for new music inside Modern Sound (p118) or catch nightly concerts at the adjoining café (p160)

❺ Posto dos Pescadores
Fishermen still head out from the post at Copacabana's southern end (p73)

❻ Produce Markets
Sample the tastes of Brazil at one of Rio's many enticing farmers markets (p122)

❼ Copacabana Palace
Dine or overnight in elegance at this symbol of Rio's golden age (p191)

JUDY BELLAH

JOHN MAIER JR

RICARDO GOMES

JOHN MAIER JR

JOHN MAIER JR

RICARDO GOMES

LEE FOSTER

BOTAFOGO & URCA

Botafogo is a traditional neighborhood with some intriguing museums, a lively boteco *(neighborhood bar) scene and several bohemian nightclubs. Urca is famed for Pão de Açúcar (Sugarloaf) soaring over its tree-lined streets; it's also an idyllic neighborhood for wandering.*

JOHN PENNOCK

1 Urca's Seawall
One of the many tranquil spots in Urca for enjoying the view (p80)

2 Pão de Açúcar
For an adrenaline rush, climb to the top of the famous peak (p79)

3 Praia do Botafogo
For sunset views, go to Botafogo's picturesque inlet (p78)

4 Praia Vermelha
A jewel-box-sized beach with a marvelous panorama (p80)

JOHN MAIER JR

FLAMENGO, LARANJEIRAS & COSME VELHO

The major attraction here is Rio's most recognizable symbol, Cristo Redentor (Christ the Redeemer). In addition to the open-armed savior, you'll find the long Parque do Flamengo set with sports fields and museums, and there's some great exploring among the shady streets.

❶ Cristo Redentor
Gaze out over the city from the Savior's lofty perch (p85)

❷ Belmonte
Have a drink, make a friend inside one of Rio's all-time favorite *botecos* (p155)

❸ Casa Rosa
Head to the Sunday samba parties here for great music and a fun crowd (p162)

❹ Parque do Flamengo
Spend time exploring one of the world's largest urban parks (p83)

1

RICARDO GOMES

3

RICARDO GOMES

2

JOHN MAIER JR

4

JOHN PENNOCK

RICARDO GOMES

1 Museu de Arte Moderna
Superb exhibits inside Rio's green Parque do Flamengo (p83)

2 Confeitaria Colombo
This ornate 1800s café makes a fine setting for a heavenly *pastel de nata* (custard tart; p144)

3 Theatro Municipal
One of many striking buildings in downtown Rio, home to some great performances (p94)

4 Igreja de Nossa Senhora de Candelária
Pray for good weather at this baroque church (p89)

5 Centro Cultural Banco do Brasil
Home to some of Rio's best exhibitions (p89)

6 Museu Histórico Nacional
History is everywhere in Centro, with key relics preserved in this former royal armory (p89)

7 Travessa do Comércio
Join Cariocas (residents of Rio) for a happy-hour drink on this narrow colonial lane (p94)

CENTRO & CINELÂNDIA

Rio's bustling commercial center is a medley of office towers and historic colonial buildings, with baroque churches, a photogenic opera house, lively plazas and the city's best museums. Narrow pedestrian streets crisscross Centro, many of which fill with drinkers and diners when the day's work is done.

KRZYSZTOF DYDYNSKI

JOHN MAIER JR

JOHN PENNOCK

RICARDO GOMES

JOHN MAIER JR

JOHN MAIER JR

1

JOHN MAIER JR

SANTA TERESA & LAPA

Bohemian Rio thrives at these edgy arts centers. Old-fashioned dance halls pack the streets of Lapa, with the rhythmic sound of samba spilling out of doorways. High up on the hill, Santa Teresa has lovely mansions where artists, intellectuals and Rio's free spirits hold court.

JOHN MAIER JR

RICARDO GOMES

RICARDO GOMES

RICARDO GOMES

JOHN MAIER JR

❶ Arcos da Lapa
The former viaduct is now the backdrop to Lapa's incredible music scene (p100)

❷ Antique Stores
Along Rua do Lavradio, this is one of numerous shops on Rio's antique row (p121)

❸ Bonde
The best way up to Santa Teresa is on this old-fashioned tram (p97)

❹ Parque das Ruínas
There are great views from many spots in Santa Teresa, including the ruins of a former mansion (p99)

❺ B&Bs
For the inside scoop on Santa Teresa, stay in the colonial house of a local (p196)

❻ Bar do Mineiro
This neighborhood classic serves tasty home-cooked meals and strong caipirinhas (cane-liquor cocktails; p146)

❼ Democráticus
An old-time samba club with a heart of gold (p163)

JOHN MAIER JR

RICARDO GOMES

GREATER RIO

Rio's outer regions have some highly recommended sights, including a national park with protected rain forest, a car-free island and dozens of serene beaches that get wilder as you get further out of town. Other adventures include sailing trips and boat parties on the bay and joining the revelry at the Feira Nordestina.

CARO/ALAMY

1 Museu do Arte Contemporânea
Oscar Niemeyer's whimsical museum has stunning views (p104)

2 Ilha de Paquetá
This easy-to-reach island in the bay provides an idyllic escape from the city (p103)

3 Rocinha
Support the community by buying handicrafts directly from the source (p49)

4 Sítio Burle Marx
A verdant wonderland, the house and gardens on this lush estate warrant the trip (p106)

JOHN MAIER JR

RICARDO GOMES

CONTENTS

THE AUTHOR

Regis St Louis

Regis' longtime admiration for the *Cidade Maravilhosa* (marvelous city) has led to his deep involvement with the country, both as a traveler and as a writer. The city's vibrant music scene, its colorful *botecos* (neighborhood bars) and samba clubs, and the alluring energy of the Cariocas (residents of Rio) are just a few of the reasons why he's returned so often over the past 10 years. Regis speaks both Portuguese and Spanish, and his articles on Brazil and Latin America have appeared in the *Chicago Tribune*, the *LA Times* and the *San Francisco Chronicle*, among other publications. He is also the coordinating author of Lonely Planet's *Brazil* guide and *South America on a Shoestring*. He splits his time between New York City and the tropics.

REGIS' TOP RIO DAY

Since this is my ideal day, the sun is shining when I rise and it's still early as I step outside. I decide to go for a long stroll along Copacabana beach, pausing for *agua de coco* (coconut water) at one of the sparkling new kiosks (p137) along the sands. Afterwards, I grab an *açaí* – the world's most delicious (non-alcoholic) beverage – at the nearest juice bar, take a look at *O Globo* newspaper and contemplate the day ahead. As there's an exhibition I'm eager to see at the Centro Cultural Banco do Brasil (p89), I decide to take the metro up to Centro. Afterwards, I'll grab a coffee and a snack at Brasserie Rosário (p144), and have a browse at the books and music before strolling over to the bay-fronting Restaurante Albamar (p143) for some fresh seafood. Over lunch, I'll take a look at my walking tour of Centro (p95) and see if I can find some new places to add. Happily fed, I take a stroll west through the pedestrian streets, stopping at shops and taking in the street scene before ultimately making my way to the music vendors who make up the small open-air Feira de Música (p112) on Rua Pedro Lessa. I'll buy a few albums then catch the *bonde* (tram) up to Santa Teresa. There I'll stop in on a few friends, grab an afternoon drink at Cafecito (p147) or at the Bar dos Descasados (p157) and make plans for the evening. If I'm lucky, a friend will call and invite me to the opening of a new samba club in Lapa; otherwise, I'll consider my options and go either to Semente (p164) if today is a Monday, Democráticus (p163) if it's Thursday or Beco do Rato (p161) if it's Friday. Afterwards, I'll taxi down to Ipanema for a final drink at Devassa (p151).

LONELY PLANET AUTHORS

Why is our travel information the best in the world? It's simple: our authors are passionate, dedicated travelers. They don't take freebies in exchange for positive coverage so you can be sure the advice you're given is impartial. They travel widely to all the popular spots, and off the beaten track. They don't research using just the internet or phone. They discover new places not included in any other guidebook. They personally visit thousands of hotels, restaurants, palaces, trails, galleries, temples and more. They speak with dozens of locals every day to make sure you get the kind of insider knowledge only a local could tell you. They take pride in getting all the details right, and in telling it how it is. Think you can do it? Find out how at **lonelyplanet.com**.

GETTING STARTED

Before dashing off to Brazil, find out whether you need a visa. Many nationalities require them, including citizens from the US, Canada and Australia. See p228 for more details.

If you plan to visit during the high season, it's wise to book accommodations at least two or three months in advance. For Carnaval or Reveillon (New Year's Eve), it's never too early to start planning, with some hotels filling up six months in advance.

Aside from accommodations, Rio is an easygoing place, and you can reserve most other things (tours, outdoor activities, tables at top restaurants) after your arrival.

Money is, of course, the other major consideration – and no small one, given the ongoing surge of the Brazilian *real* in recent years. In general, prices for most things are about the same as in cities in North America and Western Europe, with ample options for both budget travelers and visitors on generous expense accounts.

WHEN TO GO

There is never really a bad time to visit Rio, but whether you want to party like a rock star or escape the masses may help in deciding when to go. Rio's high season coincides with the Brazilian summer, running from December to March. This is when the country fills with both foreign visitors and vacationing Brazilian families. Hotel-room prices are about 30% higher at this time and you'll face more crowds, though this is also the most festive time in Rio. The low season runs from May to September; if you're looking to beat the crowds and don't mind cooler weather, this is a fine time to visit.

If you plan any side trips, be mindful that Búzios, Paraty, Ilha Grande and other nearby destinations get packed on summer weekends. You'll have more luck going mid-week.

Rio lies just inside the tropics, with rainfall and humidity playing no small part in the city's seasons. Though it rains all year, in winter, blue skies and mild weather are the norm.

Summer days are warm to hot (see p220), and sometimes the humidity can be downright stifling – though nights often bring a welcome respite from the heat (and gentle ocean breezes near the coast). Summer is also the rainiest time of year and powerful showers that erupt and pass within a few hours are not uncommon (it's always worth keeping a rain jacket in your bag).

FESTIVALS

Rio's Carnaval (February/March) is deservedly popular, but that's not the end of the celebrating. Reveillon (New Year's Eve) is another citywide celebration, when Cariocas (residents of Rio) and visitors pack Copacabana beach. Other *festas* (parties) occur throughout the year. For the dates of Rio's many public holidays, see p222.

January & February

DIA DE SÃO SEBASTIÃO Jan 20

The patron saint of Rio is commemorated with a procession that carries the image of São Sebastião from Igreja (church) de São Sebastião dos Capuchinos in Tijuca to the Catedral Metropolitana (p100), where the image is blessed in a Mass celebrated by the Archbishop of Rio de Janeiro.

ADVANCE PLANNING

In addition to organizing your visa (if you need one) and booking accommodations, there are a few things you might look into before flying to Rio.

The best guides (see p225) are often booked up well in advance, so get in touch early if there's something particular you want to do (such as scuba diving or rock-climbing up the face of Pão de Açúcar, p177). If you plan on tandem gliding, get in touch with a pilot (p179) and find out which day might be best for flying.

Check whether there will be any football (soccer) games on while you're in town (get the lowdown with www.sambafoot.com), and browse through listings on Riotur (www.rioguiaoficial.com.br/en) to read about upcoming concerts and special events. Catch up on the latest news stories and political gossip with the *Rio Times* (www.riotimesonline.com).

CARNAVAL
In February or March the city puts on its famous no-holds-barred party. For more information, see p50.

VERÃO DO MORRO
www.veraodomorro.com.br, in Portuguese
In February or March, the Verão do Morro (summer on the mountain) party kicks off, with a month of weekend concerts in a fabulous setting above Rio. Top Brazilian bands and DJs headline the all-night fest. The event usually kicks off a week after Carnaval. Tickets, available at the Pão de Açúcar cable-car station (p79), among other locations, cost around R$90.

March & April

DIA DA FUNDAÇÃO DA CIDADE Mar 1
The city commemorates its founding in 1565 by Estácio de Sá with a Mass in the church of its patron saint, Igreja de São Sebastião dos Capuchinos.

SEXTA-FEIRA DA PAIXÃO
In March or April (depending when Easter falls), Good Friday is celebrated throughout the city. The most important ceremony re-enacts the Stations of the Cross under the **Arcos da Lapa** (p100), with more than 100 actors.

FESTIVAL INTERNACIONAL DE DOCUMENTÁRIOS
www.etudoverdade.com.br
Latin America's most important documentary film festival takes place over 10 days in March or April when more than 100 films from Brazil and abroad are screened at theaters in Rio and São Paulo.

DIA DO ÍNDIO Apr 19
April 19 is recognized in Brazil as Indians' day, with a week of special events held at the **Museu do Índio** (p78). Exhibitions, dance and film presentations are staged daily.

DIA DE SÃO JORGE Apr 23
Igreja de São Jorge, Rua da Alfândega 382, Centro
On April 23 the city pays its respects to St George, an important figure in the Afro-Brazilian community. St George is the alter-ego of the god Ogum in the Candomblé religion (originating in Africa). There's a Mass and procession, and food vendors abound.

May & June

RIO DAS OSTRAS JAZZ E BLUES FESTIVAL
www.riodasostrasjazzeblues.com
Located 170km east of Rio, on the way to Búzios, Rio das Ostras boasts lovely beaches and mangrove forests. In early June, it's the setting for one of Brazil's best jazz and blues fests, with five days of concerts on outdoor stages by international performers (John Hammond Quartet, Spyro Gyra, Coco Montoya and DJ Logic have played here in the past).

FESTAS JUNINAS
Spanning the month of June, the feast days of various saints mark some of the most important folkloric festivals in Brazil. In Rio, celebrations are held in various public squares, with lots of food stands, music, fireworks and the occasional bonfire or two. The big feast days are June 13 (Dia de Santo Antônio), June 24 (São João) and June 29 (São Pedro). See Riotur (p228) for details.

RIO MARATHON
www.maratonadorio.com.br
Set along the coast, with the ocean always at your side, this marathon course must be one of the most beautiful in the world. Rio hosts its annual 42km run in mid- to late June, when the weather is mild and the skies are clear and blue. There are also 6km and 21km runs.

July & August

PORTAS ABERTAS
www.artedeportasabertas.com.br, in Portuguese
Artists in Santa Teresa open their studios for a week in July during this lively annual festival. Expect music, a diverse crowd and inventive installations that make good use of the atmospheric bohemian 'hood.

FESTA DA SÃO PEDRO DO MAR Jul 3
The fishing fraternity pays homage to its patron saint in a maritime procession as decorated boats leave from the fishing community of Caju and sail to the statue of São Pedro in Urca.

FESTA LITERÁRIA INTERNACIONAL DE PARATI

www.flip.org.br

This important literary festival brings authors from around the world to Paraty for five days in July or August. Celebrated writers like JM Coetzee, Michael Ondaatje, Julian Barnes, Don DeLillo and Hanif Kureishi were among the featured guests in years past.

FESTA DE NS DA GLÓRIA DO OUTEIRO Aug 15

A solemn Mass is held at the historic church overlooking Glória and the bay to mark the Feast of the Assumption. From the church (ablaze with decorated lights), a procession travels out into the streets of Glória. This *festa* includes music and colorful stalls set up set up in front of the Igreja de NS da Glória do Outeiro (p88). Festivities start at 8am and continue all day.

RIO JAZZ FESTIVAL

www.jazzfestivalbrasil.com.br

Although dates for this jazz festival vary (currently held in August), it's an opportunity for Rio's beautiful people to come together for three nights of great music. Local, national and international acts present a wide variety of music, playing jazz and its many relatives – samba-jazz, bossa nova, samba and Música Popular Brasileira (MPB).

September & October

SAMBA SCHOOL REHEARSALS

In September (though some start as early as July or August), samba schools begin hosting open gatherings once a week (usually on Friday or Saturday night). In spite of the name, these are less a dress rehearsal than just an excuse to dance (to samba, of course), celebrate and pass on the good vibe before the big show come Carnaval time. Anyone can come, and it's a mixed crowd of Cariocas and tourists, though it gets more and more crowded (and the admission prices rise) the closer it is to Carnaval. For more information on attending the open rehearsals, see p163.

DIA DE INDEPENDÊNCIA DO BRASIL Sep 7

Independence Day is celebrated with a large military parade down Av Presidente Vargas. It starts at 8am at Candelária (p89) and goes down just past Praça XI.

FESTIVAL DO RIO

www.festivaldorio.com.br

Rio's international film festival is one of the biggest in Latin America. More than 200 films from all over the world are shown at some 35 theaters in Rio. Often the festival holds open-air screenings at locations around town. It runs from the last week of September through the first week of October.

FESTA DA PENHA

One of the largest (and most popular) religious festivals in the city takes place every Sunday in October and on the first Sunday in November. The festa draws thousands of pilgrims who somberly ascend the 365 steps to the dramatically set church. In the plaza below, food and drink stalls and live music create a festive environment. The lively celebrations commence in the northern suburb of Penha at Igreja NS da Penha de França, Largo da Penha 19.

GAY PRIDE RIO

www.gaypridebrazil.org

Although not as large as São Paulo's massive parade, the Rio gay pride event gets bigger each year, with over a million people turning out in recent years. It usually takes place in October or November.

November & December

FESTIVAL PANORAMA DE DANÇA

www.panoramafestival.com

Spanning two weeks in November, the Festival Panorama showcases the work of dozens of contemporary dance groups from across the globe, bringing together a mix of experimental troupes as well as traditional performers.

NOITES CARIOCAS

www.noitescariocas.com.br, in Portuguese

The biggest summer concert series in Rio runs for two weeks in January or February, with all-night rock and MPB concerts held on weekend nights at Pier Mauá, just north of Centro. Previous years have seen performances by Brazil's biggest stars – Jorge Ben Jor, Lulu Santos, Elza Soares and others.

LIGHTING OF THE LAGOA CHRISTMAS TREE

From early December to the first week of January, the world's largest floating Christmas tree (85m) glows brightly on Lagoa de Rodrigo de Freitas (p71). To celebrate its lighting, the city throws a concert in Parque Brigadeiro Faria Lima, usually on the first Saturday in December.

FESTA DE IEMANJÁ

Dec 31

Dwarfed by secular New Year's Eve celebrations, this Candomblé (a religion originating from Africa) festival celebrates the feast day of Iemanjá, the goddess of the sea. Celebrants dress in white and place their petitions on small boats, sending them out to sea. If their petitions return, their prayers will not be answered. Along with the petitions, celebrants send candles, perfumes and talcum powder to appease the blue-cloaked *orixá* (spirits or deities). Until recently, devotees gathered in Copacabana, Ipanema and Leblon but, owing to the popularity of Reveillon, and its chaotic spillover, they are seeking more tranquil spots – Barra da Tijuca and Recreio dos Bandeirantes – to make their offerings.

REVEILLON

Dec 31

Rio's biggest holiday after its spectacular and rowdy Carnaval takes place on the famed Copacabana Beach, where some two million people pack the sands to welcome the new year. A spectacular fireworks display lights up the night sky as top bands perform on stages built on the sands. The hardiest of revelers keep things going all night long, then watch the sunrise the next morning.

COSTS & MONEY

Rio is less expensive than some cities in Western Europe and North America, but Brazil's booming economy and strong *real* mean that it isn't the bargain it once was. Still, it is possible to enjoy the city without breaking the bank.

Ascetics could get by on about R$60 a day, staying in cheaper hostels, preparing their own meals and avoiding pricey nights out. Midrange travelers should budget around R$300 a day if traveling solo or R$200 each for a couple – which will cover decent lodging near (but not directly facing) the beach and a good assortment of restaurant and bar expenses, plus a few day tours and adventure outings. High-end travelers will spend upwards of R$500 each per day, which will cover hotel rooms with ocean views, Rio's best restaurants, and drinks at top music halls and dance clubs.

Accommodations will probably be your biggest expense. The cheapest rooms in town can go for as little as R$29 per night for a bed in a hostel outside the Zona Sul (hostels in Ipanema, however, typically charge R$45 or $50 a night). A clean, fairly decent double room in Copacabana goes for about R$250 and up. In Ipanema, good rooms start around R$330. If you have money to burn, Rio's top hotel rooms will set you back a cool R$750 or more.

Restaurants cater to an equally broad range of budgets. At the low end are inexpensive per-kilo restaurants and cheap set lunches, which can fill a person up for R$20. If you're not scraping by, you can enjoy a good selection of local places with mains averaging R$25 to R$35, or enjoy a dinner for two for R$80 to R$120. Dinner at Rio's most expensive places will cost R$200 or so, including a few drinks. Keep in mind that many restaurants list their menu prices for two. If you're not sharing, be sure to clarify before ordering (and you can usually order a *meia porção,* or half portion).

Getting around town is fairly inexpensive, with cheap bus and metro tickets (R$2.80 one way), while taxi rides will run to a bit more (R$25 to zip up to Lapa from Ipanema). Renting a car is expensive (starting at R$100), with high petrol prices to match, and it's not worth recommending unless you plan to do a lot of exploring outside of the main towns.

Brazil is not the cheapest destination for solo travelers. The cost of a single room in a hotel is not much less than for a double.

HOW MUCH?

1L of gas **R$2.25**

1L of bottled water **R$1.50**

Glass of chope (draft beer) **R$4**

Souvenir T-shirt **R$20 to R$60**

Agua de coco (coconut water) on the beach **R$3**

Metro ticket **R$2.80**

Pair of Havaianas **R$18 to R$46**

Admission to samba club **R$10 to R$25**

Dinner for two at Sobrenatural **R$120**

Cable-car ride to the top of Pão de Açúcar **R$44**

TRAVELING RESPONSIBLY

Since our inception in 1973, Lonely Planet has encouraged our readers to tread lightly, travel responsibly and enjoy the serendipitous magic independent travel affords. We still firmly believe in the benefits that international travel can bring – but, as always, we encourage you to consider the impact your visit will have on both the global environment and the local economies, cultures and ecosystems.

With the increasing use of 'eco' splashed about, it can be hard to separate the green from the greedy. With a little research and a bit of adventure your trip can have a positive impact.

Accommodations & Food

Stay clear of chain hotels and all-inclusive resorts. These places are often owned by foreign investors who take all profit out of the country. You're much better off staying in family-run *pousadas* (guesthouses), where your money will remain in the hands of the local people.

With food, Brazil requires some tough choices. Although Brazilian beef is top notch, the explosion of cattle farming continues to fuel the Amazon's destruction, with old-growth forests cleared to make way for pastures. A growing number of restaurants serve organic and vegetarian fare. Avoid major fast-food chains, as these have played a significant role in fueling the country's deforestation.

Responsible Travel Organizations

Brazil has no certification system to identify the 'green-ness' of accommodations and tour operators. However, various organizations are working to establish sustainable-travel criteria, and the situation may change. Environmentally responsible organizations in Brazil include the following:

- Rainforest Alliance (www.rainforestalliance.org)
- ResponsibleTravel.com (www.responsibletravel.com)
- Sustainable Travel International (www.sustainabletravelinternational.org)

You can also take an organized tour based on sustainable itineraries, including those that visit favelas or involve hiking (p225), or you can volunteer your time (p229).

During the December-to-February holiday season, lodging costs are higher than at other times of the year (and sometimes more in places such as Búzios and other popular resorts). You'll pay a premium if you come during Carnaval or Reveillon, with the price of accommodations doubling or even tripling – with the added requirement of four-night minimum stays.

INTERNET RESOURCES

Brazzil (www.brazzil.com) In-depth articles touching on Brazilian politics, economy, literature, arts and culture.

Carioca Forever (www.cariocaforever.com) Articles written by English-speaking expats living in Brazil, with info on cultural events, life in Rio and language-learning tips.

Gringoes (www.gringoes.com) Articles written by Anglophones living in Brazil.

Hip Guide to Brazil (www.brazilmax.com) Excellent guide to Brazilian culture and society; good, selective articles and links.

Insider's Guide to Rio (www.ipanema.com) One of the best internet introductions to Rio, this guide has up-to-date tips on hotels, restaurants, nightlife and shopping, with special sections on Carnaval and Rio for gays.

Lana Lapa (www.lanalapa.com.br, in Portuguese) Up-to-date listings of live concerts and other events in Lapa, plus a rundown of restaurants and bars in the area.

Lonely Planet (www.lonelyplanet.com) For summaries on Brazil travel, the popular Thorn Tree forum, online accommodations booking and links to a variety of other web resources.

Maria-Brazil (www.maria-brazil.org) An expat's recommendations of favorite dining, drinking, shopping and sightseeing in Rio, plus extensive recipes and links to blogs by other expats.

Rio This Week (www.riothisweek.com) Flashy photos and listings of what's on around town, plus restaurant recommendations and other tips. You can download a colorful PDF of the current guide.

Riotur (www.rioguiaoficial.com.br) Rio's tourist information agency has a current website of what's on around town, as well as comprehensive listings of museums, restaurants and other info.

Rio Times (www.riotimesonline.com) This new online weekly is an excellent English-language resource for news and current events in Rio and around Brazil.

HISTORY

THE PORTUGUESE ARRIVAL

In the 15th century Portugal, ever infatuated with the sea, began its large-scale explorations that would eventually take Portuguese explorers to the coast of Brazil in 1500. A little over a year later, Gonçalo Coelho sailed from Portugal and entered a huge bay in January 1502. It was his chief pilot, Amerigo Vespucci, however, who would give the name to this bay. Mistaking it for a river (or possibly making no mistake at all since the old Portuguese 'rio' is another word for bay), he dubbed it Rio de Janeiro (River of January).

Although the Portuguese were the first European *arrivistes,* the French would become the first non-natives to settle along the bay. Like the Portuguese, the French had been harvesting dyewood along the Brazilian coast, but unlike the Portuguese they hadn't attempted any permanent settlements in this region until Rio. Regardless, the Portuguese were far from being the first to set foot on the tropical shoreline, as the land had already been inhabited for at least 10,000 years.

OF NOBLE SAVAGES & SAVAGE NOBLES

Some believe that the Guanabara *índios* (Indians; indigenous people), the Tupinambá (better known as the Tupi), inspired works such as Sir Thomas Moore's *Utopia* (1516) and would later inspire Rousseau's Enlightenment-era idea of the 'noble savage'. This all started from the letters credited to Amerigo Vespucci on his first voyage to Rio in 1502. The idea common at the time was that there existed on earth an Eden, and that it lay undiscovered. Vespucci claimed to have found that Eden, from his cursory observations of the Tupi. They were described as innocent savages, carefree and well groomed, with the unusual custom of taking daily baths in the sea. The fact that native women were freely offered to the strange foreigners probably added to the enthusiasm with which they spoke about the region upon their return to Portugal.

In fact, the honeymoon didn't last long. The conquerors soon came to see the forest-dwelling *índios* as raw manpower for the Portuguese empire, and enslaved them and set them to work on plantations. The *índios,* too, turned out to be different than the Europeans imagined. The Tupinambá were warlike and ate their enemies – through ritualistic cannibalism they believed they would receive the power and strength of the consumed opponent. They also didn't take to the work as the Portuguese had expected, and were dying off in large numbers from introduced diseases. By the 17th century the Tupinambá had been completely eradicated. To fulfill their growing labor demands, the Portuguese eventually turned to Africa.

AFRICANS IN BRAZIL

The Portuguese began bringing blacks, stolen from Africa, into the new colony shortly after Brazil's founding. Most blacks were brought from Guinea, Angola and the Congo and would

TIMELINE

8000 BC

Ancestors of Tupinambá settle along Baía de Guanabara; they are descendents of hunter-gatherers who crossed the Bering Strait from East Asia sometime between 10,000 BC and 12,000 BC.

AD 1502

Portuguese explorer Gonçalo Coelho leads an expedition from Portugal, sailing into Baía de Guanabara after an eight-month voyage. His chief pilot, Amerigo Vespucci (after whom 'America' is named), dubbed the lovely setting Rio de Janeiro.

1567

After successfully driving the French and their Indian allies off the land, the Portuguese set up the first settlement on Morro do Castelo. It's called São Sebastião do Rio de Janeiro (after Portuguese king São Sebastião).

top picks

HISTORICAL SITES

- **Paço Imperial** (p92) The former imperial palace was home to the royal family when they arrived from Portugal.
- **Praça Quinze de Novembro** (p92) Named after the date Brazil declared itself a republic (November 15, 1822), this plaza has witnessed a lot of historical action, including the crowning of two emperors and the abolition of slavery.
- **Travessa do Comércio** (p94) This narrow alley is a window into colonial Rio, with 18th-century buildings converted into bars and restaurants.
- **Museu Histórico Nacional** (p89) Set in the 18th-century royal arsenal, this museum houses Rio's best assortment of historical artifacts.
- **Jardim Botânico** (p70) Prince Regent Dom João VI insured the city would have no shortage of green spaces, and ordered this verdant garden planted in 1808.
- **Museu da República** (p87) Formerly known as the Palácio do Catete, this mansion was Brazil's presidential home from 1896 to 1954. Getúlio Vargas was the last president to live here, and committed suicide in one of the upstairs rooms.
- **Praça Floriano** (p95) Centro's picturesque main square has long been the meeting ground for popular demonstrations, including student uprisings against the military dictatorship in the 1960s and victory celebrations following World Cup finals.
- **Garota de Ipanema** (p131) Famed spot where Tom Jobim and Vinícius de Moraes penned the 'Girl from Ipanema', whose international success was a major moment in the history of bossa nova.

constitute some four million souls brought to Brazil over its three-and-a-half centuries of human trafficking. The port of Rio had the largest number of slaves entering the colony – as many as two million in all. At open-air slave markets these new immigrants were sold as local help or shipped to the interior, initially to work on the thriving sugar plantations, and later – when gold was discovered in Minas Gerais in 1704 – to work back-breaking jobs in the mines.

Although slavery was rotten anywhere in the New World, most historians agree that the Africans in Rio had it better than their rural brethren. Those that came to Rio worked in domestic roles as maids and butlers and out on the streets as dock workers, furniture movers, delivery boys, boatmen, cobblers, fishermen and carpenters. The worst job was transporting the barrels of human excrement produced in town and emptying them into the sea.

As Rio's population grew, so too did the number of slaves imported to meet the labor needs of the expanding coffee plantations in the Paraíba Valley. By the early 19th century African slaves made up two-thirds of Rio's population.

Lots of illicit liaisons occurred between master and slave, and children born into mixed backgrounds were largely accepted into the social sphere and raised as free citizens. This contributed considerably to creating Brazil's melting pot. While escape attempts were fewer in Rio than in the more brutal climate of the northeast, there were attempts. Those seeking freedom often set their sights on *quilombos* (communities of runaway slaves). Some were quite developed – as was the case with Palmares, which had a population of 20,000 and survived through much of the 17th century before it was wiped out by Federal troops.

Rio's nearest *quilombo* in the 19th century was in Leblon – then quite distant from the city. Unlike other *quilombos,* it was headed by a white, progressive businessman who was in favor of slave abolition. Luggage manufacturer Jose de Seixas Magalhães kept farmland in Leblon, which was staffed entirely by runaway slaves, whom he hid and protected in his Leblon man-

1580

The Portuguese bring 2000 slaves to the new colony. Over the next 300 years, more than four million blacks stolen from Africa will be relocated to Brazil.

1763

With gold flowing from the mines of Minas Gerais through Rio, the city grows wealthy and swells in population to 50,000; the Portuguese court transfers the capital of Brazil from Salvador to Rio.

1807

Napoleon invades Portugal and the Portuguese prince regent (later known as Dom João VI) and his entire court of 15,000 flee for Brazil. The royal coffers shower wealth upon Rio.

sion. This was during Brazil's incipient abolition movement, and the farm operated under the eyes of the government. Magalhães, however, enjoyed the special patronage of Princesa Isabel, daughter of Dom Pedro II and regent of the Empire while he traveled overseas. Abroad, the country was receiving pressure to outlaw slavery, and trafficking in human cargo was eventually outlawed in 1830. This move, however, did nothing to improve the lives of slaves already in Brazil, who would have to wait another two generations to gain their freedom. Despite the ban, shipment of human cargo continued well into the 1850s, with 500,000 slaves smuggled into Brazil between 1830 and 1850. The British (out of economic self-interest) finally suppressed Brazil's trafficking with naval squadrons.

Pressure from home and abroad reached boiling point toward the end of the 19th century until finally, in 1888, from the steps of Royal Palace overlooking Praça Quinze de Novembro, slavery was declared abolished. Brazil was the last country in the New World to end slavery.

RIO'S EARLY DAYS

In order to get the colony up and running, the Portuguese built a fortified town on Morro do Castelo in 1567 to maximize protection from European invasion by sea and *índios* attack by land. They named their town São Sebastião do Rio de Janeiro, in honor of King Sebastião of Portugal. Cobbled together by the 500 founding Cariocas (residents of Rio), early Rio was a poorly planned town with irregular streets in the medieval Portuguese style. It remained a small settlement through the mid-17th century, surviving on the export of brazilwood and sugarcane. In Rio's first census (in 1600), the population comprised 3000 *índios*, 750 Portuguese and 100 blacks.

With its excellent harbor and good lands for sugarcane, Rio became Brazil's third most important settlement (after Salvador da Bahia and Recife-Olinda) in the 17th century.

The gold rush in Minas Gerais had a profound effect on Rio and caused major demographic shifts on three continents. The rare metal was first discovered by *bandeirantes* (explorers and hired slave-hunters) in the 1690s, and as word spread gold seekers arrived in droves. Over the next half-century an estimated 500,000 Portuguese arrived in Brazil and many thousands of African slaves were imported. Rio served as the natural port of entry for this flow of people and commerce to and from the Minas Gerais goldfields.

In the 18th century Rio morphed into a rough-and-tumble place attracting a swarthy brand of European immigrant. Most of the settlement was built near the water (where Praça XV de Novembro stands today), beside rows of warehouses, with noisy taverns sprinkled along the main streets. Rio was a rough city full of smugglers and thieves, tramps and assassins, and slaves on the run. Smuggling was rampant, with ships robbed and the sailors murdered, with bribes given over to the cops. Gold flowing through the city created the constant menace of pirates. Adding a note of temperance to the place were the religious orders that came in small bands and built Rio's first churches.

RIO UNDER THE KING

In 1807 Napoleon's army marched on Lisbon. Two days before the French invasion, 40 ships carrying the Portuguese prince regent (later known as Dom João VI) and his entire court of 15,000 set sail for Brazil under the protection of British warships. After the initial landing in Bahia (where their unkempt state was met with bemusement), the royal family moved down to Rio, where they settled.

1822

Left in charge of Brazil after his father Dom João VI returns to Portugal, the prince regent Dom Pedro I declares independence from Portugal and crowns himself 'emperor' of Brazil.

1831

Brazil's first homegrown monarch, Dom Pedro I, proves incompetent and abdicates the throne. His son Pedro II takes power and ushers in a long period of growth and stability.

1888

Slavery is abolished in Brazil, the last country in the New World to do so. The law is signed into effect by Princesa Isabel, admired by many blacks as their benefactress.

This had momentous consequences for the city as the king, missing the high culture of Europe, lavished his attention on Rio, envisioning a splendid European-style city for his new hometown. European artisans flooded the city. The British, rewarded for helping the king safely reach Brazil, gained access to Brazil's ports, and many Anglo traders and merchants set up shop in the town center. Anti-Napoleon French also arrived, as did other Europeans, creating an international air unknown until then. When the German prince and noted naturalist Alexander Philip Maximilian arrived in Brazil in 1815 he commented on the many nationalities and mixtures of people he encountered.

Dom João VI fell in love with Rio. A great admirer of nature, he founded the botanical gardens and introduced sea bathing to the inhabitants of Rio. He had a special pier built at Caju, with a small tub at the end, in which he would immerse himself fully clothed as the waves rocked gently against it. (His wife Carlota Joaquina bathed in the nude.) This was long before Copacabana was opened to the rest of the city, remaining a virgin expanse of white sand framed by rain-forest covered mountains, reachable only by an arduous journey.

With the court came an influx of money and talent that helped build some of the city's lasting monuments, such as the palace at the Quinta da Boa Vista. Within a year of his arrival, Dom João VI also created the School of Medicine, the Bank of Brazil, the Law Courts, the Naval Academy and the Royal Printing Works.

Dom João VI was expected to return to Portugal after Napoleon's Waterloo in 1815, but instead stayed in Brazil. The following year his mother, mad Queen Dona Maria I, died, and Dom João VI became king. He refused demands to return to Portugal to rule, and declared Rio the capital of the United Kingdom of Portugal, Brazil and the Algarves. Brazil became the only New World colony to ever have a European monarch ruling on its soil.

Five years later Dom João VI finally relented to political pressure and returned to Portugal, leaving his 23-year-old son Pedro in Brazil as prince regent. In Portugal the king was confronted with the newly formed Côrtes, a legislative assembly attempting to reign in the powers of the monarchy. The Côrtes had many directives, one of which was restoring Brazil to its previous status as subservient colony. Word was sent to Dom Pedro that his authority was greatly diminished. According to legend, when Pedro received the directive in 1822, he pulled out his sword and yelled *'Independência ou morte!'* ('Independence or death!'), putting himself at the country's head as Emperor Dom Pedro I.

Portugal was too weak to fight its favorite son, not to mention the British, who had the most to gain from Brazilian independence and would have come to the aid of the Brazilians. Without spilling blood, Brazil had attained its independence and Dom Pedro I became the head of the Brazilian 'empire' (despite Pedro's claims to the contrary, Brazil was a regular monarchy, not an empire since it had no overseas colonies).

Dom Pedro I ruled for only nine years. From all accounts, he was a bumbling incompetent who scandalized even the permissive Brazilians by siring numerous illegitimate children. He also strongly resisted any attempts to weaken his power by constitutional means. Following street demonstrations in Rio in 1831, he surprised everyone by abdicating, leaving the power in the hands of his five-year-old, Brazilian-born son.

Until Dom Pedro II reached adolescence, Brazil suffered through a turbulent period of unrest, which finally ended in 1840 when Dom Pedro II, at the age of 14, took the throne. Despite his youth he proved to be a stabilizing element for the country, and ushered in a long period of peace and relative prosperity. The period of industrialization began with the

1889

A military coup, supported by Brazil's wealthy coffee farmers, overthrows Pedro II. The monarchy is abolished and the Brazilian Republic is born. Pedro II goes into exile in Paris and dies a few years later.

1900

Rio's mayor Pereira Passos ushers in a period of urbanization, with the creation of grand boulevards, the opening up of Copacabana (via a tunnel to Botafogo), and improving public health and sanitation.

1915

Praça Onze becomes the center of Afro-Brazilian culture, with Bahian immigrants gathering for music, dance and Candomblé celebrations. Samba is soon born, with the first songs heard on the radio by 1917.

THE ORIGINS OF THE FAVELA

The end of the 19th century may have brought an end to slavery, but newly freed blacks weren't welcomed into a new and equitable society. They faced enormous obstacles finding work and a place to live. Some of the newly freed fled to *quilombos*, which were runaway slave communities that sprang up throughout Brazil – including on forested areas outside of Rio; there was even a small *quilombo* in present-day Leblon.

Freed slaves weren't the only group struggling for survival at the end of the 19th century. In the northeast terrible droughts in the 1870s and '80s, coupled with the decline of the sugar industry, brought economic devastation. Offering a vision of hope, Messianic popular movements gained support among Brazil's poor. The most famous was that of Canudos. Its leader, Antônio Conselheiro (Antônio the Counselor), had wandered for years through the backlands preaching and prophesying the appearance of the Antichrist and the end of the world, defending the poor and antagonizing the authorities. He railed against the new republican government and in 1893 eventually settled with his followers at Canudos, in the interior of northern Bahia. Within 1½ years Canudos had grown to a city of 35,000.

The republican government sensed plots in Canudos to return Brazil to the monarchy. Miraculously, the rebels first defeated a force of state police, and then two subsequent attacks by the federal army. Hysterical demonstrations in the cities demanded that the republic be saved from the rebels. That's when a federal force of 8000 well-supplied soldiers – many of whom hailed from Rio – eventually took Canudos after vicious, hand-to-hand, house-to-house fighting. It was a war of extermination that nearly wiped out every man, woman and child from Canudos. The settlement was then burned to the ground to erase it from the nation's memory.

The soldiers and their wives – some of whom were survivors taken from the Canudos massacre – returned to Rio, where they were promised land in exchange for their victory. The government, however, reneged on the promise. The soldiers, who had camped out in front of the Ministry of War, then occupied the nearby hillside of Morro da Providência. Oddly enough, as the first tenants put up makeshift shelters and settled in, they came across the same hardy shrub they found in the arid lands surrounding Canudos. Called 'favela', this plant caused skin irritations in all who came in contact with it – according to some accounts, the protective shrub even helped repel the army's initial invasions. Soon hillside residents began calling their new home the Morro da Favela (perhaps in hopes that the plant would have protective benefits for those who took part in the war), and the name caught on. Soon the word favela was used to describe the ever-increasing number of informal communities appearing around Rio – which quickly gathered a mix of former slaves and poverty-stricken inhabitants from the interior, who came to the city seeking a better life.

introduction of the steamship and the telegraph, and the king encouraged mass immigration from Europe.

Dom Pedro II's shortcomings during his half-century of rule were a bloody war with Paraguay (1865–70) and his slowness at abolishing slavery. He was well liked by his subjects, but they finally had enough of the monarchy and he was pushed from power in 1889.

THE BELLE ÉPOQUE

Rio experienced boom days in the latter half of the 19th century. The spreading wealth of coffee plantations in Rio state (and in São Paulo) revitalized Brazil's economy, just as the city was going through substantial growth and modernization. Regular passenger ships began sailing to London (1845) and Paris (1851), and the local ferry service to Niterói began in 1862. A telegraph system and gas streetlights were installed in 1854. By 1860 Rio had more than 250,000 inhabitants, making it the largest city in South America.

1923

The Copacabana Palace opens its doors. The hotel quickly becomes an icon of Rio's tropical glamour, with jet-setters from Hollywood and Europe flying down to the city during its pre-Depression boom days.

1928

Deixa Falar becomes the first *escola de samba* (samba school; called a 'school' because it's located next to a primary school), followed by Mangueira later that year. In 1932 Rio holds its first Carnaval parade.

1930

Getúlio Vargas comes into power. Inspired by European fascists, President Vargas presides over an authoritarian state, playing a major role in Brazilian politics until his suicide in 1951.

For the wealthy, the goal of creating a modern European capital grew ever closer, as the city embraced all things European – with particular influence from the customs, fashion and even cuisine of Paris. The poor, however, had a miserable lot. In the 1870s and 1880s, as the rich moved to new urban areas by the bay or in the hills, Rio's marginalized lived in tenement houses in the old center of town. There conditions were grim: streets were poorly lit and poorly ventilated, with a stench filling the narrow alleyways.

Rio's flood of immigrants added diversity to the city. On the streets, you could hear a symphony of languages – African, Portuguese, English, French – mixing with the sounds of the *bonde* (tram), of carts drawn by mules, as the cadence of various dances – maxixes, lundus, polkas and waltzes – interpreted by anonymous performers.

The city went through dramatic changes in the first decade of 1900, owing in large part to the work of mayor Pereira Passos. He continued the work of 'Europeanization' by widening Rio's streets and creating grand boulevards such as Av Central and Mem de Sá. The biggest of these boulevards required the destruction of 600 buildings to make way for Av Central (later renamed Rio Branco), which became the Champs Elysées of Rio, an elegant boulevard full of sidewalk cafés and promenading Cariocas.

Passos also connected Botafogo to Copacabana by building a tunnel, paving the way for the development of the southern beaches. Despite his grand vision for Rio, his vision for the poor was one of wide-scale removal from the city center – a short-sighted policy that would dog Rio (and Brazilian) government for the next 80 years. In truth, the *cortiços* (poor, collective lodgings) were breeding grounds for deadly outbreaks of smallpox, yellow fever and typhus. Sighting the widespread health and sanitation problems, the city destroyed thousands of shacks. With no homes, the poor fled to the hills, later creating some of the earliest favelas (shanty towns). The city also exterminated rats and mosquitoes and created a modern sewage system.

By the time Passos' term ended in 1906, Rio was the Belle Époque capital par excellence of Latin America. Its only possible rival in beauty was Buenos Aires. One visitor who commented on Rio's transformation was former US President Teddy Roosevelt. In 1913, during a tour through town, he noted that since Brazil had become a republic in 1889, Rio de Janeiro had gone 'from a picturesque pest-hole into a singularly beautiful, healthy, clean and efficient modern great city.'

BOOM DAYS, REFORM & REPRESSION UNDER VARGAS

At the end of the 19th century, the city's population exploded because of European immigration and internal migration (mostly ex-slaves from the declining coffee and sugar regions). By 1900 Rio boasted more than 800,000 inhabitants, a quarter of them foreign born (by contrast, São Paulo's population was only 300,000).

Following Passos' radical changes, the early 1920s to the late 1950s were one of Rio's golden ages. With the inauguration of some grand luxury resort hotels (the Glória in 1922 and the Copacabana Palace in 1923), Rio became a romantic, exotic destination for Hollywood celebrities and international high society, with Copacabana its headquarters. In some ways Rio's quasi-mythic status as a tropical arcadia spans its entire history, but in the 1940s and 50s its reputation as the urban Eden of Latin America was vouchsafed as the world was introduced to Carmen Miranda, a Rio icon.

1960

President Juscelino Kubitschek moves the capital of Brazil from Rio to the newly constructed Brasília, which leads to a decline in Rio's political and sociocultural prominence.

1964

President Goulart is overthrown by a military coup. Troops arrive in Rio and seize power. So begins the era of dictatorship, with generals running the show for the next 20 years.

1968

The government passes the repressive Institutional Act 5, which purges opposition legislators, judges and mayors from public office; most political parties are banned. Over 100,000 people take to the streets in protest.

MOTHER OF SAMBA

In the early 20th century, one of Rio's most momentous events was transpiring inside the working-class neighborhood of Praça Onze near downtown. In 1915 this was considered 'Africa in miniature' for the influx of immigrants from Bahia, who had been flocking to the region since the end of slavery in 1888. In Praça Onze, Afro-Brazilian culture – music, dance and religion (Candomblé) – thrived in the homes of old Bahian matriarchs, called *tias* (aunts). At the center of this thriving community was Tia Ciata, something of a self-made woman who rented out costumes for the Carnaval balls, worked as a healer (she was even consulted by president Wenceslau Brás, who had a leg wound that Ciata allegedly healed) and hosted large parties on Candomblé saints' days – all while looking after her 15 children. Within time, Ciata's house became the meeting point for the city's journalists, bohemians, Bahian expats and musicians. Today's now-legendary names – Pixinguinha, Donga, Heitor dos Prazeres and others – met regularly to play music and experiment with new forms, never imagining that their result – samba – would become one of the world's great musical forms. Coincidentally, this was also around the time that African Americans in New Orleans were playing the music that would later be called jazz.

After the earliest musical creations, the performers gathering at Tia Ciata's went on to make records, and samba's popularity spread like wildfire across the city. They came first through the working class and, after initial resistance, on into the houses of the wealthy. Samba continued to evolve throughout the next few decades as it was adopted for Carnaval, yet the songs developed in those early years would live on (many are still played), and laid the foundation on which so much of Brazilian music is based today.

This was also when radical changes were happening in the world of music (see p31) and when Rio was beginning to celebrate its 'Brazilianness', or its mixed heritage and multicolored population. Sociologist Gilberto Freyre's influential book *Masters and Slaves* (1933) turned things upside down as Brazilians, conditioned to think of their mixed-race past with shame, began to think differently about their heritage – as an asset that set them apart from other nations of the world.

The 1930s was the era of President Vargas, who formed the Estado Novo (New State) in November 1937, making him the first Brazilian president to wield absolute power. Inspired by the fascist governments of Salazar in Portugal and Mussolini in Italy, Vargas banned political parties, imprisoned political opponents, and censored artists and the press.

Despite all this, many liked Vargas. The 'father' of Brazil's workers, he created Brazil's minimum wage in 1938. Each year he introduced new labor laws to coincide with Workers' Day on May 1, to sweeten the teeth of Brazil's factory workers. His vision for Brazil was not to increase the country's output, but to improve the level of education among all Brazilians.

THE MILITARY DICTATORSHIP

The world's fascination with Rio was severely curtailed during the rise of the military dictatorship of the 1960s. The era of repression began with press censorship, silencing of political opponents (sometimes by torture and violence) and an exodus of political defectors abroad (including musicians, writers and artists). There were numerous protests during that period (notably in 1968 when some 100,000 marched upon the Palácio Tiradentes). And even Rio's politicians opposed the military regime, which responded by withholding vital federal funding for certain social programs.

Despite the repression, the 60s and 70s witnessed profound changes in the city, with the opening of tunnels and the building of viaducts, parks and landfills. (Perversely, this time of autocratic rule was also marked by a booming economy.) In the realm of public transporta-

1985

Following a cautious period of *abertura* (opening), Brazil holds an indirect presidential election. Civilian rule returns to Brazil under José Sarney, though he proves unable to handle the rampant inflation and huge debt left by his predecessors.

1994

The Favela-Bairro project is unveiled. Over the next decade US$180 million in funding will be spent providing neglected communities with access to decent sanitation, health clinics and public transportation.

2002

After four unsuccessful attempts, Lula is elected president. The former union leader serves a moderate first term, despite upper-class fears of radical agendas. Meanwhile, Brazil wins its fifth World Cup.

tion, modernization was on the way. In the 1970s builders connected Rio with Niterói with the construction of the bay-spanning bridge, while beneath the city, the first metro cars began to run. This outmoded *bonde* has nearly disappeared: Rio's last streetcar line runs from Centro to Santa Teresa, and still conjures up those nostalgic prewar days.

Meanwhile, the Zona Sul saw skyscrapers rising over the beaches of Copacabana and Leblon, with a shift of the wealthy to places further away from neglected downtown Rio. The moving of Brazil's capital to Brasília in 1960 seemed to spell the end for Centro, which became a ghost town after hours and retained none of the energy of its past. By the 1970s, its plazas and parks were dangerous places, surrounded by aging office towers.

The center of old Rio remained a bleak place until around 1985, when Brazil held its first direct presidential election in 20 years. With the slow return to civilian rule, Cariocas turned their attention to sadly abandoned parts of the city, like downtown. Over the next decade citizens, particularly local shop owners, launched a downtown revitalization campaign, sometimes collecting money by going door-to-door.

By 1995 it was clear that the drive was a success. Whole blocks in downtown received much-needed facelifts. Handsomely restored buildings attracted new investment, with new shops and cultural centers opening their doors alongside book publishers and art galleries. And nightlife returned to Lapa.

A CITY DIVIDED

Unfortunately, the latter half of the 20th century was also an era of explosive growth in the favelas, as immigrants poured in from poverty-stricken areas of the northeast and the interior, swelling the number of urban poor in the city. The *Cidade Maravilhosa* began to lose its gloss as crime and violence increased, and in the 1990s it became known as the *cidade partida* (divided city), a term that reflected the widening chasm between the affluent neighborhoods of the Zona Sul and the shanty towns spreading across the region's hillsides.

As Rio entered the new millennium, crime remained one of the most pervasive problems afflicting the city. Violence continued to take thousands of lives – particularly in the favelas – with no signs of letting up; some 1300 people were killed by police alone in 2007. Rio's middle and upper classes seemed mostly resigned to life inside gated and guarded condos, while poverty and violence surged in the slums nearby.

The government solution often failed to solve the problem. Crack troops would be sent in to take out a drug lord yet, whether or not their mission was successful, the heavy caliber raids often claimed innocent lives. This left many residents with a deep-rooted disdain for the police. Declaring war on the favelas was clearly not working; once the police left, drug lord in hand (or more likely dead), there was always someone else to take his place.

For insight into the problem, see the film *Tropa Elite* (Elite Squad, 2007), researched by former police officers and drug traffickers.

A NEW DAWN

As a result of a worsening situation, Brazilian officials began to take a new approach. President Lula (full name Luiz Inácio Lula da Silva), who astutely saw the link between poverty and crime, announced in 2007 that Rio's favelas would receive US$1.7 billion to invest in running water, sanitation, roads and housing. He even paid a visit to the Cantagalo favela, a first for a Brazilian

2007

Rio hosts the Pan American Games, spending an estimated US$2 billion. Brazilian athletes rank third overall in total medal rankings (behind the US and Cuba). Increased police presence helps insure relative calm in the city.

2009

The jubilation returns as Rio is named host city of the 2016 Summer Olympics, making Brazil the first South American country in history to stage the event. Tens of thousands celebrate on Copacabana beach.

2010

Rio hosts its biggest Carnaval in history, with more than 400 street parties and some 700,000 visitors arriving to fete the big event. The city also experiences its hottest summer on record as temperatures soar to 46°C (115°F).

WORLD CUP DREAMS

Bringing the World Cup back to Brazil has long been a dream of the football-crazed nation. In 2007, the dream became reality when FIFA announced that Brazil had won the rights to host the World Cup in 2014. The South American giant last staged the big sporting event in 1950 when Brazil lost in the dramatic final against Uruguay before 200,000 fans in Rio's Maracanã stadium (which has since been modified to hold smaller crowds). The unforgettable day of infamy was later called '*maracanazo*' and is still in common parlance.

Brazil, the most successful football nation in the history of the games (with five World Cup victories), will become the fifth country to host the event twice. The 2014 World Cup will be staged all across the country in 12 different cities, including Rio.

Much work and expense lies ahead with stadium construction and remodeling. Another huge sum is earmarked for infrastructure projects – including upgrading ports, highways and airports (most importantly Rio's and São Paulo's) to cope with the massive influx of fans – an estimated 500,000 visitors.

As of early 2010, Brazil had already fallen behind on its construction schedules, and FIFA had grown increasingly worried that Brazil wouldn't be ready in time for the big event. There is even speculation that Brazil will have to cut its host cities from 12 down to eight.

But no matter how it pans out in the end, Brazil is likely to throw a spectacular World Cup – if only for the animation of its fans and for the huge parties that will accompany the event.

Rio for its part will most likely play a starring role in the 2014 World Cup, possibly hosting both the opening match and the final; it will play an even bigger role two years later when it hosts the Summer Olympics. For more details on preparations in the *Cidade Maravilhosa*, see p47.

president. He later told a reporter that such investment – providing adequate services for the people – was the only way to combat drug lords.

On the local level, police began implementing a new approach to dealing with the drug traffickers in the favela. Led by a new wing called the Pacifier Police Division, they would drive the drug lords out as they had done before, after which the police would stay behind in the community. In 2008 the favela Dona Marta became one of the first to be 'pacified', and millions of reais were invested in the community, repairing or sometimes replacing houses, improving sanitation and adding a new football (soccer) pitch – though the most dramatic improvement was adding a new funicular railroad that saved residents the 788-step slog to the top of the favela.

Although it's early, the strategy has shown signs of success and it's been implemented in eight other favelas around Rio (affecting some 100,000 residents who now live in a free community that was once controlled by drug lords). Lula himself visited Dona Marta in 2009 (as an aside, Dona Marta is also where Michael Jackson filmed part of his 1996 video, *They don't care about us.*) In an interview with the BBC Lula said, 'We are working in a way that the state is present in the day-to-day lives of poor people,' and later said, 'We have the biggest investment program of favela urbanization, basic sanitation and house building that Brazil has ever had.'

Pulling people out of poverty has long been one of Lula's overarching goals, and Brazil has had marked success in achieving this, with 10.4 million people leaving poverty-level conditions over the past decade. The city for its part continues to focus on bringing these dramatic improvements to other slums in the city, setting a goal of reaching 100 favelas by 2011 and the entire city by 2016.

Speaking of 2016, this is the year that seems to be on everyone's minds – at least when they're not thinking of 2014. The great moment for Rio – and Brazil – seems just over the horizon as it prepares to host first the FIFA World Cup, followed two years later, by the Summer Olympics. The latter will require enormous investment. During its ultimately successful pitch to IOCC, Brazil promised to spend US$14 billion – twice as much as the next highest contender – to overcome daunting logistical and social challenges. Some market analysts say the games could bring as much as $50 billion in new investments.

On other fronts, Rio, along with Brazil fared relatively well during the global financial crisis. The nation suffered a mild recession in 2009, with GDP contracting by 0.2% – the first time its economy had contracted in 17 years. In 2010, however, the economy was already on the rebound, with Brazilian Finance Minister Guido Mantega predicting 5.7% growth over the course of the year.

ARTS

Since its founding 500 years ago, Rio has made enormous contributions to the arts. Its world-class music scene continues to dominate center stage, but there's much more ablaze than just samba in the *Cidade Maravilhosa*. The city's museums, cinemas, theaters and concert halls continue to be a strong source of innovation – and inspiration – just like its venerated music clubs. Support for the arts is strong, with a good mix of the classic and daring vying for attention on the many stages throughout town.

Music is undoubtedly one of Rio's great legacies. The memorable talents from the 1930s may have disappeared, but a new crop of singers and musicians has taken their place. The revitalized neighborhood of Lapa is the center of samba, its old *gafieiras* (dance halls) drawing a diverse crowd who come to dance and hear the latest rising star. But samba can be heard all over town, at tiny storefront bars in Copacabana, spacious clubs in Centro and the verandas of Santa Teresa. Rio also has its great contributors of rock, Música Popular Brasileira (MPB), *choro*, jazz, hip-hop and even a few nostalgic bossa nova voices, which you can still hear in certain parts of town. Other distinctly Carioca innovations include *baile funk* (enormous dance parties in the favelas).

Like its music, Rio's fine arts scene is a dynamic one, with well-attended museums and galleries hosting some of Brazil's best exhibitions. At avant-garde galleries like the Centro de Arte He'lio Oitícica (p92), wall space is the domain of Rio's experimental artists. More venerable institutions showcase Brazil's most talented artists, with the Museu de Arte Moderna (MAM; p89) and Centro Cultural Banco do Brasil (p89) leading the way. There's also plenty of evocative street art, with certain boulevards – such as the southern end of Rua Jardim Botânico – hosting a riotous medley of color in its imaginative graffiti. Other artists use Rio as their backdrop, as is the case when Santa Teresa hosts its annual Portas Abertas (p21).

Brazilian cinema continues to speed ahead. Each year, the film industry produces some excellent homegrown productions, and Cariocas also have a healthy appetite for foreign and independent films. There are dozens of theaters about town, and some notable film festivals, including the Festival do Rio (p22), which screens over 300 films from across the globe and attracts huge audiences.

Theater, dance and classical music also play an important role in the city's cultural life. Enormous stages like the modern Teatro Nelson Rodrigues (p171) host some of the city's biggest and best productions, while the historic venues of Theatro Municipal (p171) and Sala Cecília Meireles (p171) also host some excellent performances.

Those with good Portuguese can immerse themselves in the literary world, catching local poets at spoken-word events like those hosted at Leblon's Da Conde (p111) and other bookstores in town. Literary lights such as José Saramago and Paulo Coelho also give readings when in town.

Rio's calendar is packed with festivals, and new events pop up all the time. These are great places to see what's hot and new in the city. See p20 for special events happening during your stay. For a complete list of venues to catch music, theater, dance and more, see p160 and p170.

MUSIC

Rio boasts an enormous musical heritage. Rock, jazz, electronic music and uniquely Brazilian styles all showcase the talents of an astounding pool of musical talent. Foremost of all is the city's signature sound of samba – a deeply ingrained part of life that is heard everywhere on the streets.

Samba

The birth of Brazilian music essentially began with the birth of samba, first heard in the early 20th century in a Rio neighborhood near present-day Praça Onze. Here, immigrants from northeastern Brazil (mostly from Bahia) formed a tightly knit community in which traditional African customs thrived – music, dance and the Candomblé religion. Local homes provided the setting for impromptu performances and the exchange of ideas among Rio's first great instrumentalists. Such an atmosphere nurtured the likes of Pixinguinha, one of samba's founding fathers, as well as Donga, one of the composers of 'Pelo Telefone,' the first recorded samba song (in 1917) and an enormous success at the then-fledgling Carnaval.

Samba continued to evolve in the homes and *botequims* (bars) around Rio. The 1930s are known as the golden age of samba. By this point, samba's popularity had spread beyond the working-class neighborhoods of central Rio, and the music evolved at the same time into diverse, less percussive styles of samba. Sophisticated lyricists like Dorival Caymmi, Ary Barroso and Noel Rosa popularized *samba-canção* (melody-driven samba). (For insight into Noel Rosa's poetically charged and tragically brief life, check out the 2006 film *Noel: Poeta da Vila.*) Songs in this style featured sentimental lyrics and an emphasis on melody (rather than rhythm), foreshadowing the later advent of cool bossa nova. Carmen Miranda, one of the big radio stars of the 1930s, would become one of the first ambassadors of Brazilian music.

The 1930s were also the golden age of samba songwriting for the Carnaval. *Escolas de samba* (samba schools), which first emerged in 1928, soon became a vehicle for samba songwriting, and by the 1930s samba and Carnaval would be forever linked. Today's theme songs still borrow from that golden epoch.

Great *sambistas* (samba singers) continued to emerge in Brazil over the next few decades, although other emerging musical styles diluted their popularity. Artists such as Cartola, Nelson Cavaquinho and Clementina de Jesus made substantial contributions to both samba and styles of music that followed from it.

Traditional samba went through a rebirth over a decade ago with the opening of old-style *gafieiras* (dance halls) in Lapa (see p36). Today, Rio is once again awash with great *sambistas.* Classic *sambistas* like Alcione and Beth Carvalho still perform, while rising stars like Teresa Christina and Grupo Semente are intimately linked to Lapa's rebirth. Other talents on Rio's stages include Thais Villela, a rising star on the Lapa scene, and Diogo Nogueira, the deep-voiced samba son of legendary singer João Nogueira. Another singer carrying on the tradition of her father is Mart'nália, daughter of samba legend Martinho da Vila. Check out her 2006 album *Menino do Rio.*

Rio's best-known young samba singer is probably Maria Rita, the talented singer and songwriter whose voice is remarkably similar to that of her late mother, Elis Regina – one of Brazil's all-time greats. Although much of Rita's work often falls into the MPB camp, her 2007 album *Samba Meu* is still her best, with a brilliant collection of sambas.

Bossa Nova

In the 1950s came bossa nova (literally, new wave), sparking a new era of Brazilian music. Bossa nova's founders – songwriter and composer Antonio Carlos (Tom) Jobim and guitarist João Gilberto, in association with the lyricist-poet Vinícius de Moraes – slowed down and altered the basic samba rhythm to create a more intimate, harmonic style. This new wave initiated a new style of playing instruments and of singing.

Bossa nova's seductive melodies were very much linked to Rio's Zona Sul, where most bossa musicians lived. Songs such as Jobim's *'Corcovado'* and Roberto Meneschal's *'Rio'* evoked an almost nostalgic portrait of the city with their quiet lyricism. Bossa was also associated with the new class of university-educated Brazilians, and its lyrics reflected the optimistic mood of the middle class in the 1950s.

By the 1960s, bossa nova had become a huge international success. The genre's initial development was greatly influenced by American jazz and blues, and over time, the bossa nova style came to influence those music styles as well. Bossa nova classics were adopted, adapted and recorded by such musical luminaries as Frank Sinatra, Ella Fitzgerald and Stan Getz, among others.

In addition to the founding members, other great Brazilian bossa nova musicians include Marcos Valle, Luiz Bonfá and Baden Powell, whose talented son Marcel Powell carries on the musical tradition (catch him live around Rio). Bands from the 1960s like Sergio Mendes & Brasil '66 were also influenced by bossa nova, as were other artists who fled the repressive years of military-dictatorship rule to live and play abroad. More recent interpreters of the seductive bossa sound include the Bahian-born Rosa Passos and the Carioca Paula Morelenbaum.

For the full story, check out Ruy Castro's book *Bossa Nova: The Story of the Brazilian Music that Seduced the World.*

Tropicália

One of Brazil's great artistic movements, emerging in the late 1960s, was *tropicália,* a direct response to the repressive military dictatorship that seized power in 1964 (and remained in power until 1984). Bahian singers Caetano Veloso and Gilberto Gil led the movement, making

THE DANCE HALLS OF OLD *Carmen Michael*

If you're interested in Brazilian music and dance, shine up your dancing shoes and head for some of Rio's old-school-style dance halls, known as *gafieiras*. Originally established in the 1920s as dance halls for Rio's urban working class, *gafieiras* nowadays attract an eclectic combination of musicians, dancers, *malandros* (con men) and, of course, the radical chic from Zona Sul. Modern and sleek they are not. Typically held in the ballrooms of old colonial buildings in Lapa, the locations are magnificently old-world. Bow-tied waiters serve ice-cold *cerveja* (beer) under low, yellow lights and, while the setup initially looks formal, give it a few rounds and it will dissolve into a typically raucous Brazilian evening.

Before *gafieiras* were established, Rio's different communities were polarized by their places of social interaction, whether it was opera and tango for the Europeans or street *choro* (romantic, intimate samba) for the Africans. Responding to a social need and in tandem with the politics of the time, *gafieiras* quickly became places where musicians and audiences of black and white backgrounds alike could mix and create new sounds. Through the *gafieiras,* the street-improvised *choro* formations became big-band songs and a new Brazilian sound was born. The best and oldest dance halls are Democráticus (p163), attracting a young yet fashionably bohemian crowd on Wednesday, and Estudantina (p164) on Praça Tiradentes, which operates from Friday to Sunday.

The standard of dancing is outstanding in Brazil, so expect to see couples who would be considered professional in Europe or the US dancing unnoticed across the polished floors. While just about anything goes in Rio, it's an opportunity for the Cariocas to dress up a little, so you will see quite a few dresses and smart shoes. Don't be intimidated by the other dancers. Unlike in Buenos Aires, where the tango is for experts only, Brazilians are pretty relaxed about newcomers dancing. For those traveling solo, *gafieiras* are fantastic places to meet some intriguing locals and learn a few steps. Dance around the edge of the dance floor with the rest of the dancers to get a closer look at how the dance works – if you are a woman, you won't wait long before someone asks you to dance. Alternatively you can take a lesson and perhaps meet some fellow beginners to dance with. There are a number of places where you can sign up for a group or a private lesson. See p181 for details.

waves with songs of protest against the national regime. (Gil, ironically, is today's Minister of Culture – see p39.) In addition to penning defiant lyrics, *tropicalistas* introduced the public to electric instruments, fragmentary melodies and wildly divergent musical styles. In fact, the *tropicalistas'* hero was poet Oswald de Andrade, whose 1928 *Manifesto Antropofágico* (Cannibalistic Manifesto) supported the idea that anything under the sun could be devoured and re-created in one's music. Hence, the movement fused elements of US rock and roll, blues, jazz and British psychedelic styles into bossa nova and samba rhythms. Important figures linked to *tropicália* include Gal Costa, Jorge Benjor, Maria Bethânia, Os Mutantes and Tom Zé. Although *tropicália* wasn't initially embraced by the public, who objected to the electric and rock elements (in fact, Veloso was booed off the stage on several occasions), by the 1970s its radical ideas had been absorbed and accepted, and lyrics of protest were ubiquitous in songwriting of the time.

The world is still coming to grips with the complex musical legacy of the *tropicalistas.* A 2006 exposition at London's Barbican Centre was dedicated to the movement, and included the music of AfroReggae, one of Rio's leading funk groups, whose songs have elements of *tropicália*. Os Mutantes also helped reignite interest in *tropicália* during their 2006 world reunion tour (which unfortunately did not include Rita Lee).

Those who want a deeper understanding of the movement and its aftermath should read Caetano Veloso's self-congratulatory book *Tropical Truth*.

Música Popular Brasileira (MPB)

Música Popular Brasileira (MPB) is a catchphrase to describe all popular Brazilian music after bossa nova. It includes *tropicália, pagode* (relaxed and rhythmic form of samba), and Brazilian pop and rock. All Brazilian music has roots in samba; even in Brazilian rock, heavy metal, disco or pop, the samba sound is often present.

MPB first emerged in the 1970s along with talented musicians such as Edu Lobo, Milton Nascimento, Elis Regina, Djavan and dozens of others, many of whom wrote protest songs not unlike the *tropicalistas.* Chico Buarque is one of the first big names from this epoch, and is easily one of Brazil's greatest songwriters. His music career began in 1968 and spanned a time during which many of his songs were banned by the military dictatorship – in fact his music became a symbol of protest during that era. Today the enormously successful Carioca artist continues to write new albums, though lately he has turned his hand to novel writing.

Jorge Benjor is another singer whose career, which began in the 1960s, has survived up to the present day. Highly addictive rhythms are omnipresent in Benjor's songs, as he incorporates African beats and elements of funk, samba and blues in his eclectic repertoire. The celebratory album *África Brasil,* alongside his debut album *Samba Esquema Novo* (with recognizable hits like 'Mas, Que Nada!') are among his best.

Carlinhos Brown is another popular artist (and workaholic) who continues to make immeasurable contributions to Brazilian music, particularly in the realm of Afro-Brazilian rhythms. Born in Bahia, Brown has influences that range from *merengue* (fast-paced dancehall music originating in the Domincan Republic) to Candomblé music to straight-up James Brown–style funk (the US artist from whom Carlinhos took his stage name). In addition to creating the popular percussion ensemble Timbalada, he has a number of excellent albums of his own (notably *Alfagamabetizado*).

Rock, Pop & Hip Hop

MPB tends to bleed into other genres, particularly into rock and pop. One artist who moves comfortably between genres is Bebel Gilberto (the talented daughter of João Gilberto), who blends bossa nova with modern beats on jazz-inflected bilingual albums like *All in One* (2009). Another heiress of Brazilian traditions is the Rio-born Marisa Monte, popular at home and abroad for her fine singing and songwriting. Mixing samba, *forró* (traditional, fast-paced music from the northeast), pop and rock, Marisa has been part of a number of successful collaborations in the music world, most recently with Arnaldo Antunes and Carlinhos Brown to create the hit album *Tribalistas* (2003). Other notable young singers who hail from a bossa line include Roberta Sá (with an excellent live album *Pra se Ter Alegria,* 2009) and Fernanda Porto (whose music is often described as drum 'n' bossa, a blend of electronica and bossa grooves – check out her 2009 album *Auto-Retrato*). The expat singer-songwriter and performance artist Cibelle incorporates a mix of pop, folk and Brazilian sounds in her lush (mainly English-language) recordings like those on *The Shine of Dried Electric Leaves* (2006). She came to prominence as the main vocalist on Suba's noteworthy album São Paulo Confessions (1999). An emerging star both at home and abroad, Céu sings dreamlike melodies with elements of Tropicália, samba, reggae and jazz (indeed she's hard to peg on her two well-received albums, the latest of which is *Vagarosa,* released in 2009).

Brazilian hip-hop emerged from the favelas of Rio sometime in the 1980s, and has been slowly attracting followers ever since. Big names such as Racionais MCs first emerged out of São Paulo, but Rio has its share of more recent success stories. One of the best on the scene is Marcelo D2 (formerly of Planet Hemp) impressing audiences with albums like *A Procura da Batida Perfeita* (2005) and *Meu Samba É Assim* (2006). Seu Jorge, who

THE IPOD 25: SOUNDS FROM BRAZIL

One of the world's great music cultures, Brazil has an astounding array of talented musicians. A list of our favorite songs could easily fill this chapter, but we've limited our highly subjective pick to 25 songs from 25 different artists.

- 'Canto de Ossanha' – Baden Powell
- 'Soy Loco Por Ti, America' – Caetano Veloso
- 'Alvorado' – Cartola
- 'Samba de Orly' – Chico Buarque and Toquinho
- 'Flor de Lis' – Djavan
- 'Aguas de Março' – Elis Regina (written by Tom Jobim)
- 'Hoje É Dia da Festa' – Elza Soares
- 'Sou Brasileiro' – Fernando Abreu and Mart'nália
- 'Namorinho de Portão' – Gal Costa
- 'Quilombo, O El Dorado Negro' – Gilberto Gil
- 'Desafinado' – João Gilberto
- 'Filho Maravilha' – Jorge Benjor
- 'A Procura da Batida Perfeita' – Marcelo D2
- 'Novo Amor' – Maria Rita
- 'Carinhoso' – Marisa Monte (written by Pixinguinha)
- 'Travessia' – Milton Nascimento
- 'Ultimo Desejo' – Noel Rosa
- 'Besta é Tu' – Novos Baianos
- 'Panis et Circenses' – Os Mutantes
- 'Acenda O Farol' – Tim Maia
- 'Garota de Ipanema' – Tom Jobim
- 'Aquarela do Brasil' – Toquinho (written by Ary Barroso)
- 'Velha Infância' – Tribalistas
- 'Não me deixe só' – Vanessa da Mata
- 'Felicidade' – Vinicius de Moraes

starred in the film *Cidade de Deus* (as well as singing brilliant Portuguese versions of Bowie songs on Wes Anderson's film *The Life Aquatic*). His best solo work is *Cru* (2005), an inventive hybrid of hip-hop and ballads, with politically charged beats. The Carioca rapper MV Bill is a man with a message. His songs focus on youth facing the ever-present threats of drugs and violence. He's even written a book *(Falcão – Meninos do Tráfico)* and created a network of youth centers in Rio that offer kids – who might otherwise be on the street – classes in dancing, music and art.

Rock has its promoters, though it enjoys far less airtime than samba. Rio gets its share of mega-rockers on the world tour (the Rolling Stones played before an estimated 1.5 million on Copacabana Beach in 2006). It also has a few homegrown talents. The group Legião Urbana from Brasília remains a national favorite even after the death of its lead singer in 2007. Skank, O Rappa, Paralamas Sucesso and the Rio-based Barão Vermelho are other essential names.

In other genres, indie-rock favorites Los Hermanos are among the best bands competing for airtime. Check out their excellent album *Ventura*. Vanguart, fitting somewhere in the folk-rock genre, are also a group to watch. Their self-titled debut album (2007) channels samba, blues and classic rock. Another indie favorite is Monokini, a group that blends pop with electro grooves – think vaguely Stereolab in the tropics. Their best album, if you can find it, is *Mondo Topless* (2004).

There's no doubt that more great artists will emerge by the time you read this. Your best bet: after arriving, head straight to a record store in Rio (try Modern Sound, p118) and find out who's the hottest pop star of the moment. It's unlikely the store clerk will answer Beyoncé, or any non-Brazilian artist for that matter. For a more detailed history of Brazilian music, check out Chris McGowan and Ricardo Pessanha's recently updated *The Brazilian Sound* (2008). McGowan's blog, with links to Brazilian artists, is also worth checking out: http://thebrazil iansound.blogspot.com.

CINEMA

Brazil has a prolific film industry, though much of what it makes doesn't venture beyond the country's borders. *Lula, O Filho do Brasil* (Lula the Son of Brazil, 2010), directed by Fábio Barreto, is one of the nation's most recent high-profile films (and to date its costliest at R$17 million). The biopic of outgoing president Lula from shoeshine boy to union leader wasn't well received at home (some critics complained of a whitewashing of some darker episodes in Lula's life), though it may fare better abroad.

Beyond Ipanema (2009), written and directed by Béco Dranoff and Guto Barra, is an excellent documentary about one of Brazil's most important exports: music. Featuring interviews with Caetano Veloso, Seu Jorge, Bebel Gilberto, David Byrne and many others, the film explores the influence of Brazilian music on the world stage.

One of the most-talked about films of 2007 was *Tropa de Elite* (Elite Squad), which depicts police brutality in the favelas; it also makes a very clear link between middle-class college kids who buy drugs and the deaths of young children in the favelas who are recruited by drug lords to help meet the demand for coke and other substances. It was made by José Padilha, the acclaimed director of the disturbing documentary *Bus 174,* which depicts a high-profile bus hijacking that took place in Rio de Janeiro in 2000. (Do yourself a favor and watch it *after* your trip, rather than before!)

The beautifully set *Casa da Areia* (House of Sand, 2006), directed by Andrucha Waddington, follows three generations of women as they struggle in the dramatic but desolate landscape of Maranhão. It stars real-life mother and daughter Fernanda Montenegro and Fernando Torres, with Seu Jorge in a supporting role.

Slightly more uplifting is *Dois Filhos do Francisco* (The Two Sons of Francisco, 2005), based on the true story of two brothers – Zeze and Luciano di Camargo – who overcame their humble origins to become successful country musicians. Despite some unfortunate melodrama, the film has plenty of merit, including a curious soundtrack created under the direction of Caetano Veloso. It is also the highest grossing film at the box office in the last 20 years.

Although made by two Americans, *Favela Rising* (2005) is so quintessentially 'Rio' that it deserves mention. A fine counterpoint to *Cidade de Deus* (more on that later), this documentary shows a different side of the favela through the eyes of Anderson Sá, founder of the very

BRAZIL'S FAVORITE VOICE *Tom Phillips*

One of Brazil's best-loved musicians still active on the scene today is Gilberto Gil, a Grammy-award winning singer and former minister of culture (from 2003 to 2008), who wasn't averse to singing a few songs following a meeting at, say, the World Economic Forum in Davos. The pop star made an unlikely government bureaucrat, considering his musical beginnings as an *engajado* (activist). During the 1960s he spent two years exiled in London after offending the dictatorship with his provocative lyrics.

A household name for decades, Gil hails from the northeastern state of Bahia. Born in 1942, he was raised in a middle-class family near Salvador. His career as a troubadour began in 1965, when he moved south to São Paulo with another Bahian musician, Caetano Veloso. Between them they were responsible for *tropicália,* an influential though short-lived cultural movement that blended traditional Brazilian music with the electric guitars and psychedelia of the Beatles. Years later Veloso even recorded a Tupiniquim (an indigenous group in the northeast) tribute to the Liverpudlian rockers – called *Sugar Cane Fields Forever*.

Over the decades Gil has notched up hit after hit – morphing from quick-footed *sambista* (samba singer) to Stevie Wonderesque balladeer to dreadlocked reggae icon.

Since the release of *Louvaçao* in 1967, Gil has recorded dozens of albums, including *Kaya N'Gan Daya,* a tribute to his idol Bob Marley. He's shared the stage with many performers over the years, even playing with the former UN general Secretary Kofi Annan (on bongos) in New York.

In between world tours, book launches and his ministerial duties, the slender 60 something year old even finds time for the beach. Keep your eyes peeled – it's not uncommon to find Gil sunning himself at Ipanema's Posto 9.

Here is some essential listening:

- *Gilberto Gil (Frevo Rasgado, 1968)* – Gilberto Gil
- *Acoustic* (1994) – Gilberto Gil
- *Quanta* (1997) – Gilberto Gil
- *Refazenda* (1996) – Gilberto Gil
- *Tropicália 2* (1994) – Gilberto Gil and Caetano Veloso
- *Tropicália, ou Panis et Circencis* (1968) – Gilberto Gil, Caetano Veloso, Gal Costa and Os Mutantes

talented *Grupo Cultural Afro Reggae* (Afro-Reggae Group) and a massive symbol of hope for many poor children growing up in the favela. In the film, Sá, who turned his life around after involvement in gangs, starts a music school for youths and makes an enormous contribution to a number of lives as the Afro-Reggae movement spreads to other favelas.

Another worthwhile documentary is *Vinícius* (2005), a paean to the great poet and songwriter Vinícius de Moraes, directed by his ex-son-in-law Miguel Faria Jr. The film features archival footage of old interviews as well as performances of Vinícius' music as played by some of Brazil's best artists.

The documentary *Rio de Jano* (2003) shows an outsider perspective via interviews with the French cartoonist Jano. Jean le Guay (aka Jano) carefully avoids the stereotypes but captures the Carioca sense of humor while drawing a mixed gang at work (in blue-collar jobs), at the beach, dancing at a funk party and basking on the beach. Director Anna Azevedo did a marvelous job bringing Jano's vision to life.

For a trip back to the 1930s Lapa, check out Karim Aïnouz's compelling *Madame Satã* (2002). Rio's gritty red-light district of that time (which hasn't changed much in the last 75 years) is the setting for the true story of Madame Satã (aka João Francisco dos Santos), the troubled but good-hearted *malandro* (con artist), transvestite, singer and a master of *capoeira* (a Brazilian martial art), who became a symbol of Lapa's mid-century bohemianism.

One of Brazil's top directors, Fernando Meirelles earned his credibility with *Cidade de Deus* (City of God), the 2002 film based on a true story by Paolo Lins. The film, which shows brutality and hope co-existing in a Rio favela, earned four Oscar nominations, including one for best director. More importantly, it brought much attention to the plight of the urban poor in Brazil. After his success with *Cidade de Deus,* Meirelles went to Hollywood with *The Constant Gardener* (2004), a conspiracy film shot in Africa. His most recent film is *Blindness* (2008), a dark allegory in which the entire world loses its sight, based on the Portuguese novel by Nobel prize–winning author José Saramago.

Eu, Tu, Eles (Me, You, Them), Andrucha Waddington's social comedy about a northeasterner with three husbands, was also well received when it was released in 2000. It has beautiful cinematography and a score by Gilberto Gil (see p39) that contributed to the recent wave of popularity of that funky northeastern music, *forró*.

Walter Salles is one of Brazil's best-known directors, whose Oscar award-winning *Central do Brasil* (Central Station, 1998) should be in every serious Brazilophile's film library. The central character is an elderly woman who works in the main train station in Rio writing letters for illiterate people with families far away. A chance encounter with a young homeless boy leads her to accompany him into the real, unglamorized Brazil on a search for his father. Salles' latest foray into film is his big-budget biopic *Diarios de Motocicleta* (The Motorcycle Diaries, 2004), detailing the historic journey of Che Guevara and Alberto Granada across South America.

As with many filmmakers, some of Salles' best works came much earlier. In fact, his first feature film *Terra Estrangeiro* (Foreign Land, 1995) holds an important place in the renaissance of Brazilian cinema. The film won seven international prizes and was shown at over two dozen film festivals. It was named best film of the year in Brazil in 1996, where it screened for over six months. Salles is also a great documentary filmmaker; *Socorro Nobre* (Life Somewhere Else, 1995) and *Krajcberg, O Poeta dos Vestígios* (Krajcberg, the Poet of the Remains, 1987) have won awards at international festivals.

Bruno Barreto's *O Que É Isso Companheiro* (released as *Four Days in September* in the US, 1998) is based on the 1969 kidnapping of the US ambassador to Brazil by leftist guerrillas. It was nominated for an Oscar in 1998.

Another milestone in Brazilian cinema is the visceral film *Pixote* (1981), directed by the acclaimed Hector Babenco. This film shows life through the eyes of a street kid in Rio, who gets swept along on a journey from innocent waif to murderer by the currents of the underworld. The film is a damning indictment of Brazilian society, made all the more poignant when the actor who played Pixote was killed by police during a bungled robbery six years after the making of the film.

Another important film is *Bye Bye Brasil* (1980) by Carlos Diegues. The first major film produced after the end of the dictatorship, it chronicles the adventures of a theater troupe as it tours the entire country, charting the profound changes in Brazilian society in the second half of the 20th century. Diegues went on to direct *Orfeu* (1999), a lackluster remake of the Camus classic.

Prior to the military dictatorship (1964–85), which stymied much creative expression in the country, Brazil was in the grip of Cinema Novo. This 1960s movement focused on Brazil's bleak social problems, and was influenced by Italian neorealism. One of the great films made during this epoch is *O Pagador de Promessas* (The Payer of Vows, 1962), a poetic story about a man who keeps his promise to carry a cross after the healing of his donkey. It won the Palme d'Or at the Cannes Film Festival. Another great pioneer of Cinema Novo is the director Glauber Rocha. In *Deus e o Diabo na Terra do Sol* (Black God, White Devil, 1963), Rocha touches on many of the elements in northeastern Brazil of struggle, fanaticism and poverty. It's one of the great films of the period.

Another important film of the 20th century is Marcel Camus' *Orfeu Negro* (Black Orpheus, 1959), which opened the world's ears to bossa nova by way of the Jobim and Bonfá soundtrack. Music aside, the film did a clever job recasting Ovid's original Orpheus-Eurydice myth in the setting of Rio's Carnaval (a fertile ground for mythmaking). Having an arguably larger impact on Brazilian cinema was the Nelson Pereira dos Santos film *Rio 40 Graus* (1955). This classic of Cinema Novo follows a number of characters and plots that intertwine at an electric pace. Because of its unglamorized portrait of the poor, it was banned on release and wasn't shown in theaters until a year later.

Brazilian cinema began in Rio; appropriately, the city itself starred in the first film made in the country – a slow pan of Baía de Guanabara, made in 1898.

LITERATURE

Carioca author Paulo Coelho, whose books have sold more than 100 million copies, is one of the world's most widely read novelists. While critics tend to knock his simplistic New Age spiritual fables, books such as *The Pilgrimage* (1987), *The Alchemist* (1988) and *The Witch of Portobello* (2006) have struck a nerve with his global fan base, bringing him rock-star fame.

CLARICE LISPECTOR: QUEEN OF THE LITERARY AVANT-GARDE

'I am so mysterious that even I don't understand myself,' Clarice Lispector once wrote.

For readers outside of Brazil, one of Latin America's great 20th-century novelists remains little known. Yet in Brazil, Lispector (1920–77) enjoys the status of a literary luminary, with her books widely available and adaptations of her work in heavy rotation on theater stages around the country. Why her fame has not spread beyond Brazil is something of an unknown. The American poet Elizabeth Bishop, who translated some of Lispector's work, raved about her in letters to friends. 'I think she is better than JL Borges – who is good, but not all that good!'

Other critics raved of her work – including her biographer who hailed *The Passion According to GH* as 'one of the greatest novels of the 20th century.' Perhaps part of her obscurity may be owing to her complicated life and the cult of mystery that seemed to surround her. She was born in the Ukraine to Jewish parents who fled the pogroms following WWI. Her family immigrated to Recife in the Northeast of Brazil. There her mother died when she was nine – from syphilis she contracted from Russian soldiers who raped her – and her father took her and her two sisters to Rio. She excelled at her studies (even graduating from a well-known law school) but decided early on that she wanted to be a writer. At 22 she published her first novel, a stream-of-consciousness work entitled *Near to the Wild Heart* that earned her critical acclaim and comparisons to Woolf, Joyce and Proust, among others.

In 1944 her life took a turn when she married a Brazilian diplomat. She lived abroad for the next eight years, as he was posted to Naples, Berne (Switzerland), Torquay (England) and Washington, DC. From her correspondence, she missed Rio desperately, describing Switzerland as 'a cemetery of sensations,' and became discontent with the diplomatic milieu: 'I hated it, but I did what I had to.' In 1959 she left her husband and returned to Rio with her two sons. There her lifestyle grew increasingly unconventional. She consulted with astrologers and card readers and became increasingly difficult to be around – storming out of social engagements and giving erratic, sometimes absurd, interviews. Before her death in 1977, she had become something of a recluse.

Lispector published eight other novels as well as volumes of short stories and children's books, though only a handful have been translated into English. A new study of Lispector, *Why This World: A Biography of Clarice Lispector* (2009), written by Benjamin Moser, may help bring her to a larger audience.

A writer of 'actual' rock-star fame is talented singer and songwriter Chico Buarque. The author of two rather mediocre novels, Buarque seemed to jump the fence successfully in his third effort, *Budapest* (2003), an engaging and meditative novel of love and language set in Budapest and Rio.

A far-different worldview is presented in works from the detective genre, with popular novels finally available in English. Often called the Raymond Chandler of Brazil, Luis Alfredo Garcia-Roza writes hard-boiled page-turners, often set in his Copacabana neighborhood. To explore the noir side of Rio check out his novels *Southwesterly Wind* (2004) and *Window in Copacabana* (2005). Patrícia Melo is another Brazilian crime novelist (and playwright), who's received praise from both readers and academics for her smart, psychologically complex thrillers. Among her best works are *The Killer* (1998) and *Inferno* (2002).

More widely respected in literary circles is the great Brazilian writer Jorge Amado, who died in 2001. Born near Ilhéus in 1912, and a longtime resident of Salvador, Amado wrote colorful romances of Bahia's people and places, with touches of magical realism. His early work was strongly influenced by communism. His later books were lighter in subject, but more picturesque and intimate in style. The most acclaimed are *Gabriela, Clove and Cinnamon* (1958), set in Ilhéus, and *Dona Flor and Her Two Husbands* (1966), set in Salvador. The latter relates the tale of a young woman who must decide between two lovers – the first being the man she marries after her first husband drops dead at Carnaval, the second being her deceased husband who returns to her as a (still amorous) ghost. Amado's other works include *Tent of Miracles* (1969), which explores race relations in Brazil, and provides an excellent introduction to Candomblé (Amado himself was a practitioner). *The Violent Land* (1943) is an early Amado classic – something of a dark frontier story. *Shepherds of the Night* (1964), three short stories about a group of Bahian characters, provides another excellent and witty portrait of Bahia.

In the 19th century, José de Alencar became one of Brazil's most famous writers. Many of his works are set in Rio, including *Cinco Minutos* and *Senhora,* both published in 1875. Another author from that era, Joaquim Manoel de Macedo was a great chronicler of the customs of his time. In addition to such romances as *A Moreninha,* he wrote *Um Passeio Pela Cidade do Rio de Janeiro* (1863) and *Memórias da Rua do Ouvidor* (1878). Joaquim Maria Machado de Assis, another Carioca, is widely regarded as Brazil's greatest writer. The son of a freed slave, Assis worked as a typesetter and journalist in late-19th-century Rio. A tremendous stylist with a great command of humor and irony, Assis had a sharp understanding of human relations, which he used to great effect in his brilliantly cynical works. He used Rio as the background for most of the works he produced in the late 19th century, such as *The Posthumous Memoirs of Bras Cubas* (1881) and *Quincas Borba* (1891).

Mario de Andrade led the country's artistic renaissance in the 1920s, and became one of the leading figures in the modernist movement in Brazil. In works such as *Macunaíma* (1928) he pioneered the use of vernacular language in national literature. He stressed the importance of Brazilian writers drawing from their own rich heritage. His work showed elements of surrealism and was later seen as a precursor to magical realism.

VISUAL ARTS

Although currently little known outside of Brazil, Rio's artists are slowly carving a name for themselves in the contemporary art world. At the forefront of the art movement are avant-gardists such as Ducha, who utilizes the city's unique topography to create some of his boldest works. His best-known work is his 2001 *Projeto Cristo Redentor,* in which he turned the Christ statue blood-red by covering the white spotlights surrounding it with red gelatin film. This of course required breaking the law, which earned him a fair bit of notoriety.

Another Rio-based artist doing daring work is Jarbas Lopes. His politically and socially incisive work often takes aim at the corruption inherent in many spheres of Brazilian government. Lopes' *O Debate* (The Debate) series was created by manipulating posters, found on the street, of political candidates. Taking the posters of two opposing candidates, he'd weave them together, then place them back on the street, offering his views on the lack of choice in the elections.

Often associated with the *tropicália* movement, Lygia Clark (1920–88) had an art career spanning three decades. Her earliest pieces were monochrome constructivist paintings of the 1950s; in the '60s, her work became more conceptual, morphing finally into highly experimental explorations of sensory perception, ultimately entering a kind of psychotherapeutic realm. Her work continues to appear in exhibits around the globe.

Although he's not from Rio, the photographer Sebastião Salgado is Brazil's best-known contemporary artist outside the country. Noted for his masterful use of light, the black-and-white photographer has earned international acclaim for his stunningly beautiful and highly evocative photos of migrant workers and others on the fringes of society.

Going back a few years, the Carioca artist Hélio Oiticica (1937–80) was one of the most significant figures of the avant-garde of the '60s and '70s. He's best known for interactive works, like his controversial *Cosmococa,* an installation that invited viewers to lie on sand covered with plastic sheeting, while watching a projection in which lines of cocaine were arranged across a photo of Marilyn Monroe. Despite his short life, his impact on Brazilian art was profound. Today there's even a cultural center, Centro de Arte Hélio Oiticica, named after him.

Rio-born artist Cildo Meireles (b 1948) has also made a sizeable contribution to the contemporary art movement. Creating at the height of the military dictatorship, Meireles focused on the social environment, using silk screens and installations to question the legitimacy of the regime. In the US he garnered much attention for his designing and printing of fake banknotes that featured an image of Uncle Sam on one side and Fort Knox on the other, which he reintroduced into circulation.

Anna Bella Geiger (b 1933) is another important artist active since the 1960s. Following the warm reception of her early photographic work, she expanded her range, becoming one of Brazil's pioneers in video art. Her most recent work was her 2004 exhibition at Paço Imperial, entitled *Obras em Arquipélago,* a sublime composition uniting the language and design of cartography with the geography of the human body.

Getting his start a few decades earlier was the experimental artist Abraham Palatnik, one of the first Brazilians to explore the use of technology in art. He delighted critics with his masterful mixing of light and movement, which he fused in 'cinechromatic machines' – projections of colored light forms onto clear surfaces, innovative work for the 1950s. His last solo exhibition was held in Rio in 1986.

Throughout Brazil's recent history, the influence of European and other foreign art on Brazilian work is significant. In the 19th and 20th centuries, Brazilian artists followed international trends

LIVING ART

Street art sometimes comes to life in extraordinary forms in Rio de Janeiro. Take for example the sprawling exhibit held in the Centro Cultural Banco do Brasil (p89) in 2009, which featured the enormous wall murals and sculptures done by celebrated (but renegade) Brazilian street artists Os Gemeos (www.lost.art.br/osgemeos.htm).

A year earlier, an even more daring 'installation' took place in one of Rio's most notorious favelas, Morro da Providência. French photographer and graffiti artist JR came to Rio to create a project called 'Women are Heroes'. He went into Providência and (after earning the trust of the local drug lords) interviewed and photographed women who've had tough lives – losing their children to violence, suffering from corruption first-hand. After hearing their stories and carrying out photo shoots, he then enlarged their portraits to mural size and pasted them onto buildings, stairwells and other spaces around the favela, creating a giant gallery of evocative images for anyone who happened to pass by. His project, which was repeated in several countries in Africa, as well as in Cambodia, aims to bring light not only to the extraordinary hardships faced by many women across the world, but to also acknowledge their courage and crucial roles in their communities. You can view images from the favela on www.womenareheroes.be.

such as neoclassicism, romanticism, impressionism and modernism. The best-known Brazilian painter internationally is Cândido Portinari (1903–62). Early in his career he made the decision to paint only Brazil and its people. Strongly influenced by the Mexican muralists, such as Diego Rivera, he fused native, expressionist influences with a sophisticated, socially conscious style.

Rio's earliest painters were quite taken with the landscape – a tradition that continues today. The 19th-century French artists Jean-Baptiste Debret and Nicolas Taunay, who came via the French artistic mission, set the tone for the development of art over the next 100 years (some critics say they stifled Brazilian art by keeping it rooted in old-fashioned traditions). Regardless, Debret's and Taunay's works in watercolor are some of the first visual records of life in the colony. The neoclassical strand was continued in later works such as Victor Meirelles' *A Primeira Missa* (the First Mass, 1861), which depicts the first Mass celebrated in the new colony, with Pedro Álvarez Cabral (Portuguese discoverer of Brazil) and his men in attendance.

THEATER & DANCE

One of the big names in Brazilian theater today is the avant-garde director Gerald Thomas. Raised in Rio, Thomas now lives in New York, but continues to have some of his biggest successes on Rio's stages. His work, which he calls Dry Opera, features the almost cinematic use of blackouts and atmospheric lighting, along with pre-recorded music and marionette-like acting. For some, it amounts to a complete reinvention of theater. The political comedy *Um Circo de Rins e Fígados* (A Circus of Kidneys and Livers) remains one of his long-running successes (already seen by over 80,000 people in both Brazil and Argentina). His drama isn't strictly limited to his plays: in 2003, following his production of *Tristan und Isolde,* several belligerent audience members shouted at the director, and he mooned them from onstage. This led to criminal proceedings, though his name was eventually cleared.

Equal parts dance, theater and performance art, Intrépida Trupa has been showcasing its avant-garde pieces since 1986. Expertly choreographed acrobatics, impressive special effects and dramatic tension have earned comparisons to Cirque du Soleil. Its popular show Metegol returns periodically to Rio, usually staged at Fundição Progresso (p100), where the troupe also gives classes in acrobatics (p181).

Rio's lively theater scene began long before the term 'indecent exposure' was in circulation. In fact, the first theater troupes were founded just after Brazil's independence in 1822, and playwrights soon developed a national style. The poet and writer Gonçalves Dias (1823–64) was among the first Brazilians to write plays. Only a handful of Dias' work survives, and the romantic figure (who later died in a shipwreck) is better known for his poetry. His lyric 'Canção do Exílio' (Song of Exile) is his dedication to Brazil's natural beauty.

During the early days of the republic, other great theater works were produced. Well-known writers, such as José de Alencar, Machado de Assis and Artur Azevedo, wrote plays in addition to literary works, expanding the national repertoire of Brazil's proliferating theaters.

In the 1940s, Nelson Rodrigues (1912–80), who's often characterized as the Eugene O'Neill of Brazil, was instrumental in transforming theater. His socially conscious plays revealed the moral hypocrisy of upper-class Brazilian families. The 1950s saw a flourishing of the theater arts as playwrights like Gianfranco Guarnieri, Jorge Andrade and Ariano Suassuna created more experimental works, creating a dynamic theater scene in Rio and São Paolo.

ARCHITECTURE

The capital of Brazil for many years, Rio has been the architectural setting for the beautiful, the functional and the avant-garde. Today one can see a sweeping range of styles that span the 17th to 20th centuries in archetypal buildings that often jockey for attention alongside one another.

Vestiges of the colonial period live on in downtown Rio. Some of the most impressive works are the 17th-century churches built by the Jesuits. The best examples from this, the baroque period, are the Convento de Santo Antônio (p92) and the Mosteiro de São Bento (p93). The incredibly ornate interiors, which appear almost to drip with liquid gold, show little of the restraint that would later typify Brazilian architecture.

The artist mission (a group of artists and architects chosen to bring new life to the city) that arrived from France in the early 19th century introduced a whole new design aesthetic to the budding Brazilian empire. Neoclassicism became the official style and was formally taught in the newly founded Imperial Academy. The works built during this period were grandiose and monumental, dominated by classical features such as elongated columns and wide domes. Among the many fine examples of this period are the Instituto Nacional de Belas Artes, the Theatro Municipal (p94) and the Casa França-Brasil (p93) – considered the most important from this period. There are a few curious features of the Casa: its alignment to the cardinal points, the large cross-shaped space inside and its monumental dome.

The end of the 19th century saw the continuation of this trend of returning to earlier forms and featured works such as the Real Gabinete Português de Leitura (p94). Completed in 1887, the Royal Reading Room shows inspiration from the much earlier manueline period (early 1500s), with a Gothic facade and the highlighting of its metallic structure.

During the 20th century, Rio became the setting for a wide array of architectural styles – including neoclassical, eclectic, art deco and modernist works. During the same period, Rio also restored some of its colonial gems (others fell to the wrecking ball), becoming one of Latin America's most beautiful cities.

This, of course, did not happen by chance. In the early 20th century, as capital of Brazil, Rio de Janeiro was viewed as a symbol of the glory of the modern republic and the president lavished beautiful neoclassical buildings upon the urban streetscape.

The early 1900s was also the period when one of Rio's most ambitious mayors, Pereira Passos, was in office. These twin factors had an enormous influence in shaping the face of Brazil's best-known city.

Mayor Passos (1902–06) envisioned Rio as the Paris of South America, and ordered his engineers to lay down grand boulevards and create manicured parks, as some of Rio's most elegant buildings rose overhead. One of the most beautiful buildings constructed during this period was the Palaçio Monroe (1906), a re-creation of a work built for the 1904 St Louis World's Fair. The elegant neoclassical Monroe Palace sat on the Praça Floriano and housed the Câmara dos Deputados (House of Representatives). Unfortunately, like many other of Rio's beautiful buildings, it was destroyed in 1976 in the gross 'reurbanization' craze that swept through the city.

The fruits of this early period were displayed at the International Exposition held in Rio in 1922. This was not only the showcase for neocolonial architecture and urban design;

top picks

ARCHITECTURAL ICONS

- Copacabana Palace (p191) The neoclassical gem that came to represent a glitzy new era.
- Arcos da Lapa (p100) Often used as a symbol of Lapa's bohemian rebirth.
- Maracanã football stadium (p103) Brazil's temple to football and its largest stadium will play a prominent role in the 2014 World Cup and 2016 Olympics.
- Cristo Redentor (p85) Voted one of the new seven modern wonders of the world, Christ the Redeemer still looms large over Rio's landscape.
- Theatro Municipal (p94) The flower of the Belle Époque and also the costliest opera house constructed outside of Europe.

it also introduced Brazil's most modern city to the rest of the world. Another big event of the 1920s was the completion of the Copacabana Palace (p191), the first luxury hotel in South America. Its construction would lead to the rapid development of the beach regions.

Rio's 1930s buildings show the currents of modern European architecture, which greatly impacted upon the city's design. Rio's modernism was born along with the rise of President Vargas, who wanted to leave his mark on federal Rio through the construction of public ministries, official chambers and the residences of government power. The Ministry of Health & Education, the apotheosis of the modernist movement in Brazil, is one of the city's most significant public buildings, as it's one of the few works designed by French architect Le Corbusier, in conjunction with several young Brazilian architects. (Another Le Corbusier-influenced design is the Aeroporto Santos Dumont, completed in 1937.)

The 1930s was also the era of the art-deco movement, which was characterized by highly worked artistic details and an abundance of ornamentation. Good specimens include the central train station and the statue of Cristo Redentor (p85) on Corcovado.

Oscar Niemeyer, one of the young Brazilians who assisted on Le Corbusier's project, would turn out to be a monumental name in architectural history. Working in the firm of Lúcio Costa at the time of his initial collaboration with Le Corbusier, Niemeyer – along with Costa – championed the European avant-garde style in Brazil, making a permanent impact on the next 50 years of Brazilian design. Costa and Niemeyer collaborated on many works, designing some of the most important buildings in Brazil.

In Rio, Niemeyer and Costa broke with the neoclassical style and developed the functional style, with its extensive use of steel and glass, and lack of ornamentation. The Museu de Arte Moderna (inaugurated in 1958, p89) and the Catedral Metropolitana (begun in 1964, p100) are good examples of this style. One of the most fascinating modern buildings close to Rio is the Niemeyer-designed Museu do Arte Contemporânea (MAC; p104) in Niterói. Its fluid form and delicate curves are reminiscent of a flower in bloom (though many simply call it spaceship like). It showcases its natural setting and offers stunning views of Rio.

Niemeyer, whose work has often been described as harmonious, graceful and elegant, has continued to design innovative buildings for over half a century. He collaborated with Le Corbusier and other architects on the design of the UN headquarters in New York, completed in 1953. Now over 100, Niemeyer shows no sign of slowing down, and he still maintains an office in Copacabana. (Niemeyer, incidentally, was forced into exile in 1964 for his association with the Communist party, and he still maintains ties today.)

More recent building projects in Rio include the completion of Hotel Fasano (p186), Philippe Starck's first project in Brazil. It opened in 2007 and is a stylish blend of wood, glass and steel, with mid-century elegance (harking back to Rio's golden days in the 1950s and 60s). It also has whimsical Starck touches, like amoeba-shaped mirrors and a huge 5m-long block of wood that serves as the front check-in desk. One project that was nearing completion as this book went to press is the futuristic 1800-seat concert hall Cidade de Música (Music City) in Barra da Tijuca. The new base of the Brazilian Symphony Orchestra was designed by the Pritzker prize-winning architect Christian de Portzamparc at a cost of US$518 million.

ENVIRONMENT & PLANNING

THE LAND

Rio – with its spectacular scenery – is more than blessed by nature. Its location between the mountains and the sea, bathed by the sun, has entranced visitors for many centuries. Darwin called it 'more magnificent than anything any European has ever seen in his country of origin.'

It all started millions of years ago, when the movement of the earth pushed rock crystal and granite, already disturbed by faults and fractures, into the sea. Low-lying areas were flooded and the high granite peaks became islands.

The plains and swamps on which the city is built were slowly created through centuries of erosion from the peaks and the gradual accumulation of river and ocean sediment.

The mountains, their granite peaks worn by intense erosion and their slopes covered with Atlantic rain forest, form three ranges: the Rural da Pedra Branca massif, the Rural Marapicu-Gericinó massif and the Tijuca-Carioca massif.

The Tijuca-Carioca massif can be seen from almost everywhere in Rio and is responsible for the coastline, which alternates between bare granite escarpments and Atlantic beaches. Its most famous peaks are Pão de Açúcar (Sugarloaf, p79), Morro do Leme, Ponta do Arpoador, Morro Dona Marta, Corcovado and Dois Irmãos at the end of Praia de Leblon.

The sea has also played its part. The stretch of coast between Dois Irmãos and Arpoador was once a large spit, and Lagoa Rodrigo de Freitas (p71) was a bay. Between Arpoador and Morro do Leme, the sea created the beautiful curved beach of Copacabana. Praia Vermelha, the smallest of Rio's Atlantic beaches, is the only one with yellow sand instead of white. Inside Baía de Guanabara, river sediment and reclamation projects formed the present bay rim.

GREEN RIO

Rio still has a long way to go toward protecting its natural beauty, and there are serious environmental problems affecting the city.

Although nowhere near as bad as burgeoning São Paulo to the south, the air quality in Rio is poor, a result of both the heavy volume of traffic throughout the metropolitan area and industrial emissions in neighboring regions. The mountains that surround the city enclose the air pollution, aggravating the problem. (One effect of this air pollution is high rates of asthma among children.)

Despite initial efforts to clean up the Baía de Guanabara following the Earth Summit (the UN Conference on Environment and Development) in 1992, an oil spill in 2000 brought further ecological damage to the bay, and no concerted efforts have been made to clean it up since then. It is foolish to swim at bay beaches. Ocean beaches are also polluted, although less so than the bay. Ipanema is cleaner than Copacabana, and the further you get from the city, the cleaner the waters will be. Refuse from storm drains and the open sewers still prevalent in the city add to the pollution after heavy rains – after which its inadvisable to swim (some 30% of households still lack access to sewer connections).

Another disturbing problem in the city is the continued destruction of Mata Atlântica (Atlantic rain forest) that remains on some of the hillsides around the city, as favelas continue to spread. Until recently, very few citizens took much interest in environmental cleanups. New projects, however, are beginning to reflect a growing concern over the degradation of Rio's natural beauty. Beach clean-up groups, spearheaded by nongovernmental organizations (NGOs) such as Aqualung, have begun appearing on the shores of Rio, and other groups have even set their sights on cleaning up the polluted Baía de Guanabara.

Although Rio is nothing like it was when tropical rain forest covered its landscape, there is still a variety of wildlife to be found in the city. In Campo de Santana, *agoutis* (hamster-like native rodents), egrets, peacocks, white-faced tree ducks, geese and curassows abound.

The greenery surrounding Forte Duque de Caxias (p77) has many plants and birds native to the Atlantic rain forest, such as saddle and bishop tanagers, thrushes and the East Brazilian house wren, which has a distinctive trill. Parque Nacional da Tijuca (p105) contains many more rain-forest species.

The Jardim Botânico (p70) has a huge variety of native and imported plant species, including the Vítoria Régia water lilies from the Amazon and impressive rows of royal palms, whose seeds originally came from France. It has over 8000 plant species, including 600 varieties of orchid. Watch for the brightly plumed hummingbirds, known in Brazil as *beija-flores* (literally, flower-kissers).

top picks

GREEN SPACES

- **Floresta (Forest) da Tijuca** (p105) Rio's crown jewel of green spaces, with rain forests teeming with plant and animal life.
- **Sítio Burle Marx** (p106) Out of the way, but worth the trip, with thousands of plant species on an old, lushly landscaped estate.
- **Parque do Flamengo** (p83) Best on Sunday when through-streets close to traffic and joggers, cyclists and rollerbladers claim the myriad pathways through the seaside park.
- **Jardim Botânico** (p70) Stately royal gardens best suited to leisurely strolls.
- **Parque do Catete** (p87) This small but elegant park is complete with swan-filled pond and garden-side bistro.

OLYMPIC FEVER

Cynics have already started fanning the flames, saying that Rio, with its social problems and inadequate infrastructure, won't be able to pull off a smooth Olympic Games in 2016. The city, however, has already started asking the tough questions and seems determined to show the world they can throw down a memorable and glitch-free Olympics.

Rio certainly has its work cut out. The city will need a total of 34 separate venues to host the events; 18 are already in place; nine new permanent venues and seven temporary ones (including four on Copacabana beach) will be built. Maracanã football stadium, set to become the star of the Olympics, will host the opening and closing ceremonies; it's currently undergoing a US$280 million renovation in preparation for the event (and for the 2014 World Cup, in which it will also play a starring role). The stadium is not scheduled to reopen until early 2013.

Rio currently has a severe shortage of rooms (which is one reason why hotels can get away with charging exorbitant rates during Carnaval). In all, the city would need to more than double its current number of hotel rooms from 22,000 to more than 48,000 to cope with the Olympic influx. Brazil's pitch to the IOC floated the idea of housing people on six cruise ships (a logistical challenge), plus building a 20,000-room Olympic village in Barra. The IOC said it would have to pay 'particular attention' to these ideas. Meanwhile some city officials have lampooned the idea of housing people on cruise ships, and the notion that the needed hotel rooms will be built.

Transportation, no small consideration on Rio's bus-clogged avenues, is a critical factor, and the city is at the drawing board considering a full gamut of ideas – from building aerial trams over the mountains (a green but ultimately impractical idea) to extending the metro to Barra (not going to happen by 2016), and implementing dedicated bus lanes to create 'surface metros' (the most likely scenario). Airports will also need to be upgraded.

Other parts of the city will receive a makeover in preparation for the games, including the port – which at the moment has an unsavory reputation for crumbling buildings, squatters and crime.

The projected cost of the games is a staggering US$14.4 billion. The return? A São Paulo business school estimated the games would pump US$51 billion into the economy through 2027. More immediately, the games would add 120,000 jobs through the year 2016.

Even if the games don't go perfectly, visitors will probably find enough redeeming features – caipirinhas (cocktails) on Ipanema Beach, colorful matches at Maracanã – to feel that the overall experience was worthwhile.

Micos (capuchin monkeys) and other wildlife can be seen in surprising places in the city, including Pista Cláudio Coutinho (p79) in Urca and Parque Lage (p71) on the south side of Corcovado.

URBAN PLANNING & DEVELOPMENT

One of the world's 25 most populous cities, Rio suffers from the same urban sprawl that affects many large cities. Today Rio occupies around 1200 sq km, with 4800 people packed into each square kilometer.

Favelas contribute much to this urban density. The number of people living in them grows at an annual rate three times that of overall population growth. Some believe there are now over 500 favelas, with an estimated one million Cariocas living in them.

In earlier decades, federal officials paid very little attention to the problems of the urban poor. Things first began to change in 1994 with the city's launch of Favela-Bairro, a program aimed at bringing city infrastructure to some of the favelas. Although the project was imperfect, it was a good first step. Brazil's strong economy has allowed politicos to continue investing in favelas. In 2007, President Lula pledged around US$1.7 billion to improve conditions in Rio's favelas, by putting money into transportation, sanitation and education. Since then, some favelas have received substantial improvements in infrastructure – noticeable, for example, in Dona Marta, which now has a funicular whisking residents up the hillside.

One of the big civic successes in recent years was the Pan American Games, which Rio hosted in 2007. Although the city scrambled to complete projects on time, the games ran smoothly. Brazil spent around US$2 billion on the event, bringing an estimated 80,000 visitors (and athletes from 42 countries) into the city. Unfortunately, it missed a big opportunity to invest in new roads, rail links and public transport. The smooth running of the games, however, helped the city secure the winning bid to host the Olympic Games in 2016 – beating out Barcelona, Tokyo and Chicago. Massive preparations are now under way for the big event; for details see above.

GOVERNMENT & POLITICS

Rio de Janeiro is the capital of the eponymous state (Brazil has 26 states), which manages its affairs in the Palácio Tiradentes (p94) under the guidance of the state assembly. The head of Rio state is the governor, who is elected for four-year terms. On a city level, Rio is headed by a mayor, also elected for four years, and a *câmara municipal* (municipal council), which meets at Praça Floriano (p95).

Political parties proliferate in Brazil; at present there are over two dozen, the majority having formed in the last 10 years.

Sérgio Cabral, elected in 2006, is the current governor of Rio state. In Brazil, where it's business as usual in many public offices, the 40-something governor of Rio brings a bold new vision to the state. One of his role models is former New York City mayor Rudolph Giuliani, whose 'zero tolerance' crime policies are often credited with cleaning up New York City. Cabral has made corruption one of his big targets, with a focus on making changes in the police force and the justice system. He helped kick off the zero-tolerance drunk-driving law, with police checkpoints (and un-bribable cops) and stringent penalties for those caught driving under the influence.

Cabral has also overseen new infrastructure and city services flowing into favelas, and created new police units designed to break the stranglehold gangs have on communities there (see p32 for details). He has jumpstarted a family-planning program in poor neighborhoods, making condoms and the contraceptive pill more widely available.

Critics of Cabral's 'tough-on-crime' approach say it's the same message that's been tried and has failed in the past. Whether Cabral can bring meaningful change to Rio will undoubtedly play out on the city streets in the coming years.

MEDIA

Like many other cities in the world, Rio's news outlets are concentrated in the hands of the few. The Organizações (O) Globo empire, which was founded by patriarch Roberto Marinho in Rio in the 1920s, today has the world's fourth-largest TV network (behind NBC, CBS and ABC in the US). O Globo also includes Brazil's major radio network (Radio Globo), the country's second-biggest publishing house (Editora Globo) and of course the leading Rio newspaper *(O Globo)*. Today *O Globo* receives half of the total amount spent annually in Brazil on advertising.

Major dailies in Rio include the sometimes sensationalist *O Dia*, as well as the nationwide *Jornal do Brasil*, a more moderate publication (not unlike *O Globo* in its political slant).

The variety of magazines on newsstands is astounding. Aside from Portuguese translations of popular magazines like *Cosmopolitan*, there are hundreds of glossies, covering everything from science, history and literature to sailing, dogs and astrology. Brazil's most popular magazines are *Veja*, a glossy mag full of journalism lite (not unlike *Time* magazine); *Época*, which has a similar format; and the more sophisticated *Isto É*, with more in-depth articles on politics and economic issues.

For news in English, visit the website of the *Rio Times* (www.riotimesonline.com). Although internet usage is growing, there are still few conduits of alternative news sources in Brazil. Globo

THE NATIONAL ADDICTION

Although football is certainly near the top of the list of Brazil's national obsessions, *novelas* (soap operas) are more watched than anything else on TV. Aired nightly between 6pm and 9pm, these one-hour soaps feature some of Brazil's top actors and certainly Brazilian TV's racier subject matter – unlike American soaps, *novelas* aren't afraid to show some nudity and bloodshed. The plots tend to deal with historical themes, in settings ranging from 17th-century Salvador to a 19th-century coffee plantation or an estate in 1930s Minas Gerais. Period costume is just part of the fun. Also unlike US variants, Brazilian soaps run for a finite period – usually six to nine months – with wild finales often featuring over-the-top gun battles or improbable marriages. Incidentally, directors aren't averse to killing off a few characters along the way; this only adds to the excitement – particularly when audiences give unfavorable reviews of the death, and the screenwriter is compelled to resurrect the deceased character.

Despite the widespread popularity of *novelas*, there are a few critics. The most common gripe is the role to which blacks are relegated in the soaps. The maid, butler and chauffeur are invariably black, while the majority of leading characters have the fairest of skin. Defenders say this is merely a reflection of reality, particularly when filming period pieces. Regardless, things may be beginning to change as a few *novelas* are introducing meatier roles for their once-typecast actors.

FASHION CONSCIENCE

Coopa Roca (www.coopa-roca.org.br) is one favela organization that is garnering attention in some surprising places – top London fashion shows included. This craftwork and sewing collective began in Rocinha in the early 1980s under the guidance of sociologist Maria Teresa Leal. The idea began during Leal's repeat trips to the favela with her housekeeper, a Rocinha resident. During her stays, Leal encountered many women who were talented seamstresses but who had no opportunity to earn money for their skills. Wanting to give something to the community, Leal set up Coopa Roca, and the organization was off and running. Initially a small group of women joined the co-op, each working from home to produce quilts, pillows and craft items made of recycled fabrics and other materials.

The work grew more complex over the years, with more women joining the ranks, and soon the co-op began creating truly eye-catching pieces, using delicate techniques such as *fuxico* (embroidering with pieces of fabric).

The fashion world came calling in the early 1990s, with commissions from Brazilian designers Osklen and Carlos Miele, as well as the ubiquitous department store C&A. More recently, Coopa Roca has made pieces for luxury lingerie maker Agent Provacateur and the French label Lacoste, which recently hired Coopa-Roca to sew hundreds of limited-edition polo shirts. In 2009, the Clinton Global Initiative (CGI) gave Leal a grant to help Coopa-Roca produce its own label for the first time.

Today the co-op employs more than 150 women, most of whom would have little opportunity to earn money otherwise. All of the women continue to work from home and share the production and administrative responsibilities. Despite their growing success, the headquarters of Coopa Roca remains in the favela, where it continues to play a prominent role within the community.

Online tends to dominate this field as well. For further details of newspapers and magazines available in Rio, see p224.

FASHION

Rio's fashion has a lot to do with the belief in the body beautiful: Cariocas have beautiful bodies and they're not afraid to display them.

Top European labels must now jockey for attention beside rising homegrown luminaries. The city's biggest fashion event is the annual Fashion Rio, a week during which some three dozen or so Brazilian designers – the majority based in Rio – launch their upcoming spring and summer collections. What began as a small event in 2002 has grown to become a major media circus, with top models such as Gisele Bündchen showcasing the work of Lenny, Salinas, Walter Rodrigues, Blue Man, Complexo B and others slowly emerging onto the world stage.

In addition to the many boutiques in Ipanema and Leblon, a good opportunity to peruse the talents of upcoming designers is at the Babilônia Feira Hype market (see p112), held throughout the year.

Although the French invented the bikini in 1946, it's Brazilian designers – and the models promoting them – that breathe new life into it every season. *Fio dental* ('dental floss' bikinis) emerged in the 80s, and are still an icon on beaches here. Exposed *bundas* (bottoms), at least for the women, are generally the style. Whether you're six or 60, fat or skinny, the rule on the beach is to wear as little as possible, while still covering up the essentials (topless bathing is not allowed in Rio, by the way) – this applies to men, to some extent. Maybe 15% of men wear Bermudas, while the vast majority stick to *sungas* (hip-hugging briefs).

Off the beach, women show up the men quite a bit; they wear short skirts or dresses (sometimes in bold patterns or vivid colors), or more often slim-fitting designer jeans with a couture top. For most men, a night out means putting on a clean T-shirt and jeans. They are, according to one disgruntled Carioca woman, seriously fashion challenged. This is perhaps a bit unfair, as men are beginning to catch on; a growing number of boutiques in Ipanema, Leblon and the *shoppings* (shopping malls) are dedicated to converting men to their cause.

Regardless of gender or socioeconomic background, Havaianas are the quintessential item you'll find in every Carioca's wardrobe. The nifty rubber sandals are also one of Brazil's leading exports, with well over two billion pairs created since the inception of the company in 1962. Aside from sandals, a tan is the most common fashion accessory, and it's rare to find a Carioca who doesn't have at least some color to their skin, if not an outright deep, dark glow.

For insight into the latest ins and outs of the fashion scene, check what they're saying in the blog http://madeinbrazil.typepad.com.

CARNAVAL

If you haven't heard by now, Rio throws one of the world's best parties, with music and dancing filling the streets for days on end. Officially, Carnaval is just five days of revelry – from Friday to Tuesday before Ash Wednesday – but Cariocas (residents of Rio) begin partying months in advance. The culmination of the big fest is the brilliantly colorful parade through the Sambódromo, with giant mechanized floats, pounding drummers and whirling dancers – but there's lots of action in Rio's many neighborhoods for those seeking more than just the stadium experience.

Out-of-towners add to the mayhem, joining Cariocas in the street parties and costumed balls erupting throughout the city. There are free live concerts to be found (in Largo do Machado, Arcos da Lapa and Praça General Osório, among other places), while those seeking a bit of decadence can head to the various balls. Whatever you do, prepare yourself for sleepless nights, an ample dose of caipirinhas (cane-liquor cocktails) and samba, and mingling with the joyful crowds spilling out of the city.

Joining the *bandas* and *blocos* (street parties) is one of the best ways to have the Carioca experience. These marching parades consist of a procession of brass bands (in the case of *bandas*) or drummers and vocalists (in the case of *blocos*) followed by anyone who wants to dance through the streets. Some *bandas* suggest costumes (drag, Amazonian attire etc), while others simply expect people to show up and add to the good cheer.

Although the city is blazing with energy during Carnaval, don't expect the party to come to you. To get more information on events during Carnaval, check *Veja* magazine's *Veja Rio* insert (sold on Sunday at newsstands) or visit Riotur (Map p90; ☎ 2271-7000; www.rioguiaoficial.com.br; 9th fl, Praça Pio X; 9am-6pm Mon-Fri), the tourist organization in charge of Carnaval. Also see p51 to get some ideas on how to celebrate the return of King Momo, the lord of the Carnaval. For those unacquainted with Momo, he's the modern embodiment of Momos, the Greek god of trickery; when the chosen Momo is announced, Cariocas expect a portly, jolly ruler who can dance a mean samba. The revelry officially begins when the mayor hands King Momo the keys to the city on the Friday before Carnaval. The afternoon event usually takes place in front of the Palácio da Cidade (Map p80; Rua São Clemente 360) in Botafogo.

Other useful websites for Carnaval info are www.ipanema.com and www.rio-carnival.net.

HISTORY

Although the exact origins of Carnaval are shrouded in mystery, some believe the fest originated as a pagan celebration of spring's arrival sometime during the Middle Ages. The Portuguese brought the celebration to Brazil in the 1500s but it took on a decidedly local flavor by the adopting of Indian costumes and African rhythms. (The origin of the word itself probably derives from the Latin *'carne vale'* – 'farewell, meat' – whereby the Catholic population would give up meat and other fleshly temptations during the 40 days of Lent.)

The first festivals in Rio de Janeiro were called *entrudo*, with locals dancing through the streets in colorful costumes and throwing mud, flour and various suspect liquids at one another. In the 19th century Carnaval meant attending a lavish masked ball or participating in the orderly and rather vapid European-style parade. Rio's poor citizens, bored by the finery but eager to participate in a celebration, began holding their own parades, dancing through the streets to African-based rhythms. Then, in the 1920s, the new sound of samba emerged in Rio. It was the music full of African flavors that was brought to the

CARNAVAL DATES

The following are the Carnaval dates (Friday to Shrove Tuesday) in coming years:

2011 March 4–8

2012 February 17–21

2013 February 8–12

2014 February 28 – March 4

CARNAVAL PARTY PLANNER *Marcos Silviano do Prado*

Cariocas start partying long before the big Sambódromo parades take place, but the city is at its wildest from Friday to Tuesday before Ash Wednesday. To make the most of your time, check out the long-standing *festas* (parties) listed below. You can dance through the streets in a *banda,* party like a rock star at one of many dance clubs scattered throughout town or find your groove at one of the samba school rehearsals listed under Nightlife, p163. Those looking for free, open-air, neighborhood-wide celebrations shouldn't miss Rio Folia, in front of Arcos da Lapa (Lapa Arches, p100) in Lapa.

Saturday – two weeks before Carnaval

- Banda de Ipanema (p52) at 4pm
- Rehearsals at samba schools (p163)

Weekend before Carnaval

- Banda Simpatia é Quase Amor (p52), Saturday at 2pm
- Rehearsals at samba schools

Carnaval Friday

- Carnaval King Momo is crowned by the mayor at 1pm
- Shows start at Terreirão do Samba (Samba Land; p55) from 8pm
- Children's samba schools parade at the Sambódromo (p53) from 5pm
- Ball at the Scala (p52) from 11pm
- Gay ball at Le Boy (p52)

Carnaval Saturday

- Cordão do Bola Preta (p52) from 9:30am
- Banda de Ipanema at 4pm
- Parade of Group A samba schools at the Sambódromo from 7pm
- Street band competition (Av Rio Branco, Centro; admission free) from 8pm
- Shows at Terreirão do Samba (Samba Land; p55) and Rio Folia (p55) from 8pm
- Copacabana Palace Luxury Ball (p52) from 10pm – costume or black tie mandatory
- Carnaval balls at Scala, Rio Scenarium (p164) and other venues (p52) from 11pm
- Gay balls at Le Boy and The Week (p167)
- X-Demente Party at Fundição Progresso (p100)
- Parties at 00 (p166) and other dance clubs

Carnaval Sunday

- Banda Simpatia é Quase Amor (p52) at 2pm
- Shows at Terreirão do Samba and Rio Folia from 8pm
- Samba parade at the Sambódromo from 9pm
- Carnaval balls at Scala and Rio Scenarium from 11pm
- Gay balls at Le Boy
- Parties at dance clubs

Carnaval Monday

- Shows at Terreirão do Samba and Rio Folia from 8pm
- Samba parade at the Sambódromo from 9pm
- Carnaval balls at Scala, Rio Scenarium and others from 11pm
- Gay balls at Le Boy
- Parties at dance clubs

Carnaval Tuesday

- Banda de Ipanema at 4pm
- Shows at Terreirão do Samba and Rio Folia from 8pm
- Parade of Group B samba schools at the Sambódromo from 9pm
- Scala Gay Costume Ball from 11pm
- Carnaval balls from 11pm
- Gay balls at Le Boy and The Week
- X-Demente Party at Marina da Glória (Map p87)
- Parties at dance clubs

Weekend after Carnaval

- Parade of champions, Sambódromo, Saturday 9pm
- Monobloco, Ave Rio Branco in Centro, Sunday from 8am

city by former slaves and their poor descendents – a sound that would forever more be associated with Carnaval.

Since those days, Carnaval has grown in leaps and bounds, with elaborate parades spreading from Rio de Janeiro to other parts of Brazil. It has also become a huge commercial enterprise, with the city spending in excess of R$100 million (US$56 million) to throw the party each year.

SIGHTS & ACTIVITIES

There are many ways to take part in Rio's Carnaval, whether joining an informal *banda,* attending a masked ball or catching the parade up close at the Sambódromo. If you'd rather not be a spectator on the big night, you can don a costume and dance with a samba school – an experience that's rated highly by those who've done it (see p53).

CARNAVAL ON THE STREETS

Rio's street parties – the *bandas* and *blocos* – have exploded in recent years. Ten years ago, there were only a handful of these events happening around town. In 2010 there were over 400 street parties, filling every neighborhood in town with the sound of pounding drums and old-fashioned Carnaval songs – not to mention thousands of merrymakers. For many Cariocas, this is the highlight of Carnaval. You can don a costume (or not), learn a few songs and join in; all you have to do is show up – and for Zona Sul fests, don't forget to bring your swimsuit afterwards, for a dip in the ocean.

For complete listings, pick up a free *Carnaval de Rua* guide from Riotur (p228). The following are some of the better known street parties, each attracting anywhere from 1000 to several hundred thousand (in the case of Cordão do Bola Preta). Although the dates usually stay the same, the times sometimes change, so it's wise to confirm before heading out.

Banda de Ipanema (Praça General Osório, Ipanema; 4pm 2nd Sat before Carnaval, Carnaval Sat & Carnaval Tue) This long-standing *banda* attracts a wild crowd, complete with drag queens and others in costume. Don't miss it.

Banda de Sá Ferreira (cnr Av Atlântica & Rua Sá Ferreira, Copacabana; 4pm Carnaval Sat & Sun) This popular Copacabana *banda* marches along the ocean from Posto 1 to Posto 6.

Banda Simpatia é Quase Amor (Praça General Osório, Ipanema; 2pm 2nd Sat before Carnaval & Carnaval Sun) Another Ipanema favorite, with a 50-piece percussion band.

Barbas (cnr Rua Assis Bueno & Rua Arnoldo Quintela, Botafogo; 1pm Carnaval Sat) One of the oldest *bandas* of the Zona Sul parades through the streets with a 60-piece percussion band. A water truck follows along to spray the crowd of some 2500, all decked out in red and white.

Bloco do Bip Bip (Rua Almirante Gonçalves 50, Copacabana; 6pm Carnaval Fri & 5pm Carnaval Tue) Meets in front of the old samba haunt Bip Bip (p161).

Carmelitas (cnr Rua Dias de Barros & Ladeira de Santa Teresa, Santa Teresa; 2pm Carnaval Fri & 8am Carnaval Tue) Crazy mixed crowd (some dressed as Carmelite nuns) parades through Santa Teresa's streets.

Céu na Terra (Curvelo, Santa Teresa; 8:30am Carnaval Sat) Follows along the *bonde* (tram) on a memorable celebration through Santa Teresa en route to Largo das Neves.

Cordão do Bola Preta (cnr Rua Evaristo da Veiga & Rua 13 de Maio, Centro; 8am Carnaval Sat) The oldest and biggest *banda* still in action. Costumes are always welcome, especially those with black-and-white spots.

Dois Pra Lá, Dois Pra Cá (Carlinho de Jesus Dance School, Rua da Passagem 145, Botafogo; 2pm Carnaval Sat) This fairly long march begins at the dance school and ends at the Copacabana Palace.

Monobloco (Ave Rio Branco, Centro; 8am 1st Sun after Carnaval) Rise and shine! This huge *bloco* attracts upwards of 400,000 revelers who, nursing hangovers (or perhaps still inebriated), gather in Centro for a final farewell to the Carnaval mayhem.

Rola Preguiçosa (Rua Maria Quiteria, Ipanema; 7pm Carnaval Fri) Marches behind a giant phallus.

Suvaco de Cristo (Rua Jardim Botânico, Jardim Botânico; 8am Sun before Carnaval) Very popular *bloco* (which means 'Christ's armpit' – in reference to open-armed Redeemer looming overhead), it also meets on Carnaval Saturday, but doesn't announce the time (to avoid overcrowding), so ask around.

Vem Ni Mim Que Eu Sou Facinha (Praça General Osório, Ipanema; 5pm Carnaval Fri) A *banda* that stays put.

CARNAVAL BALLS

Carnaval balls are giant, sometimes costumed, parties with live music and dancing, and an ambience that runs the gamut from staid and formal to wild and a bit tawdry. The most famous and formal ball (you'll need a tux) is held at the Copacabana Palace (p191), where you'll have the opportunity to celebrate with Rio's glitterati as well as international stars. Tickets cost R$1100 to R$3200.

Popular but less pricey balls (around R$40) are held at Rio Scenarium (p164) and at Scala (Map p66; ☎ 2239-4448; Leblon & Gávea; Av Afrânio de Melo Franco 296, Leblon). The most extravagant gay balls are found at Le Boy (Map p76; ☎ 2513 4993; www.leboy.com.br, in Portuguese; Rua Raul Pompéia 102, Copacabana). To help get in the mood, these are good places to don a costume.

Tickets go on sale about two weeks beforehand, and the balls are held nightly during Carnaval. The *Veja Rio* insert in *Veja* magazine has details.

SAMBA SCHOOL PARADES

The highlight of any Carnaval experience is attending (or participating in) a parade at the Sambódromo (Map p60; Rua Marquês do Sapuçai). There, before a crowd of some 90,000 (with millions more watching on TV), each of 12 samba schools has its 80 minutes to dance and sing through the open Oscar Niemeyer–designed stadium. The pageantry is not simply eye candy for the masses. Schools are competing for top honors in the parade, with winners announced (and a winner's parade held) on the Saturday following Carnaval.

Here's what to expect: each school enters the Sambódromo with amped energy levels, and dancers take things up a notch as they dance through the stadium. Announcers introduce the school, the group's theme colors and the number of *alas* (literally, wings – subgroups within a school, each playing a different role). Far away the lone voice of the *puxador* (interpreter) starts the samba. Thousands more voices join him (each school has 3000 to 5000 members), and then the drummers kick in, 200 to 400 per school. The pounding drums drive the parade. Next come the main wings of the school, the big allegorical floats, the children's wing, the drummers, the celebrities and the bell-shaped *baianas* (women dressed as Bahian aunts) twirling in elegant hoopskirts. The *baianas* honor the history of the parade itself, which was brought to Rio from Salvador da Bahia in 1877.

Costumes are fabulously lavish, with 1.5m feathered headdresses; long, flowing capes that sparkle with sequins; and rhinestone-studded G-strings.

The whole procession is also an elaborate competition. A handpicked set of judges chooses the best school on the basis of many components, including percussion, the *samba do enredo* (theme song), harmony between percussion, song and dance, choreography, costumes, story line, floats and decorations. The dance championship is hotly contested, with the winner becoming the pride not just of Rio but all of Brazil.

The Sambódromo parades start with the *mirins* (young samba-school members) on the evening of Carnaval Friday, and continue on through Saturday night when the Group A samba schools strut their stuff. Sunday and Monday are the big nights, when the 12 best samba schools in Rio (the Grupo Especial) parade: six of them on Sunday night and into the morning, and six more on Monday night. The following Saturday, the six top schools strut their stuff again in the Parade of Champions – which generally has more affordable tickets than on the big nights. Each event starts at 9pm and runs until 4am.

Most visitors stay for three or four schools, and come to see their favorite in action (every self-respecting Carioca has a school they support, just as they have a favorite football team). If you're really gung-ho, wear your school's colors and learn the theme song (the words are found on each of the school's websites) so you can sing along when it marches through the Sambódromo.

Tickets

Getting tickets for the parades at legitimate prices can be tough. LIESA (liesa.globo.com), the official samba school league, begins selling tickets in December or January, most of which get immediately snatched up by travel agencies – then later resold at higher prices). Check with Riotur about

JOINING A SAMBA SCHOOL

Those who have done it say no other part of Carnaval quite compares to donning a costume and dancing through the Sambódromo (see above) before roaring crowds. Anyone with the desire and a little extra money to spare can march in the parade. Most samba schools are happy to have foreigners join one of the wings. To get the ball rolling, you'll need to contact your chosen school in advance; it will tell you the rehearsal times and when you need to be in the city (usually a week or so before Carnaval). Ideally, you should memorize the theme song as well, but it's not essential (you can always lip sync). For a list of samba schools and contact information, see p163. The biggest investment, aside from the airfare to Rio, is buying a *fantasia* (costume), which will cost upwards of R$600. If you speak some Portuguese, you can contact a school directly; many Rio travel agencies can also arrange this. One recommended outfit (this author paraded with them in 2010) is Rio Charm (www.riocharm.com.br), which brings a group of travelers together to parade with a Grupo A school (which some say is less formal and more fun). Costumes are around R$400.

Those seeking an insider's perspective on samba schools should read Alma Guillermoprieto's excellent book, *Samba*.

where you can get them, as the official outlet can vary from year to year. At face value, tickets run from R$110 to R$300, though you'll probably have to pay about twice that (or more) if you buy just before Carnaval. The best seating areas, in order of preference, are sectors 9, 7, 11, 5 and 3. The first two (9 and 7) have great views and are in the center, which is the liveliest place to be.

By Carnaval weekend, most tickets will have sold out, but there are lots of scalpers. If you buy a ticket from a scalper (no need to worry about looking for them – they'll find you!), make sure you get both the plastic ticket with the magnetic strip and the ticket showing the seat number. The tickets for different days are color coded, so double-check the date as well.

If you haven't purchased a ticket but still want to go, you can show up at the Sambódromo during Carnaval at around midnight, three or four hours into the show, when you can get grandstand tickets for about R$30 from scalpers outside the gate. Make sure you check which sector your ticket is for. Most ticket sellers will try to pawn off their worst seats.

And if you can't make it during Carnaval proper, there's always the cheaper Parade of Champions the following Saturday.

Getting to the Sambódromo

Don't take a bus to or from the Sambódromo. It's much safer to take a taxi or the metro (the Sambódromo is near Praça Onze metro station), which runs round the clock during Carnaval, from Saturday morning until Tuesday evening. This is also a great opportunity to check out the paraders commuting in costume.

Make sure you indicate to your taxi driver which side of the stadium your seats are on. If you take the metro, the stop at which you get off depends on the location of your seats. For sectors 2, 4 and 6, exit at Praça Onze. Once outside the station, turn to the right, take another right and then walk straight ahead (on Rua Júlio Carmo) to Sector 2. For sectors 4 and 6, turn right at Rua Carmo Neto and proceed to Av Salvador de Sá. You'll soon see the Sambódromo and hear the roar of the crowd. Look for signs showing the entrance to the sectors. If you are going to sectors on the other side (1, 3, 5, 7, 9, 11 and 13), exit at the metro stop Central. You'll then walk about 700m along Av Presidente Vargas until you see the Sambódromo.

SAMBA GLOSSARY FOR PARADE-GOERS

Alas – literally the 'wings.' These are groups of samba-school members responsible for a specific part of the central *samba do enredo* (theme song). Special *alas* include the *baianas* (women dressed as Bahian 'aunts' in full skirts and turbans). The *abre ala* of each school is the opening wing or float.

Bateria – the drum section is the driving beat behind the school's samba and is the 'soul' of the school.

Carnavalesco – the artistic director of each school, responsible for the overall layout and design of the school's theme.

Carros alegóricos – the dazzling floats, usually decorated with near-naked women. The floats are pushed along by the school's maintenance crew.

Desfile – the parade. The most important samba schools *desfilar* (parade) on the Sunday and Monday night of Carnaval. Each school's *desfile* is judged on its samba, drum section, master of ceremonies and flag bearer, floats, leading commission, costumes, dance coordination and overall harmony.

Destaques – the richest and most elaborate costumes. The heaviest ones usually get a spot on one of the floats.

Diretores de harmonia – the school organizers, who usually wear white or the school colors; they run around yelling and 'pumping up' the wings, making sure there aren't any gaps in the parade.

Enredo – the central theme of each school. The *samba do enredo* is the samba that goes with it. Radio stations and dance halls prime Cariocas with classic *enredos* on the weeks leading up to Carnaval.

Passistas – the best samba dancers of a school. They roam the parade in groups or alone, stopping to show off some fancy footwork along the way. The women are usually dressed in short, revealing skirts, and the men usually hold tambourines.

Puxador – the interpreter of the theme song. He (a *puxador* is invariably male) works as a guiding voice, leading the school's singers at rehearsals and in the parade.

RIO FOLIA

Lapa becomes one of the major focal points during Carnaval. In front of the cinematic Arcos da Lapa, the Praça Cardeal Câmara (Map p98) transforms into an open-air stage, with concerts running through Carnaval. About half a dozen different bands play each night (samba of course). The music starts at 10pm and runs past 2am, though revelers pack Lapa until well past sunrise.

SAMBA LAND & SAMBA CITY

Another festive space for concerts is the Terreirão do Samba (Samba Land), an open-air courtyard next to the Sambódromo's sector 1, where bands play to large crowds throughout Carnaval (beginning the weekend before). There are also dozens of food and drink vendors, and a wide variety of bands playing. The action starts around 8pm and continues until 5:30am. Admission is R$10.

One of the biggest developments in Rio's Carnaval world is Cidade do Samba (Samba City; Map p60; ☎ 2213-2503; cidadedosambarj.globo.com; Rua Rivadávia Correa 60, Gamboa; 🕑 10am-5pm Tue-Sat), which opened in 2006. Located north of Centro near the port, the 'city' is actually made up of 14 large buildings in which the top schools assemble the Carnaval floats.

Visitors can take a tour through the area (R$5) or attend a live show (R$190), which features costumed dancers, live music and audience participation, plus free drinks and appetizers. It's touristy and pricey, but some visitors enjoy the Carnaval-style show nonetheless. It's currently held every other Thursday, beginning at 8pm; confirm times with Cidade do Samba or check with Riotur.

NEIGHBORHOODS

top picks

What's your recommendation? www.lonelyplanet.com/rio-de-janeiro

NEIGHBORHOODS

The *Cidade Maravilhosa* (marvelous city) is justly famed for its beaches and nightlife, but the city has lots more going on beyond its steamy seashore and samba-filled nights. Rio, after all, was once the mighty 'capital of the Brazilian empire' (as one Portuguese king crowned it), and its European settlement dates back more than five centuries. History lives on in its colonial quarters, cobbled lanes and 19th-century mansions, with many relics from the past waiting to be discovered.

Wanderers and adventurers have a wealth of options when tackling the city. Our recommendation is to head up to the heights of Pão de Açúcar (Sugarloaf) or Cristo Redentor (Christ the Redeemer) for an overview of the city. There you'll see the city's wild urban diversity, with beaches, mountains, skyscrapers and favelas (shanty towns) all woven into the landscape. The city itself can be divided into two zones: the Zona Norte, which consists of industrial, working-class neighborhoods in the northern part of the city, and the Zona Sul, with its middle- and upper-class neighborhoods and well-known beaches in the city's southern half. Centro, Rio's business district, forms the boundary between the two.

After getting an overview, it's time to dive in. We've organized our neighborhoods chapter generally from south to north, and have included a number of walking tours for exploring the city streets.

The Zona Sul has the city's star attractions. At the far southern tip, the upscale neighborhoods of Ipanema and Leblon share the same stretch of south-facing shoreline. Rio's beautiful people flock to these beaches, while the tree-lined streets just inland hide some of the best eating, drinking and shopping in the city.

The northern border of Ipanema and Leblon is the Lagoa Rodrigo de Freitas, a saltwater lagoon fronted by the high-rent districts of Gávea, Jardim Botânico and Lagoa. Here you'll find open-air dining and drinking at lakeside restaurants, as well as the verdant botanical gardens to the west.

East of Ipanema begins the scalloped beach of Copacabana. Once a destination for international jetsetters, Copacabana is the city's somewhat ragged tourist magnet, with dozens of oceanfront hotels and sidewalk restaurants. The population density is high here with old-timers, favela kids and tourists all on the streets, and you'll find an equal mix of high and low culture.

Botafogo lies just north of Copacabana, and is a desirable neighborhood with an active *boteco* (small local bar) culture and some intriguing museums in the area's old mansions. Next door, Urca retains a peaceful vibe that seems a world away from the Zona Sul's busier neighborhoods, and is famed for the iconic mountain Pão de Açúcar overshadowing its leafy streets.

Continuing north are more residential neighborhoods, including low-key Flamengo, leafy Laranjeiras and further west Cosme Velho, where Cristo Redentor opens his arms atop Corcovado. Following the curve of the bay north is the Parque do Flamengo, a tree-lined park that is home to cycling trails, football (soccer) pitches and several monuments and museums. Inland from there, Catete and Glória hide much history in their battered streets, including the former presidential home.

One metro stop up, Centro is Rio's business hub; it's also one of Rio's oldest areas, with baroque churches, former palaces and excellent museums. On the southeastern edge of Centro is Lapa, Rio's nightlife nexus with dozens of samba-filled bars and clubs. Uphill from Lapa is Santa Teresa, a picturesque neighborhood of winding streets and old mansions that have been restored by the many artists who have settled there.

Greater Rio includes Zona Norte destinations such as Maracanã soccer stadium, the Feira Nordestina (Northeastern Fair) and the Quinta da Boa Vista, former residence of the imperial family. It also includes the Baía de Guanabara, with the picturesque island of Paquetá. Across the bay is Niterói, home to one of Oscar Niemeyer's architectural creations. Another place to explore is the region west of Leblon, where you'll find lush rain forest and the beach of Barra da Tijuca. Other beaches dot the coast heading west, and get wilder and less populated the further out you go.

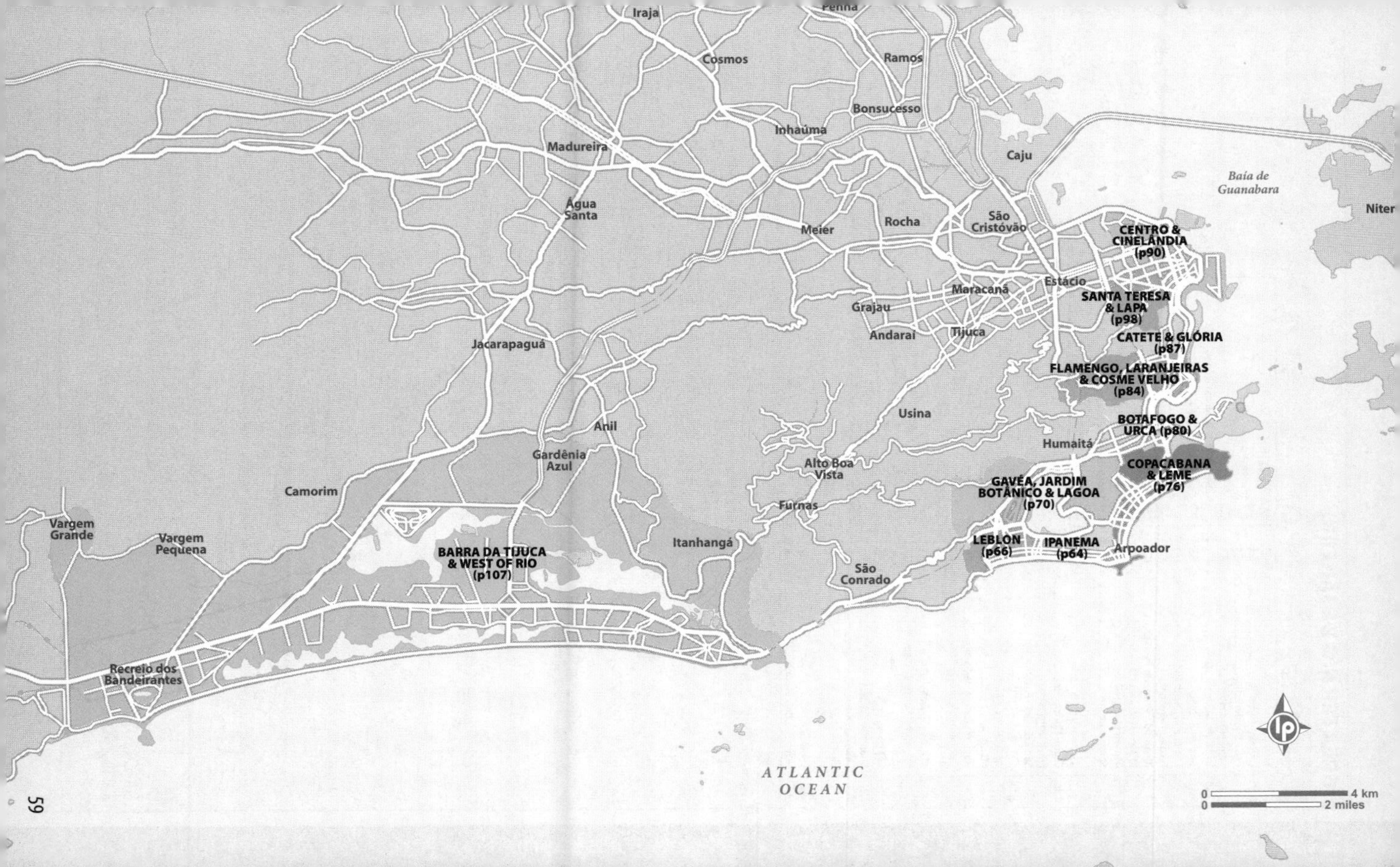
Iraja
Penha
Cosmos
Ramos
Bonsucesso
Inhaúma
Madureira
Caju
Baía de Guanabara
Niter
Água Santa
Meier
Rocha
São Cristóvão
CENTRO & CINELÂNDIA (p90)
Estácio
Maracanã
Grajau
SANTA TERESA & LAPA (p98)
Andarai
Tijuca
CATETE & GLÓRIA (p87)
Jacarapaguá
FLAMENGO, LARANJEIRAS & COSME VELHO (p84)
Usina
BOTAFOGO & URCA (p80)
Anil
Humaitá
Gardênia Azul
Alto Boa Vista
COPACABANA & LEME (p76)
GAVÉA, JARDIM BOTÂNICO & LAGOA (p70)
Camorim
Furnas
Vargem Grande
Vargem Pequena
BARRA DA TIJUCA & WEST OF RIO (p107)
Itanhangá
LEBLON (p66)
IPANEMA (p64)
Arpoador
São Conrado
Recreio dos Bandeirantes
ATLANTIC OCEAN
0
4 km
0
2 miles

GREATER RIO DE JANEIRO

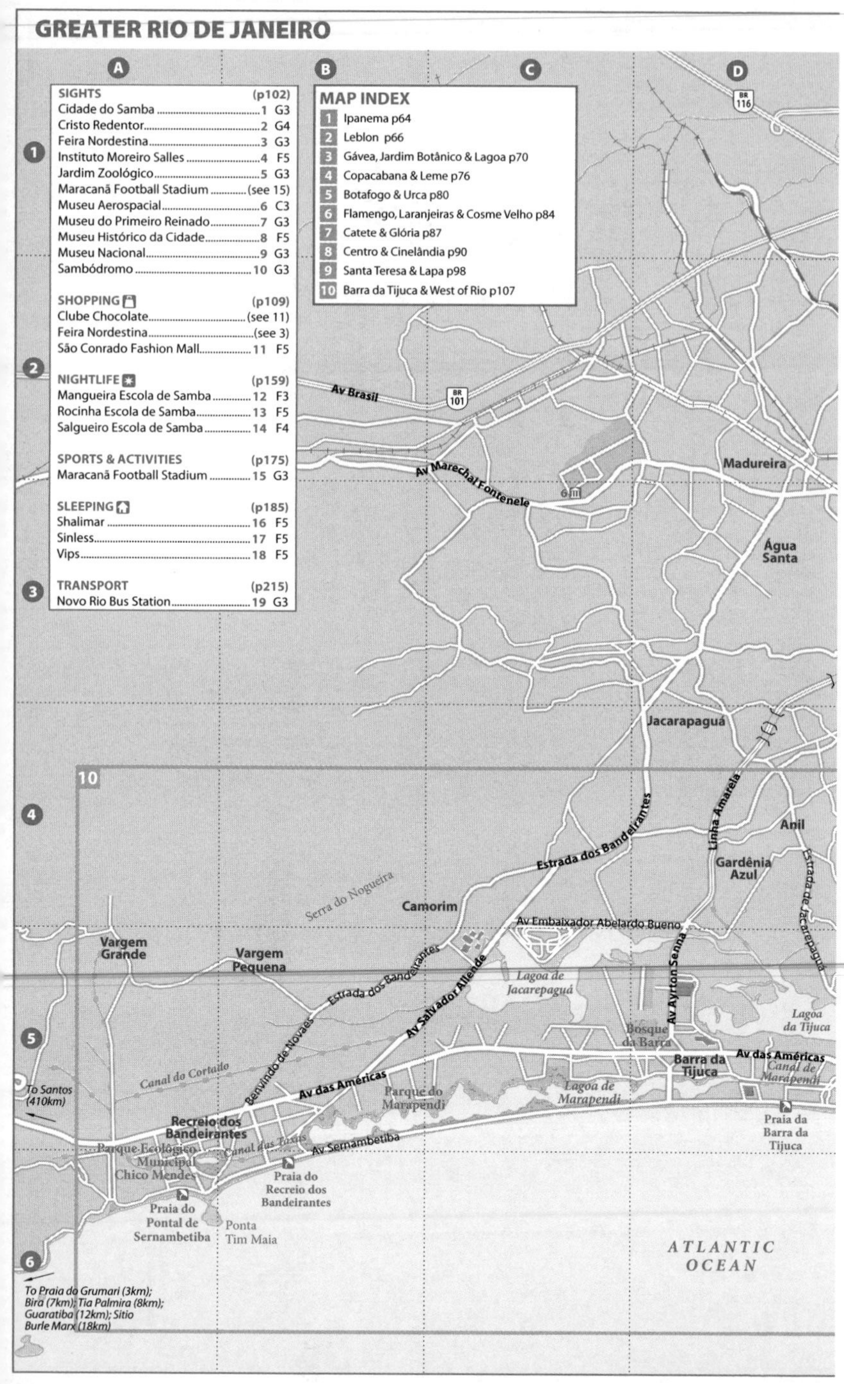

A
B
C
D
SIGHTS (p102)
Cidade do Samba 1 G3
Cristo Redentor 2 G4
Feira Nordestina 3 G3
Instituto Moreiro Salles 4 F5
Jardim Zoológico 5 G3
Maracanã Football Stadium (see 15)
Museu Aerospacial 6 C3
Museu do Primeiro Reinado 7 G3
Museu Histórico da Cidade 8 F5
Museu Nacional 9 G3
Sambódromo 10 G3
SHOPPING (p109)
Clube Chocolate (see 11)
Feira Nordestina (see 3)
São Conrado Fashion Mall 11 F5
NIGHTLIFE (p159)
Mangueira Escola de Samba 12 F3
Rocinha Escola de Samba 13 F5
Salgueiro Escola de Samba 14 F4
SPORTS & ACTIVITIES (p175)
Maracanã Football Stadium 15 G3
SLEEPING (p185)
Shalimar 16 F5
Sinless 17 F5
Vips 18 F5
TRANSPORT (p215)
Novo Rio Bus Station 19 G3
MAP INDEX
1 Ipanema p64
2 Leblon p66
3 Gávea, Jardim Botânico & Lagoa p70
4 Copacabana & Leme p76
5 Botafogo & Urca p80
6 Flamengo, Laranjeiras & Cosme Velho p84
7 Catete & Glória p87
8 Centro & Cinelândia p90
9 Santa Teresa & Lapa p98
10 Barra da Tijuca & West of Rio p107
1
2
3
4
5
6
BR 116
BR 101
Av Brasil
Av Marechal Fontenele
Madureira
Água Santa
Jacarepaguá
10
Estrada dos Bandeirantes
Linha Amarela
Anil
Gardênia Azul
Estrada de Jacarepaguá
Serra do Nogueira
Camorim
Av Embaixador Abelardo Bueno
Vargem Grande
Vargem Pequena
Estrada dos Bandeirantes
Av Salvador Allende
Lagoa de Jacarepaguá
Av Ayrton Senna
Lagoa da Tijuca
Bosque da Barra
Benvindo de Novaes
Canal do Cortado
Av das Américas
Parque do Marapendi
Lagoa de Marapendi
Barra da Tijuca
Av das Américas
Canal de Marapendi
To Santos (410km)
Recreio dos Bandeirantes
Canal das Taxas
Av Sernambetiba
Praia da Barra da Tijuca
Parque Ecológico Municipal Chico Mendes
Praia do Recreio dos Bandeirantes
Praia do Pontal de Sernambetiba
Ponta Tim Maia
ATLANTIC OCEAN
To Praia do Grumari (3km); Bira (7km); Tia Palmira (8km); Guaratiba (12km); Sítio Burle Marx (18km)

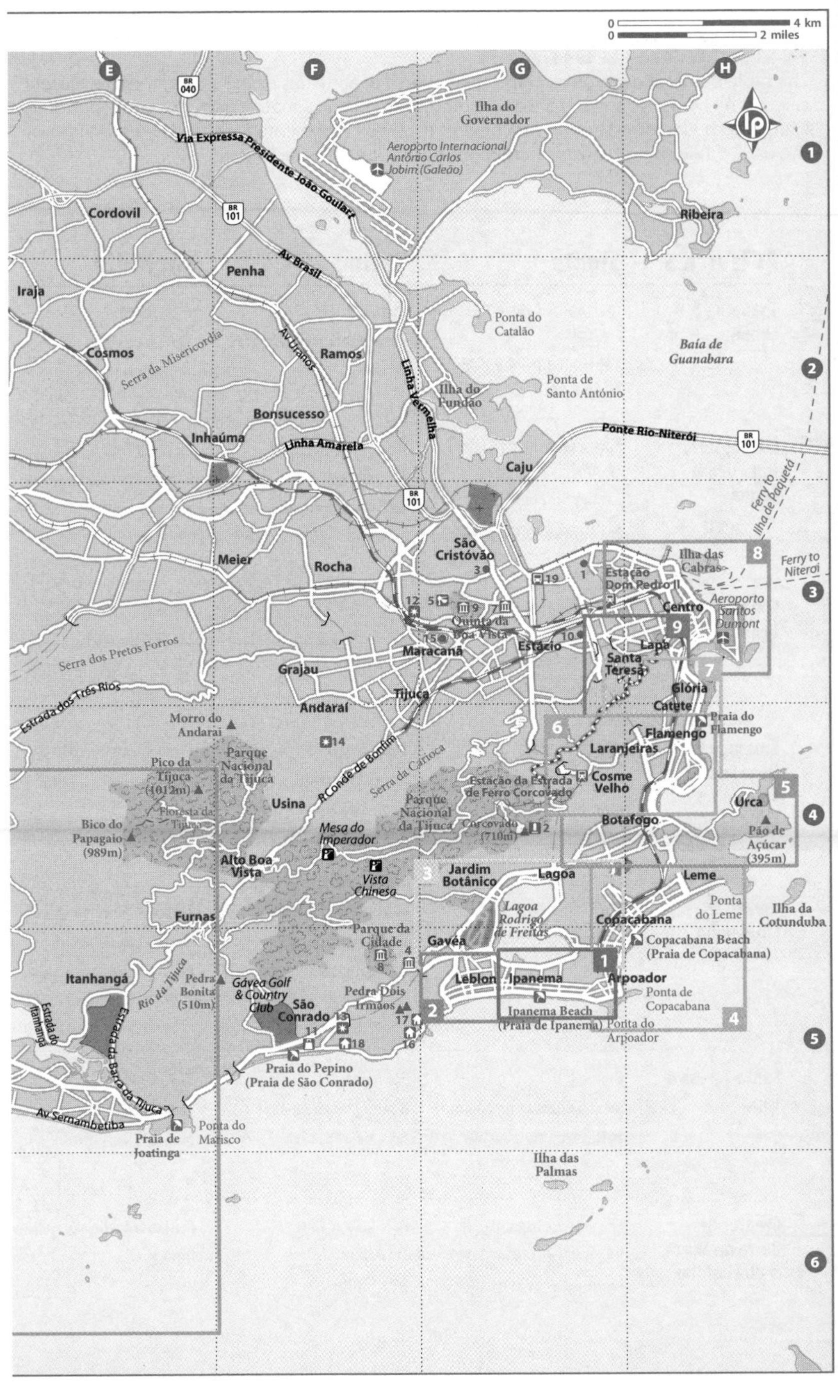

0 4 km
0 2 miles
E
F
G
H
Ilha do Governador
Aeroporto Internacional Antônio Carlos Jobim (Galeão)
Via Expressa Presidente João Goulart
Av Brasil
Cordovil
Ribeira
Penha
Iraja
Ponta do Catalão
Baía de Guanabara
Cosmos
Serra da Misericórdia
Av Uranos
Ramos
Linha Vermelha
Ilha do Fundão
Ponta de Santo António
Bonsucesso
Inhaúma
Linha Amarela
Ponte Rio-Niterói
Caju
Ferry to Ilha de Paquetá
São Cristóvão
Meier
Rocha
Ilha das Cabras
Estação Dom Pedro II
Ferry to Niterói
Centro
Aeroporto Santos Dumont
Quinta da Boa Vista
Maracanã
Estácio
Lapa
Santa Teresa
Serra dos Pretos Forros
Grajau
Tijuca
Glória
Catete
Estrada dos Três Rios
Andaraí
Morro do Andaraí
Praia do Flamengo
Flamengo
Laranjeiras
Parque Nacional da Tijuca
Pico da Tijuca (1012m)
R Conde de Bonfim
Serra da Carioca
Estação da Estrada de Ferro Corcovado
Cosme Velho
Usina
Floresta da Tijuca
Bico do Papagaio (989m)
Parque Nacional da Tijuca
Urca
Botafogo
Mesa do Imperador
Corcovado (710m)
Pão de Açúcar (395m)
Alto Boa Vista
Vista Chinesa
Jardim Botânico
Lagoa
Leme
Lagoa Rodrigo de Freitas
Ponta do Leme
Ilha da Cotunduba
Furnas
Parque da Cidade
Copacabana
Gávea
Copacabana Beach (Praia de Copacabana)
Itanhangá
Pedra Bonita (510m)
Rio da Tijuca
Gávea Golf & Country Club
São Conrado
Pedra Dois Irmãos
Leblon
Ipanema
Arpoador
Ponta de Copacabana
Ipanema Beach (Praia de Ipanema)
Ponta do Arpoador
Estrada do Itanhangá
Estrada da Barra da Tijuca
Praia do Pepino (Praia de São Conrado)
Av Sernambetiba
Praia de Joatinga
Ponta do Marisco
Ilha das Palmas

ITINERARY BUILDER

The table below allows you to plan a day's worth of activities in any area of the city. Simply select which area you wish to explore, and then mix and match from the corresponding listings to build your day. The first item in each cell represents a well-known highlight of the area, while the other items are more off-the-beaten-track gems.

AREA / ACTIVITIES	Sights	Eating	Nightlife
Ipanema & Leblon	**Ipanema & Leblon Beaches** (opposite) **Ponta do Arpoador** (opposite) **Mirante do Leblon** (opposite)	**Zuka** (p133) **Zazá Bistrô Tropical** (p133) **Bazzar** (p134)	**Melt** (p169) **Devassa** (p153) **Baronneti** (p169)
Gávea, Jardim Botânico & Lagoa	**Lagoa Rodrigo de Freitas** (p73) **Jardim Botânico** (p72) **Instituto Moreira Salles** (p71)	**Olympe** (p138) **Bráz** (p138) **Guy Restaurante** (p138)	**00 (Zero Zero;** p169) **Braseiro da Gávea** (p154) **Palaphita Kitch** (p155)
Copacabana & Leme	**Copacabana & Leme Beach** (p75) **Forte de Copacabana** (p77) **Forte Duque de Caxias** (p77)	**Amir** (p141) **Siri Mole & Cia** (p140) **La Trattoria** (p141)	**Bip Bip** (p163) **Clandestino** (p169) **Botequim Informal** (p156)
Botafogo & Urca; Flamengo, Laranjeiras & Cosme Velho; Catete & Glória	**Pão de Açúcar** (p80) **Cristo Redentor** (p85) **Museu da República** (p86)	**Yorubá** (p143) **Intihuasi** (p144) **Tacacá do Norte** (p145)	**Praia Vermelha** (p164) **Champanharia Ovelha Negra** (p166) **Casa Rosa** (p165)
Centro & Cinelândia	**Paço Imperial** (p92) **Museu Histórico Nacional** (p89) **Centro Cultural Banco do Brasil** (p89)	**Confeitaria Colombo** (p147) **Brasserie Rosário** (p147) **Restaurante Albamar** (p146)	**Trapiche Gamboa** (p168) **Boteco Casual** (p158) **Central Cultural Carioca** (p164)
Santa Teresa & Lapa	**Bonde** (p97) **Museu Chácara do Céu** (p97) **Parque das Ruínas** (p99)	**Sobrenatural** (p148) **Bar do Mineiro** (p149) **Aprazível** (p148)	**Rio Scenarium** (p167) **Carioca da Gema** (p165) **Democráticus** (p166)
Greater Rio, Barra da Tijuca & West of Rio	**Feira Nordestina** (p103) **Ilha de Paquetá** (p104) **Parque Nacional da Tijuca** (p105)	**Barreado** (p150) **Tia Palmira** (p150) **Bira** (p149)	**Feira Nordestina** (p103) **Nuth** (p170)

IPANEMA & LEBLON

Eating p128; Shopping p110; Sleeping p186

The favored address for Rio's young, beautiful and wealthy Cariocas (residents of Rio), these twin neighborhoods boast a magnificent beach and tree-lined streets full of enticing open-air cafés, restaurants and bars. It's also the city's high-end shopping district, with dozens of colorful boutiques and multistory *galerias* (shopping centers) selling pretty things that can quickly deplete a budget. While traditional sights are few, you can fill many days just exploring the leafy streets. Ipanema is also Rio's gay district, which revolves around the café and bar scene on the streets just west of Praça General Osório.

Ipanema acquired international fame in the early 60s as the home of the bossa nova character 'Girl from Ipanema.' It became the hangout of artists, intellectuals and wealthy liberals, who frequented the sidewalk cafés and bars. After the 1964 military coup and the resulting crackdown on liberals, many of these bohemians were forced into exile. During the 70s, Leblon became the nightlife center of Rio. The restaurants and bars of Baixo Leblon, on Av Ataúlfo de Paiva between Rua Aristides Espínola and Rua General Artigas, were the meeting point for a new generation of artists and musicians. While Lapa is where the live music is, Leblon still has its allure. Some of the city's best old-fashioned bars are sprinkled about this neighborhood, many dating from the 1950s.

IPANEMA & LEBLON BEACHES Map p66

Av Delfim Moreira & Av Vieira Souto

Although the beaches of Ipanema and Leblon are one long beach, the *postos* (posts) along them subdivide the beach into areas as diverse as the city itself. Posto 9, right off Rua Vinícius de Moraes, is Garota de Ipanema, which is where Rio's most lithe and tanned bodies tend to migrate. The area is also known as the Cemetério dos Elefantes because of the handful of old leftists, hippies and artists who sometimes hang out there. In front of Rua Farme de Amoedo the beach is known as Bolsa de Valores or Crystal Palace (this is the gay section), while Posto 8 further up is mostly the domain of favela kids. Arpoador, between Ipanema and Copacabana, is Rio's most popular surf spot. Leblon attracts a broad mix of single Cariocas, as well as families from the neighborhood. Posto 10 is for sport lovers, with ongoing volleyball, soccer and *frescobal* (played with wooden racquets and a rubber ball) games. There's also Baixo Bebê, between posts 11 and 12, where affluent parents with children migrate.

Whatever spot you choose, you'll enjoy cleaner sands and sea than those in Copacabana. Keep in mind that if you go on Saturday or Sunday, the sands get crowded. Go early to stake out a spot.

Incidentally, the word *ipanema* is an indigenous word for 'bad, dangerous waters' – not so far off given the strong undertow and often oversized waves crashing on the shore. Be careful, and swim only where the locals do.

TRANSPORTATION: IPANEMA & LEBLON

(Bus) Botafogo (571); Corcovado train station (583); Urca (511); Copacabana (571); São Conrado (177); Centro (132); Novo Rio bus station (473)

(M) Ipanema/General Osório

Metrô na Superfície 'Metro buses' connect Ipanema/General Osório station with western Ipanema and Leblon (see p218 for more information).

PONTA DO ARPOADOR Map p64

Far eastern end of Av Vieira Souto

This rocky point juts out into the water and serves as one of Rio's best places for watching the sunset. Throughout the day, you'll spot fishermen casting off the rock, couples stealing a few kisses and photographers snapping that iconic stretch of Ipanema beach stretching off toward the towering peaks of Dois Irmãos. You'll also see large flocks of surfers jockeying for position offshore. Around the western edge of the rock is the tiny, secluded Praia do Diabo (Devil's Beach), a fine place to take in the views – but swim with caution. A very rustic gym is built into the rocks (think barbells with concrete weights and chin-up bars).

MIRANTE DO LEBLON Map p66

Av Niemeyer

A few fishermen casting out to sea mingle with couples admiring the view at this overlook at the western end of Leblon

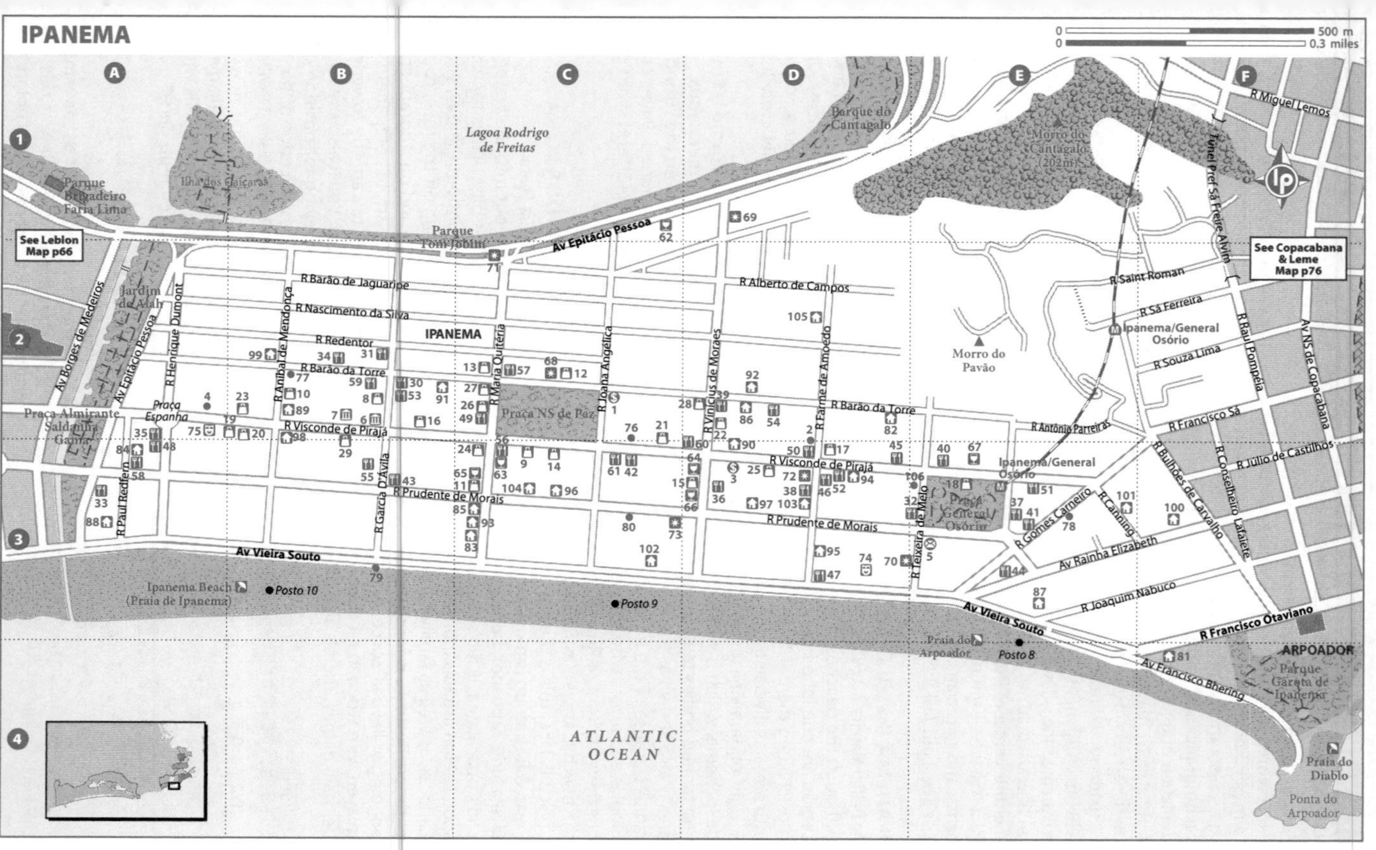

IPANEMA
500 m
0.3 miles
Lagoa Rodrigo de Freitas
Parque Brigadeiro Faria Lima
Ilha dos Caiçaras
See Leblon Map p66
See Copacabana & Leme Map p76
Parque Tom Jobim
Parque do Cantagalo
Morro do Cantagalo (202m)
Morro do Pavão
Túnel Pref Sá Freire Alvim
Av Epitácio Pessoa
Av Borges de Medeiros
Jardim de Alah
Praça Almirante Saldanha da Gama
Praça Espanha
R Miguel Lemos
R Saint Roman
R Sá Ferreira
Ipanema/General Osório
R Souza Lima
R Raul Pompéia
Av NS de Copacabana
R Francisco Sá
R Júlio de Castilhos
R Conselheiro Lafaiete
R Bulhões de Carvalho
R Antônio Parreiras
R Barão de Jaguaripe
R Nascimento da Silva
R Redentor
R Barão da Torre
R Visconde de Pirajá
R Prudente de Morais
R Alberto de Campos
R Henrique Dumont
R Aníbal de Mendonça
R Paul Redfern
R Garcia D'Ávila
R Maria Quitéria
R Joana Angélica
R Vinícius de Moraes
R Farme de Amoedo
R Teixeira de Melo
R Gomes Carneiro
R Canning
Av Rainha Elizabeth
R Joaquim Nabuco
R Francisco Otaviano
Av Francisco Bhering
IPANEMA
Praça NS da Paz
Praça General Osório
Av Vieira Souto
Ipanema Beach (Praia de Ipanema)
Posto 10
Posto 9
Posto 8
Praia do Arpoador
ARPOADOR
Parque Garota de Ipanema
Praia do Diabo
Ponta do Arpoador
ATLANTIC OCEAN

IPANEMA

beach. The luxury Sheraton Hotel looms to the west, with the not so luxurious favela of Vidigal nearby.

TOCA DO VINÍCIUS Map p64

☎ 2247-5227; www.tocadovinicius.com.br; Rua Vinícius de Moraes 129, Ipanema; 🕑 10am-7pm Mon-Fri, 10am-6pm Sat & Sun

A quintessential stop off for bossa nova fans, Toca do Vinícius is a music store (p115) named in honor of the famous Brazilian musician, Vinícius de Moraes. The 1st floor has a good selection of bossa, while upstairs a tiny museum displays original manuscripts and photos of the great songwriter and poet. Live bossa nova concerts are held on the sidewalk in front once a month.

MUSEU AMSTERDAM SAUER Map p64

☎ 2512-1132; www.amsterdamsauer.com; Rua Garcia D'Ávila 105; admission free; 🕑 9am-7pm Mon-Fri, 9am-4pm Sat

Next door to Museu H Stern, the Amsterdam Sauer Museum houses an impressive collection of precious stones – over 3000 items in all. Visitors can also take a peek at the two life-sized replicas of mines.

LEBLON

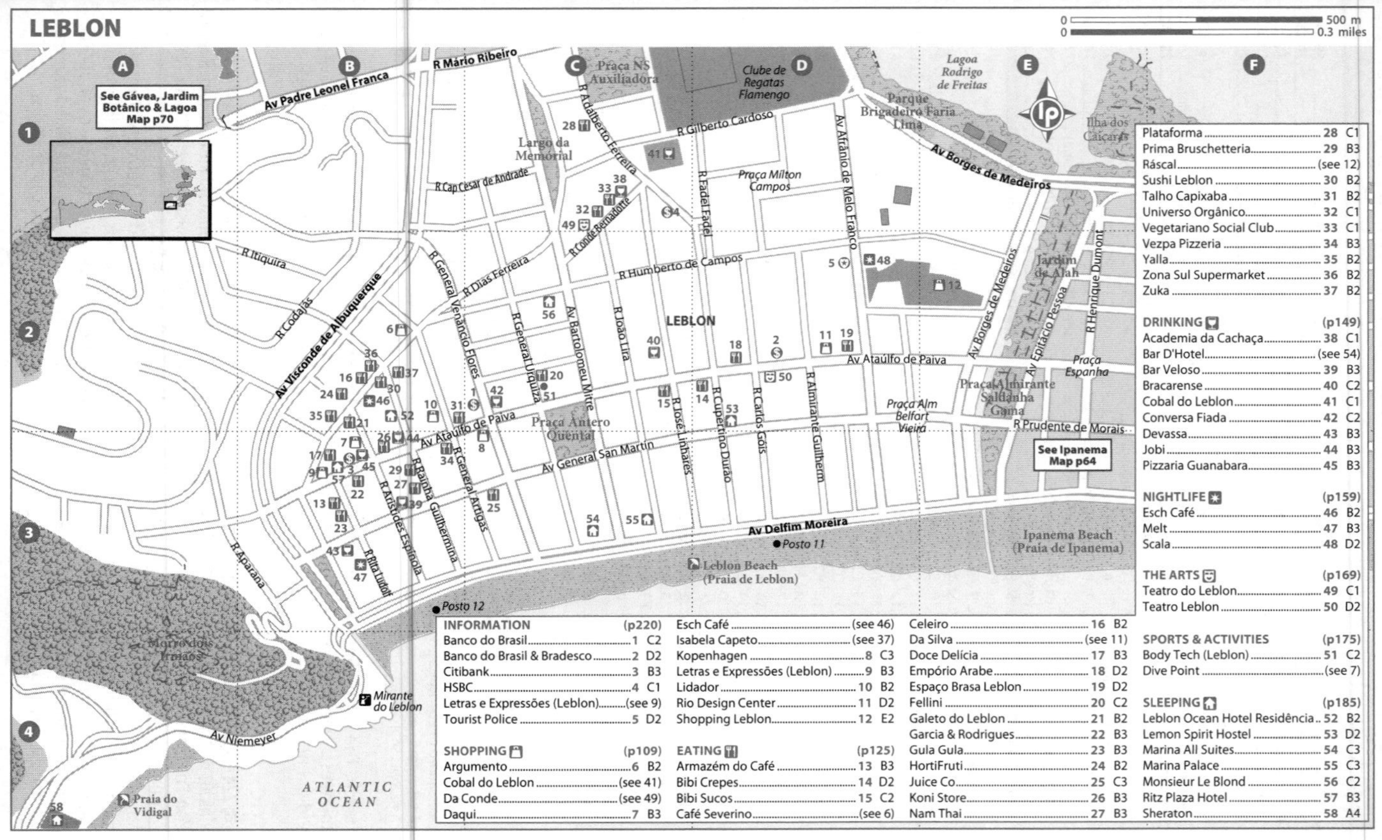

INFORMATION (p220)
- Banco do Brasil 1 C2
- Banco do Brasil & Bradesco 2 D2
- Citibank 3 B3
- HSBC 4 C1
- Letras e Expressões (Leblon) .... (see 9)
- Tourist Police 5 D2

SHOPPING (p109)
- Argumento 6 B2
- Cobal do Leblon .... (see 41)
- Da Conde .... (see 49)
- Daqui 7 B3
- Esch Café .... (see 46)
- Isabela Capeto .... (see 37)
- Kopenhagen 8 C3
- Letras e Expressões (Leblon) 9 B3
- Lidador 10 B2
- Rio Design Center 11 D2
- Shopping Leblon 12 E2

EATING (p125)
- Armazém do Café 13 B3
- Bibi Crepes 14 D2
- Bibi Sucos 15 C2
- Café Severino .... (see 6)
- Celeiro 16 B2
- Da Silva .... (see 11)
- Doce Delícia 17 B3
- Empório Arabe 18 D2
- Espaço Brasa Leblon 19 D2
- Fellini 20 C2
- Galeto do Leblon 21 B2
- Garcia & Rodrigues 22 B3
- Gula Gula 23 B3
- HortiFruti 24 B2
- Juice Co 25 C3
- Koni Store 26 B3
- Nam Thai 27 B3
- Plataforma 28 C1
- Prima Bruschetteria 29 B3
- Rascal .... (see 12)
- Sushi Leblon 30 B2
- Talho Capixaba 31 B2
- Universo Orgânico 32 C1
- Vegetariano Social Club 33 C1
- Vezpa Pizzeria 34 B3
- Yalla 35 B2
- Zona Sul Supermarket 36 B2
- Zuka 37 B2

DRINKING (p149)
- Academia da Cachaça 38 C1
- Bar D'Hotel .... (see 54)
- Bar Veloso 39 B3
- Bracarense 40 C2
- Cobal do Leblon 41 C1
- Conversa Fiada 42 C2
- Devassa 43 B3
- Jobi 44 B3
- Pizzaria Guanabara 45 B3

NIGHTLIFE (p159)
- Esch Café 46 B2
- Melt 47 B3
- Scala 48 D2

THE ARTS (p169)
- Teatro do Leblon 49 C1
- Teatro Leblon 50 D2

SPORTS & ACTIVITIES (p175)
- Body Tech (Leblon) 51 C2
- Dive Point .... (see 7)

SLEEPING (p185)
- Leblon Ocean Hotel Residência 52 B2
- Lemon Spirit Hostel 53 D2
- Marina All Suites 54 C3
- Marina Palace 55 C3
- Monsieur Le Blond 56 C2
- Ritz Plaza Hotel 57 B3
- Sheraton 58 A4

MUSEU H STERN

Map p64

☎ 2274-8897; www.hstern.com.br; Rua Visconde de Pirajá 490; admission free; 9am-6pm Mon-Fri, 9am-2pm Sat

The headquarters of the famous jeweler H Stern incorporates a museum displaying a permanent exhibition of fine jewelry, some rare mineral specimens and a large collection of tourmalines. There is a 12-minute tour, which displays the process of turning the rough stones into flawlessly cut jewels as the gems pass through the hands of craftsmen, cutters, goldsmiths and setters.

PARQUE GAROTA DE IPANEMA

Map p64

Off Rua Francisco Otaviano, near Rua Bulhões Carvalho

This small park next to the Arpoador rock features a tiny playground, a concrete area popular with skaters and a lookout with a view of Ipanema Beach. On weekends in summer, there are occasional concerts here.

EAT, DRINK LEBLON

Walking Tour

The neighborhood bar is something of a Leblon institution, with ice-cold beer, delicious-but-terrible-for-you appetizers, and a festive, all-ages crowd that isn't averse to solving the problems of the Fluminense football team or just having a laugh with friends over a few rounds. We recommend doing the pub tour on a weekend afternoon – particularly on game days, when things are at their liveliest. Obviously, if you're planning a late-night drinking event, it's wise to take a taxi between bars.

1 Academia da Cachaça

There's nothing like a shot of *cachaça* (cane liquor) to take the edge off before a big evening out. In addition to tasty cocktails (try the passion-fruit caipirinha), the festive Academia da Cachaça (p150) serves up traditional Brazilian dishes. If you can't find a table, there are a handful of other bars next door.

2 Cobal do Leblon

Just across the way, is the flower and vegetable market Cobal do Leblon (p150), which transforms into a festive open-air drinking spot most nights. While it's nothing fancy – think plastic tables and chairs – this place is popular, particularly with the 20-something crowd.

3 Chico & Alaíde

Once your thirst is slaked (but not too slaked – the night is young), head west to Chico & Alaíde (☎ 2512-0028; Rua Dias Ferreira 679), a new hot spot with a festive crowd, sidewalk seating and tasty appetizers (*Veja Rio* declared it the best bar cuisine of Rio in 2010).

4 Tio Sam

Further west on this well-shaded street, you'll find a classic watering hole that's been around for three decades. Despite the name, Tio Sam (Uncle Sam; ☎ 2512-2413; Rua Dias Ferreira 605) is pure Carioca, with Brahma on tap, fried sardines and bowls of crabmeat on the menu, and a crowd that may or may not know why their bar is painted red, white and blue (a US school was once their neighbor).

5 Belmonte

A short stroll west leads to Belmonte (☎ 2294-2849; Rua Dias Ferreira 521), an open-sided place with an old-fashioned feel, despite its relative youth (built in the last decade). The reason to stop here is to sample the *pastel de camarão* (shrimp pastry); and of course there's beer.

6 Venga!

From Belmonte it's a three-block walk along a restaurant-packed street (stay focused) to Venga! (☎ 2512-9826; Rua Dias Ferreira 113), a pocket-sized tapas bar with warm lighting, a mean *polvo com batatas e paprica picante* (octopus with potatoes and paprika) and good-looking sangria- and wine-swilling patrons.

7 Pizzaria Guanabara

From here, go back to Rua Aristides Espínola and turn right. In a few paces, you'll reach Pizzaria Guanabara (p152), home to a youngish beer-drinking crowd and a major destination in the wee hours (it stays open until 7am), when the post-party crowd comes for food. Keep in mind that the pizza is not particularly good, but tastes great when hunger strikes at 3am.

8 Jobi

Go one block east to another classic old-timer, Jobi (p151), a tiny bar opened in the 1960s that everyone in the Zona Sul has been to at least once. Good appetizers, droll waiters and the

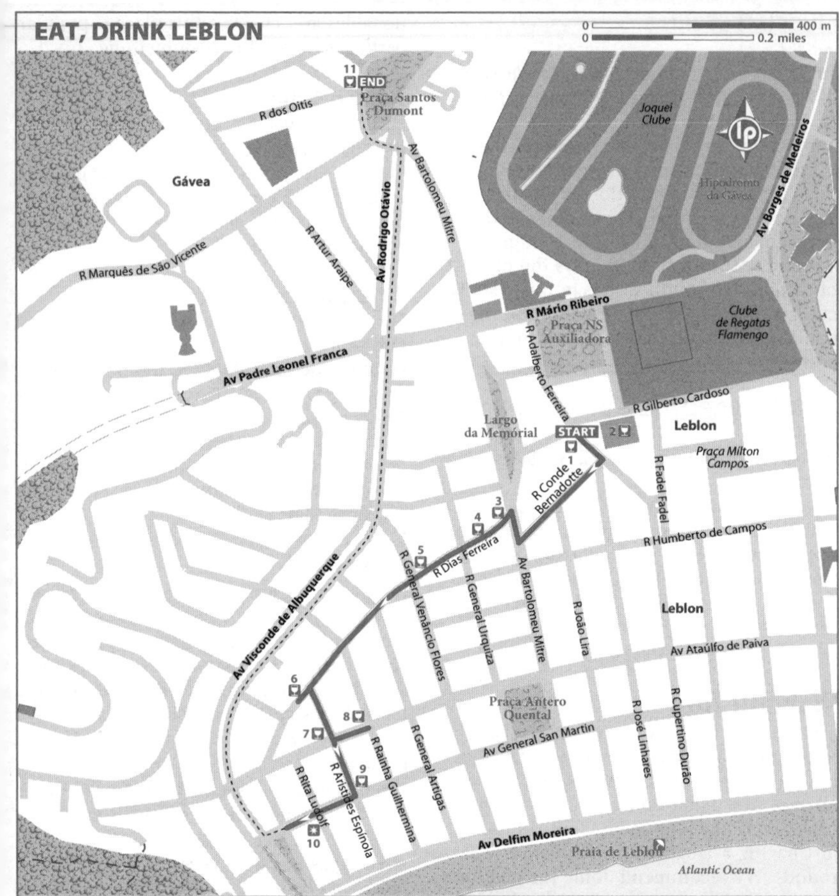

WALK FACTS

Start Rua Conde de Bernadotte
End Praça Santos Dumont
Distance 2km
Duration three to six hours
Fuel stop Braseiro da Gávea

ever-flowing ice-cold *chope* (draft beer) are a few reasons for its longevity.

9 Bar Veloso

Head south on Rainha Guilhermina and one block west to Bar Veloso (p151), a newish two-story place named after the famous bar where Vinícius and Jobim hung out. The open-sided ground floor brings a chatty, flirty crowd.

10 Melt

If suddenly you feel like dancing – or just sitting somewhere and watching other people dance – Melt (p168) is just up the street (head one block west on Av General San Martin). You'll find a comfy lounge on the 1st floor, with DJs or bands performing on the 2nd floor. Things don't kick off until late (midnight).

11 Baixo Gávea

If you're not ready to call it a night but ready for a change of venue, catch a taxi up to the Praça Santos Dumont. Most nights of the week, the bars, such as Braseiro da Gávea (p152), facing the square pack with 20-something revelers, making for one of Rio's best open-air drinking scenes.

GÁVEA, JARDIM BOTÂNICO & LAGOA

Eating p135; Shopping p116

Rio's picturesque lake is the focal point of these well-heeled neighborhoods north of Ipanema and Leblon. The Lagoa Rodrigo de Freitas is actually a saltwater lagoon and is much utilized by Cariocas. Joggers and cyclists zip along the shoreline trail by day, while at night, the lakeside restaurants fill with couples and friends enjoying a meal and live music in the open air. Two small islands in the lake, Ilha Piraqué and Ilha dos Caiçaras, are private country clubs.

West of the lake are the botanical gardens for which the neighborhood is named. Here you'll find stately palms and a variety of flowering plants. South of the gardens is Gávea, home to Rio's premier horse-racing track, and a planetarium. Aside from their natural attractions, these neighborhoods also have some excellent restaurants, lively nightlife and one of the Zona Sul's best cultural centers.

Much of the development of this area is linked to the lake. Prior to the Portuguese arrival, the Tupinambá indigenous group dubbed the lake Sacopenapã (place of the soco birds), but it was later changed to Rodrigo de Freitas, in honor of the Portuguese settler who made his fortune off the sugarcane fields surrounding the lake in the 16th century. Factories blighted the landscape in the 1900s, and it took much of the 20th century for the area to recover. Although the lake is still too polluted for swimming, some wildlife has returned, and visitors might see egrets on the lookout for fish in the lake.

GÁVEA

INSTITUTO MOREIRA SALLES

Map p60

☎ 3284-7400; www.ims.com.br, in Portuguese; Rua Marquês de Sao Vicente 476; admission free; 1-8pm Tue-Sun

This beautiful cultural center is next to Parque da Cidade and contains an archive of more than 80,000 photographs, many portraying old streets of Rio as well as the urban development of other Brazilian cities over the last two centuries. It also hosts impressive exhibitions, often showcasing the works of some of Brazil's best photographers and artists. Check its website for details of what's on when you're in town.

The gardens, complete with artificial lake and flowing river, were designed by Brazilian landscape architect Burle Marx. There's also a craft shop and a quaint café here that serves lunch or afternoon tea.

TRANSPORTATION: GÁVEA, JARDIM BOTÂNICO & LAGOA

Jardim Botânico and Gávea: Centro (170); Botafogo, Flamengo and Glória (176, 178); Leblon, Ipanema and Copacabana (571, 572, 574)

Metrô na Superfície Metro buses connect Ipanema/General Osório station with Gávea, stopping at Av Bartolomeu Mitre (near the Hospital Miguel Couto) and continuing west on Av Padre Leonel Franca.

MUSEU HISTÓRICO DA CIDADE

Map p60

☎ 2512-2353; www.rio.rj.gov.br/cultura, in Portuguese; Estrada de Santa Marinha 505; admission R$5; 10am-4pm Tue-Fri, 10am-3pm Sat & Sun

The 19th-century mansion located on the lovely grounds of Parque da Cidade now houses the City History Museum. In addition to its permanent collection, which portrays Rio from its founding in 1565 to the mid-20th century, the museum has exhibitions of furniture, porcelain, photographs and paintings by well-known artists. The park itself is free, open from 7am to 6pm.

PLANETÁRIO

Map p70

☎ 2274-0046; www.rio.rj.gov.br/planetario, in Portuguese; Av Padre Leonel Franca 240; museum only adult/child R$8/4, museum & planetarium show adult/child R$16/8; 9am-5pm Tue-Fri, 3-6pm Sat & Sun

Gávea's stellar attraction, the Planetário (Planetarium) features a museum, a *praça dos telescópios* (telescopes' square) and a couple of state-of-the-art operating domes, each capable of projecting over 6000 stars onto its walls (40-minute sessions in the domes take place on weekends and holidays). Visitors can also take a peek at the night sky (free) through the telescopes on Tuesday, Wednesday and Thursday from 7:30pm to 8:30pm (6:30pm to 7:30pm in winter). The modern Museu do Universo

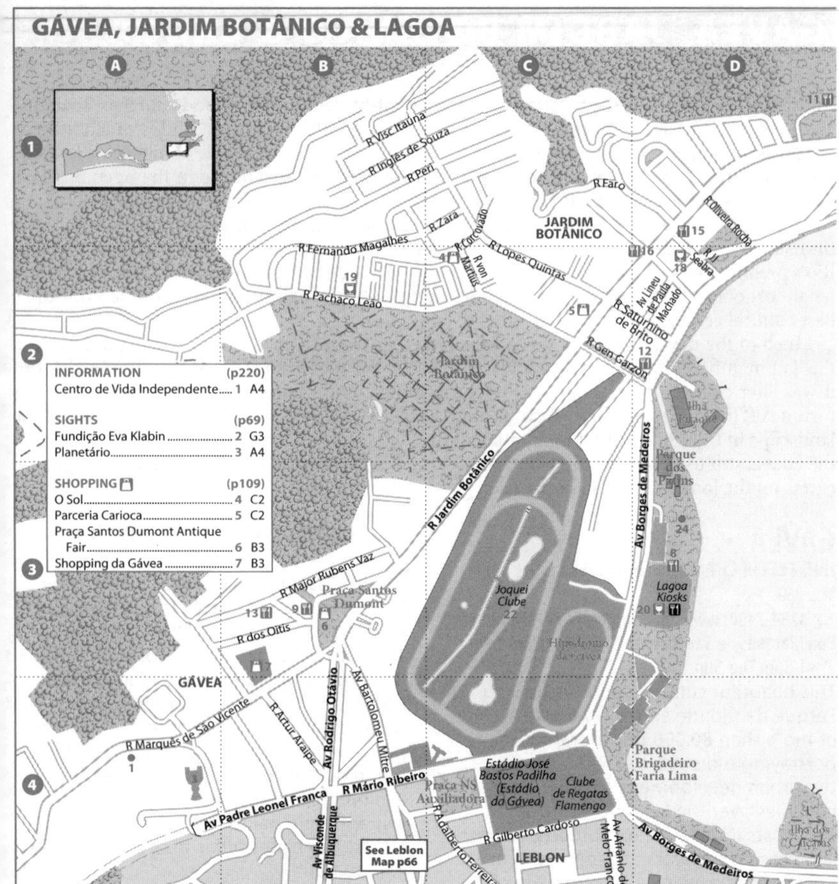

(Universe Museum) houses sundials, a Foucault's Pendulum and other permanent exhibitions, plus temporary displays. Periodically, the planetarium hosts live concerts (Musica nas Estrelas) on Sundays. Check the website or the newspaper for more information.

JARDIM BOTÂNICO

JARDIM BOTÂNICO Map p70

☎ 3874-1808; www.jbrj.gov.br, in Portuguese; Rua Jardim Botânico 920; admission R$5; ⏲ 8am-5pm

This exotic 137-hectare garden, with over 8000 plant species, was designed by order of the Prince Regent Dom João (later to become Dom João VI) in 1808. The garden is quiet and serene on weekdays and blossoms with families and music on weekends. Highlights of a visit here include the row of palms (planted when the garden first opened), the Amazonas section, the lake containing the huge Vitória Régia water lilies and the enclosed orquidário, home to 600 species of orchids. Also onsite is the Museu do Meio Ambiente (Environmental Museum; ☎ 3204-2504; Rua Jardim Botânico 1008; ⏲ 10am-5pm Tue-Sun), which opened in 2008 and houses temporary environmentally focused exhibits. English-language tours can be arranged by appointment. A pleasant outdoor café overlooks the gardens. Be sure to take insect repellent.

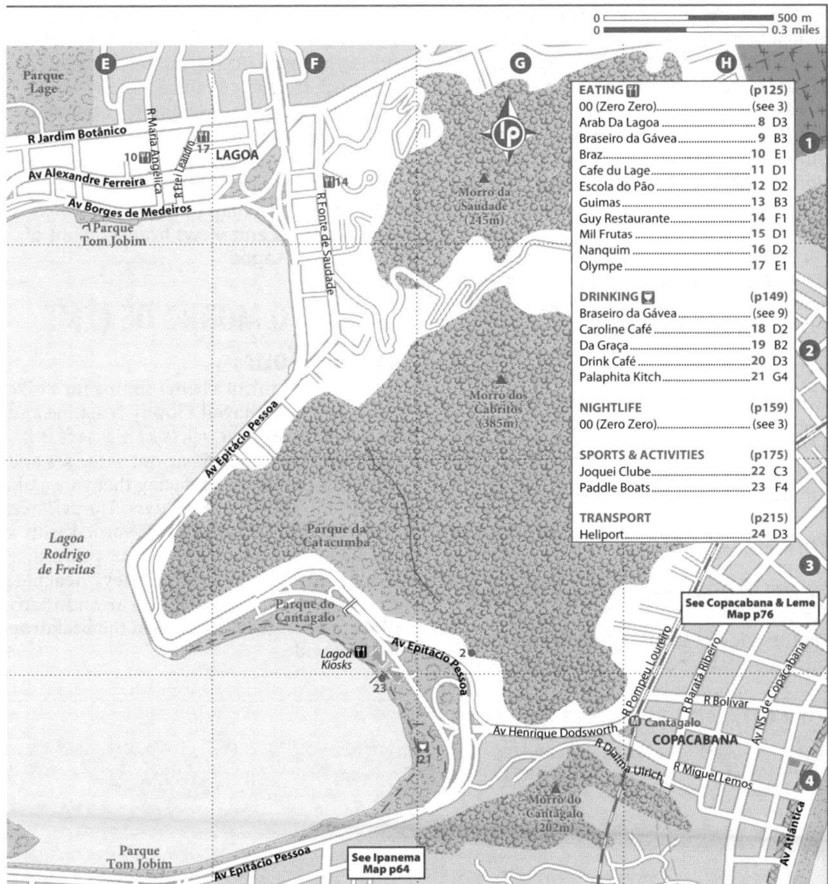

PARQUE LAGE

Map p70

☎ 3257-1819; www.eavparquelage.rj.gov.br, in Portuguese; Rua Jardim Botânico 414; 9am-5pm

This beautiful park, at the base of Parque Nacional da Tijuca, is about 1km from Jardim Botânico. It has English-style gardens, little lakes and a mansion that houses the Escola de Artes Visuais (School of Visual Arts), which often hosts free art exhibitions and occasional performances. The park is a tranquil place and particularly popular on weekends when the Café du Lage (p136) whips up a delightful brunch. Native Atlantic rain forest surrounds Parque Lage. This is the starting point for challenging hikes up Corcovado (but it's best to go with a guide).

LAGOA

LAGOA RODRIGO DE FREITAS

Map p70

One of the city's most picturesque spots, Lagoa has 7.2km of cycling/walking path around the lake. Bikes are available for hire, for around R$10 an hour, near Parque Brigadeiro Faria Lima. And there's also a helipad (p226) on the shoreline for those who want a bird's-eye of the *Cidade Maravilhosa*. It may sound cheesy, but hiring a paddle boat is another way to enjoy the lake, especially when the Christmas tree is lit up across the water. Boat rental is available on the lake's east side in Parque do Cantagalo, December through early January. For those who prefer caipirinhas to plastic swan boats, the kiosks in Parque dos Patins offer lakeside dining al fresco, often accompanied by live *forró* (traditional music from the northeast).

FUNDAÇÃO EVA KLABIN

Map p70

☎ 3202-8557; www.evaklabin.org.br; Av Epitácio Pessoa 2480; admission R$10; guided visits by appointment 2:30 & 4pm Tue-Fri

An old mansion full of antiques, the former residence of Eva Klabin houses the works of art she collected for 60 years. Reflecting Eva's diverse interests, the collection has 1100 pieces from ancient Egypt, Greece and China. Paintings, sculptures, silver, furniture and carpets are also on display.

PARQUE DA CATACUMBA

Map p70

☎ 2247-9949; Av Epitácio Pessoa; 8am-5pm Tue-Sun

On the edge of the lake (but across the busy road), this park and sculptural garden added some new adventure activities in 2010, including a 7m rock-climbing wall (R$15), a zipline (R$10), rappelling down a 30m rock-face (R$40) and a canopy walk (R$30) through the treetops. It's operated by Lagoa Aventuras (☎ 4105-0079; www.lagoaaventuras.com.br). It's free to simply stroll through the park, and there's a short but steep trail (15 minutes' walking) to the Mirante do Sacopã, which offers scenic views from a height of 130m above Lagoa.

LAGOA TO MORRO DE LEME

Cycling Tour

It is hard to think of a better setting for a bike ride than the Zona Sul's lovely coastline and its nearby lakeside jewel, Lagoa Rodrigo de Freitas (p71). The mountains rising out of the sea and the white-sand beaches facing them are a big part of the allure of the *Cidade Maravilhosa* and you will find yourself rewarded with a number of panoramic views as you cruise along on this fabulous journey. Beaches, bay, Corcovado, Pão de Açúcar and many of Rio's other lush peaks form the backdrop for your ride.

LAGOA TO LEME CYCLING TOUR

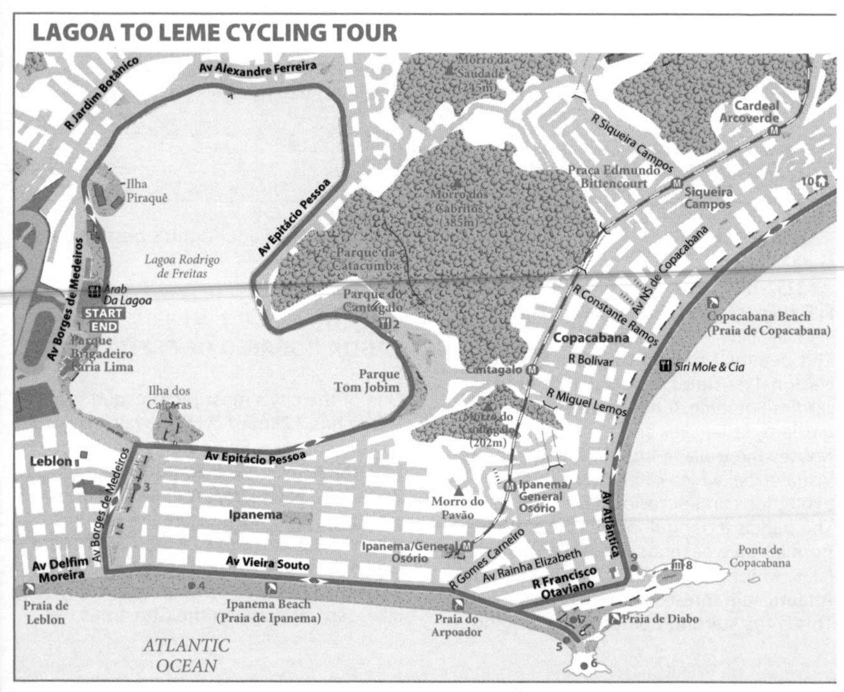

Bring some money for snacks and *agua de coco* (coconut water) – both prevalent along the beach – and a meal at the end of your ride. You'll work up an appetite out in the sun.

Most of this journey follows a bike path separate from – but sometimes annoyingly close to – the traffic on the street. Sunday is the best day to do this ride, as the beach road bordering the bike path is closed then – giving you more room to connect to your inner Armstrong.

1 Parque Brigadeiro Faria Lima

Begin in this park on the edge of Lagoa. Conveniently, there's a bike-rental place right there. You can also rent bikes at a number of other places in town (p216).

2 Lagoa kiosks

Once you are on the bike path, follow it north as it loops around the lake, beneath the outstretched arms of Cristo up above you. About 4km from your starting point, you will pass some of the Lagoa kiosks, which are quite popular spots for al fresco dining in the evening.

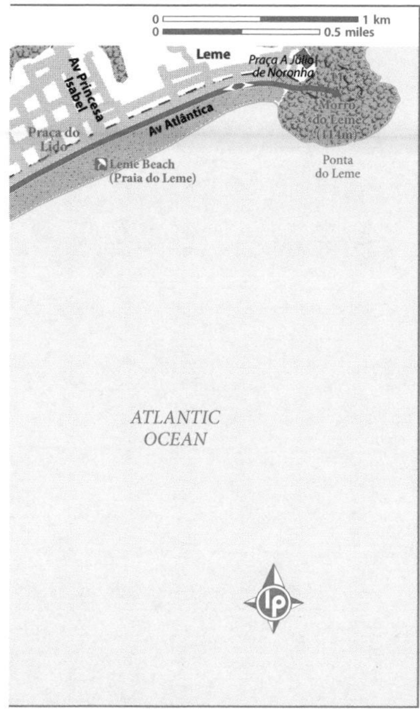

RIDE FACTS

Start Parque Brigadeiro Faria Lima
End Parque Brigadeiro Faria Lima
Distance 25km
Duration Three hours
Fuel stop Siri Mole & Cia kiosk (p137)

3 Jardim de Alah

After passing the kiosks, pedal for another 2km and you'll pass the Ilha dos Caiçaras on your right. Go just past it and take Av Borges de Medeiros south, following along the canal and the Jardim de Alah opposite. In a few blocks you'll reach the beach.

4 Posto 10

Once you reach the beach, look for a cycle path that goes along the south side of Av Vieira Souto and turn left. After about 500m, you'll catch an eyeful of *frescobal,* football and volleyball games, with plenty of good people watching.

5 Praça do Arpoador

Another 1.5km further, you'll reach Arpoador. Pull off the bike path for your first *agua de coco* from a kiosk near the beach. You'll need to walk your bike here, as it's usually full of pedestrians. Take a seat under a palm tree and enjoy the fine view west, with Dois Irmãos towering over Leblon.

6 Ponta do Arpoador

The rock outcropping to your left is Ponta do Arpoador (p63), which offers decent waves. It's a rare day when there aren't at least a dozen surfers jockeying for good breaks.

7 Parque Garota de Ipanema

After your rest, get back on the bike – either pushing your bike through the Parque Garota de Ipanema (p67), or going back up to Rua Francisco Otaviano, where the bike path continues.

8 Forte de Copacabana

Following the path, you'll pass the entrance to Forte de Copacabana (p75) and will soon have a splendid view of Morro do Leme, which is at the north end of curving Copacabana Beach.

9 Posto dos pescadores

At the beginning of Copacabana you'll see the *posto dos pescadores* (fishermen's place), where fishermen haul in their catch for the day in the morning. As you continue along the bike path, be sure to stop for a cool drink at **kiosks** along the beach.

10 Copacabana Palace

Although you'll probably be watching the beach, the mountains and the sea, keep an eye out for the whitewashed **Copacabana Palace** (p191), Copa's first hotel (1923) back when the beach was still a remote getaway from Centro.

11 Morro do Leme

In Leme the path ends at the Morro do Leme, where you'll probably see kids leaping off the rocks. Take a break, perhaps exploring the forested paths around Forte Duque de Caxias (p77) before starting the return journey, which follows the same route back. If you haven't eaten by the time you return to Lagoa, grab a meal at **Arab da Lagoa** (p136) or one of the other lakeside restaurants.

COPACABANA & LEME

Eating p136; Shopping p117; Sleeping p191

Synonymous with Rio's golden age, Copacabana was once an icon of Brazil, with ritzy beachfront hotels frequented by international celebrities. One look around the place today, and you'll note that a lot has changed since the 1940s. On the surface, today's Copa is a chaotic mix of discount stores and noisy traffic-filled avenues, with a humming red-light district and a slight edginess to the streets. While paradise it clearly is not, the beach is undeniably beautiful. Framed by mountains and deep blue sea, the magnificent curve of shoreline stretches more than 4km from end to end.

Packing the beach are sun-worshippers of every age and background – from favela kids to aging socialites, with tourists and families from the Zona Norte thrown into the mix. Perhaps because of the democratic mix, Copacabana is a fascinating place to explore, with rare finds hidden in its narrow back streets. Old-school *botecos,* eclectic restaurants and nightclubs, myriad shops and of course the handsome shoreline still entrance many visitors. While the cool kids cling to Ipanema and Leblon, Copacabana seems poised on the edge of a renaissance. Its new glassy kiosks (p137) have brought a touch of class to the neighborhood, while the recently dubbed 'Baixo Copa' (p153) is becoming a nightlife destination in its own right.

As in Ipanema, part of the beachside street (Av Atlântica in this case) closes on Sunday and holidays (until 6pm), giving freer reign to the joggers, cyclists and inline skaters normally jostling for space on the narrow bike path.

The name Copacabana comes from a small Bolivian village on Lake Titicaca. Historians believe a statue of the Virgin Mary (Our Lady of Copacabana) was brought to Rio and consecrated inside a small chapel near Arpoador. Copacabana remained a small fishing village until Túnel Velho opened in 1891, connecting it with the rest of the city.

The construction of the neoclassical Copacabana Palace Hotel in 1923 heralded a new era for Copacabana – and Rio – as South America's most elegant destination. Copacabana remained Rio's untarnished gem until the 1970s, when the area began to fall into decline.

COPACABANA & LEME BEACHES

Map p76

Av Atlântica

A magnificent confluence of land and sea, the long, scalloped beach of Copacabana and Leme runs for 4km, with a flurry of activity always stretching along its length: over-amped soccer players singing their team's anthem, Cariocas and tourists lining up for caipirinhas at kiosks, favela kids showing off their soccer skills, beach vendors shouting out their wares among the beached and tanned bodies.

As in Ipanema, each group stakes out its stretch of sand. Leme is a mix of older residents and favela kids, while the area between the Copacabana Palace hotel and Rua Fernando Mendes is the gay and transvestite section, known as the Stock or Stock Market – easily recognized by the rainbow flag. Young football and *futevôlei* (soccer volleyball) players hold court near Rua Santa Clara. Posts 5 and 6 are a mix of favela kids and Carioca retirees, while the beach next to Forte de Copacabana is the fishermen's community beach. In the morning, you can buy the fresh catch of the day.

The beach is lit at night and police are in the area, but it's still not wise to wander the sands after dark. It's fine to go for a drink at one of the kiosks at night, just try to avoid deserted areas. Av NS de Copacabana (NS stands for *Nossa Senhora,* meaning Our Lady) is also sketchy late at night and on weekends, when the shops are closed and few locals are around.

FORTE DE COPACABANA Map p76

☎ 2521-1032; Av Atlântica & Rua Francisco Otaviano; admission R$4; 10am-4pm Tue-Sun

Built in 1914 on the promontory of the old Our Lady of Copacabana chapel, the fort of Copacabana was one of Rio's premier defenses against attack. You can still see

TRANSPORTATION: COPACABANA & LEME

Bus: Ipanema (570), Leblon (574), Gávea (432), Centro (123)

Metro: Siqueira Campos, Cardeal Arcoverde, Cantagalo, Ipanema/General Osório

COPACABANA & LEME

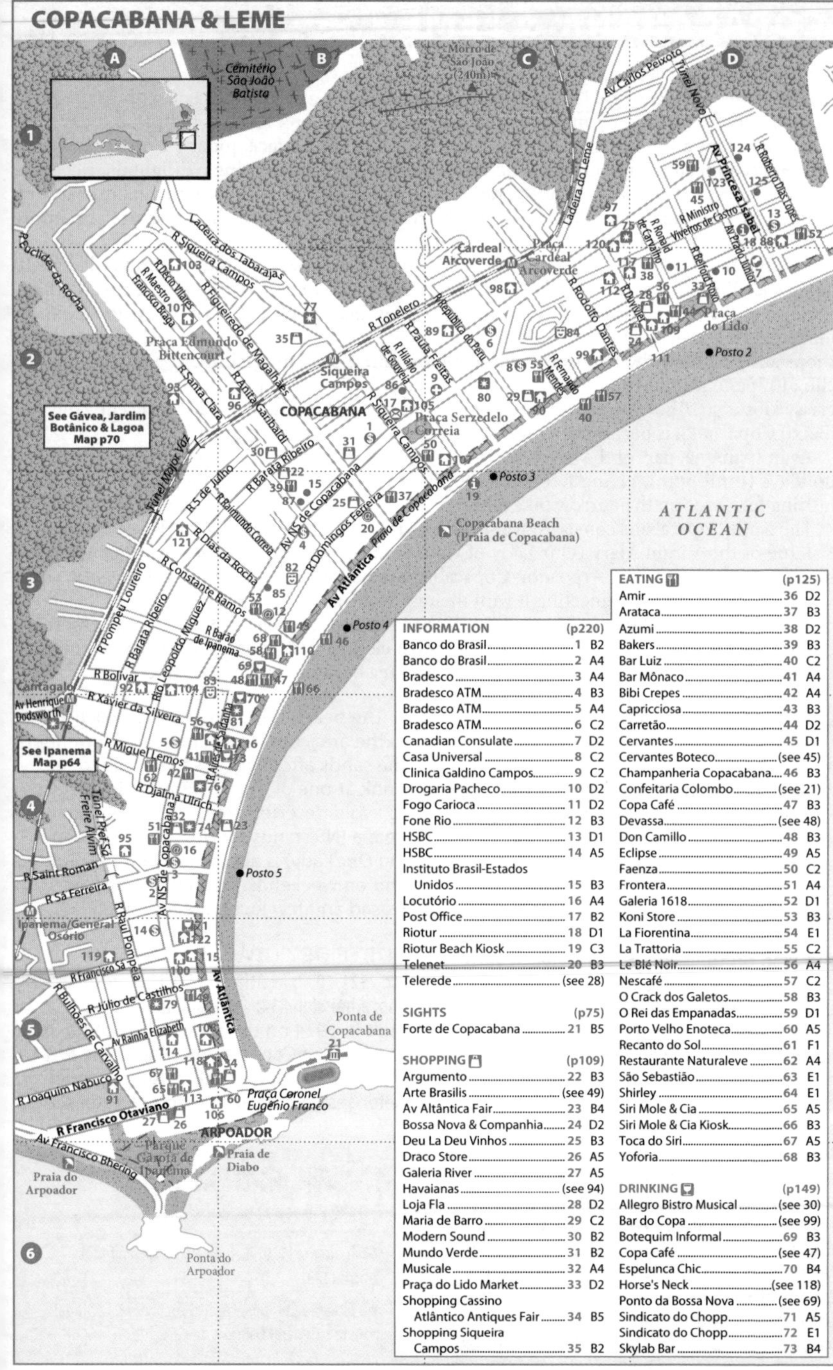

See Gávea, Jardim Botânico & Lagoa Map p70
See Ipanema Map p64
COPACABANA
ARPOADOR
ATLANTIC OCEAN
Copacabana Beach (Praia de Copacabana)
Praia do Arpoador
Praia de Diabo
Ponta do Arpoador
Ponta de Copacabana
Posto 2
Posto 3
Posto 4
Posto 5
INFORMATION (p220)
Banco do Brasil 1 B2
Banco do Brasil 2 A4
Bradesco 3 A4
Bradesco ATM 4 B3
Bradesco ATM 5 A4
Bradesco ATM 6 C2
Canadian Consulate 7 D2
Casa Universal 8 C2
Clinica Galdino Campos 9 C2
Drogaria Pacheco 10 D2
Fogo Carioca 11 D2
Fone Rio 12 B3
HSBC 13 D1
HSBC 14 A5
Instituto Brasil-Estados Unidos 15 B3
Locutório 16 A4
Post Office 17 B2
Riotur 18 D1
Riotur Beach Kiosk 19 C3
Telenet 20 B3
Telerede (see 28)
SIGHTS (p75)
Forte de Copacabana 21 B5
SHOPPING (p109)
Argumento 22 B3
Arte Brasilis (see 49)
Av Altântica Fair 23 B4
Bossa Nova & Companhia 24 D2
Deu La Deu Vinhos 25 B3
Draco Store 26 A5
Galeria River 27 A5
Havaianas (see 94)
Loja Fla 28 D2
Maria de Barro 29 C2
Modern Sound 30 B2
Mundo Verde 31 B2
Musicale 32 A4
Praça do Lido Market 33 D2
Shopping Cassino Atlântico Antiques Fair 34 B5
Shopping Siqueira Campos 35 B2
EATING (p125)
Amir 36 D2
Arataca 37 B3
Azumi 38 D2
Bakers 39 B3
Bar Luiz 40 C2
Bar Mônaco 41 A4
Bibi Crepes 42 A4
Capricciosa 43 B3
Carretão 44 D2
Cervantes 45 D1
Cervantes Boteco (see 45)
Champanheria Copacabana 46 B3
Confeitaria Colombo (see 21)
Copa Café 47 B3
Devassa (see 48)
Don Camillo 48 B3
Eclipse 49 A5
Faenza 50 C2
Frontera 51 A4
Galeria 1618 52 D1
Koni Store 53 B3
La Fiorentina 54 E1
La Trattoria 55 C2
Le Blé Noir 56 A4
Nescafé 57 C2
O Crack dos Galetos 58 B3
O Rei das Empanadas 59 D1
Porto Velho Enoteca 60 A5
Recanto do Sol 61 F1
Restaurante Naturaleve 62 A4
São Sebastião 63 E1
Shirley 64 E1
Siri Mole & Cia 65 A5
Siri Mole & Cia Kiosk 66 B3
Toca do Siri 67 A5
Yoforia 68 B3
DRINKING (p149)
Allegro Bistro Musical (see 30)
Bar do Copa (see 99)
Botequim Informal 69 B3
Copa Café (see 47)
Espelunca Chic 70 B4
Horse's Neck (see 118)
Ponto da Bossa Nova (see 69)
Sindicato do Chopp 71 A5
Sindicato do Chopp 72 E1
Skylab Bar 73 B4

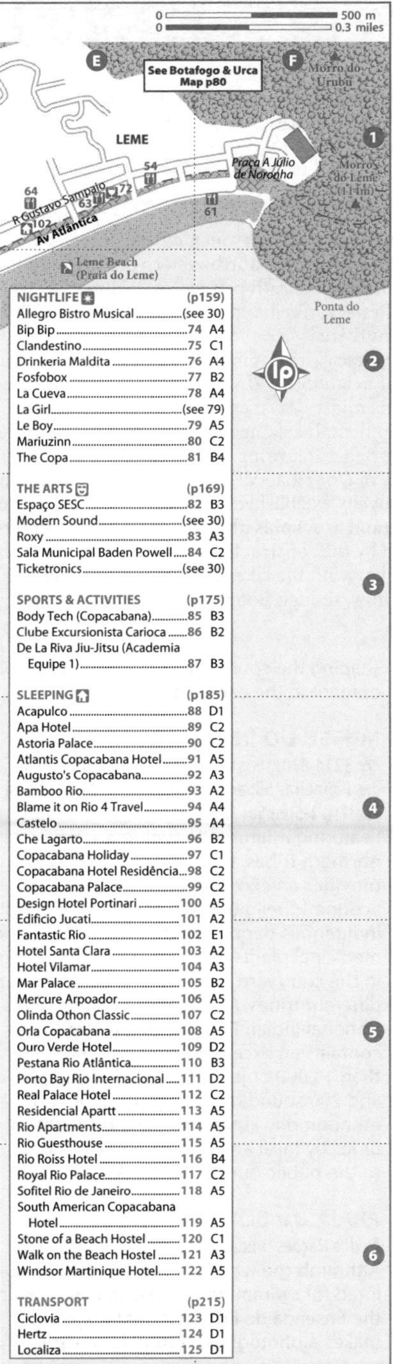

its original features, including walls up to 12m thick, defended by Krupp cannons. Inside is a museum with several floors of exhibits tracing the early days of the Portuguese colony to the mid-19th century; the exhibits aren't the most tastefully done, but the view alone is worth a visit. Be sure to stop in the beautifully sited Confeitaria Colombo (p139).

FORTE DUQUE DE CAXIAS

☎ 3223-2034; Praça Almirante Júlio de Noronha; admission R$4; 9am-5pm Sat & Sun

More commonly known as Forte do Leme, this military base is open to the public on weekends, when visitors can access the forested trail skirting up to the top of Morro de Leme. The short but steep trail passes through Atlantic rain forest and by the ruins of an earlier 18th-century fort that stood here. The views from the top are magnificent.

BOTAFOGO & URCA

Eating p140; Shopping p119; Sleeping p195

The traditional, middle-class neighborhood of Botafogo may not have the beaches of its neighbors to the south, but it doesn't lack for much else. There's a lot going on in this neighborhood, with intriguing museums, several movie theaters, quaint bookshops, a shopping center (with great views) and festive, open-air bars set along tranquil back streets. There are also a couple of vibrant nightclubs and a boulevard dotted with old mansions.

Neighboring Urca is even more idyllic, with shaded, quiet streets. Here, you'll find an eclectic mix of architecture, with art-deco and modernist houses backed by manicured gardens, as local residents stroll past them. Along the seawall, which forms the northwestern perimeter of Pão de Açúcar, fishermen cast for dinner as couples lounge beneath palm trees, taking in views of Baía de Guanabara and Cristo Redentor. Tiny Praia Vermelha in the south has one of Rio's finest beach views. A pleasant walking trail begins there.

Although it was the site of one of the first Portuguese garrisons in the region, almost 300 years elapsed before Urca developed into a residential neighborhood. Today it is one of the safest and – in spite of the Pão de Açúcar cable car in its midst – least explored by foreign visitors.

Botafogo, on the other hand, saw early development. It's named after the Portuguese settler João Pereira de Souza Botafogo, and grew in importance following the arrival of the Portuguese court in the late 1800s. Carlota Joaquina, the wife of Dom João VI, had a country villa, and she used to bathe in the Baía de Guanabara. With royalty established in the area, arriving aristocrats built many mansions, some of which still stand as schools, theaters and cultural centers.

In the 19th century, development was spurred by the construction of a tram that ran to the botanical garden (Jardim Botânico), linking the bay with the lake (Lagoa Rodrigo de Freitas). This artery still plays a vital role in Rio's traffic flow, though Botafogo's main streets are now extremely congested.

BOTAFOGO

MUSEU CASA DE RUI BARBOSA

Map p80

☎ 3289-4600; www.casaruibarbosa.gov.br, in Portuguese; Rua São Clemente 134; admission R$2; 9am-5:30pm Tue-Fri, 2-6pm Sat & Sun

The former mansion (completely restored in 2003) of famous Brazilian journalist and diplomat Rui Barbosa is now a museum housing his library and personal belongings, along with an impressive archive of manuscripts and first editions of other Brazilian authors, such as Machado de Assis and José de Alençar. Barbosa played a major role in shaping the country's socioeconomic development in the early 20th century.

TRANSPORTATION: BOTAFOGO & URCA

Botafogo

Bus: Ipanema, Leblon and Copacabana (571 & 573), Jardim Botânico and Gávea (170 & 176)

M Botafogo

Urca

Bus: Centro (107), Leblon, Ipanema and Copacabana (511 & 512)

MUSEU DO ÍNDIO Map p80

☎ 3214-8702; www.museudoindio.org.br; Rua das Palmeiras 55; admission R$3; 9am-5:30pm Tue-Fri, 1-5pm Sat & Sun

Featuring multimedia exhibitions on Brazil's northern tribes, the small Museu do Índio provides an excellent introduction to the economic, religious and social life of Brazil's indigenous people. Next to native food and medicinal plants, the four life-size dwellings in the courtyard were actually built by four different tribes. As a branch of Funai (the National Indian Foundation), the museum contains an excellent archive of more than 14,000 objects, 50,000 photographs and 200 sound recordings. Its indigenous ethnography library containing 16,000 volumes by local and foreign authors is open to the public during the week.

PRAIA DO BOTAFOGO Map p80

Av dos Naçoes Unidas

Although the waters of the bay are too polluted for swimming, the beach overlooking the Enseada de Botafogo (Botafogo Inlet) makes a photogenic setting for a stroll.

Hopeful football stars play pick-up games along the shore, against the backdrop of sailboats bobbing on the water and Pão de Açúcar off in the background.

PASMADO OVERLOOK Map p80

Rua Bartolomeu Portela

Sweeping views of Enseada de Botafogo, Pão de Açúcar and Corcovado await visitors who make the journey up Pasmado. It's best reached in early morning or late afternoon, when the light is at its best for capturing the postcard panorama. Visitors will also be able to see details of a favela from above. The overlook is best reached by taxi via Rua General Severiano.

MUSEU VILLA-LOBOS Map p80

☎ 2266-3845; Rua Sorocaba 200; admission free; 🕙 10am-5pm Mon-Fri

Housed in a century-old building, the modest museum is dedicated to the memory of Brazil's greatest classical composer – and founder of the Brazilian Academy of Music – Heitor Villa-Lobos. In addition to scores, musical instruments – including the piano on which he composed – and personal items, the museum contains an extensive sound archive. Classical concerts are sometimes held in the adjoining courtyard.

URCA

PÃO DE AÇÚCAR Map p80

☎ 2461-2700; www.bondinho.com.br; Praça General Tibúrcio; adult/child R$44/22; 🕙 8am-7:50pm

One of Rio's dazzling icons, Pão de Açúcar (Sugarloaf) offers a vision of Rio at its most disarming. Following a steep ascent up the mountain, you'll be rewarded with superb views of Rio's gorgeous shoreline, and the city planted among the green peaks. For prime views of the *Cidade Maravilhosa,* go around sunset on a clear day.

Everyone must go to Pão de Açúcar but, if you can, avoid it from about 10am to 11am and 2pm to 3pm, which is when most tourist buses arrive. Avoid cloudy days as well.

To reach the summit, 395m above Rio and the Baía de Guanabara, you take two cable cars. The first ascends 215m to Morro da Urca. From here, you can see Baía de Guanabara and along the winding coastline. On the ocean side of the mountain is Praia Vermelha, in a small, calm bay. Morro da Urca has a restaurant, souvenir shops, a playground, outdoor theater and a helipad (p226).

top picks

FOR CHILDREN

- Playing in the sand in the family-friendly beach area (between posts 11 and 12) in Leblon (p63).
- Meeting some of Brazil's native creatures at the Jardim Zoológico (p103).
- Admiring the city skyline at sunset during a cruise (p224) along the bay.
- Riding the bonde (tram, p97) up to Santa Teresa.
- Renting bikes (p216) for a cycle around Lagoa, followed by lunch at one of the lakeside kiosks.
- Checking out the submarine and nautical equipment at the Museu Naval (p94).
- Stargazing at the Planetário (p69).
- Slipping and sliding along waterfalls at the gigantic Rio Water Planet (p108).

The second cable car goes up to Pão de Açúcar. At the top, the city unfolds beneath you, with Corcovado mountain and Cristo Redentor off to the west, and the long curve of Copacabana beach to the south. If the breathtaking heights unsteady you, a café is on hand to serve caipirinhas and other drinks. There's also a restaurant, an ice-cream shop and the obligatory souvenir shop. The two-stage cable cars depart every 20 minutes.

Those who'd rather take the long way to the summit should sign up with one of the granite-hugging climbing tours (p177) offered by various outfits in Rio.

There's a new *churrascaria* (barbecue meat restaurant at the base of the mountain). It's touristy but not a bad place for a bite or a drink if you have time to kill after booking your tickets to the top.

PISTA CLÁUDIO COUTINHO Map p80

🕙 6am-sunset

Everyone loves this paved 2km trail winding along the southern contour of Morro do Urca. It's a lush treed area, with the waves crashing on the rocks below. Look out for families of capuchin monkeys with their gray fur, striped tails and tiny faces. To get there, walk 100m north along the edge of Praia Vermelha (with your back to the cable-car station) and you'll see the entrance to the path straight ahead, just past the beach. About 300m along the path, there's a small unmarked trail leading off to Morro da

BOTAFOGO & URCA

Urca. From there you can go up to Pão de Açúcar by cable car, saving a few reais. Pão de Açúcar can also be climbed – but it's not recommended without climbing gear.

PRAIA DA URCA Map p80

Av João Luis Alves

This tiny beach is popular with neighborhood kids who gather here for pick-up footbal games when school is not in session (and sometimes when it is). A small restaurant, Garota da Urca (p140), lies near the beach.

PRAIA VERMELHA Map p80

Praça General Tibúrcio

Beneath Morro da Urca, narrow Praia Vermelha has superb views of the rocky coastline from the shore. Its coarse sand gives the beach the name *vermelha* (red). Because the beach is protected by the headland, the water is usually calm.

MUSEU DE CIÊNCIAS DA TERRA

Map p80

☎ 2295-4746; Av Pasteur 404; admission free; 🕑 10am-4pm Tue-Sun

With curved staircases and statues out the front, this majestic building went through many incarnations before it housed the Earth Science Museum. The four-room exhibit gives an overview of the natural history of Brazil. Other rooms showcase the museum's extensive collection of minerals, rocks and meteorites – 5000 pieces in all.

URCA, THE VILLAGE BY THE SEA

Walking Tour

One of Rio's most charming neighborhoods is also one of its least explored. The peaceful streets are lined with trees, beautiful houses and lush gardens. Out by the bay, fishermen cast their lines just beyond the rocky shoreline as couples lounge on the seawall, Corcovado framing the scene.

1 Cassino da Urca

Our walk begins where Rua Marechal Cantuária meets Av São Sebastião. On your left, you'll see the former Cassino da Urca, a once-popular gambling and nightspot, where Carmen Miranda and Josephine Baker both performed. Today it has been restored to house a branch of the European Design Institute.

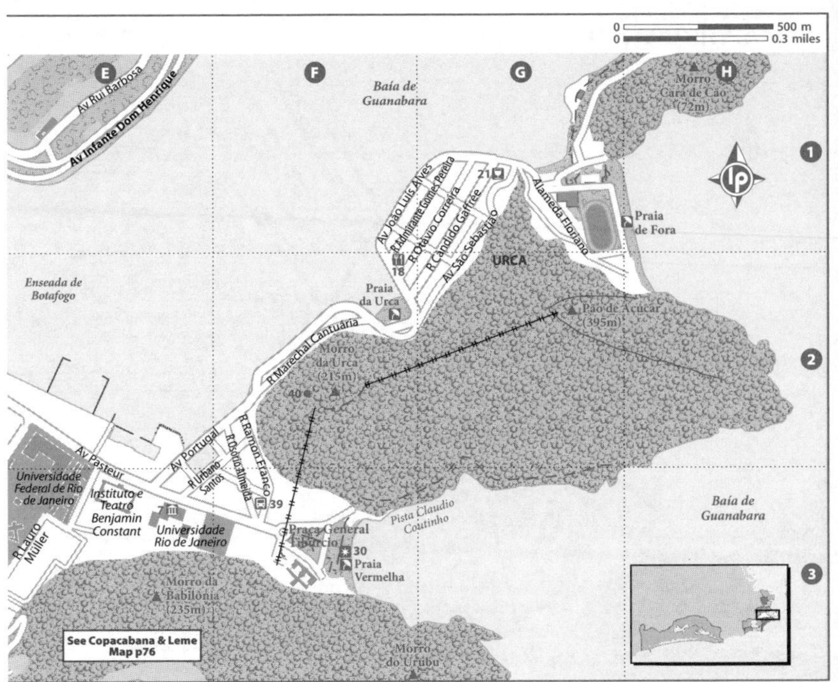

BOTOFOGO & URCA

INFORMATION (p220)
Banco do Brasil 1 C2
Bradesco ATM 2 A3
Bradesco ATM 3 C2
Bradesco ATM 4 D3
Post Office 5 C1

SIGHTS (p78)
Museu Casa de Rui Barbosa 6 C2
Museu de Ciências da Terra 7 E3
Museu do Índio 8 B2
Museu Villa-Lobos 9 B2
Pasmado Overlook 10 D2

SHOPPING (p109)
Artíndia (see 8)
Botafogo Praia Shopping 11 C2
Cobal de Humaitá 12 A3
Livraria Prefácio 13 C2
Ponto Fotográfica 14 C2
Rio Off-Price Shopping 15 D3
Rio Sul Shopping 16 D3

EATING (p125)
Cafe Botânico 17 A3
Emporium Pax (see 11)
Garota da Urca 18 F2
Miam Miam 19 D3
Yorubá 20 C3

DRINKING (p149)
Bar Urca 21 G1
Botequim 22 A3
Champanharia Ovelha Negra 23 C2
Cobal de Humaitá (see 12)
Espirito do Chopp 24 A3
Garota da Urca (see 18)
O Plebeu 25 A3

NIGHTLIFE (p159)
Bar Bukowski 26 C3
Canecão 27 D3
Casa da Matriz 28 B3
Far Up (see 24)
Pista 3 29 B3
Praia Vermelha 30 F3

THE ARTS (p169)
Espaço de Cinema 31 D2
Estação Botafogo 32 C2

SPORTS & ACTIVITIES (p175)
Casa de Dança Carlinhos de Jesus 33 D3
Sivananda Center 34 B2

SLEEPING (p185)
Ace Hostel 35 C2
El Misti 36 C2
Tupiniquim 37 D3
Vila Carioca 38 C2

TRANSPORT (p215)
Buses to Centro or Zona Sul 39 F3
Heliport 40 F2

2 Carmen Miranda's former residence

Veer to the right along Av São Sebastião, following the road uphill. You'll pass Carmen Miranda's former residence at No 131 and soon reach the wall that separates the military fort from the neighborhood.

3 Bar Urca

At the end of the street, take the steps down to Av João Luis Alves. Stop for a cold drink at Bar Urca (p154), while admiring the splendid views across the bay. On clear nights and weekends, the bar becomes a popular open-air gathering spot.

URCA, THE VILLAGE BY THE SEA

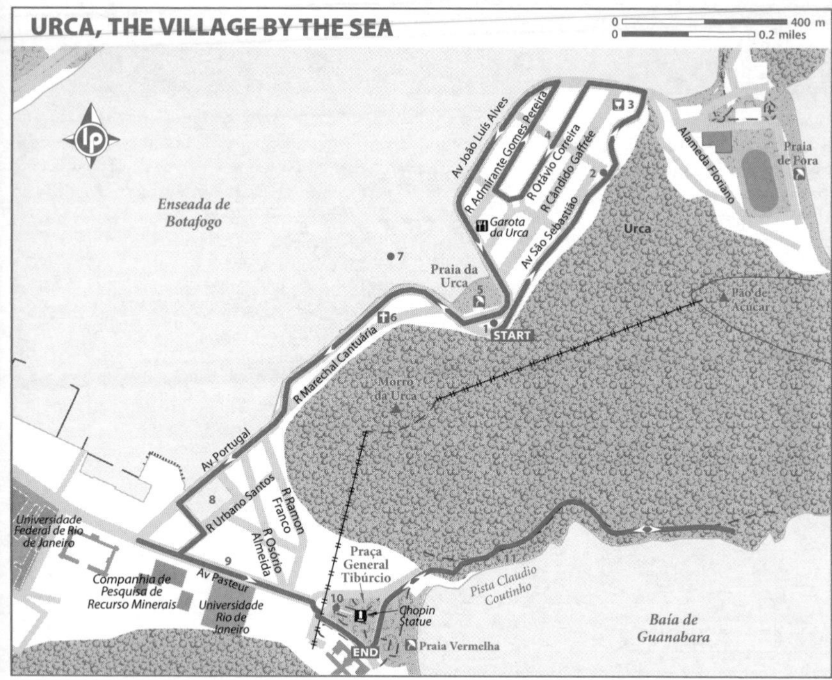

WALK FACTS

Start Rua Marechal Cantuária
End Praia Vermelha
Distance 4km
Duration Three hours
Fuel stop Garota da Urca (p140)

4 Rua Otávio Correira

Explore the tree-lined backstreets by heading down Rua Otávio Correira and looping back along Rua Admirante Gomes Pereira. Along the way, you'll get a glimpse of the handsomely maintained private houses of Urca.

5 Praia da Urca

Cut back to Av João Luis Alves and follow it to Praia da Urca (p79), a tiny beach with more fine views of the bay. You can walk across the sand or take the road around.

6 Igreja de Nossa Senhora do Brasil

Stay on the bay side as the road forks. Peek inside Igreja de Nossa Senhora do Brasil (the chapel is on the ground floor; the church upstairs), noting the small Brazilian flag on the Madonna's cloak.

7 São Pedro no Mar statue

Facing the church is the floating statue of São Pedro no Mar. On June 29, St Peter's feast day, the fishermen process across the bay, past the statue, scattering flowers across the water.

8 Quadrado da Urca

Go along what is now Av Portugal to a bridge. On the left is Quadrado da Urca, a harbor. Go left onto Rua Elmano Cardim and right onto Rua Urbano Santos, which runs into Av Pasteur.

9 Av Pasteur

Follow this avenue southeast past majestic buildings such as Companhia de Pesquisa de Recursos Minerais (guarded by a lion) and neoclassical Universidade Federal do Rio de Janeiro.

10 Praça General Tibúrcio

Just beyond the cable-car station is Praça General Tibúrcio. Keep on toward the sea to the statue of Chopin, donated by Rio's Polish community.

11 Pista Cláudio Coutinho

Following paved Pista Cláudio Coutinho (p79) out and back, look for capuchin monkeys and parrots, and enjoy the waves crashing on the rocks.

FLAMENGO, LARANJEIRAS & COSME VELHO

Eating p141; Shopping p119; Sleeping p195

Running east from the bay out to Corcovado, these three residential neighborhoods have much history hidden in their old streets. Some even believe Flamengo was the site of Rio's first Portuguese-built house. The neighborhood was certainly Rio's finest residential district in the 19th century, though it lost its luster when the tunnel to Copacabana was completed, and the upper classes migrated south. Today this region contains both remnants from the colonial past and some highly successful urban development projects from more recent times.

The Parque do Flamengo dominates the region. Also known as the *aterro* (landfill), this beach-fronting green space is one of the world's largest urban parks, with a nationally recognized art museum, biking and running trails, sports fields, and thousands of trees and flowering plants. Inland from the park, the shaded streets of Flamengo are sprinkled with a few cafés, historic *botecos* and gossip-filled juice bars.

West of Flamengo, Laranjeiras is a tightly interwoven community with a small-town feel to the district. Charming plazas such as the Praça São Salvador are a great spot for just taking in the neighborhood.

Cosme Velho lies beyond Laranjeiras and is a major destination for visitors heading up to the statue of Cristo Redentor by the old-fashioned cog train. Nearby is the colorful Largo do Boticário, a frozen-in-time plaza from 19th-century Rio. Cosme Velho and Laranjeiras both have a few nightlife options, including several jazz cafés and nightclubs.

FLAMENGO

PARQUE DO FLAMENGO

Map p84

Officially called Parque Brigadeiro Eduardo Gomes, Parque do Flamengo was the result of a landfill project that leveled the São Antônio hill in 1965, and now spreads all the way from downtown Rio through Glória, Catete and Flamengo, and on around to Botafogo. The 1.2 sq km of land reclaimed from the sea now stages every manner of Carioca outdoor activity. Cyclists and rollerbladers glide along the myriad paths, while the many football fields and sports courts are framed against the sea. On Sundays and holidays, the avenues through the park are closed (from 7am to 6pm).

Designed by famous Brazilian landscaper Burle Marx (who also landscaped Brasília), the park features some 170,000 trees of 300 different species. In addition there are three museums in the park: the Museu de Arte Moderna (p89), the Monumento Nacional aos Mortos da II Guerra Mundial (p95) and the Museu Carmen Miranda (p83).

ARTE SESC CENTRO CULTURAL Map p84

☎ 3138-1343; www.sescrio.org.br, in Portuguese; Rua Marquês de Abrantes 99; admission free; guided visits noon-8pm Tue-Sat, 11am-5pm Sun

This small cultural center is housed in an early-20th-century mansion built by Czech entrepreneur Frederico Figner. His record company is better known than he is – Odeon records being one of the top labels in the country. The small gallery features changing exhibits, often highlighting Rio's development in the early 20th century.

MUSEU CARMEN MIRANDA Map p84

☎ 2334-4293; facing Av Rui Barbosa 560; admission free; 10am-5pm Tue-Fri, 1-5pm Sat

Once the highest-paid entertainer in the USA, Carmen Miranda was the only Brazilian to leave her prints in Hollywood's Walk of Fame. Although she's largely forgotten there, the talented Brazilian singer still has her fans in Rio and has become a cult icon among the gay community. This poorly maintained museum (which vaguely resembles a public toilet from outside) doesn't do

TRANSPORTATION: FLAMENGO, LARANJEIRAS & COSME VELHO

Flamengo

Bus: Leblon, Ipanema and Copacabana (571 and 573)

M: Flamengo, Largo do Machado

Laranjeiras & Cosme Velho

Bus: Leblon (570 & 583), Ipanema (569 & 583), Copacabana (569 & 583)

FLAMENGO, LARANJEIRAS & COSME VELHO

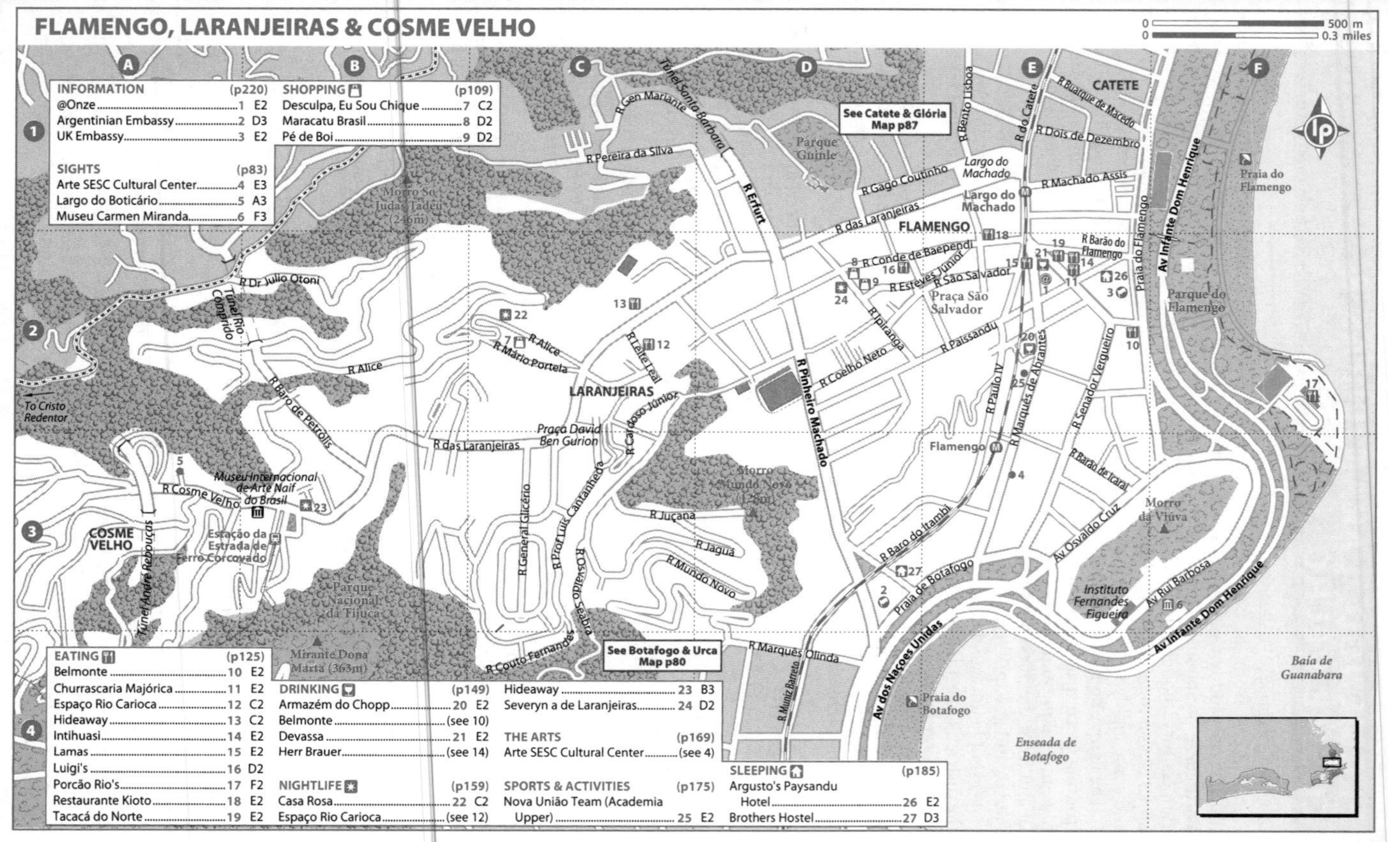

RIO'S FAVORITE REDEEMER

Named one of the world's seven new wonders in 2007, Cristo Redentor is Brazil's largest monument and certainly its most widely recognized. The Redeemer, who turns 80 in 2011, is not a gift from the French – as popular urban legend has it. In fact, Cristo was designed by the Carioca architect-engineer Heitor Silva Costa (1873–1947), who also designed the Cathedral of Petropólis. Many organizations helped make the statue a reality, including several individuals who went door-to-door asking for contributions. The idea of the statue originated in 1921 when a group called Círculo Carioca held a competition for a religious monument to commemorate Brazil's upcoming 100 years of independence. Heitor's winning project, which took 10 years to build, was considered particularly ambitious at the time – naysayers doubted whether it could be accomplished at all. Heitor's original idea depicted Christ as a vertical form with a long cross held against his side, but the committee wanted something recognizable from a great distance, so the crosslike outstretched arms were chosen instead. Today it's one of Brazil's most visited sites, welcoming more than 600,000 people a year.

a very good job of capturing one of Brazil's old-time stars – though you can peek at photographs, hear music, watch a few film clips and check out some of Miranda's over-the-top platform heels.

COSME VELHO

CRISTO REDENTOR Map p60

☎ 2558-1329; www.corcovado.com.br; Rua Cosme Velho 513 (cog station); cog train & admission R$36; 8:30am-6:30pm

One of Rio's most identifiable landmarks, the magnificent 38m-high Cristo Redentor (Christ the Redeemer) looms large atop Corcovado. From here, the statue – all 1145 tons of him – has stunning views over Rio (which explains the contented expression on his face). Corcovado, which means 'hunchback,' rises straight up from the city to a height of 710m, and at night the brightly lit statue is visible from nearly every part of the city. See above for details on its history.

When you reach the top, you'll notice the Redeemer's gaze directed at Pão de Açúcar (p79), with his left arm pointing toward the Zona Norte, and Maracanã football stadium crowding the foreground. You can also see the international airport on Ilha do Governador just beyond and the Serra dos Órgãos mountain range in the far distance. Beneath Christ's right arm you can see Lagoa Rodrigo de Freitas, Hipódromo de Gávea, Jardim Botânico, and over to Ipanema and Leblon.

Corcovado lies within the Parque Nacional da Tijuca. The most memorable way to the top is by cog train (departures every 30 minutes). For the best view, sit on the right-hand side going up.

There's also a road going up to the base of the monument. A private car or taxi will go only as far as Paineiras parking lot, from which you must transfer to an authorized van to go the 2km further to the top (R$15 per person).

Be sure to choose a clear day to visit.

LARGO DO BOTICÁRIO Map p84

Rua Cosme Velho 822

The brightly painted houses on this picturesque plaza date from the early 19th century. Largo do Boticário was named in honor of the Portuguese gentleman – Joaquim Luiz da Silva Souto – who once ran a *boticário* (apothecary) utilized by the royal family. The sound of a brook coming from the nearby forest adds to the plaza's charm. Occasional art and cultural events are hosted here.

CATETE & GLÓRIA

Eating p142; Sleeping p195

The aging buildings of bustling Catete and Glória have certainly seen better days. Like Flamengo, these twin districts flourished in the mid-19th century. In those days, their location at the outskirts of the city made them highly desirable places to live. Many noblemen and merchants built stately homes in this district, including the Barão de Novo Friburgo, who built the stately Palácio do Catete. By the end of the century, though, the wealthy began moving further out as the inner city expanded – a trend that continues today.

The Palácio do Catete, which once served as the republic's seat of power, remains the jewel of the neighborhood, and its attached gardens are a peaceful refuge from the often chaotic streets outside.

A few blocks north lies another historic beauty, the Igreja de Nossa Senhora da Glória do Outeiro. Atop a small hill overlooking the bay, the baroque church dates from the 18th century and was a favorite of Dom Pedro II and the royal family.

Aside from these vestiges of the past, most of the area is now a working-class area of greasy lunch counters, discount clothing and hardware shops, and unkempt juice bars. Some of the once magnificent mansions now house second-rate hotels in serious need of renovation. With many budget options among these crumbling facades, Glória and Catete attract shoestring travelers who don't mind the workaday bustle.

CATETE

MUSEU DA REPÚBLICA Map p87

☎ 3235-2650; www.museudarepublica.org.br; Rua do Catete 153; admission R$6, free on Wed; 🕒 10am-5pm Tue-Fri, 2-6pm Sat & Sun

The Museu da República, located in the Palácio do Catete, has been wonderfully restored. Built between 1858 and 1866 and easily distinguished by the bronze condors on the eaves, the palace was home to the president of Brazil from 1896 until 1954, when President Getúlio Vargas committed suicide here.

He had made powerful enemies in the armed forces and the political right wing, and was attacked in the press as a communist for his attempts to raise the minimum wage and increase taxes on the middle and upper classes. Tensions reached a critical level when one of Vargas' bodyguards fired shots at a journalist. Although the journalist was unharmed, an air force officer guarding him was killed, giving the armed forces the pretext they needed to demand the resignation of Vargas. In response, Vargas committed suicide, and his emotional suicide note read, 'I choose this means to be with you [the Brazilian people] always…I gave you my life; now I offer my death.' The bedroom in which the suicide occurred is eerily preserved on the 3rd floor.

The museum has a good collection of art and artifacts from the Republican period, and also houses a good lunch restaurant, an art-house cinema and a bookstore.

CENTRO CULTURAL OI FUTURO

Map p87

☎ 3131-3060; www.oifuturo.org.br; Rua Dois de Dezembro 63; admission free; 🕒 galleries 11am-5pm Tue-Sun, lobby to 8pm Tue-Sun

One of Rio's most visually exciting new additions is this modern arts center on the edge of Flamengo. With 2000 sq meters of exhibition space spread across six floors, the center features temporary multimedia installations that run the gamut from architecture and urban design to pop art, to photo-journalism and to eye-catching video art. There's also a permanent exhibition on the history of telecommunications in Brazil. The top floor houses an auditorium where visitors can attend concerts and plays, or catch a documentary.

PARQUE GUINLE

Map p87

Rua Paulo Cesar de Andrade 407

This handsomely landscaped park is a pleasant refuge from busy Rua das Lar-

TRANSPORTATION: CATETE & GLÓRIA

🚌 Ipanema, Leblon and Copacabana (571 & 573)

Ⓜ Largo do Machado, Catete, Glória

anjeiras outside its sphinx-guarded gates. There's a small wooded area, a tiny lake with ducks and always a few Cariocas enjoying a lounge on the grass. Designed by French landscape architect Gochet (with later flourishes by Roberto Burle Marx), the park is also home to the dramatic Palácio das Laranjeiras, the state governor's residence, and currently closed to visitors. The palace overlooks the west side of the park and is partially hidden by the thicket of trees.

MUSEU DE FOLCLÓRICO EDSON CARNEIRO Map p87

☎ 2285-0441; Rua do Catete 179; admission free; 🕑 11am-6pm Tue-Fri, 3-6pm Sat & Sun

Created in 1968, the museum is an excellent introduction to Brazilian folk art, particularly from the northeast. Its permanent collection comprises 1400 pieces, and includes Candomblé costumes, ceramic figurines and religious costumes used in festivals. The museum also features a folklore library and a small shop, selling handicrafts, books and folk music. The museum is located next door to the Palácio do Catete.

PARQUE DO CATETE

Map p87

Rua do Catete 181; admission free; 🕑 8am-8pm

The small landscaped park on the grounds of the Palácio do Catete provides a quiet refuge from the city. Its pond and shade-covered walks are popular with neighborhood strollers and children. Special performances in the park include concerts and plays.

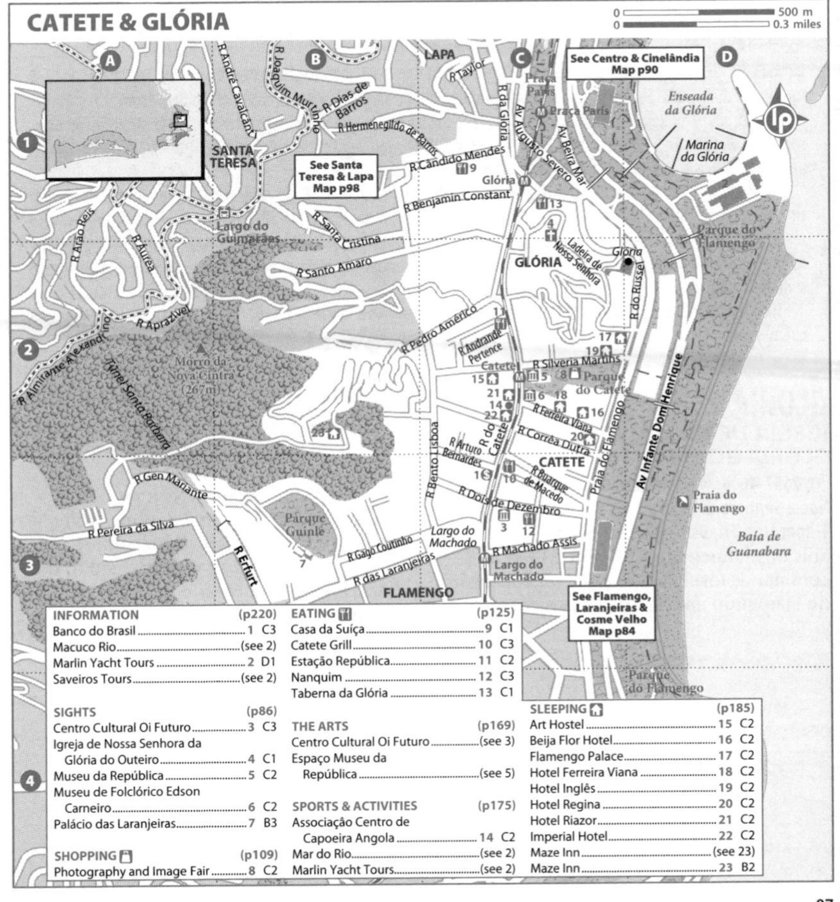

HOPE IN RIO'S FAVELAS

Residents of Rio de Janeiro's favelas (shanty towns) face enormous obstacles. Many families live in communities lacking basic essentials (sewers, medical clinics, roads). Children attend some of the city's worst schools (many, indeed, drop out). The long bus commute to work can often take hours on traffic-snarled roads for a salary that may not even meet living expenses. There's also the social stigma of living in the slums, some of which are run by local drug lords.

Yet it isn't all gloom for Rio's estimated one million favela residents. In the last two decades locally managed organizations have begun appearing in favelas across the city. While small in scale, these nonprofits offer residents the chance to learn new skills, gain a sense of pride, and give something often in short supply: hope.

For many poor favela children, the Grupo Cultural Afro Reggae (GCAR) is a lifeline. In 1997 in the Vigário Geral favela, GCAR opened a cultural center offering workshops in music, theatre, dance, hip-hop and *capoeira* (Brazilian martial art). The center provided kids with a chance to get off the street, tap into their Afro-Brazilian heritage and gain self-esteem in setting and fulfilling goals. Owing to the center's wide popularity, the ideas have spread. GCAR and its favela affiliates now offer more than 60 different programs for poor residents around Rio.

Rocinha, Brazil's largest favela, creates similar opportunities for local residents at its Casa da Cultura. Founded in 2003 by Gilberto Gil, Minister of Culture, singer and neighbor, the center draws on the favela's rich artistic tradition, and offers classes in music, theater and painting. The favela next door, Vidigal, perched on a hillside overlooking Ipanema Beach, is the base of the group Nos do Morro (Us from the Favela). This theater group won fame after some of its young actors appeared in the award-winning film *Cidade de Deus* (City of God). Ten of its members performed in *The Two Gentlemen of Verona* for the Royal Shakespeare Company in August 2006.

As many have discovered, the favela has a deep well of talent, but few opportunities. Opportunity is exactly what sociologist Maria Teresa Leal had in mind when she founded a sewing collective in Rocinha in the 1980s. The idea began during Leal's repeat trips to the favela where she encountered many talented seamstresses who had no chance to earn money for their skills. So began Coopa Roca (www.coopa-roca.org.br), a small group of women, each working from home to produce quilts, pillows and craft items made of recycled fabrics and other materials. Today the co-op employs some 150 women, and has even caught the eye of the fashion world, with commissions from Brazilian designers Osklen and Carlos Miele, as well as British designer Paul Smith.

For their part, favelas have made numerous contributions to the city. Rio's biggest party, Carnaval, was born in the favelas, and they continue to be pivotal to the fest. That favelas throw the best parties has long been known to many Cariocas. Today, Baile Funks are a well-known aspect of the party scene, luring both rich and poor to the gritty neighborhoods on the hillsides. There, DJs spin a blend of Rio's bass-heavy tunes (with almost no relation to American-style funk) to packed dance floors.

Travelers interested in peering beneath the stereotypes can visit a favela on a tour (p225), volunteer (p229), or stay overnight in a favela such as Maze Inn (p196) or Pousada Favelinha (p198).

GLÓRIA

IGREJA DE NOSSA SENHORA DA GLÓRIA DO OUTEIRO Map p87

☎ 2557-4600; www.outeirodagloria.org.br; Praça Nossa Senhora da Glória 135; 🕑 9am-noon & 1-4pm Mon-Fri, 9am-noon Sat & Sun

This tiny church atop Ladeira da Glória commands lovely views out over Parque do Flamengo and the bay. Considered one of the finest examples of religious colonial architecture in Brazil, the church dates from 1739 and became the favorite of the royal family upon their arrival in 1808. Some of the more fascinating features of the church are its octagonal design, its single tower (through which visitors enter), the elaborately carved altar (attributed to the Brazilian sculptor Mestre Valentim) and its elegant 18th-century tiles.

CENTRO & CINELÂNDIA

Eating p143; Shopping p120

Rio's business and financial hub is a wild architectural medley of old and new, with striking baroque churches and narrow colonial streets juxtaposed with looming office towers and wide, traffic-filled boulevards. During the week, it's all fuss and hurry as Rio's lawyers, secretaries and clerks jostle among the crowded streets. But despite the pace, it's well worth joining the fray as Centro has some of the city's best museums and its most intriguing historical sights, with avant-garde art galleries, 18th-century cathedrals and sprawling royal collections in former imperial buildings.

Many pedestrian-only areas crisscross Centro, and for the urban wanderer, there's no better destination in Rio. The most famous sub-district is known as Saara, a giant street bazaar crammed with discount stores and sprinkled with Lebanese restaurants.

Speaking of eating, Centro's restaurants suit every taste and budget, from greasy diners to elegant French bistros, with excellent per-kilo spots, art-nouveau cafés and old-fashioned pubs. After lunch, Cariocas browse the bookstores, music shops, galleries and curio shops. By workday's end, the bars and streetside cafés buzz with life as Cariocas unwind over ice-cold draughts.

At the southern edge of the business district, Cinelândia's shops, bars, restaurants and movie theaters are popular day and night. The bars and restaurants get crowded at lunch and after work, when street musicians sometimes wander the area. There's a greater mix of Cariocas here than in any other section of the city.

CENTRO

MUSEU DE ARTE MODERNA Map p90

☎ 2240-4944; www.mamrio.org.br, in Portuguese; Av Infante Dom Henrique 85; admission R$8; ⏲ noon-6pm Tue-Fri, noon-7pm Sat & Sun

At the northern end of Parque do Flamengo, the Museu de Arte Moderna (MAM) is immediately recognizable by the striking postmodern edifice designed by Alfonso Eduardo Reidy. The landscaping of Burle Marx is no less impressive.

After a devastating fire in 1978 that consumed 90% of its collection, the Museu de Arte Moderna is finally back on its feet, and now houses 11,000 permanent works, including pieces by Brazilian artists Bruno Giorgi, Di Cavalcanti and Maria Martins. Curators often bring excellent photography and design exhibits to the museum, and the cinema hosts regular film festivals throughout the year.

CENTRO CULTURAL BANCO DO BRASIL Map p90

☎ 3808-2020; Rua Primeiro de Março 66; admission free; ⏲ 10am-9pm Tue-Sun

Reopened in 1989, the Centro Cultural Banco do Brasil (CCBB) is housed in a beautifully restored 1906 building. It's one of Brazil's best cultural centers, with more than 120,000 visitors per month. Facilities include a cinema, two theaters and a permanent display of the evolution of currency in Brazil. CCBB hosts excellent exhibitions that are among the city's best. A recent display of African art garnered international attention.

There is always something going on at the CCBB, from exhibitions, lunchtime and evening concerts, to film screenings, so look at *O Globo*'s entertainment listings before you go. Don't miss this place, even if you only pass through the lobby while you're on a walking tour.

MUSEU HISTÓRICO NACIONAL Map p90

☎ 2550-9224; www.museuhistoriconacional.com.br; off Av General Justo near Praça Marechal Âncora; admission R$6; ⏲ 10am-5:30pm Tue-Fri, 2-6pm Sat & Sun

One of Rio de Janeiro's best museums, the large National History Museum contains over 250,000 historic relics relating to the history of Brazil – from its founding to its early days as a republic. Its extensive collection is housed on the old arsenal (built in 1764) and includes a full-sized model of a colonial pharmacy, enormous canvases depicting the bloody war with Paraguay, imperial carriages and tiny relics like the writing quill Princesa Isabel used to sign the document abolishing slavery in Brazil.

IGREJA DE NOSSA SENHORA DE CANDELÁRIA Map p90

☎ 2233-2324; Praça Pio X; admission free; ⏲ 8am-4pm Mon-Fri, 8am-noon Sat, 9am-1pm Sun

The construction of the original church (dating from the late 16th century) on the

CENTRO & CINELÂNDIA

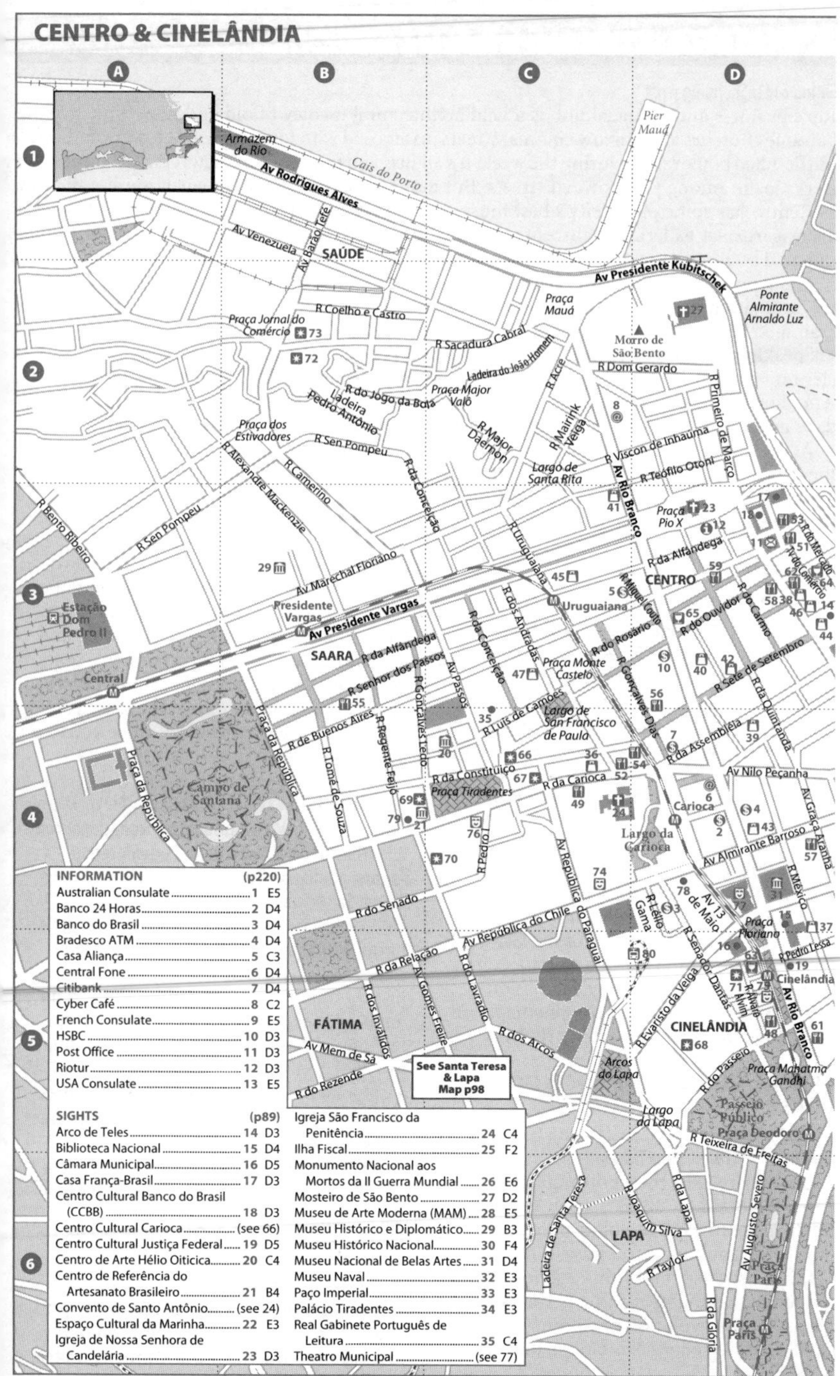

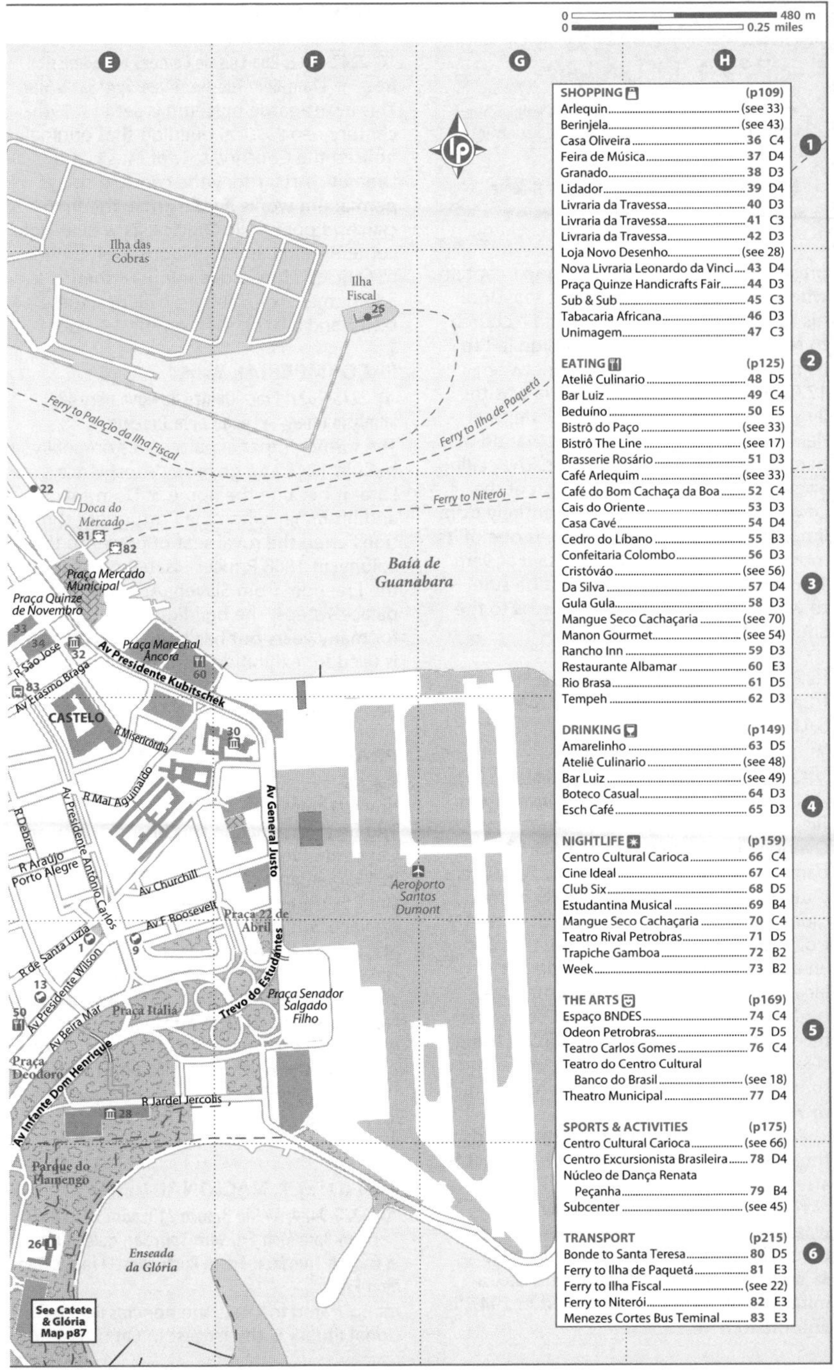

0 480 m
0 0.25 miles
E
F
G
H
1
2
3
4
5
6
SHOPPING (p109)
Arlequin (see 33)
Berinjela (see 43)
Casa Oliveira 36 C4
Feira de Música 37 D4
Granado 38 D3
Lidador 39 D4
Livraria da Travessa 40 D3
Livraria da Travessa 41 C3
Livraria da Travessa 42 D3
Loja Novo Desenho (see 28)
Nova Livraria Leonardo da Vinci 43 D4
Praça Quinze Handicrafts Fair 44 D3
Sub & Sub 45 C3
Tabacaria Africana 46 D3
Unimagem 47 C3
EATING (p125)
Ateliê Culinario 48 D5
Bar Luiz 49 C4
Beduíno 50 E5
Bistrô do Paço (see 33)
Bistrô The Line (see 17)
Brasserie Rosário 51 D3
Café Arlequim (see 33)
Café do Bom Cachaça da Boa 52 C4
Cais do Oriente 53 D3
Casa Cavé 54 D4
Cedro do Líbano 55 B3
Confeitaria Colombo 56 D3
Cristóvão (see 56)
Da Silva 57 D4
Gula Gula 58 D3
Mangue Seco Cachaçaria (see 70)
Manon Gourmet (see 54)
Rancho Inn 59 D3
Restaurante Albamar 60 E3
Rio Brasa 61 D5
Tempeh 62 D3
DRINKING (p149)
Amarelinho 63 D5
Ateliê Culinario (see 48)
Bar Luiz (see 49)
Boteco Casual 64 D3
Esch Café 65 D3
NIGHTLIFE (p159)
Centro Cultural Carioca 66 C4
Cine Ideal 67 C4
Club Six 68 D5
Estudantina Musical 69 B4
Mangue Seco Cachaçaria 70 C4
Teatro Rival Petrobras 71 D5
Trapiche Gamboa 72 B2
Week 73 B2
THE ARTS (p169)
Espaço BNDES 74 C4
Odeon Petrobras 75 D5
Teatro Carlos Gomes 76 C4
Teatro do Centro Cultural Banco do Brasil (see 18)
Theatro Municipal 77 D4
SPORTS & ACTIVITIES (p175)
Centro Cultural Carioca (see 66)
Centro Excursionista Brasileira 78 D4
Núcleo de Dança Renata Peçanha 79 B4
Subcenter (see 45)
TRANSPORT (p215)
Bonde to Santa Teresa 80 D5
Ferry to Ilha de Paquetá 81 E3
Ferry to Ilha Fiscal (see 22)
Ferry to Niterói 82 E3
Menezes Cortes Bus Teminal 83 E3
Ilha das Cobras
Ilha Fiscal
25
Ferry to Palácio da Ilha Fiscal
Ferry to Ilha de Paquetá
Ferry to Niterói
22
Doca do Mercado
81
82
Baía de Guanabara
Praça Mercado Municipal
Praça Quinze de Novembro
33
34
32
R São José
Praça Marechal Âncora
60
Av Presidente Kubitschek
83
Av Erasmo Braga
CASTELO
R Misericórdia
30
R Mal Aguinaldo
Av General Justo
R Debret
Av Presidente Antônio Carlos
R Araújo Porto Alegre
Av Churchill
Aeroporto Santos Dumont
Av F Roosevelt
Praça 22 de Abril
R de Santa Luzia
1
9
Av Presidente Wilson
13
50
Trevo do Estudantes
Praça Senador Salgado Filho
Praça Itália
Av Beira Mar
Praça Deodoro
Av Infante Dom Henrique
R Jardel Jercolis
28
Parque do Flamengo
26
Enseada da Glória
See Catete & Glória Map p87

TRANSPORTATION: CENTRO & CINELÂNDIA

From the Zona Sul look for the following destinations printed in the window: 'Rio Branco,' 'Praça XV' and 'Praça Tiradentes'.

M Cinelândia, Carioca, Uruguaiana, Presidente Vargas

present site was credited to a ship's captain who was nearly shipwrecked at sea. Upon his safe return he vowed to build a church to NS de Candelária. A later design led to its present-day grandeur. Built between 1775 and 1894, NS de Candelária was the largest and wealthiest church of imperial Brazil. The interior is a combination of baroque and Renaissance styles. The ceiling above the nave reveals the origin of the church. The cupola, fabricated entirely from limestone shipped from Lisbon, is one of its most striking features. Mass is said at 9am, 10am and 11am on Sunday. But be sure to watch out for traffic as you cross to the church.

IGREJA SÃO FRANCISCO DA PENITÊNCIA & CONVENTO DE SANTO ANTÔNIO

Map p90

2262-0197; Largo da Carioca 5; admission R$2; church 8am-6pm, convent 9am-noon & 1-4pm Tue-Fri

Overlooking the Largo da Carioca is the baroque Igreja São Francisco da Penitência, dating from 1726. Restored to its former glory, the church's sacristy, which dates from 1745, has blue Portuguese tiles and an elaborately carved altar made out of jacaranda wood. It also has a roof panel by José Oliveira Rosa depicting St Francis receiving the stigmata. The church's statue of Santo Antônio is an object of great devotion to many Cariocas in search of a husband or wife.

A garden on the church grounds leads to the catacombs, used until 1850. Visits must be arranged in advance.

Next door, the Convento de Santo Antônio was built between 1608 and 1615. It contains the chapel of Nossa Senhora das Dores da Imaculada Conceição. Fabiano de Cristo, a miracle-working priest who died in 1947, is entombed here.

CENTRO DE ARTE HÉLIO OITICICA

Map p90

2242-1012; Rua Luis de Camões 68; admission free; 11am-6pm Tue-Fri, 11am-5pm Sat & Sun

This avant-garde museum is set in a 19th-century neoclassical building that originally housed the Conservatory of Music and Dramatic Arts. Today the center displays permanent works by the artist, theoretician and poet Hélio Oiticica, as well as bold contemporary art exhibitions, well-tuned to Oiticica's forward-leaning aesthetics. In addition to six exhibition galleries, there's a bistro and a book shop on the 1st floor.

PAÇO IMPERIAL Map p90

2215-2622; Praça Quinze de Novembro 48; admission free; noon-6pm Tue-Sun

The former imperial palace was originally built in 1743 as a governor's residence. Later it became the home of Dom João and his family when the Portuguese throne transferred the royal seat of power to the colony. In 1888 Princesa Isabel proclaimed the Freedom from Slavery Act from the palace's steps. The building was neglected for many years but has been restored and is used for exhibitions and concerts; its cinema frequently screens foreign and art-house films.

PRAÇA XV (QUINZE) DE NOVEMBRO

Map p90

Near Rua Primeiro de Março

The first residents on this historic site were Carmelite fathers who built a convent here in 1590. It later came under the property of the Portuguese crown and became Largo do Paço, which surrounded the royal palace (Paço Imperial). The square was later renamed Praça XV (Quinze) de Novembro after Brazil declared itself a republic on November 15, 1822. A number of historic events took place here: the coronation of Brazil's two Emperors (Pedro I and Pedro II), the abolition of slavery and the overthrow (deposition) of Emperor Dom Pedro II in 1889.

BIBLIOTECA NACIONAL Map p90

2220-9484; Av Rio Branco 219; admission R$2; 9am-8pm Mon-Fri, 9am-3pm Sat, guided tours in English 1pm Mon-Fri, in Portuguese 11am & 3pm Mon-Fri

Inaugurated in 1910, the neoclassical national library is the largest in Latin America, with more than nine million volumes, including many rare books and manuscripts. Among the treasure trove are original letters written by Princess Isabel, the first newspapers printed in the country and two copies of the precious Mainz Psalter Bible, printed in 1492.

CAMPO DE SANTANA Map p90

Praça da República & Rua Frei Caneca

Campo de Santana is a pleasant park that, on September 7, 1822, was the scene of the proclamation of Brazil's independence from Portugal by Emperor Dom Pedro I of Portugal. The landscaped park with an artificial lake and swans is a fine place for a respite from the chaotic streets, and you're liable to see a few agoutis (a hamster-like rodent native to Brazil) running wild here.

CASA FRANÇA-BRASIL

Map p90

☎ 2332-5120; www.casafrancabrasil.rj.gov.br, in Portuguese; Rua Visconde de Itaboraí 78; admission free; 🕑 10am-8pm Tue-Sun

In a neoclassical building dating from 1820, the Casa França-Brasil sponsors changing exhibitions often dealing with political and cultural facets of Carioca society. The classical revival building once served as a customs house. There's a restaurant attached (p143).

CENTRO CULTURAL CARIOCA

Map p90

☎ 2242-9642; www.centroculturalcarioca.com.br, in Portuguese; Rua do Teatro 37; 🕑 11am-8pm Mon-Fri & 4:30-8:30pm Sat

This restored theater on Praça Tiradentes is once again a major contributor to the arts in downtown Rio. Its exposed brick walls and large wood-framed windows form the backdrop to superb musical groups – often samba – performing throughout the week (p163), and there are dance recitals, book releases and ongoing exhibitions. Dance classes are also offered here (p181).

CENTRO CULTURAL JUSTIÇA FEDERAL Map p90

☎ 3261-2550; Av Rio Branco 241; admission free; 🕑 noon-7pm Tue-Sun

The stately building overlooking the Praça Floriano served as the headquarters of the Supreme Court (Supremo Tribunal Federal) from 1909 to 1960. Following its recent restoration, it's become the Federal Justice Cultural Center, featuring exhibitions focused above all on photography and Brazilian art, though some fascinating exhibits from abroad sometimes make their way here. There's a pleasant café on the ground floor.

MOSTEIRO DE SÃO BENTO Map p90

☎ 2206-8100; Rua Dom Gerardo 68; guided visits R$8; 🕑 7am-6pm

This is one of the finest colonial churches in Brazil. Built between 1617 and 1641 on Morro de São Bento, the monastery has an excellent view over the city. The simple facade hides a baroque interior richly decorated in gold. Among its historic treasures are wood carvings designed by Frei Domingos da Conceição (and made by Alexandre Machado) and paintings by José de Oliveira Rosa. On Sunday, the High Mass at 10am includes a choir of Benedictine monks singing Gregorian chants.

To reach the monastery from Rua Dom Gerardo, go to No 40 and take the elevator to the 5th floor.

MUSEU HISTÓRICO E DIPLOMÁTICO

Map p90

☎ 2253-2828; Av Marechal Floriano 196; 🕑 tours 2pm, 3pm & 4pm Mon, Wed & Fri

Housed in the neoclassical Palácio Itamaraty, the Museum of History and Diplomacy served as the private presidential home from 1889 until 1897. The museum has an impressive collection of art, antiques and maps. Visits are by guided 45-minute tours. Call ahead to ensure you get an English-speaking guide. The museum is just a short walk west from Presidente Vargas metro station.

MUSEU NACIONAL DE BELAS ARTES

Map p90

☎ 2240-0068; Av Rio Branco 199; admission R$5, Sun free; 🕑 10am-6pm Tue-Fri, noon-5pm Sat & Sun

Rio's fine arts museum houses more than 18,000 original paintings and sculptures, some of which date back to works brought over from Portugal by Dom João VI in 1808. One of its most important galleries is the Galeria de Arte Brasileira, with 20th-century classics such as Cândido Portinari's *Café*. Other galleries display Brazilian folk art, African art and furniture, as well as contemporary exhibits. Guided tours are available in English (call ahead).

MUSEU NAVAL

Map p90

☎ 2104-5506; Rua Dom Manuel 15, Praça Quinze de Novembro; admission free; ⏲ noon-5pm Tue-Sun

Chronicling the history of the Brazilian navy from the 16th century to the present, the museum also has exhibitions of model warships, maps and navigational instruments.

Naval enthusiasts should also visit the nearby Espaço Cultural da Marinha (ECM; Map p90; ☎ 2104-5592; admission free; ⏲ noon-5pm Tue-Sun), on the waterfront near the eastern end of Av Presidente Vargas. It contains the *Riachuelo* submarine, which you can wander through, the *Bauru* (a WWII torpedo boat) and the royal family's large rowboat. The boat tour to Ilha Fiscal (Map p90; p104) leaves from the docks here.

CENTRO DE REFERÊNCIA DO ARTESANATO BRASILEIRO Map p90

☎ 3380-1850; Praça Tiradentes 71; admission free; ⏲ 10am-5pm Mon-Fri

This new museum, which opened in 2009, showcases the craft-making traditions all across Brazil. Changing exhibits feature woodcarvings, ceramics, textiles, jewelry, metal work, basket weaving and even recycled materials in the creation of both popular and sacred art. Although nothing here is for sale, if you're interested in a particular piece, the staff can provide contact information for any of the artists represented.

PALÁCIO TIRADENTES Map p90

☎ 2588-1411; Rua Primeiro de Março; admission free; ⏲ 10am-5pm Mon-Sat, noon-5pm Sun

In the looming building overlooking the bay, the stately Tiradentes Palace today houses the seat of the legislative assembly. Exhibits on the 1st and 2nd floors relate the events that took place there between 1926 and the present. One of its darkest hours was when the National Assembly was shut down in 1937 under the Vargas dictatorship; it later served as his Department of Press and Propaganda. Most information is in Portuguese, though you can listen to a rundown of history in English at the interactive machine in the foyer. The statue in front, incidentally, is not a likeness of Russian mystic Rasputin, but rather that of martyr Tiradentes, who led the drive toward Brazilian independence in the 18th century.

PASSEIO PÚBLICO Map p90

Rua do Passeio; admission free; ⏲ 9am-5pm

The oldest park in Rio, the Passeio Público was built in 1783 by Mestre Valentim, a famous Brazilian sculptor, who designed it after Lisbon's botanical gardens. In 1860 the park was remodeled by French landscaper Glaziou. The park features some large trees, a pond with islands and an interesting crocodile-shaped fountain. The entrance gate was built by Valentim. Before the Parque do Flamengo landfill, the sea came right up to the edge of the park.

REAL GABINETE PORTUGUÊS DE LEITURA Map p90

☎ 2221-3138; Rua Luís de Camões 30; admission free; ⏲ 9am-6pm

Built in the Portuguese manueline style in 1837, the gorgeous Portuguese Reading Room houses over 350,000 works, many dating from the 16th, 17th and 18th centuries. It also has a small collection of paintings, sculptures and ancient coins.

THEATRO MUNICIPAL

Map p90

☎ 2332-9195; www.theatromunicipal.rj.gov.br; Praça Floriano

Built in 1905 in the style of the Paris Opera, the magnificent Municipal Theater is the home of Rio's opera, orchestra and ballet. Its lavish interior contains many beautiful details – including the stage curtain painted by Italian artist Eliseu Visconti, which contains portraits of 75 major figures from the arts including Carlos Gomes, Wagner and Rembrandt. At research time, the theater was closed for restoration. When it reopens, call to find out when guided tours are on offer; better yet, come see a performance here (see p171).

TRAVESSA DO COMÉRCIO

Map p90

Near Praça XV (Quinze) de Novembro

Beautiful two-story colonial townhouses line this narrow cobblestone street leading off Praça XV (Quinze) de Novembro. The archway, called Arco de Teles, leading into the area was once part of an old viaduct running between two buildings. Today, Travessa do Comércio contains half a dozen restaurants and drinking spots that open onto the streets. It's a favorite spot for Cariocas after work.

CINELÂNDIA

PRAÇA FLORIANO Map p90

Av Rio Branco

The heart of modern Rio, the Praça Floriano comes to life at lunchtime and after work when the outdoor cafés are filled with beer drinkers, samba musicians and political debate. The square is also Rio's political marketplace and is the site of daily speechmaking, literature sales and street theater. Most city marches and rallies culminate here on the steps of the old Câmara Municipal (Town Hall) in the northwestern corner of the plaza.

MONUMENTO NACIONAL AOS MORTOS DA II GUERRA MUNDIAL

Map p90

☎ 2240-1283; Av Infante Dom Henrique 75; admission free; 🕑 10am-4pm Tue-Sun

This delicate monument to the soldiers who perished in WWII contains a museum, a mausoleum and the Tomb of the Unknown Soldier. The museum exhibits uniforms, medals and documents from Brazil's Italian campaign. There's also a small lake and sculptures by Ceschiatti and Anísio Araújo de Medeiros.

HISTORIC CENTRO

Walking Tour

A mélange of historic buildings and young skyscrapers, the center of Rio is an excellent place to discover the essence of the city away from its beaches and mountains. Among the hustle and bustle of commerce, you'll find fascinating museums, atmospheric bars and theaters, open-air bazaars and the colonial antique stores set near old samba clubs. This tour is best done during the week, as it gets rather deserted (and unsafe) on weekends.

1 Praça Floriano

Start at the Praça Floriano (p95), the heart of modern Rio. Praça Floriano comes to life at night when the outdoor cafés are filled with beer

> **WALK FACTS**
>
> Start Praça Floriano (metro Cinelândia)
> End Praça Pio X
> Distance 4.4km
> Duration Four hours
> Fuel stop Confeitaria Colombo (p144)

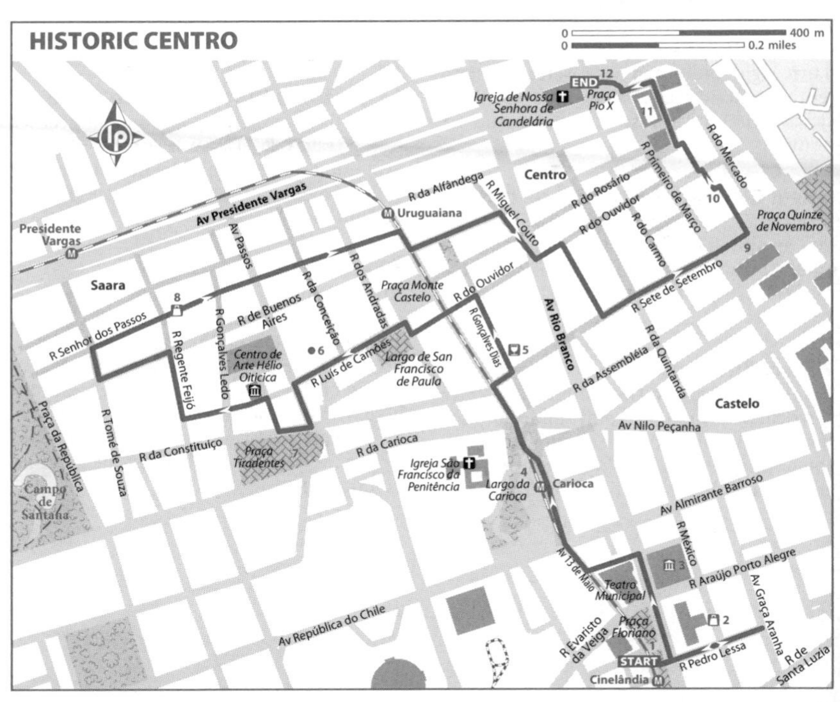

drinkers and political debate. The neoclassical Theatro Municipal (p171) overlooking the plaza is one of Rio's finest buildings.

2 Feira de Música

On the east side of Av Rio Branco facing Praça Floriano is the Rua Pedro Lessa, where you can browse through the record and CD stalls at the open-air music market called the Feira de Música (p112).

3 Museu Nacional de Belas Artes

Stroll up a few blocks along busy Av Rio Branco to get a glimpse of the neoclassical Museu Nacional de Belas Artes (p93). It's worth venturing inside for a look at some of Rio's best-known 19th-century painters.

4 Largo da Carioca

Cross over Av Rio Branco and turn right onto Av 13 de Maio. You'll soon pass through the Largo da Carioca, a bustling area with a small market. Up on the hill is the Igreja São Francisco da Penitência (p92), a 17th-century church which you can reach via elevator near the Carioca metro station.

5 Confeitaria Colombo

After taking in the views, descend to the streets and continue along Av 13 de Maio. Turn right onto Rua Sete Setembro and left onto Gonçalves Dias to reach Confeitaria Colombo (p144) for a dose of caffeine and art nouveau.

6 Real Gabinete Português de Leitura

From Rua Gonçalves Dias, turn left on Rua do Ouvidor, following it across the Largo de San Francisco de Paula. One block further is the Real Gabinete Português de Leitura (p94), a historic reading room that's well worth a look.

7 Praça Tiradentes

Go one block west and one south to the Praça Tiradentes, an old square surrounded by century-old buildings. It's a bit run down, though some entrepreneurs have begun restoring the area. Head around the corner to the Centro de Arte Hélio Oiticica (p92), which hosts avant-garde art exhibitions.

8 Saara

Walk over to Rua Regente Feijó and loop around to Rua Senhor dos Passos. This will take you into the heart of Saara (Portuguese for 'Sahara'), a narrow neighborhood bazaar packed with discount shops, pedestrians and a few Lebanese restaurants. Walk, shop and snack your way east to Rua Miguel Couto and turn right.

9 Paço Imperial

Leaving Saara, turn left on Rua do Ouvidor and jog down to Rua Sete de Setembro. Follow it until it ends at Rua Primeiro de Março. Across the road, the Paço Imperial (p92) was once the seat of imperial power in Brazil. This is a good spot to check out current exhibitions in the galleries or browse for music in the bookshop.

10 Travessa do Comércio

As you leave the imperial building, cross Praça Quinze de Novembro and take the narrow lane beneath the arch. You'll walk along one of Centro's oldest lanes, through Travessa do Comércio (p94), with open-air restaurants and bars that fill with revelers around happy hour.

11 Centro Cultural Banco do Brasil

If you still have energy, pop around the corner to the Centro Cultural Banco do Brasil (p89), a huge exhibition space (with a cinema, theater and cafés), where you can often find Rio's best exhibitions.

12 Praça Pio X

After taking care crossing a very busy boulevard, you reach the Igreja de NS de Candelária (p89), the last stop on the tour. Have a rest in the cool interior of the church while taking in one of Rio's baroque masterpieces. From here, you can walk a few blocks to the Uruguaiana metro station or back to Travessa do Comércio for a much-deserved drink at an outdoor café.

SANTA TERESA & LAPA

Eating p145; Shopping p121; Sleeping p196

Icons of bohemian Rio, Santa Teresa and Lapa are two rough-and-tumble neighborhoods that have contributed considerably to the city's artistic and musical heritage. On a hill overlooking the city, Santa Teresa has an impressive collection of 19th-century mansions set along winding lanes, with an old tram still rattling through the neighborhood. The Carmelite convent founded here in 1750 gave the district its name and became the first of many impressive buildings in the area. Santa Teresa was the uppermost residential neighborhood in the 19th century, when Rio's upper class lived here and rode the *bonde* (tram) to work in Centro. Many beautiful colonial homes stretch skyward, their manicured gardens hidden behind gabled fences. Like other areas near Centro, the neighborhood fell into neglect in the early 20th century as the wealthy moved further south. During the 1960s and 70s many artists and bohemians moved into Santa Teresa's mansions, initiating a revitalization process that still continues. Today, Santa Teresa is a buzzword about Rio for its vibrant arts scene. Throughout the year, impromptu festivals and street parties fill the air, ranging from *maracatu* drumming along Rua Joaquim Murtinho to live jazz at the Parque das Ruínas to the annual Portas Abertas event, where dozens of artists open their studios and cover the streets with living installations.

The neighborhood's ongoing restoration has led to an influx of boutique hotels, restaurants and cafés, and some have compared Santa Teresa to Paris' Montmartre. Yet this rugged neighborhood is unlikely to ever completely lose its edginess, if only for the omnipresent favelas spreading down the hillsides. Be cautious when walking around Santa Teresa, and avoid deserted streets. The best time to explore is on Saturday or Sunday when the neighborhood is at its liveliest.

The streets of Lapa lie down the hill from Santa Teresa and south of Cinelândia. Formerly a residential neighborhood of the wealthy, Lapa became a red-light district in the 1930s, its brothels and taverns the stomping ground for bohemians, intellectuals, politicians and *malandros*. Although Lapa is still a derelict area, it's also one of the music capitals of Brazil. At night, revelers from all over the city mingle among its samba clubs and music-filled bars. The music scene has brought some gentrification to the area, including new restaurants and hostels. Despite some signs of renewal, Lapa still has its share of crime. Take care when strolling around the neighborhood, which is actually safer on busy weekend nights than it is during the day.

Lapa's landmark aqueduct, Arcos da Lapa (Lapa Arches), is one of the neighborhood's most prominent features. Narrow tracks course over the 64m-high structure, carrying the famous *bonde* to and from Santa Teresa.

SANTA TERESA

BONDE

Map p90

☎ 2240-5709; station at Rua Lélio Gama 65; fare R$0.60; ⏲ departures every 30min

The *bonde* that travels up to Santa Teresa from Centro is the last of the historic streetcars that once crisscrossed the city. Its romantic clatter through the cobbled streets has made it the archetype for bohemian Santa Teresa. The two routes currently open have been in operation since the 19th century. Both travel high atop the narrow Arcos da Lapa (p100) and along curving Rua Joaquim Murtinho before reaching Largo do Guimarães (p100). From there, one line (Paula Matos) takes a northwestern route, terminating at Largo das Neves (p100). The longer route (Dois Irmãos) continues from Largo do Guimarães uphill and southward before terminating near the water reservoir at Dois Irmãos (Two Brothers – named after the twin stone pyramids used to collect water from the Carioca River).

Although Santa is safer than its been, a policeman often accompanies the tram as the favelas down the hillsides still make this a high-crime area. Go by all means, but don't take any valuables with you. Local kids jumping on and off the tram lend a festive air to the journey. An unspoken tradition states that those who ride on the running board ride for free.

MUSEU CHÁCARA DO CÉU Map p98

☎ 3970-1126; Rua Murtinho Nobre 93; admission R$3; ⏲ noon-5pm Wed-Mon

The former mansion of art patron and industrialist Raymundo Ottoni de Castro Maya contains a small but diversified collection of modern art – formerly Ottoni's

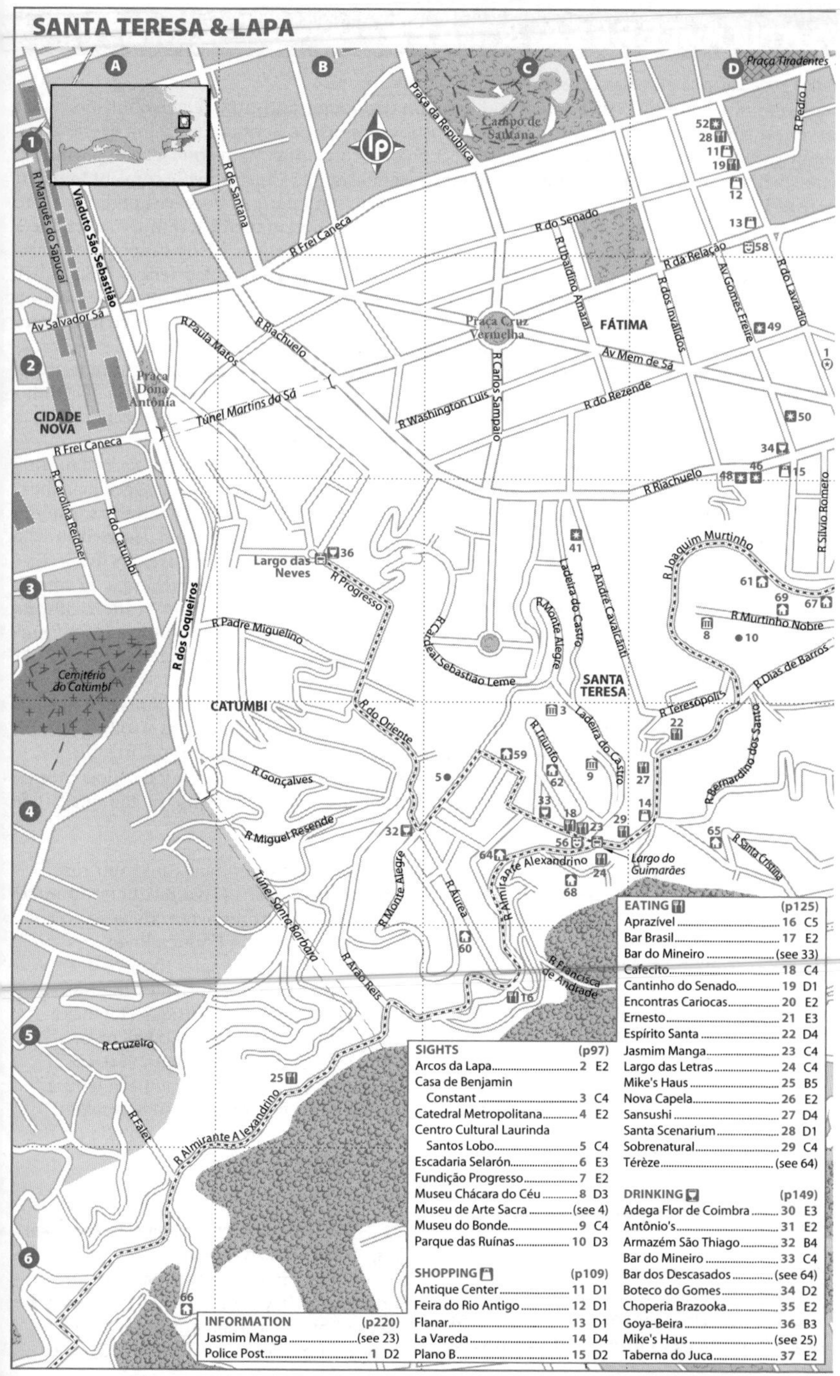
SANTA TERESA & LAPA
A
B
C
D
1
2
3
4
5
6
Praça Tiradentes
Praça da República
Campo de Santana
R Pedro I
R Marquês do Sapucaí
Viaduto São Sebastião
R de Santana
R Frei Caneca
R do Senado
R Ubaldino Amaral
R da Relação
Av Gomes Freire
R do Lavradio
R dos Inválidos
FÁTIMA
Praça Cruz Vermelha
Av Mem de Sá
Av Salvador Sá
R Paula Matos
R Riachuelo
Praça Dona Antônia
CIDADE NOVA
Túnel Martins de Sá
R Washington Luís
R Carlos Sampaio
R do Rezende
R Carolina Reidner
R do Catumbi
R Silvio Romero
R Joaquim Murtinho
Largo das Neves
R Progresso
R dos Coqueiros
R Padre Miguelino
R Cardeal Sebastião Leme
R Monte Alegre
Ladeira do Castro
R André Cavalcanti
R Murtinho Nobre
R Dias de Barros
Cemitério do Catumbi
CATUMBI
SANTA TERESA
R Teresópolis
R do Oriente
R Triunfo
R Gonçalves
R Bernardino dos Santos
R Miguel Resende
R Almirante Alexandrino
Largo do Guimarães
R Santa Cristina
Túnel Santa Bárbara
R Áurea
R Francisca de Andrade
R Arão Reis
R Cruzeiro
R Falet
R Almirante Alexandrino
INFORMATION (p220)
Jasmim Manga (see 23)
Police Post 1 D2
SIGHTS (p97)
Arcos da Lapa 2 E2
Casa de Benjamin Constant 3 C4
Catedral Metropolitana 4 E2
Centro Cultural Laurinda Santos Lobo 5 C4
Escadaria Selarón 6 E3
Fundição Progresso 7 E2
Museu Chácara do Céu 8 D3
Museu de Arte Sacra (see 4)
Museu do Bonde 9 C4
Parque das Ruínas 10 D3
SHOPPING (p109)
Antique Center 11 D1
Feira do Rio Antigo 12 D1
Flanar 13 D1
La Vareda 14 D4
Plano B 15 D2
EATING (p125)
Aprazível 16 C5
Bar Brasil 17 E2
Bar do Mineiro (see 33)
Cafecito 18 C4
Cantinho do Senado 19 D1
Encontras Cariocas 20 E2
Ernesto 21 E3
Espírito Santa 22 D4
Jasmim Manga 23 C4
Largo das Letras 24 C4
Mike's Haus 25 B5
Nova Capela 26 E2
Sansushi 27 D4
Santa Scenarium 28 D1
Sobrenatural 29 C4
Térèze (see 64)
DRINKING (p149)
Adega Flor de Coimbra 30 E3
Antônio's 31 E2
Armazém São Thiago 32 B4
Bar do Mineiro 33 C4
Bar dos Descasados (see 64)
Boteco do Gomes 34 D2
Choperia Brazooka 35 E2
Goya-Beira 36 B3
Mike's Haus (see 25)
Taberna do Juca 37 E2

private collection, which he bequeathed to the nation. In addition to works by Portinari, Di Cavalcanti and Lygia Clark, the museum displays furniture and Brazilian maps dating from the 17th and 18th centuries. Unfortunately, some of the museum's most valuable pieces were stolen during a robbery in 2006 and never recovered. Beautiful gardens surround the building, and a panoramic view of Centro and Baía de Guanabara awaits visitors.

PARQUE DAS RUÍNAS

Map p98

☎ 2252-1039; Rua Murtinho Nobre 169; admission free; 🕑 8am-8pm Tue-Sun

This park contains the ruins – exterior brick walls and a newly built staircase – of the mansion belonging to Brazilian heiress Laurinda Santos Lobo. Her house was a meeting point for Rio's artists and intellectuals for many years until her death in 1946. The real reason to come here is for the excellent view from up top. There's a small outdoor café and occasional open-air concerts are held here.

CASA DE BENJAMIN CONSTANT

Map p98

☎ 2509-1248; Rua Monte Alegre 255; admission R$3, Sun free; 🕑 guided tours 1-5pm Wed-Sun

This country estate served as the residence for one of Brazil's most influential politicians in the founding of the young republic. Benjamin Constant (1837–91) was an engineer, military officer and professor before taking an active role in the Provisional Government. He is also remembered for founding a school for blind children. Painstakingly preserved, his house provides a window into his life and times. The lush gardens surrounding his estate provide a fine view over Centro and the western side of Santa Teresa.

CENTRO CULTURAL LAURINDA SANTOS LOBO

Map p98

☎ 2224-3331; Rua Monte Alegre 306; admission free; 🕑 9am-5pm Tue-Sun

This large mansion built in 1907 once served as a salon for artists from Brazil and abroad as socialite Laurinda Santos Lobo hosted her parties here. Guests included Villa-Lobos and Isadora Duncan. Today, as a the cultural center, the building still plays an active role in the neighborhood by hosting exhibitions and open-air concerts throughout the year.

LARGO DAS NEVES Map p98

End of Rua Progresso

A slice of small-town life in the city, this small plaza is the gathering point for neighborhood children and families, who lounge in the benches by day. At night, the bars surrounding the square come alive with revelers crowding the walkways. At times, MPB bands perform to a young crowd here. Largo das Neves is the terminus of the Paula Matos *bonde* line.

LARGO DO GUIMARÃES Map p98

Rua Almirante Alexandrino

The plaza named after Joaquim Fonseca Guimarães (a local resident whose house became Hotel Santa Teresa just up the road) now forms the center of bohemian Santa Teresa. A festive Carnaval street party originates here, and a number of restaurants, handicrafts and thrift shops lie within a short distance.

MUSEU DO BONDE Map p98

☎ 2242-2354; Rua Carlos Brant 14; admission free; 🕒 9am-4:30pm

The tiny one-room Tram Museum at the depot close to Largo do Guimarães offers a history of Rio's tramways since 1865 – when the trams were pulled by donkeys. A few photographs, trip-recorders and conductor uniforms are just about the only objects documenting their legacy. Uplifting music plays overhead. The term *bonde,* incidentally, means just that: bond, indicating the way in which the first electric trams were financed – through public bonds. While you're at the museum, wander down to the old workshop that houses the trams. Cineastes may remember the depot from the opening sequence of the film *Orfeu Negro*.

> **TRANSPORTATION: SANTA TERESA & LAPA**
>
> **Santa Teresa**
>
> 🚌 Centro (206 & 214) from Carioca metro station
>
> 🚋 Paula Matos, Dois Irmãos
>
> **Lapa**
>
> 🚌 Leblon, Ipanema & Copacabana (571) to Largo da Lapa
>
> Ⓜ Cinelândia

LAPA

ARCOS DA LAPA Map p98

Near Av Mem de Sá

The landmark aqueduct dates from the mid-1700s when it was built to carry water from the Carioca River to downtown Rio. In a style reminiscent of ancient Rome, the 42 arches stand 64m high. Today, it carries the famous *bonde* on its way to and from Santa Teresa atop the hill.

CATEDRAL METROPOLITANA Map p98

☎ 2240-2669; Av República do Chile 245; admission free; 🕒 7am-6pm

The enormous cone-shaped cathedral was inaugurated in 1976 after 12 years of construction. Among its sculptures, murals and other works of art, the four vivid stained-glass windows, which stretch 60m to the ceiling, are breathtaking. The Museu de Arte Sacra (Museum of Sacred Art) in the basement contains a number of historical items, including the baptismal font used at the christening of royal princes and the throne of Dom Pedro II. The cathedral can accommodate up to 20,000 worshippers.

ESCADARIA SELARÓN Map p98

Stairway btwn Rua Joaquim Silva in Lapa & Rua Pinto Martins in Santa Teresa

An ever-expanding installation, the staircase leading up to the Convento de Santa Teresa from Rua Joaquim Silva became a work of art when Chilean-born artist Selarón decided to cover the steps with colorful mosaics. Originally a homage to the Brazilian people, the 215 steps feature ceramic mosaics in green, yellow and blue. He uses mirrors as well as tiles collected from around the world to create the illustrious effects. A hand-painted sign in English and Portuguese explains Selarón's vision, which has expanded to include mosaics near the Arcos da Lapa. In the morning, you can often find him at work, and he welcomes visitors to bring tiles from other countries, which he'll then add to the Lapa landscape.

FUNDIÇÃO PROGRESSO Map p98

☎ 2220-5070; Rua dos Arcos 24; admission free; 🕒 9am-6pm Mon-Fri

Once a foundry for the manufacturing of safes and ovens, the building today hosts avant-garde exhibitions, concerts and excellent samba performances throughout the year. It is one of the few buildings in the area that survived the 1950s neighborhood redistricting project to widen the avenue.

EXPLORE SANTA TERESA

Walking Tour

Colorful colonial buildings, narrow brick-lined streets and sweeping views of downtown are a few of the reasons artists flocked here in the mid-70s. Today the 'hood is still experiencing a cultural renaissance. You never know what you'll find here: old mansions hosting African drumming, bossa-jazz in a bombed-out building or impromptu music jams. No other neighborhood has quite the energy that Santa Teresa has. Do be careful when exploring this neighborhood, as muggings still occur. The weekends are the liveliest time to visit, but if you plan to take the *bonde* then, travel to the *bonde* station by taxi as Centro is deserted (and dangerous) on Saturday and Sunday.

1 Largo do Guimarães

Our saunter begins in the heart of the neighborhood at the *bonde* stop of Largo do Guimarães (p100), which is where you'll find the densest concentration of Santa Teresa shops and restaurants.

2 Museu do Bonde

Head downhill along Rua Carlos Brandt to visit the tiny Museu do Bonde (p100) for a symphonic journey back to the *bonde*'s once-glorious day in the sun.

3 La Vareda

After checking out the museum and the tram-storage building next door, walk back up to Largo do Guimarães and turn left along Rua Almirante Alexandrino to La Vareda (p122), where you can browse handicrafts, some of which are made by local artists.

4 Curvelo

Keep following the tracks downhill. Soon you'll reach Curvelo, a roofed stop on the *bonde* line. Here, turn right onto Rua Dias de Barros and have a look at the view over the bay from the small plaza at the start of

WALK FACTS

Start Largo do Guimarães
End Rua Carlos Magno
Distance 2.5km
Duration 2½ hours
Fuel stop Bar do Mineiro (p146)

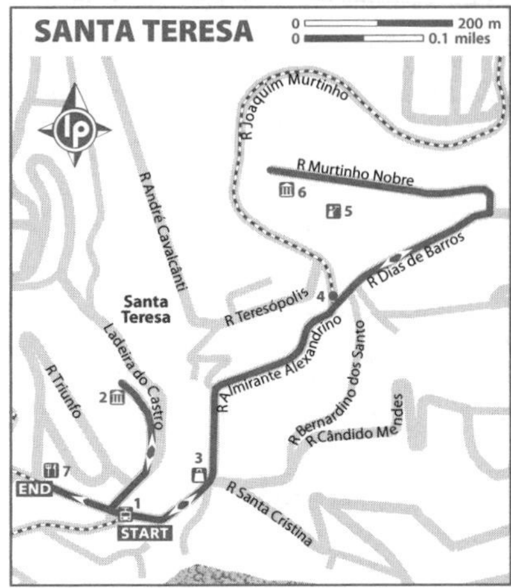

the street. Follow this road until you reach a road branching off to the left (Rua Murtinho Nobre).

5 Parque das Ruínas

Loop around and head up to the Parque das Ruínas (p99), a former mansion that's now just a brick shell. Climb the iron staircases to the top level for amazing views over the city.

6 Museu Chácara do Céu

Continue to the end of the street and wind your way up through the lush gardens of Museu Chácara do Céu (p97). Go inside for a look at an intriguing assortment of modern art from all corners of the globe.

7 Bar do Mineiro

After exploring, walk back up to Largo do Guimarães and keep following the *bonde* tracks one block further to the old-fashioned Bar do Mineiro (p146), one of Rio's best-loved *botecos*, and a great spot for a cold drink or some Brazilian fare.

GREATER RIO

Shopping p122

Attractions here are fewer than those in the Zona Sul and Centro, but you'll still find some excellent reasons to venture out, including soccer rowdiness at Maracanã and island allure on the bay.

The neighborhood of São Cristóvão is home to the Quinta da Boa Vista, a large somewhat scruffy park containing the Museu Nacional and the zoo. It's also the site of the soccer stadium and the Feira Nordestina, one of Brazil's biggest weekend markets. In the 19th century the suburb was the home of the nobility, including the monarchs themselves. It has since become a heavily populated, working-class suburb.

Rio's lovely but heavily polluted Baía de Guanabara lies east and north of Centro. This is a fine setting for a cruise to either Ilha de Paquetá or Niterói. The bay has a prominent place in Rio's history. In 1502 Portuguese explorers sailed into the bay and, mistaking it for the entrance to a large river, named it Rio de Janeiro (River of January). Even though they were mistaken in their geography, the name stuck and was later extended to the new settlement as a whole. Of course, the history doesn't begin with the Portuguese arrival. The indigenous Tamoio people lived along the shore long before their arrival, and the bay provided much of their sustenance. They were the ones who named the bay 'Guanabara,' which means 'arm of the sea.' In those days it was a tropical wilderness teeming with tapirs and jaguars. Today the wild animals (and much of the aquatic life as well) have disappeared from the bay. Owing to several landfill projects – which created Parque do Flamengo and Aeroporto Santos Dumont – the bay is also disappearing. The best way to experience the bay is by boat, taking a cruise (p225) or catching the ferry to either Niterói or Ilha de Paquetá.

SÃO CRISTÓVÃO

FEIRA NORDESTINA

Map p60

☎ 2580-5335; Campo de São Cristóvão; admission R$1; 🕒 10am-4pm Tue-Thu, 10am Fri to 10pm Sun

This enormous fair (32,000 sq meters with 658 stalls) is not to be missed. It showcases the culture from the northeast, with *barracas* (food stalls) selling Bahian dishes as well as beer and *cachaça* (cane liquor), which flows in great abundance here. The best time to go is on weekends, when you can catch live bands playing *forró,* plus samba groups and comedy troupes, MPB and *rodas de capoeira* (*capoeira* circles). The vibrant scene runs nonstop from Friday morning through to Sunday evening. In addition to food and drink, you can browse music CDs (*forró,* of course), hammocks and a wide assortment of handicrafts.

TRANSPORTATION: GREATER RIO

Maracanã

🚌 From Copacabana, Ipanema & Leblon (464); to Copacabana and Ipanema (456 & 457), to Leblon (464)

Ⓜ Maracanã

Quinta da Boa Vista

🚌 Copacabana, Ipanema and Leblon (474)

Ⓜ São Cristóvão (for Museu Nacional and Jardim Zoológico)

QUINTA DA BOA VISTA

Map p60

☎ 2562-6900; 🕒 9am-5pm

Quinta da Boa Vista was the residence of the Portuguese imperial family until the Republic was proclaimed. Today, it's a large and busy park with gardens and lakes. At weekends it's crowded with football games and families from the Zona Norte. The former imperial mansion houses the Museu Nacional (p102) and Museu da Fauna. The Jardim Zoológico (p103), Rio's zoo, is 200m away.

MUSEU NACIONAL

Map p60

☎ 2562-6900; Quinta da Boa Vista; admission R$3; 🕒 10am-4pm Tue-Sun

This museum and its imperial entrance are still stately and imposing, and the view from the balcony to the royal palms is majestic. However, the weathered buildings and unkempt grounds have clearly declined since the fall of the monarchy.

There are many interesting exhibits: dinosaur fossils, saber-toothed tiger skeletons, beautiful pieces of pre-Columbian ceramics from the littoral and high plains of Peru, a huge meteorite, hundreds of stuffed birds, mammals and fish, gruesome displays of tropical diseases, and exhibits on the peoples of Brazil.

JARDIM ZOOLÓGICO

Map p60

☎ 3878-4200; Quinta da Boa Vista; admission R$6; ⏲ 9am-4:30pm Tue-Sun

Covering over 12 hectares, the zoo at Quinta da Boa Vista has a wide variety of reptiles, mammals and birds – mostly indigenous to Brazil. Special attractions include the large walk-through aviary and the night house, which features nocturnal animals. The monkey house is also a crowd favorite. Some animal enclosures are cramped, though overall the reproduced habitats are fairly well done.

MARACANÃ FOOTBALL STADIUM

Map p60

☎ 2334-1705; Gate 15, north entrance off Rua Mata Machado

Brazil's temple of football easily accommodates 80,000 people. On certain occasions, such as the World Cup match of 1950 or Pelé's last game, it has squeezed in close to 200,000 crazed fans – although the stadium has now been modified to hold fewer people.

If you like sports in general, if you want to understand Brazil, or if you just want an intense, quasi-psychedelic experience, then by all means go see a game of *futebol* – preferably a championship game or one between local rivals Flamengo, Vasco, Fluminense or Botafogo. Check out p176 for further details.

Inside the stadium, there's a sports museum (admission R$20; ⏲ 9am-5pm Mon-Fri) – opening hours vary on game days, when it closes five hours before the match. It has photographs, posters, cups and the uniforms of Brazilian sporting greats, including Pelé's famous No 10 shirt. There's also a store where you can buy soccer shirts. Enter by the north entrance, through gate 15 off Rua Mata Machado.

The stadium closed in 2010 to undergo renovations in preparation for the 2014 World Cup. It is slated to reopen in 2012 or in 2013.

MUSEU DO PRIMEIRO REINADO

Map p60

☎ 2332-4513; Av Dom Pedro II 293; admission free; ⏲ 11am-5pm Tue-Fri

A 10-minute walk east of the Quinta da Boa Vista, this former mansion of the Marquesa de Santos depicts the history of the First Reign (the reign of bumbling Dom Pedro I before he was driven out of the country). The collection includes documents, furniture and paintings, but the main attraction is the building and its interior, with striking murals by Francisco Pedro do Amaral.

BAÍA DE GUANABARA & NITERÓI

ILHA DE PAQUETÁ

☎ ferry 0800-704-4113; www.barcas-sa.com.br

This tropical island in the Baía de Guanabara was once a very popular tourist spot and is now frequented mostly by families from the Zona Norte. There are no cars on the island. Transport is by foot, bicycle (with literally hundreds for rent) or horse-drawn cart.

There's a certain dirty, decadent charm to the colonial buildings, unassuming beaches and businesses catering to local tourism. The place gets crowded on weekends.

Go to Paquetá for the boat ride through Rio's famous bay and to see Cariocas at

BEACHES EAST OF RIO

A number of beaches lie just east of Niterói. The ones closest to town are too polluted for swimming, but as you continue out you'll reach some pristine beaches – Piratininga, Camboinhas, Itaipu and finally Itacoatiara, the most fabulous of the bunch. Framed by two looming hills on either side of the shore and backed by vegetation, the white sands of Itacoatiara seem a world away from the urban beaches of Rio. *Barracas* (food stalls) sell scrumptious plates of fish, and there are also food stands overlooking the beach. The surf is strong here – evidenced by the many surfers jockeying for position – so swim with caution. To get there, you can take bus 38 or any bus labeled 'Itacoatiara' from the ferry terminal (R$4, 50 minutes). If you're traveling in a group, you can negotiate a return fare with a taxi driver.

play – especially during the Festa de São Roque, which is celebrated with fireworks, a procession and music on the weekend following 16 August.

Boats leave from near the Praça XV (Quinze) de Novembro (Map p90) in Centro. The ferry takes 70 minutes and will cost you R$9 for a return trip. There are nine departures daily, the most useful being 7:10am, 10:30am and 1:30pm.

ILHA FISCAL

Map p90

☎ 2104-6992; admission R$10; 🕓 tours 1pm, 2:30pm & 4pm Thu-Sun

This eye-catching lime-green, neo-Gothic palace sitting in the Baía de Guanabara looks like something out of a child's fairy-tale book. It was designed by engineer Adolfo del Vecchio and completed in 1889. Originally used to supervise port operations, the palace is famous as the location of the last Imperial Ball on November 9, 1889. Today it's open for guided tours three times a day from Thursday to Sunday; tours leave from the dock near Praça Quinze (usually by boat, but sometimes by van).

NITERÓI

Niterói's principal attraction is the famous Museu do Arte Contemporânea (MAC). The cruise across the bay, however, is perhaps just as valid a reason for leaving Rio. Out on the water, you'll have impressive views of downtown, Pão de Açúcar (p79) and the other green mountains rising up out of the city; you'll also see planes (quite close) landing and taking off at Aeroporto Santos Dumont. Try to be on the water at sunset when Centro glows with golden light. The ferry (☎ 0800-704-4113; www.barcas-sa.com.br) costs R$5.60 return and leaves from Praça Quinze de Novembro in Centro every 20 minutes; it's usually packed with commuters. Once you reach the dock, there isn't much to see in the immediate area. From here catch a bus to the MAC or to one of the beaches – or just turn around and return by ferry.

MUSEU DO ARTE CONTEMPORÂNEA

☎ 2620-2400; www.macniteroi.com.br, in Portuguese; Mirante da Boa Viagem, Niterói; admission R$4; 🕓 10am-6pm Tue-Sun

Designed by Brazil's most famous architect, Oscar Niemeyer, the MAC has a wild curvilinear design that blooms like a flower (or

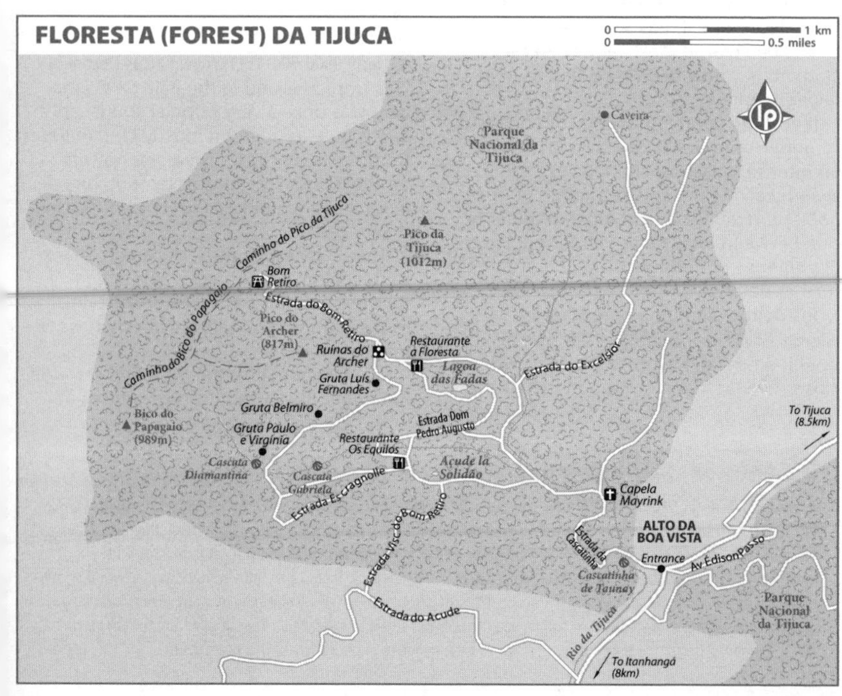

FLORESTA (FOREST) DA TIJUCA – PARQUE NACIONAL DA TIJUCA

The Tijuca is all that's left of the Atlantic rain forest that once surrounded Rio de Janeiro. In just 15 minutes you can go from the concrete jungle of Copacabana to the 120-sq-km tropical jungle of the Parque Nacional da Tijuca (Map p103). A more rapid and dramatic contrast is hard to imagine. The forest is an exuberant green, with beautiful trees, creeks and waterfalls, mountainous terrain and high peaks. It has an excellent, well-marked trail system. Candomblistas (practitioners of the Afro-Brazilian religion of Candomblé) leave offerings by the roadside, families have picnics and serious hikers climb the 1012m to the summit of Pico da Tijuca.

The heart of the forest is the Alto da Boa Vista area in the Floresta (Forest) da Tijuca, with many lovely natural and manmade features. Among the highlights of this beautiful park are several waterfalls (Cascatinha de Taunay, Cascata Gabriela and Cascata Diamantina), a 19th-century chapel (Capela Mayrink) and numerous caves (Gruta Luís Fernandes, Gruta Belmiro, Gruta Paulo e Virgínia). Also in the park is a lovely picnic spot (Bom Retiro) and two restaurants (Restaurante Os Esquilos and Restaurante a Floresta, which is near the ruins of Major Archer's house – Ruínas do Archer).

The park is home to many different bird and animal species, including iguanas and monkeys, which you might encounter on one of the excellent day hikes you can make here (the trails are well signed). Maps can be obtained at the small artisan shop just inside the park entrance, which is open from 7am to 9pm.

The entire park closes at sunset. It's best to go by car, but if you can't, catch bus 221, 233 or 234. Alternatively, take the metro to Saens Peña, then catch a bus going to Barra da Tijuca and get off at Alto da Boa Vista.

The best route by car is to take Rua Jardim Botânico two blocks past the Jardim Botânico (heading east from Gávea). Turn left on Rua Lopes Quintas and then follow the Tijuca or Corcovado signs for two quick left turns until you reach the back of the Jardim Botânico, where you turn right. Then follow the signs for a quick ascent into the forest and past the Vista Chinesa (Map p60) – get out for a good view – and the Mesa do Imperador (Map p60). As soon as you seem to come out of the forest, turn right onto the main road and you'll see the stone columns to the entrance of Alto da Boa Vista on your left after a couple of kilometers. You can also drive up to Alto da Boa Vista by heading out to São Conrado and turning right up the hill at the Parque Nacional da Tijuca signs.

Warning: there have been occasional reports of robbery within the park. Most Cariocas recommend going on weekends when there are more people around. Ask at Riotur (p228) about the present situation.

more prosaically, a flying saucer) against sweeping bay views. Unfortunately, the exhibits inside the museum are less inspiring. To get to the MAC from the Niterói ferry terminal, turn right as you leave and walk about 50m across to the bus terminal in the middle of the road; a 47B minibus will drop you at the museum door.

PONTE RIO-NITERÓI

Map p59

The Ponte (bridge) Rio-Niterói (Ponte Pres Costa E Silva) offers spectacular views of the Baía de Guanabara. It is 15.5km long, 60m high and 26.6m wide, with two three-lane roads. There's a tollbooth 3km from the Niterói city center.

BARRA DA TIJUCA & WEST OF RIO

Eating p147; Shopping p122; Sleeping p199

The Miami of Rio, Barra – as it's known locally – is a sprawling suburb with huge malls and entertainment complexes, long traffic corridors and very little pedestrian movement. The beach here is the real attraction, a wide and lovely 15km-long stretch of pristine shoreline. The commercial area feels quite different from other parts of Rio as Barra's development happened relatively recently. The middle classes first began moving here in the 1970s, when the situation in urban Rio seemed as if it had reached boiling point. Cariocas fled crime and the crowded city to live on an unpopulated stretch of beachfront. Today, Barra is still a safe neighborhood, but the influx of new residents has created crowded conditions once again.

While first-time visitors don't always make it to Barra da Tijuca, there are some extraordinary sights here, aside from the beach. The lush Sitio Burle Marx contains some of the loveliest gardens in Rio, while the Casa do Pontal houses a fascinating collection of folk art. Once you get beyond the development of Barra, the region gets less and less urban. Some of Rio's best beaches lie out this way. There are also some great restaurants in idyllic settings that seem a far cry from busy downtown Rio.

SÍTIO BURLE MARX off Map p107

☎ 2410-1412; Estrada da Barra de Guaratiba 2019, Guaratiba; admission R$5; 🕑 tours 9:30am & 1:30pm, by advance appointment only

This huge 35-hectare estate was once the home of Brazil's most famous landscape architect, Roberto Burle Marx. The estate's lush vegetation includes thousands of plant species, some of which are rare varieties from different corners of the globe. A 17th-century Benedictine chapel also lies on the estate, along with Burle Marx's original farmhouse and studio, where you can see displays of paintings, furniture and sculptures by the talented designer.

CASA DO PONTAL Map p107

☎ 2490-4013; www.popular.art.br/museucasadopontal; Estrada do Pontal 3295, Recreio dos Bandeirantes; admission R$10; 🕑 9:30am-5pm Tue-Sun

Owned by French designer Jacques Van de Beuque, this impressive collection of over 5000 pieces is one of the best folk-art collections in Brazil. The assorted artifacts are grouped according to themes, including music, Carnaval, religion and folklore. The grounds of the museum are surrounded by lush vegetation.

BOSQUE DA BARRA Map p107

☎ 3151-3428; Av das Américas 6000 (intersection of Av Ayrton Senna), Barra da Tijuca; 🕑 8am-6pm Tue-Sun

Covering 50 hectares of salt-marsh vegetation, the park is a refuge and breeding area for many small birds and animals. The woods have a jogging track and cycle path.

MUSEU AEROESPACIAL

Map p60

☎ 2108-8954; www.musal.aer.mil.br, in Portuguese; Av Marechal Fontenele 2000, Campo dos Afonsos; admission free; 🕑 9am-3pm Tue-Fri, 9:30am-4pm Sat & Sun

This museum maintains exhibitions on Santos Dumont (the Brazilian father of aviation), Air Marshal Eduardo Gomes, the history of Brazilian airmail and the role of Brazil's air force in WWII. There are lots of old planes, motors and flying instruments. Highlights are replicas of Santos Dumont's planes, the *14 Bis* and the *Demoiselle*. You can also arrange guided visits if you call at least three days in advance.

PARQUE DO MARAPENDI

Map p107

Av Sernambetiba, Recreio dos Bandeirantes; 🕑 8am-5pm Tue-Fri

At the end of Av Sernambetiba in Recreio dos Bandeirantes, this biological reserve sets aside 70 hectares for study and has a small area for leisure, with workout stations and games areas.

TRANSPORTATION: BARRA DA TIJUCA

🚌 Copacabana, Ipanema, Leblon, Flamengo, Centro (175)

Metrô na Superfície The Barra Expresso metro bus connects Ipanema/General Osório metro station with points along Barra.

BARRA DA TIJUCA & WEST OF RIO

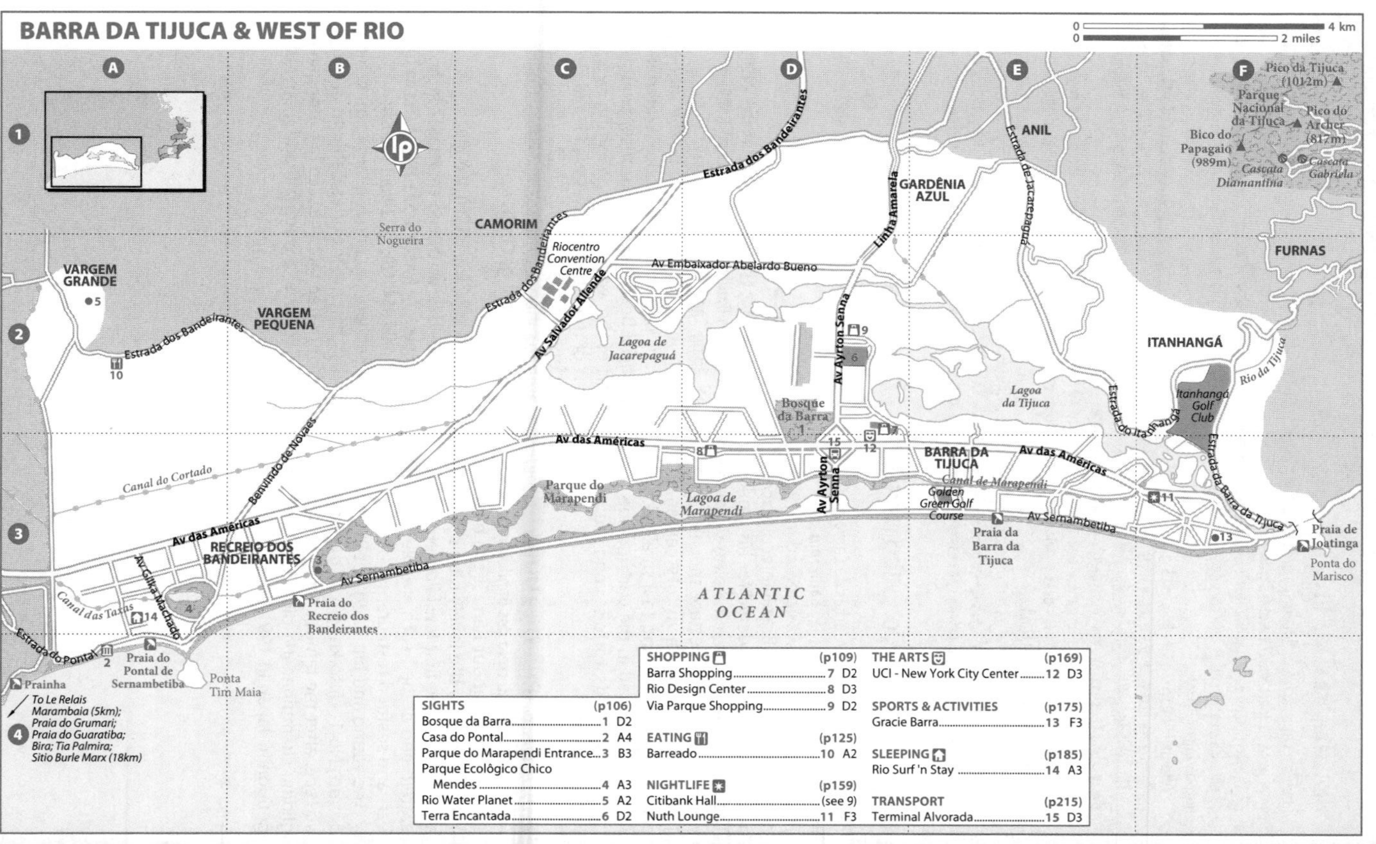

SIGHTS	(p106)
Bosque da Barra	1 D2
Casa do Pontal	2 A4
Parque do Marapendi Entrance	3 B3
Parque Ecológico Chico Mendes	4 A3
Rio Water Planet	5 A2
Terra Encantada	6 D2

SHOPPING	(p109)
Barra Shopping	7 D2
Rio Design Center	8 D3
Via Parque Shopping	9 D2

EATING	(p125)
Barreado	10 A2

NIGHTLIFE	(p159)
Citibank Hall	(see 9)
Nuth Lounge	11 F3

THE ARTS	(p169)
UCI - New York City Center	12 D3

SPORTS & ACTIVITIES	(p175)
Gracie Barra	13 F3

SLEEPING	(p185)
Rio Surf 'n Stay	14 A3

TRANSPORT	(p215)
Terminal Alvorada	15 D3

BEACHES WEST OF RIO

Although Copacabana and Ipanema are Rio's most famous stretches of sand, there are many stunning beaches in the area, some in spectacular natural settings.

The first major beach you'll reach heading west of Leblon is Praia do Pepino (Map p60) in São Conrado. Pepino is a beautiful beach, and is less crowded than Ipanema. It's also where hang-glider riders like to lounge when they're not soaring overhead.

Although it gets crowded on weekends, Recreio dos Bandeirantes (Map p107) is almost deserted during the week. The large rock acts as a natural breakwater, creating a calm bay. The 2km-long stretch of sand is popular with families.

The secluded 700m-long Prainha (Map p107) lies just past Recreio. It's one of the best surfing beaches in Rio, so it's always full of surfers. Waves come highly recommended here.

The most isolated and unspoiled beach close to the city, Grumari (off Map p107) is quiet during the week and packed on weekends with Cariocas looking to get away from city beaches. It is a gorgeous setting, surrounded by mountains and lush vegetation.

From Grumari, a narrow road climbs over a jungle-covered hillside toward Guaratiba (off Map p107). West of here is a good view of the Restinga de Marambaia (the vegetation-rich strip between the beach and the mainland), closed off to the public by a naval base. Cariocas enjoy eating lunch at several of the seafood restaurants in the area.

PARQUE ECOLÓGICO CHICO MENDES Map p107

☎ 2437-6400; Km 17, Av Jarbas de Carvalho 679, Recreio dos Bandeirantes; 🕑 8am-5pm

This 40-hectare park was created in 1989 and named after the Brazilian ecological activist who was murdered for his work. The park protects the remaining sand-spit vegetation from real estate speculators. The facilities include a visitors' center and ecological trails leading to a small lake. Animals protected in the park include butterflies, lizards, tortoises and the broad-nosed caiman.

PRAIA DA BARRA DA TIJUCA Map p107

Av Sernambetiba, Recreio dos Bandeirantes

The best thing about Barra is the beach. It's 12km long, with the lovely blue sea lapping at the shore. The first few kilometers of the eastern end of the beach are filled with bars and seafood restaurants.

The young and hip hang out in front of *barraca* No 1 – also known as the *barraca do Pepê,* after the famous Carioca hang-gliding champion who died during a competition in Japan in 1991.

The further out you go, the more deserted it gets, and the stalls turn into trailers. It's calm on weekdays and crazy on hot summer weekends.

RIO WATER PLANET Map p107

☎ 2428-9000; Estrada das Bandeirantes 24000, Recreio dos Bandeirantes; admission R$89; 🕑 10am-5pm Fri-Sun & holidays

Rio Water Planet claims to be the biggest aquatic park in Latin America. Waterfalls, artificial beaches (a bit surprising in this part of the world) and lazy rafting rivers are part of the attractions, as are Rio Kart Planet (an open-air kart track), Rio Show Planet (an area for shows) and Rio Circus Planet. Children under 1m tall get in free.

TERRA ENCANTADA Map p107

☎ 2421-9369; www.terra-encantada.com.br, in Portuguese; Av Ayrton Senna 2800, Barra da Tijuca; adult/child R$40/20; 🕑 2-9pm Thu-Sun

The Enchanted Land is a large amusement park in Barra. It includes Cabhum (a 64m, 100km/h free fall), Ressaca (a toboggan ride that goes over a waterfall) and many other rides.

SHOPPING

top picks

SHOPPING

Shopping in Rio can mean anything from browsing boutiques in peaceful Leblon to strolling the teeming stalls at the Feira Nordestina on weekends. Not surprisingly, beach and casual wear are a big part of the scene, but less well known are the great variety of stores selling antiques, custom-made handicrafts, wine and spirits, handmade jewelry, records and CDs, coffee-table books and one-of-a-kind goods found only in Rio (such as colorful Gilson Martins' handbags).

If you're looking for a hot new outfit for the night, start your shopping foray in Ipanema, and keep in mind that many stores are hidden inside multistory buildings. See p114 for a cheat sheet on some of these well-concealed boutiques. For a more colorful, chaotic experience, metro it up to Centro, where the narrow pedestrian lanes of Saara are packed with discount goods of all shapes and sizes – plus costume essentials come Carnaval time. Copacabana has a bit of high-end and plenty of frenzy for those wanting the complete experience.

Something of an institution in Rio is the *shopping* (mall), which is a good place to hide away when bad weather arrives. In addition to hunting for sales, you can grab a bite (some malls, such as Shopping Botafogo, have restaurants with panoramic views) or catch a film.

Open-air markets are never far away in Rio. Delectable tropical fruits and vegetables dominate, but you'll also find markets selling used CDs and records, furniture, clothing and handicrafts.

All listings in this chapter are organized by shopping genre (accessories, books, clothing etc) within each neighborhood.

OPENING HOURS

Most stores in Centro open from 9am to 6pm Monday to Friday. A few open on Saturday, usually from 10am to 1pm. In the Zona Sul, stores open from 10am to 6pm Monday to Friday, though some stay open until 8pm or 9pm. On Saturday, shopping hours are 10am to 2pm. Only a few of the big shopping malls open on Sunday – from about 3pm to 8pm.

CONSUMER TAXES

Most stores list their prices with the tax already included, so what you see on the price tag is the total price you'll pay for the goods.

IPANEMA & LEBLON

Ipanema and Leblon are the best hunting grounds for top fashion designs (both homegrown and foreign labels). You'll also find curio and novelty stores, galleries, bookshops, liquor stores and plenty of cafés for refueling along the way. There's a lot going on along the main thoroughfare (Rua Visconde de Pirajá in Ipanema and Av Ataúlfo de Paiva in Leblon).

GILSON MARTINS Map p64 Accessories

☎ 2227-6178; Rua Visconde de Pirajá 462, Ipanema; 🕑 10am-8pm Mon-Fri, 10am-4pm Sat

Designer Gilson Martins turns the silhouette of Corcovado into a fashion statement in his flagship store in Ipanema. In addition to glossy handbags, wallets and other accessories, the shop has a gallery in the back with ongoing exhibitions. Gilson also has a Copacabana branch (Map p76; **Rua Figueiredo Magalhães 304**).

DAQUI Map p66 Accessories & Home Decor

☎ 2529-8576; Av Ataúlfo de Paiva 1174, Leblon; 🕑 10am-8pm Mon-Fri, 10am-4pm Sat

This sweet little boutique sells graphic T-shirts made by Brazilian designers, delicate jewelry, kids' clothes (including leather slippers with animal faces), wind-up toys, colorful luminaries, kitschy vases and other crafty curiosities for the home.

INTERSTUDIO Map p64 Art & Home Decor

☎ 2511-1237; Rua Visconde de Pirajá 595, Ipanema; 🕑 10am-7pm Mon-Fri, 10am-2pm Sat

This small Ipanema shop sells some beautifully made art pieces, including large wooden carvings by Pernambuco artisans and captivating Rio landscape paintings by Italian painter Vittorio Cannone (costing around R$550). Worldwide shipping is available.

URUCUM ART & DESIGN

Map p64 Art & Home Decor

☎ 2540-9990; Rua Visconde de Pirajá 605, Ipanema; 🕑 noon-7pm Mon-Sat

In the same complex as the cinema Estação Ipanema (p172), this tiny shop sells handcrafted woodwork, sculpture, pottery, vases, block prints, playful souvenirs (we spotted monkey candles on a recent visit) and artwork, most of which is made by artists from Rio or Minas Gerais.

ARGUMENTO Map p66 — Books & Music

☎ 2239-5294; Rua Dias Ferreira 417, Leblon; 9am-midnight Mon-Sat, 10am-midnight Sun

One of Leblon's fine neighborhood bookstores, Argumento stocks a small but decent selection of foreign-language books and magazines. The charming café in the back is a perfect place to disappear with a book – or a new friend. A new branch in Copacabana (Map p76) opened recently.

DA CONDE

Map p66 — Books & Music

☎ 2274-0359; Store 125, Rua Conde de Bernadotte 26, Leblon; 11am-midnight Mon-Sat

Secreted inside a tiny shopping gallery, this little multilevel bookstore stocks a small selection of English-language titles. You'll also find CDs and a café and lounge that hosts occasional book signings and other literary events.

LETRAS E EXPRESSÕES

Map p64 — Books & Music

☎ 2247-8737; Rua Visconde de Pirajá 276, Ipanema; 8am-midnight

One of Ipanema's growing assortment of bookshops, Letras e Expressões carries a decent selection of foreign-language books from architectural tomes to fiction and travel books (including Lonely Planet titles). It also has a variety of English-language magazines and an internet café. There is also a 24-hour Leblon branch (Map p66; ☎ 2511-5085; Av Ataulfo de Paiva 1292).

LIVRARIA DA TRAVESSA

Map p64 — Books & Music

☎ 3205-9002; Rua Visconde de Pirajá 572, Ipanema; 9am-midnight Mon-Sat, 11am-midnight Sun

One of a growing chain of bookstores around the city, Livraria da Travessa has a small selection of foreign-language books and periodicals, with CDs upstairs. The buzzing 2nd-floor café (a branch of Bazzar, p128) serves salads, sandwiches, quiches and desserts. There's an even larger Livraria da Travessa inside the mall Shopping Leblon (p115).

KOPENHAGEN Map p66 — Chocolates

☎ 2511-1112; Av Ataúlfo de Paiva 1025, Leblon; 9am-7pm Mon-Fri, 9am-5pm Sat

Serving up tasty bonbons and other decadent chocolate treats, Kopenhagen has been satisfying children and chocoholics since 1928. Recent favorites include tiny bottle-shaped liqueur-filled chocolates, chocolate-dipped cookies and giant rum balls. There's another store in Copacabana (Map p76).

ESCH CAFÉ Map p66 — Cigars

☎ 2512-5651; Rua Dias Ferreira 78, Leblon; noon-1:30am Mon-Sat, to midnight Sun

This restaurant-bar is also the 'house of the Havana,' which means if you have a taste for the Cubans, this is your place. The humidor is stocked with a decent selection, which you can enjoy there over a glass of port, or a few blocks away on the beach. It also has a Centro branch (Rua do Rosário 108).

CLOTHING SIZES

Women's clothing

Aus/UK	8	10	12	14	16	18
Europe	36	38	40	42	44	46
Japan	5	7	9	11	13	15
USA	6	8	10	12	14	16

Women's shoes

Aus/USA	5	6	7	8	9	10
Europe	35	36	37	38	39	40
France only	35	36	38	39	40	42
Japan	22	23	24	25	26	27
UK	3½	4½	5½	6½	7½	8½

Men's clothing

Aus	92	96	100	104	108	112
Europe	46	48	50	52	54	56
Japan	S		M	M		L
UK/USA	35	36	37	38	39	40

Men's shirts (collar sizes)

Aus/Japan	38	39	40	41	42	43
Europe	38	39	40	41	42	43
UK/USA	15	15½	16	16½	17	17½

Men's shoes

Aus/UK	7	8	9	10	11	12
Europe	41	42	43	44½	46	47
Japan	26	27	27½	28	29	30
USA	7½	8½	9½	10½	11½	12½

Measurements approximate only; try before you buy

MARKET LOVER'S GUIDE TO RIO

Rio's many markets are ideal places for exploring the subcultures beneath the city's skin – whether brushing elbows with antique lovers, recent migrants from the northeast or the youthful flocks of fashionistas from the Zona Sul. Several markets, like the Feira Nordestina and the once-monthly Feira do Rio Antigo, are as much about food and music as they are about shopping. A little bargaining is expected when making purchases, but keep in mind that sellers generally don't over-inflate their prices and so aren't willing to haggle very much.

Av Atlântica Fair (Map p76; Av Atlântica near Rua Djalma Ulrich, Copacabana; 6pm-midnight Mon-Sat) Paintings, drawings, jewelry, clothing and a fair bit of tourist junk make up this Copacabana market. It's located on the median along Av Atlântica.

Feira de Música (Map p90; Rua Pedro Lessa, Centro; 9am-5pm Mon-Fri) On weekdays, next to the Biblioteca Nacional, record and CD stalls line the small lane. You'll find everything from American indie rock to vintage Brazilian funk, and most vendors will let you listen to any of the discs for sale.

Feira do Rio Antigo (Map p98; 2224-6693; Rua do Lavradio, Centro; 10am-6pm 1st Sat of month) Although the Rio Antiques Fair happens just once a month, don't miss it if you're in town. The colonial buildings become a living installation as the whole street fills with antiques, and samba bands add to the ambience.

Feira Nordestina (Map p60; 3860-9976; Campo de São Cristóvão, São Cristóvão; admission R$1; 10am-4pm Tue-Thu, nonstop 10am Fri to 10pm Sun) For details see p102.

Hippie Fair (Map p64; Praça General Osório, Ipanema; 7am-7pm Sun) The Zona Sul's most famous market, the Hippie Fair (aka Feira de Arte de Ipanema) has artwork, jewelry, handicrafts, clothing and souvenirs for sale. Stalls in the southeast and northeast corners of the plaza sells tasty plates of *acarajé* (croquettes, with a sauce of vatapá and shrimp, R$7), plus excellent desserts (R$3). Don't miss it.

Photography and Image Fair (Map p87; 3235-2650; Parque do Catete, Museu da República, Rua do Catete 153, Catete; 9am-5pm last Sun of month) Works from amateur and professional photographers are for sale at this once-monthly market in the verdant Parque do Catete. There's also a multimedia room, which hosts workshops, talks and slide projections.

Praça do Lido Market (Map p76; Praça do Lido, Copacabana; 8am-6pm Sat & Sun) Copacabana's response to Ipanema's widely popular Hippie Fair, this smaller weekend affair features handicrafts and souvenirs, soccer jerseys, jewelry stands and, from time to time, a man selling amazing slices of chocolate cake.

Praça Santos Dumont Antique Fair (Map p70; Praça Santos Dumont, Gávea; 9am-5pm Sun) Gávea's 80-stall antique fair features ceramics, artwork, jewelry, records, watches, books and other odds and ends.

Praça Quinze Handicrafts Fair (Map p90; Praça Quinze de Novembro, Centro; 8am-6pm Thu-Fri) Near the Imperial Palace, artisans sell works of leather, wood, porcelain, glass and silver. There are also stalls with regional Brazilian fare.

Shopping Cassino Atlântico Antiques Fair (Map p76; Av Atlântico 4240, Copacabana; 11am-7pm Sat) Inside an air-conditioned shopping center, this antique fair consists of three floors of blown glass, sculpture, carpets, silverware and jewelry. Pieces are in much better condition here, which is clearly reflected in the prices. A tearoom and live music help shoppers get in the mood.

ESAPAÇO FASHION
Map p64 Clothing

2512-8391; Av Aníbal de Mendonça 114, Ipanema; 9am-8pm Mon-Sat, 10am-6pm Sun

This long, narrow boutique has a decor and aesthetic aimed to attract a young, hip, somewhat fashion-forward group of shoppers in its form-fitting skirts, dresses and tops, flashy sneakers and one-of-a-kind jewelry. Electronic music plays overhead, and there's a tiny lounge area at the back with some art books – for the gents while the gals shop.

FORUM Map p64 Clothing

2521-7415; www.forum.com.br; Rua Barão da Torre 422, Ipanema; 10am-6pm Mon-Fri, 10am-2pm Sat

Much touted Brazilian designer Tufi Duek reigns over this curiously designed flagship store. Here you'll find beautifully made pieces from his men's and women's collections.

ISABELA CAPETO Map p66 Clothing

2540-5232; Rua Dias Ferreira 217, Leblon; 10am-8pm Mon-Fri, 10am-3pm Sat

One of Brazil's fashion stars, Isabela Capeto creates beautifully made clothing with seductive lines. Many of her pieces are embroidered and feature add-ons of vintage lace, sequins or fabric trims. Her Leblon shop is a good place to see dresses and skirts that have earned her accolades from *O Globo, Vogue* and other publications.

OSKLEN

Map p64 Clothing

☎ 2227-2911; Rua Maria Quitéria 85, Ipanema; 🕒 10am-7pm Mon-Fri, 10am-2pm Sat

One of Brazil's best-known fashion labels outside the country, Osklen is known for its stylish and well-made beachwear (particularly men's swim shorts and graphic T-shirts), sneakers and outerwear. The company was started in 1988 by outdoor enthusiast Oskar Metsavaht, the first Brazilian to scale Mont Blanc.

REDLEY

Map p64 Clothing

☎ 2287-4843; Rua Maria Quitéria 99, Ipanema

In the heart of Ipanema, this new multi-level fashion store is a fine place to browse for couture beach duds and streetwear. Unlike most other Ipanema boutiques, this one's aimed at the men, with an excellent assortment of T-shirts, shorts and swim suits.

CATHERINE LABOURÉ

Map p64 Clothing & Accessories

☎ 2287-9630; 2nd fl, Rua Visconde de Pirajá 207, Ipanema; 🕒 10am-6:30pm Mon-Fri, 10am-4pm Sat

Tucked away inside an otherwise humdrum shopping center, this intriguing shop sells vintage dresses, skirts, silk scarves, handbags, shoes and sunglasses, with labels by top international designers. There's a smaller selection for men – mostly T-shirts and button-downs – as well as a few small antiques and collectibles for the home.

ESPAÇO BRAZILIAN SOUL

Map p64 Clothing & Accessories

☎ 2522-3641; Rua Prudente de Morais 1102, Ipanema

Set in a picturesque little villa, Espaço Brazilian Soul is a two-story boutique selling designer duds (Osklen among them) in the form of board shorts, T-shirts, flip-flops and button-downs. There's more men's apparel than women's, though the dresses are still worth a peek.

GAROTA DE IPANEMA

Map p64 Clothing & Accessories

☎ 2521-3168; Rua Vinícius de Moraes 53, Ipanema

Next to the famous restaurant of the same name, this tiny boutique is an excellent place to browse for attractive, reasonably priced bikinis and beachwear. There are also eye-catching T-shirts (for men and women) as well as bags and other accessories.

LUKO

Map p64 Clothing & Accessories

☎ 2540-0589; Store 111, Rua Visconde de Pirajá 547, Ipanema; 🕒 10am-7pm Mon-Fri, 10am-4pm Sat

This charming boutique has an eclectic collection of youthful women's couture. Slim, beaded necklaces and bracelets, silk scarves, form-fitting tops and skirts, and slinky lingerie are among the items you'll find here. Rumor has it that Luko is a favorite among TV production companies looking for pieces.

top picks

RIO SOUVENIRS

- **Music** Rio is one of the world's best places to expand your CD collection. Don't overlook local favorites, like singers Maria Rita, Diogo Nogueira or Mart'nália.
- **Cachaça** (cane liquor) You can buy a quality cachaça for Minas for around R$25 and up.
- **Swimwear** You may not be able to take the beach home, but you can at least flaunt your new tan in a tiny *sunga* (Speedo) or *fio dental* (string bikini). Ipanema (along Rua Visconde de Pirajá) is the place to look.
- **Maracatu drum** If you don't think the massive northeastern instrument will fit on your coffee table, consider the smaller, gentler *cavaquinho* (small ukulele-like instrument). Maracatu Brasil (p120) and Casa Oliveira (p121) are good places to look.
- **Havaianas** You can find a pair for every mood at the spacious new shop in Copacabana (p117).
- **Paintings** A wide range of artists showcase their works at the Sunday Hippie Fair (p112).
- **Soccer jersey** Forget the well-known yellow label. Try and score a jersey for one of Rio's teams. Loja Fla (p117) is the go-to place for Flamengo fans.
- **Folk art** Tap into Brazil's handicraft traditions at stores such as Pé de Boi (p119) and Brasil & Cia (p114).

WÖLLNER OUTDOOR

Map p64 Clothing & Accessories

☎ 2512-6531; Rua Visconde de Pirajá 511, Ipanema; 🕑 10am-9pm Mon-Fri

The great outdoors, and the shirt and shorts you'll need to enjoy it, seem to be the inspiration for Wöllner. Clothes and accessories are ruggedly styled, not unlike Abercrombie and American Eagle. Once you've browsed the selections, grab a *cafézinho* (small black coffee) and a chocolate torte at the café in the front.

HAVAIANAS Map p64 Footwear

☎ 2267-7395; Rua Farme de Amoedo 76, Ipanema; 🕑 9am-8pm Mon-Fri, 10am-6pm Sat & Sun

The famous Brazilian rubber sandal finally has its own dedicated store. At this narrow shop, you'll find a colorful variety of Havaianas (flip-flops) for men, women and children, covering all price points (R$15 up to R$120). There's a bigger branch (p117) in Copacabana.

BRASIL & CIA Map p64 Handicrafts

☎ 2267-4603; Rua Maria Quitéria 27, Ipanema; 🕑 10am-7pm Mon-Sat, 10am-4pm Sun

This handicrafts shop sells colorful works in papier-mâché, porcelain and glass, showcasing Brazil's rich artisan traditions. Figurines, wooden boxes, dolls and other crafts are made by artists from Pernambuco and Alagoas. Perfect for keepsakes of your travels.

AMSTERDAM SAUER Map p64 Jewelry

☎ 2279-6237; www.amsterdamsauer.com; Rua Visconde de Pirajá 484, Ipanema; 🕑 9am-7:30pm Mon-Fri, 10am-4pm Sat

Well known for its impressive collection of precious stones, Amsterdam Sauer also sells finely crafted jewelry. Watches, pens, wallets and other accessories are available too. Visitors can also check out the museum (p65) on Garcia D'Avila while they are here.

ANTONIO BERNARDO

Map p64 Jewelry

☎ 2512-7204; Rua Garcia D'Ávila 121, Ipanema; 🕑 10am-8pm Mon-Fri, 11am-4pm Sat

Designer-goldsmith Antonio Bernardo has garnered attention for his lovely bracelets, earrings and necklaces. The designs here are unique and artfully done, and Bernardo uses high-quality materials.

MARIA OITICICA Map p64 Jewelry

☎ 3202-1011; Forum de Ipanema, Rua Visconde de Pirajá 351, Ipanema

Using native materials found in the Amazon, Maria Oiticica has created some lovely handcrafted jewelry inspired by indigenous art. Seeds, plant fibers and tree bark are just some of the ingredients of her bracelets, necklaces and earrings, and her work helps support struggling local communities with craft-making traditions.

H STERN Map p64 Jewelry & Accessories

☎ 2274-3447; www.hstern.com.br; Rua Visconde de Pirajá 490, Ipanema; 🕑 9:30am-6:30pm Mon-Fri, 10am-4pm Sat

The famous jeweler H Stern has an array of finely crafted jewelry, watches and other accessories for sale. At the company's headquarters you can also take a tour of the H Stern gem museum (p67).

MUSICALE Map p64 Music

☎ 2287-2330; Rua Visconde de Pirajá 207, Ipanema; 🕑 10am-7pm Mon-Fri, to 2pm Sat

This small music shop has narrow aisles, but you'll come across some real finds if

HIDDEN BOUTIQUES

Lovely shops abound in Ipanema and Leblon, though they're not always obvious to the eye. Some of the best finds are secreted in *galerias* (small shopping plazas) like these:

Forum de Ipanema (Map p64; Rua Visconde de Pirajá 351, Ipanema; 🕑 10am-8pm Mon-Sat) Top stores here include Via Milano shoes; Yes, Brazil apparel; and Bum Bum and Salinas (both selling men's and women's swimwear).

Ipanema 2000 (Map p64; Rua Visconde de Pirajá 547, Ipanema; 🕑 10am-8pm Mon-Fri) Ipanema's fashion-conscious shoppers flock to this store gallery in search of something new for the after-office soiree – or the upcoming trip to Búzios.

Rio Design Center (Map p66; ☎ 3206-9100; Av Ataúlfo de Paiva 270, Leblon; 🕑 10am-10pm Mon-Fri, 10am-8pm Sat, 3-9pm Sun) Four floors of galleries and stores, plus a handful of good restaurants on the ground and basement levels.

you brave the elbow-jousting at Musicale. Used and new CDs are organized somewhat by category, and you can listen to any used CD at one of the in-store decks.

TOCA DO VINÍCIUS Map p64 Music

☎ 2247-5227; www.tocadovinicius.com.br; Rua Vinícius de Moraes 129, Ipanema; 🕑 10am-7pm Mon-Fri, 10am-6pm Sat & Sun

Bossa nova fans shouldn't miss this store. In addition to its ample CD selection of contemporary and old performers (prices run R$30 to R$35), Toca do Vinícius sells music scores and composition books. Upstairs a tiny museum displays memorabilia of the great songwriter and poet Vinícius de Moraes. Once-a-month concerts in front of the store feature top-name bossa and samba artists (check the website for dates).

LOMOGRAPHY GALLERY STORE
Map p64 Photography

☎ 2267-2226; www.lomography.com.br; 2nd fl, Rua Visconde de Pirajá 437, Ipanema; 🕑 11am-8pm Tue-Fri, 11am-4pm Sat

The very first Lomography outpost in South America, this colorful shop and gallery specializes in the Lomo Kompakt Automat, a compact Russian film camera known for saturated colors and surreal effects (halos, shadowing). You can purchase different models here at the store, check out the LomoWall (of photographic art) and learn more about the growing fan base worldwide who are devoted to these analog cameras.

CASA & VIDEO
Map p64 Photography & Electronics

☎ 2508-3030; Rua Visconde de Pirajá 371, Ipanema; 🕑 9am-10pm

If you've lost your digital camera (or forgot to bring one), this electronics chain is a handy store to get a replacement. All the name brands are here – Kodak, Samsung, Sony – as well as some you probably haven't heard of. Prices are higher than what you'd pay back home (owing to high import taxes). Casa & Video has numerous other branches around town, including inside Rio Sul shopping center (p119).

SHOPPING LEBLON Map p66 Shopping Center

☎ 3138-8000; Av Afrânio de Melo Franco 290, Leblon

The best new shopping destination in Rio is this glittering multistory shopping center packed with top-name Brazilian and foreign labels. There are plenty of tempting stores that will drain your vacation funds, as well as good restaurants, a cinema and a well-placed Starbucks (one of the few outposts in Rio), complete with a live piano player.

EXPAND WINE STORE Map p64 Wine

☎ 2123-7900; Rua Barão da Torre 358, Ipanema; 🕑 9am-midnight Mon-Sat, to 5pm Sun

This well-stocked wine shop in Ipanema is a great place to buy a few bottles while exploring the neighborhood. Chile, Argentina and 14 other countries are represented among the 1000 vintages. The attached restaurant is the place to try out those velvety malbecs and merlots.

LIDADOR Map p66 Wine & Spirits

☎ 2512-1788; Av Ataúlfo de Paiva 1079, Leblon; 🕑 10am-8pm Mon-Fri, 10am-5pm Sat

One of Leblon's best wine shops, Lidador stocks Chilean and Argentinean wines as well as vintages from Europe and beyond. *Cachaças,* rums and even Brazilian wines are available if you're looking for something with a little more bite. There's also a handy location in Ipanema (Map p64; Rua Vinícius de Moraes 120).

SHOPPING IN IPANEMA

Shopping Tour

Ipanema's many boutiques make for some excellent browsing (and blessed air-conditioning) when you need a break from the beach. In addition to high-end clothing stores, you'll find shops selling wine, music, books, handicrafts and plastic Russian cameras. Off the avenue, pretty streets with cafés, ice-cream stands and open-air restaurants provide a respite from shopping.

1 Rua Farme de Amoedo

Before hitting the streets, boost up your energy levels with coffee and a pastry or two at Cafeína (p133), a pleasant open-air spot one block west of Praça General Osório. From there, walk half a block north to check out Havaianas (p114). It's a great place to pick up gifts for friends.

2 Toca do Vinícius

Walk one block west to Rua Vinícius de Moraes, named after the famed Carioca composer. One of the best little music stores in Rio, Toca do Vinícius (p115) lies along this street, and stocks all the great bossa nova hits of

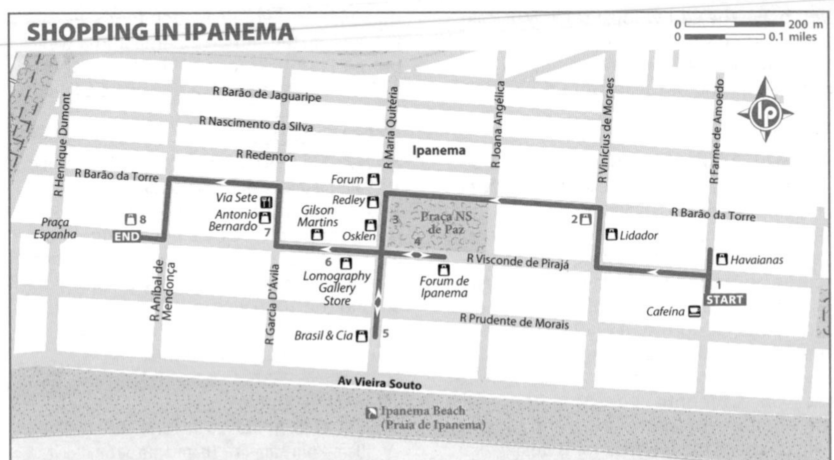

SHOPPING FACTS

Start Rua Farme de Amoedo
End Praça Espanha
Distance 2km
Duration 2½ hours
Fuel Stop Via Sete

the legend for whom it's named. You'll also find samba, MPB (Música Popular Brasileira) and a good mix of Brazilian and international labels. Just across the road is Lidador, a handy wine shop.

3 Praça NS de Paz – west side

From Rua Viníus de Moraes, walk one block west of the plaza, where you'll find a few noteworthy clothing shops, including Forum (p112), Redley (p113) and Osklen (p113). These shops stock men's and women's swimwear, T-shirts and outerwear in eye-catching styles.

4 Hidden boutiques

Down on busy Rua Visconde de Pirajá are dozens of shops, but some – like Forum de Ipanema (p114) – are hidden from view. Take a wander through this multistory center for a peak at lots of colorful fashion stores.

5 Handicrafts

One block south, you'll find Brasil & Cia (p114), one of the best handicrafts shops in the Zona Sul. Here you can check out the colorful works of artists from Minas Gerais, Bahia and other states.

6 Russian cameras & handbags

Back on Rua Visconde de Pirajá are two unique stores: Lomography Gallery Store (p115), which has a collection of quirky analog cameras and a wall of photo art; and Gilson Martins (p110), which receives much press for its iconic vinyl bags bearing images either of the Brazilian flag or of Corcovado.

7 Rua Garcia D'Ávila

Probably Ipanema's toniest street, Rua Garcia D'Ávila is the address of several high-end jewelers, a Louis Vuitton store, and equally elegant cafés and restaurants. Our picks: Antonio Bernardo (p114), maker of exquisite, custom-made jewelry, followed by a bite at Via Sete (p131), with an inviting patio overlooking the sidewalk.

8 Livraria da Travessa

Although the bookseller has a number of shops in Rio, this Livraria da Travessa (p111) is one of our favorites, if only for the cozy café on the 2nd floor. You can browse coffee-table books, listen to CDs in the music section and finish off with coffee and dessert.

GÁVEA, JARDIM BOTÂNICO & LAGOA

Aside from a few scattered shops, there isn't much of a shopping scene in Jardim Botânico or Lagoa. Residents from the neighborhood typically head to Ipanema, Leblon or the huge Shopping da Gávea mall to satisfy their retail cravings. On weekends, however, an interesting market on the Praça Santos Dumont Antique Fair (p112) makes the journey here worthwhile.

PARCERIA CARIOCA
Map p70 Clothing & Accessories

☎ 2259-1437; store 108, Rua Jardim Botânico 728, Jardim Botânico; 🕑 10am-7pm Mon-Fri, to 2pm Sat

This sweet little store sells clever T-shirts, colorful handbags and accessories, and an assortment of shoes, jewelry and decorative pieces, all of which combine elements of craftwork with contemporary fashion. As a bonus, Parceria Carioca works with NGOs and co-ops that provide jobs for artisans from poor communities. It also has stores in Forum Ipanema (Rua Visconde de Pirajá 351, Ipanema) and Shopping da Gávea (p117).

O SOL Map p70 Handicrafts

☎ 2294-5099; Rua Corcovado 213, Jardim Botânico; 🕑 9am-6pm Mon-Fri, 9am-1pm Sat

O Sol is run by Leste-Um, a nonprofit social-welfare organization. This delightful store displays the works of regional artists and sells Brazilian folk art in clay, wood and porcelain. It also sells baskets and woven rugs.

SHOPPING DA GÁVEA
Map p70 Shopping Center

☎ 2274-9896; Rua Marquês de São Vicente 52, Gávea; 🕑 10am-10pm Mon-Sat, 3-9pm Sun

Shopping da Gávea touts itself as the preferred mall of artists and intellectuals, which may or may not matter to you when you're laying down serious cash for those sneakers. There are 200 stores, four performance theaters and numerous restaurants, including La Pastaciutta, which serves tasty pastas and appetizers.

COPACABANA & LEME

Copacabana's shops, just like its local residents, are a diverse bunch, with everything from *cachaça* to football jerseys on hand, as well as shoe stores, surf shops and record stores thrown in the mix. Fashion hunters will find more lower-tier labels than in Ipanema, along with lower prices to match. Between Copa and Ipanema is the Galeria River, a low-rise shopping mall lined with surf and swimwear shops.

DRACO STORE Map p76 Clothing

☎ 2227-7393; Rua Francisco Otaviano 55, Ipanema

Like Galeria River (p118) a few doors down, this menswear store specializes in stylish beachwear, including well-made swim-shorts. You'll also find jeans, button-downs and T-shirts (in the R$50 to R$70 range) – the best of which bear the names of Rio neighborhoods (Copacabana, Ipanema, Arpoador).

LOJA FLA Map p76 Clothing & Accessories

☎ 2541-4109; Ave NS de Copacabana 219, Copacabana

With more than 30 million fans worldwide, Flamengo is one of the most-watched football (soccer) teams in all of Brazil. This new shop sells all the Flamengo goods, including jerseys, logo-emblazoned socks and soccer balls, posters and other memorabilia. The prices aren't cheap (jerseys run R$70 to R$160), but that hasn't dented the popularity of this often-packed little store.

HAVAIANAS Map p76 Footwear

☎ 2267-2418; Rua Xavier da Silveira 19, Copacabana; 🕑 9am-8pm Mon-Fri, 10am-6pm Sat & Sun

If you're out of ideas for gifts to take home, head to this sizeable Havaianas shop, where the ubiquitous Brazilian rubber sandal comes in all different styles – sporting the

top picks

SHOPPING STRIPS

- Av Ataúlfo de Paiva, Leblon Boutiques selling haute couture sprinkled among cafés, bookshops and restaurants.
- Av Nossa Senhora (NS) de Copacabana, Copacabana Packed during the week, this strip is lined with shops selling everything from chocolates to soccer balls, with plenty of street vendors hawking their wares along the sidewalks.
- Rua do Lavradio, Lapa Rows of antique stores mixed with hypermodern furniture shops, along with a few cafés and bars.
- Rua Visconde de Pirajá, Ipanema Ipanema's vibrant shopping strip has boutiques, shopping centers and scores of dining and coffee-sipping options.
- Senhor dos Passos, Centro One of the main streets coursing through the Middle Eastern bazaar–like Saara, with clothing and curio shops packing the street.

flags of Brazil, Argentina, Portugal, England and Spain – plus snazzy designs for the ladies, and even logo-bearing bags, key chains and beach towels. There are also some rather amusing Havaianas socks, which haven't exactly caught on here yet.

ARTE BRASILIS Map p76 Handicrafts

☎ 2513-1238; Av NS de Copacabana 1313, Copacabana; 🕑 9am-6pm Mon-Sat

One of Copacabana's few decent handicraft stores, Arte Brasilis sells colorful wall hangings, wooden carvings, place settings, and other handmade objects from Minas Gerais and the northeast. There are better places to shop for souvenirs, but this one is convenient if you're based in Copacabana.

MARIA DE BARRO Map p76 Handicrafts

☎ 2235-4339; Av Atlântica 1998, Copacabana; 🕑 10am-10pm Mon-Sat, 3-9pm Sun

This tiny shop sells a small selection of handcrafted pieces from the northeast of Brazil. Wooden geometric vases with animals such as capybaras carved in the side, tiny clay pots and sculptures in stone are among the simple, art-naïf pieces.

MUNDO VERDE Map p76 Health Food

☎ 2257-3183; www.mundoverde.com.br, in Portuguese; Av NS de Copacabana 630, Copacabana; 🕑 9am-6pm Mon-Fri, 9am-2pm Sat

Brazil's largest health-food retailer, Mundo Verde sells organic products, including: *salgados* (bar snacks), and other snacks besides; jams made from Amazonian fruits; and other assorted goods. The sun-care products are usually cheaper here than in pharmacies – and much better for your skin.

BOSSA NOVA & COMPANHIA
Map p76 Music

☎ 2295-8096; Rua Duvivier 37A, Copacabana; 🕑 9am-8pm Mon-Fri, 10am-5pm Sat

This well-lit music store has a fine assortment of bossa, *choro* and samba CDs and LPs, as well as musical instruments, coffee-table books, sheet music and biographies of top Brazilian composers.

MODERN SOUND Map p76 Music

☎ 2548-5005; www.modernsound.com.br; Rua Barata Ribeiro 502, Copacabana; 🕑 9am-9pm Mon-Fri, 9am-8pm Sat

One of Brazil's largest music stores, Modern Sound makes a fine setting for browsing through the many shelves of samba, electronica, hip-hop, imports, classical and dozens of other well-represented categories. The in-store café features live concerts daily.

MUSICALE Map p76 Music

☎ 2267-9607; Av NS de Copacabana 1103C, Copacabana; 🕑 10am-7pm Mon-Fri, 10am-4pm Sat

Musicale has a small but well-curated selection of used CDs (and a few new titles), most of which cost between R$16 and R$22. Albums run the gamut between samba, Música Popular Brasileira (MPB) and regional sounds, plus American and British rock and indie as well as world music (French pop, *nueva cancion*), and you can listen to used discs on one of several CD players scattered around the store. Musicale also buys and trades CDs.

GALERIA RIVER Map p76 Shopping Center

Rua Francisco Otaviano 67, Arpoador; 🕑 10am-6pm Mon-Sat

Surf shops, skateboard and rollerblade outlets, and shops selling beachwear and fashions for young nubile things fill this shopping gallery in Arpoador. Shorts, bikinis, swim trunks, party attire and gear for outdoor adventure are in abundance. The shops here – like Ocean Surf Shop – are a good place to inquire about board rentals, which cost about US$10 per day. Those interested in rock climbing and trekking should stop by the Casa do Montanhista, a hiking-apparel store, for more information about courses.

SHOPPING SIQUEIRA CAMPOS
Map p76 Shopping Center

☎ 2549-0650; Rua Siqueira Campos 143, Copacabana; 🕑 10am-8pm Mon-Sat

One of Rio's first malls, this quirky shopping mall packs an intriguing mix of stores along an upward-winding ramp. You'll find numerous antique shops, jewelry, no-nonsense art galleries, a pet shop and dozens of other surprising finds that you won't come across in Leblon. There's also a grocery store on the 1st floor.

DEU LA DEU VINHOS Map p76 Wine & Spirits

☎ 2235-7287; Rua Domingos Ferreira 66, Copacabana

Copacabana's best wine shop is hidden on a quiet street one block from the beach. In addition to a fair assortment of Chilean and Argentine vintages, you'll find a few decent Brazilian labels like Casa Vadulga and Miolo.

A wide assortment of *cachaças* and other spirits round out the offerings.

BOTAFOGO & URCA

Shopping in Botafogo usually means heading to the high-rise mall overlooking the bay. There are, however, other options, such as the Museu do Indio's small handicrafts shop (with all pieces made by Brazilian tribes) as well as a cozy bookshop near the cinemas with a back-room café. Urca, quiet old soul that she is, has nothing in the way of shopping.

LIVRARIA PREFÁCIO Map p80 Books & Music

☎ 2527-5699; Rua Voluntários da Pátria 39, Botafogo; 🕓 10am-10pm Mon-Fri, 2-10pm Sat & Sun

This charming bookshop stocks a small selection of foreign titles as well as music. And perusers need not go hungry or thirsty while they browse for titles: a slender bar in front delivers refreshing glasses of *chope* (draft beer), while seating upstairs and in the café in back offers heartier fare. The bookshop hosts an occasional poetry reading or record-release party.

ARTÍNDIA Map p80 Handicrafts

☎ 3214-8702; Museu do Índio, Rua das Palmeiras 55, Botafogo; 🕓 9am-5:30pm Mon-Fri, 1-5pm Sat & Sun

Inside the grounds of the Museu do Índio, Artíndia sells a variety of indigenous handicrafts – masks, musical instruments, toys, pots, baskets and weapons. Regional artists, mostly from northern tribes, create objects crafted from native materials like straw, clay, wood and feathers.

PONTO FOTOGRÁFICA

Map p80 Photography

☎ 2539-4994; Rua Voluntários da Pátria, Botafogo 150; 🕓 10-6pm Mon-Fri, to 2pm Sat

This professional outfit has a full range of photo services, including digital printing, enlargements, photo restorations and plenty of other services you probably don't have a use for. It uses Kodak developing and paper.

BOTAFOGO PRAIA SHOPPING

Map p80 Shopping Center

☎ 2559-9880; Praia de Botafogo 400, Botafogo; 🕓 10am-10pm Mon-Sat, 3-10pm Sun

Botafogo's large shopping center has dozens of stores, featuring Brazilian and international designers to suit every style – and clothe every part of the body. The 3rd floor's the best for top designers: check stores such as Philippe Martins, Giselle Martins, Osklen and Equatore. The mall also has a cinema and several top-floor restaurants, such as Emporium Pax (p140), with great panoramic views.

RIO OFF-PRICE SHOPPING

Map p80 Shopping Center

☎ 2542-5693; Rua General Severiano 97, Botafogo; 🕓 10am-10pm Mon-Sat, 3-9pm Sun

Near Rio Sul Shopping, Rio Off-Price Shopping is something of a factory outlet. It has many of the same stores as other malls – domestic and international designers – but prices are about 20% lower. It also has two cinemas and meal options (mostly fast food).

RIO SUL SHOPPING Map p80 Shopping Center

☎ 2545-7200; www.riosul.com.br, in Portuguese; Rua Lauro Müller 116, Botafogo; 🕓 10am-10pm Mon-Sat, 3-10pm Sun

The biggest shopping center you can reach without heading to Barra, Rio Sul has over 400 shops, featuring both the prominent and the obscure, cinemas, restaurants and, on weekends, overwhelming crowds.

FLAMENGO, LARANJEIRAS & COSME VELHO

While not a traditional shopping destination, this area offers some worthwhile exploring, particularly if you stop in the whimsical vintage shop on Rua Alice and the art gallery–handicrafts emporium known as Pé de Boi in Laranjeiras.

DESCULPA, EU SOU CHIQUE

Map p84 Clothing & Home Decor

☎ 2225-6059; Rua Alice 75, Laranjeiras; 🕓 10am-7pm Mon-Fri, 10am-8pm Sat

On bohemian Rua Alice, 'Sorry I'm Chic' is a delightful store selling a rambling assortment of vintage fashion, modish relics from the '60s and plenty of great finds from decades past. The upstairs area with a bar is also a theater space with periodic performances throughout the year.

PÉ DE BOI Map p84 Handicrafts

☎ 2285-4395; Rua Ipiranga 55, Laranjeiras; 🕓 9am-7pm Mon-Fri, 9am-1pm Sat

Although everything is for sale here, Pé de Boi feels more like an art gallery than a handicrafts shop, owing to the high quality of the wood and ceramic works, and the tapestries, sculptures and weavings. This is perhaps Rio's best place to see one-of-a-kind pieces by artists from Bahia, Amazonia, Minas Gerais and other parts of Brazil. Don't miss the upstairs area (with photos of some of the artists whose work is here).

MARACATU BRASIL

Map p84 Musical Instruments

☎ 2557-4754; www.maracatubrasil.com.br; Rua Ipiranga 49, Laranjeiras; 10am-6pm Mon-Sat

You can't miss the lime-green building that houses this small percussion store and workshop. Inside, you can buy an *afoxê* (a gourd shaker with beads strung around it), conga and bongo drums, tambourines and other Brazilian percussion instruments. Upstairs is a drum clinic, where you can study those infectious beats with local instructors; see p221 for more details.

CENTRO & CINELÂNDIA

For a break from the chrome and glass of the Zona Sul, check out the old-school shops of historic Centro. Bargains abound in the narrow pedestrian streets around Saara (p89), where shops peddle everything from clothes and cosmetics to toys, jerseys and all the fabric and sequins you'd ever need to make your own Carnaval costume. Nearby streets offer a little of everything, including discounted record stores, used bookshops and percussion stores often set behind century-old shopfronts.

top picks

RECORD STORES

- Feira de Música (p112) During the week browse through bins of records and CDs at this open-air market in Centro.
- Modern Sound (p118) One of Brazil's largest music stores stocks an impressive selection, with lots of staff recommendations, top Rio artists and imports. Live music shows are staged here daily.
- Plano B (p122) An underground favorite among local DJs, Plano B has new and used records and CDs, as well as a tattoo parlor in the back.
- Toca do Vinícius (p115) Bossa nova's smooth grooves live on in this shop dedicated to old and new artists of the genre. Upstairs, Vinícius' fans can get a glimpse of his life's work in the small museum dedicated to him.

GRANADO Map p90 Bath Products

☎ 3231-6747; Rua Primeiro de Março 14, Centro; 8am-8pm Mon-Fri, 10am-2pm Sat

A classic-looking apothecary with a name that's been around since 1870, Granado incorporates Brazilian ingredients in its all-natural products. Favorites include the Castanha do Brasil (made from chestnuts from the Amazon) line of moisturizers, shampoos and conditioners. You'll also find bright, sweet-smelling soaps and bath gels (even for pets and babies), scented candles, perfumes, shaving products and retro-looking bags. Other locations are in Lapa (Map p98; Rua do Lavradio 32) and Leblon (Map p66; Rua General Artigas 470A).

NOVA LIVRARIA LEONARDO DA VINCI Map p90 Books

☎ 2533-2237; Av Rio Branco 185, Centro; 9am-7pm Mon-Fri, 9am-1pm Sat

With one of Rio's best foreign-language book collections, da Vinci also has a wide range of art and photography books, as well as coffee-table books about Rio's history and architecture. It's one floor down; follow the spiral ramp. There's a decent coffee shop nearby.

ARLEQUIM Map p90 Books & Music

☎ 2220-8471; Paço Imperial, Praça Quinze de Novembro 48, Centro; 9am-8pm Mon-Fri, 10am-6pm Sat

Bossa nova plays overhead at this charming café (mains R$14 to R$28), bookstore and music shop. As well as new books (including foreign-language titles), Arlequim sells CDs covering bossa, samba and other styles. Most cost between R$20 and R$30.

LIVRARIA DA TRAVESSA

Map p90 Books & Music

☎ 2505-0400; Rua Sete de Setembro 54, Centro; 9am-8pm Mon-Fri, 9am-2pm Sat

The newest branch of Livraria da Travessa is a great place to browse. There are some books in English, and an array of colorful (but pricey) coffee-table books. There's another branch (Map p90; Travessa de Ouvidor 17) around the corner and a third Centro branch (Map p90) on Ave Rio Branco 44, all with in-store café-restaurants.

TABACARIA AFRICANA

Map p90 Cigars & Tobacco

☎ 2509-5333; Largo do Paço 38, Centro; ⏲ 9am-5pm Mon-Fri

The sweet fragrance of pipe tobacco is embedded in the walls and furniture of this shop facing the Praça Quinze. Regulars sit at the table in front slowly drawing on the pick of the day while the afternoon drifts by, smoke-like. In the back, the glass jars contain a variety of flavors and aromas. Let the shopkeeper put a mix together for you.

LOJA NOVO DESENHO

Map p90 Home Decor

☎ 2524-2290; Av Infante Dom Henrique 85, Centro; ⏲ noon-6pm Tue-Fri, noon-7pm Sat & Sun

Inside Museu de Arte Moderna (p89), this 'Store of New Design' sells fanciful objects that are pure eye candy. Some of Rio's best modern designs are here (created by some of the country's best industrial designers). And you'll find whimsical two-dimensional vases, surreal clock faces and other clever works.

LIDADOR Map p90 Liquor Store & Deli

☎ 2533-4988; Rua da Assembléia 65, Centro; ⏲ 9am-8pm Mon-Fri, 9am-1pm Sat

Gleaming bottles stretch high to the ceiling of this well-stocked liquor cabinet. Founded in 1924, Lidador also sells a range of smoked meats, chocolates and imported goods. A windowless pub hidden in the back is a fine place to enjoy freshly made sandwiches.

CASA OLIVEIRA Map p90 Musical Instruments

☎ 2508-8539; Rua da Carioca 70, Centro; ⏲ 9am-7pm Mon-Fri, 9am-2pm Sat

One of several excellent music shops on Rua da Carioca, Casa Oliveira sells all the pieces that make up the rhythm section of Carnaval *baterias* (percussion sections). Unique souvenirs for the musically minded include *cavaquinos* (ukulele-sized guitars), which start at around R$150, and *pandeiros* (tambourines), starting at R$35.

BERINJELA Map p90 Music & Books

☎ 2532-3646; Av Rio Branco 185, Centro; ⏲ 9am-7pm Mon-Fri, 10am-1pm Sat

Berinjela is a fine place to hunt for old records and classic samba CDs, and there's also a selection of used books (though only a handful in English). It's hidden in a small shopping center, down a spiral ramp and just past Leonardo da Vinci bookshop.

SUB & SUB Map p90 Outdoor Gear

☎ 2509-1176; subsub.com.br; Sobreloja (2nd floor), Rua da Alfândega 98, Centro; ⏲ 10am-6pm Mon-Fri

Sub & Sub has an array of gear for outdoor adventure: climbing and mountaineering, diving, snorkeling, camping and hiking. The staff can also recommend courses for those interested in learning a new skill.

UNIMAGEM

Map p90 Photography

☎ 2221-0008; Rua dos Andradas 29, Centro; ⏲ 9am-6pm Mon-Fri, 9am-noon Sat

The choice of professional photographers in the city, Unimagem has a good selection of new and used cameras (SLRs, TLRs, point-and-shoot) as well as all the accessories (tripods, film, paper). It also runs a superb developing lab: black-and-white, color, slides and, of course, digital images. It can also provide a one-hour developing service for both slide and color film.

SANTA TERESA & LAPA

Stomping ground for Rio's bohemian crowd, Santa Teresa has a growing number of handicraft shops and vintage stores with some enticing restaurants and cafés that add to the appeal. In Lapa, you'll find Rua do Lavradio, the city's best antiques street. It's at its liveliest on the first Saturday of the month.

ANTIQUE CENTER Map p98 Antiques

☎ 3147-9014; Rua do Lavradio 28, Lapa; ⏲ 9am-6pm Mon-Fri, 9am-2pm Sat

One of Lavradio's best antique shops, this place is packed with glass- and dishware, furniture, iron kettles, lamps, oil paintings and a wide variety of other displays that make for a fascinating glimpse into the past.

FLANAR Map p98 Antiques

☎ 2507-2751; Rua do Lavradio 60, Lapa; ⏲ 9am-6pm Mon-Fri, 9am-2pm Sat

The old colonial edifice hides an intriguing selection of antiques – from tables and chairs to chandeliers, glassware, ceramics and old oil paintings. Although many objects for sale here won't fit in your suitcase, it's still a fun place to browse.

FARMERS MARKETS

The *feiras* (produce markets) that pop up in different locations throughout the week are the best places to shop for fruit and vegetables. For an authentic slice of homegrown Carioca commerce, nothing beats wandering through and taking in the action.

Cobal do Humaitá (Map p80; ☎ 2266-1343; Rua Voluntários da Pátria 446, Botafogo; 🕒 7am-4pm Mon-Sat) The city's largest farmers market sells plenty of flowers, veggies and fruits; there are also cafés and restaurants on hand for those looking for a bit more.

Cobal de Leblon (Map p66; ☎ 2239-1549; Rua Gilberto Cardoso, Leblon; 🕒 7am-4pm Mon-Sat) Smaller than Humaitá's market, the Cobal de Leblon makes a fine setting for stopping to smell the flowers – or the *maracujá* (passion fruit) – before settling down to a meal at one of the open-air restaurants.

Copacabana Markets are held Wednesday on Rua Domingos Ferreira, Thursday on Rua Belford Roxo and Rua Ronald de Carvalho, and Sunday on Rua Décio Vilares.

Glória Sunday market on Rua Augusto Severo.

Ipanema Markets are held Monday on Rua Henrique Dumont, Tuesday on Praça General Osório and Friday on Praça NS da Paz.

Jardim Botânico Saturday market on Rua Frei Leandro.

Leblon Thursday on Rua General Urquiza.

Urca Sunday on Praça Tenente Gil Guilherme.

LA VEREDA

Map p98 Handicrafts

☎ 2507-0317; Rua Almirante Alexandrino 428, Santa Teresa; 🕒 10am-8pm

On the *bonde* (tram) line near Largo do Guimarães, La Vareda stocks a colorful selection of handicrafts from local artists and artisans. Handpainted clay figurines by Pernambuco artists, heavy Minas ceramics, delicate sterling silver jewelry and loosely woven tapestries cover the interior of the old store. Other cool gift ideas: T-shirts bearing a *bonde* image, block prints by local artist Erivaldo and vibrant art-naïf canvases by various Santa artists. There are several other handicraft shops and galleries also on this street.

PLANO B

Map p98 Music & Tattoos

☎ 2509-3266; www.planob.net; Rua Francisco Muratori 2A, Lapa; 🕒 noon-8pm Mon-Fri, to 6pm Sat

Only in Lapa will you encounter a place where you can pick through bins of old jazz records and new electronic mixes before stepping into the back room to get a tattoo, inspired perhaps by that old Elza Soares song playing overhead. Plano B also has a decent selection of CDs, and the young staff can advise – if samba-funk eludes you. It also hosts DJ spin sessions some weekend nights; check the website.

GREATER RIO & BARRA DA TIJUCA

Barra da Tijuca is the kingdom of shopping malls, each offering something slightly different than the one next door – one even services its 4.8km of stores with a monorail.

CLUBE CHOCOLATE Map p60 Eclectic

☎ 3322-1223; Store 202, São Conrado Fashion Mall, Estrada da Gávea 899, São Conrado; 🕒 noon-11pm Mon-Wed, to midnight Thu-Sat, to 10pm Sun

This innovative store is not to be missed on any serious shopping itinerary. Amid a spacious, handsomely designed boutique you can browse Marc Jacobs, Prada and Paul Smith clothing and all the fashionable top Brazilian stylists. You can also have a bite at the French bistro or sample some of the latest CDs, books and gadgets.

BARRA SHOPPING Map p107 Shopping Center

☎ 4003-4131; www.barrashopping.com.br, in Portuguese; Av das Américas 4666, Barra da Tijuca; 🕒 10am-10pm Mon-Sat, 1-9pm Sun

Rio's largest mall (one of the biggest in the continent) is an easy place to shop away a few hours or days as do 30 million shoppers each year. Over 500 stores clutter this 4km-long stretch, plus five movie screens, a kids' parkland and a wealth of dining options.

RIO DESIGN CENTER

Map p107 Shopping Center

☎ **2430-3024; www.riodesign.com.br, in Portuguese; Av das Américas 7777, Barra da Tijuca;** 🕒 **10am-10pm Mon-Sat, 1-9pm Sun**

This architecturally rich center features a number of excellent home-furnishing stores selling designer lamps, vases, decorative pieces and furniture. It also has some very good restaurants and a few art galleries.

SÃO CONRADO FASHION MALL

Map p60 Shopping Center

☎ **2111-4444; www.scfashionmall.com.br, in Portuguese; Estrada da Gávea 899, São Conrado;** 🕒 **10am-10pm Mon-Sat, 3-9pm Sun**

This is not only Rio's most beautiful mall but it also features all the big international names – Armani, Versace, Louis Vuitton and others – plus all of Brazil's most recognizable designers. It's located in the posh neighborhood of São Conrado, near the Hotel Intercontinental.

VIA PARQUE SHOPPING

Map p107 Shopping Center

☎ **2421-9222; www.shoppingviaparque.com.br, in Portuguese; Av Ayrton Senna 3000, Barra da Tijuca;** 🕒 **10am-10pm Mon-Sat, 3-9pm Sun**

With 280 stores, six movie theaters and an abundance of restaurants, this shopping center is the heart of Rio's thriving consumer culture. The center also houses one of the city's big, busy and diverse concert arenas, **Citibank Hall** (p166).

EATING

top picks

What's your recommendation? www.lonelyplanet.com/rio-de-janeiro

EATING

If you haven't heard of Rio's excellent restaurants, you're in good company. Despite top-notch chefs, ethnically diverse cuisine and a rich bounty from farm, forest and sea, the city hasn't earned much of a culinary reputation abroad. Inside Brazil it's a different story, with Cariocas (residents of Rio) convinced that there's no place quite like home for sitting down to a bang-up meal – whether that entails juicy grilled steaks, coconut-flavored seafood stews or glistening slices of sashimi and plump sushi rolls.

It's easy to eat well in Rio, no matter what your budget or your dietary restrictions (although counting calories is daunting in this city of temptation). Fresh tropical fruit is the basic building block for a healthy meal. Most Cariocas start their mornings off with a stop at the local juice bar, where they can enjoy two or three dozen varieties of vitamin-filled elixirs, including Amazonian flavors such as *açaí* (juice made from an Amazonian berry), *cupuaçu* (Amazonian fruit), *carimbola* (star fruit) and others. You'll also find the best restaurants make brilliant use of passion fruit, mango and other fruits. For a bit of caffeine, Cariocas opt for a *cafézinho,* short, black, strong and often quite sweet coffee.

At lunchtime, locals favor per-kilo restaurants, which range from simple, working-class affairs to sumptuous buffets lined with fresh salads, grilled meats, pastas, seafood dishes and a table packed with desserts. Like elsewhere, dinner is often as much about socializing as it is about eating, and the city has some magical settings for lingering over a long meal. You can dine at a sidewalk café overlooking the beach, book an outdoor table at a hidden spot high up in Santa Teresa or join the din of fellow diners in a traditional old-fashioned *boteco,* which are casual, open-sided bars scattered all over town.

Variety comes in many forms in Rio – which is not surprising given the large immigrant population. Lebanese, Japanese, Spanish, German, French and Italian cuisines are among the standouts, though there's an equally broad selection of regional Brazilian restaurants. Diners can sample rich, shrimp-filled *moqueca* (seafood stew cooked in coconut milk) from Bahia or tender *carne seca* (jerked meat) covered in *farofa* (manioc flour), a staple in Minas Gerais. Daring palates can venture north into Amazonia, enjoying savory *tacacá* (manioc paste, lip-numbing leaves of the vegetable *jambu,* and dried shrimp) or *tambaqui* (a large Amazonian fish) and other meaty fishes from the mighty Amazon. Cowboys and the *gaúcho* from the south bring the city its *churrascarias,* Brazil's famous all-you-can-eat barbecue restaurants where crisply dressed waiters bring piping-hot spits of fresh roasted meats to your table. Wherever you end up, try to pace yourself. Brazilian dishes are normally quite large – and some dishes are meant for two. When in doubt, ask the server to clarify.

Cafés, patisseries and ice-cream shops are also an integral part of the Rio experience. The leafy back streets of the Zona Sul (particularly restaurant-filled Ipanema) are great places to recharge with a cappuccino, a slice of chocolate torte or a creamy scoop of *sorvete* (ice cream). Juice bars whip up grilled sandwiches, and light bites like *pão de queijo* (cheese-filled rolls), but for the best assortment of snacks, plan a meal at the neighborhood *boteco. Salgados* (bar snacks) come in many satisfying, highly addictive, (and, yes unhealthy) varieties, like *bolinhos de bacalhau* (deep-fried codfish balls), *pasteis* (crispy pastries filled with meat or cheese) or *coxinhas* (pear-shaped cornmeal balls filled with chicken).

Those who'd like to get into the cuisine scene should check out *Eat Smart in Brazil* by Joan and David Peterson. It includes an overview of Brazil's culinary heritage and regional cuisines as well as recipes and a detailed glossary.

WHERE TO EAT

Ipanema and Leblon are the best places to browse for a memorable meal. There you'll find Rio's star chefs, beautifully set dining rooms and the fashion-conscious crowds that fill them. You'll also enjoy excellent meals in assorted Copacabana restaurants – though not in the most obvious places (not in the beachside strip for example). Other gems are hidden in the streets of Jardim Botânico, high up in Santa Teresa and along the narrow pedestrian lanes in Centro. For details on top streets for mealtime browsing, see boxed text, p129.

PRACTICALITIES

Opening Hours

Aside from juice bars, cafés and bakeries, few restaurants open for breakfast (those that do start serving around 8am). Cariocas don't typically order a sit-down meal until noon, the time when most places open. Restaurants in Centro typically open only during the week and only for lunch – usually from noon until 3pm. Restaurants in the Zona Sul, with its wealth of culinary options, attract larger dinner crowds, with restaurants filling up around 9pm or so. Typically, they don't close until midnight – and a few places stay open until 3am or 4am. On weekends, lunch is often the big meal of the day – Saturday being the traditional day to linger over *feijoada* (black beans and pork stew – see p146 for the recipe).

How Much?

Rio can be light or hard on the wallet, depending on where and what you eat. Juice bars are the cheapest; you can order a *misto quente* (toasted ham and cheese sandwich) and juice for around R$12. Pay-by-weight restaurants are also good value. These eateries vary in price and quality, but average about R$40 per kilo (a fairly full plate will cost R$26).

There is a vast array of midrange dining options; expect to pay between R$20 and R$30 for a main course. *Churrascarias* (traditional barbecue restaurants) offer all-you-can-eat dining options – try to fast for at least six hours before going. Prices range from around R$50 to R$80 per person, with more food than you could possibly imagine (much less *eat*).

To experience the fruits of Rio's best chefs, head to Centro by day, where power-lunching executives enjoy masterfully prepared sushi, steak or duck confit in stately environments. By night, restaurants in Leblon and Ipanema (and a handful in Copacabana) compete for annual culinary prizes. A main course in any of these locations will cost upwards of R$45 and will have decent wine cellars that range beyond the Argentine and Chilean vintages at other places.

Booking Tables

Most restaurants accept reservations for both lunch and dinner, so call ahead to avoid a wait. Restaurants that don't accept reservations often have a bar where you can have a drink while you wait for a table.

PRICE GUIDE

The price symbols in this chapter indicate the cost of a two-course meal for one person, excluding drinks.

$$$	over R$60
$$	R$25-60
$	under R$25

Unfortunately, when you call to make a reservation, the person who answers the phone is not likely to speak English. Concierges are adept at booking seats for you, but if you're game, have a stab at Portuguese – Brazilians are usually flattered at the attempt.

Tipping

In restaurants, a 10% tip is usually included in the bill. When it isn't included – and your waiter will generally tell you if it's not – it's customary to leave 10%. If the service was exceptionally bad or good, adjust accordingly. Tipping in cafés and bars isn't common, but is always appreciated.

Groceries & Takeout

Open-air markets abound in the city. Juicy pineapples, mangos, papayas and other fruits make fine snacks for the beach. Some markets (p112) feature excellent regional cuisine – such as Ipanema's Feira Hippie on Sunday with its Bahian vendors, and the northeastern restaurants at the Feira Nordestina.

Supermarkets provide another option for self-caterers. The city's most prominent supermarket chain, Zona Sul, is prevalent throughout Ipanema, Leblon and Copacabana. Zona Sul supermarket (p135) on Rua Dias Ferreira in Leblon is the best supermarket in Rio, with imported cheeses, fresh breads, deli items and salads, and wines and spirits. Nearby is Hortifruti (p135), an indoor fruit and vegetable market. Leblon's Garcia & Rodrigues (p131), which is also a restaurant, stocks a seductive selection of French and Italian wines, cheeses and other high-end deli items. The patisserie and ice-cream counters alone warrant a visit.

Downtown, the gleaming shelves at Lidador (p121) enable commuters to stock up on smoked meats, chocolates and other delicacies before they head off to the suburbs. Per-kilo places all have takeout containers, if you're in a hurry and simply want to grab something freshly cooked; juice bars also accommodate takeout customers.

One needn't, however, even step off the sidewalks to find sustenance. Throughout town, you'll find vendors selling *agua de coco* (coconut water), available by the cup or by the liter. On the beach, you're never more than a stone's throw from drink stands; Copacabana also has shiny all-glass restaurant kiosks where you can get a full meal. Favorite drinks at these places are caipirinhas (cane liquor cocktails) or beer *agua de coco*, served straight from the coconut. If you're frolicking in the waves and can't be bothered making the trek up the beach, just wait for the food to come to you. Vendors laden with heavy bags roam the beach till sundown, offering beer, soda, *globos* (a bag of puffed chips), maté (a tea-like drink) and *sanduich natural* (sandwich filled with ricotta cheese, chicken salad or tuna salad).

IPANEMA & LEBLON

Rio's best restaurants lie in the neighborhoods of Leblon and Ipanema. Here, along the tree-lined side streets abutting the major thoroughfares, you'll find a mix of trendy eateries, outdoor cafés and juice bars. Price and quality generally run high here, though the stylish new flavor of the month doesn't always live up to the hype.

GALANI

Map p64 Brazilian $$$

☎ 2525-2525; Av Vieira Souto 460, Ipanema; feijoada buffet R$79; ⌚ noon-4:30pm

On the top floor of the Caesar Park Hotel on Saturday, you'll find one of Rio's best *feijoadas*. The decadent pork and black bean recipe comes beautifully prepared, without a lot of extra fat, and you can sample nearly a dozen varieties of pork dishes. The view is spectacular.

FASANO AL MARE Map p64 Seafood $$$

☎ 3202-4000; Av Vieira Souto 80, Ipanema; mains R$70-95; ⌚ noon-3:30pm & 7pm-1am

Under the helm of award-winning Italian chef Luca Gozzani, the lavish Fasano Al Mare serves excellent seafood dishes. Top picks include risotto with saffron and rock lobster, seared tuna and whole fish baked in salt. Reservations are essential.

CELEIRO Map p66 Salads $$$

☎ 2274-7843; Rua Dias Ferreira 199, Leblon; per kg R$77; ⌚ 10am-6pm Mon-Sat

This casual spot on one of Leblon's main restaurant strips packs crowds in during lunchtime. Celeiro is famed for its organic salads and roasted vegetables, though the small eatery serves excellent soups, pastries and quiches. Get there early to avoid the rush.

BAZZAR Map p64 Eclectic $$$

☎ 3202-2884; Rua Barão da Torre 538, Ipanema; mains R$50-60; ⌚ noon-midnight Mon-Thu, to 2am Fri & Sat, 10am-6pm Sun

Set on a peaceful tree-lined street, this nicely designed restaurant serves a wide variety of cuisine, making it a good spot if you're not sure what you're in the mood for, but want something dazzling. Top choices are grilled *namorado* with whole-grain rice, citrus and pesto; pumpkin risotto; and lamb with red wine sauce and sweet potatoes. There's a smaller branch hidden on the 2nd floor of Ipanema's Livraria da Travessa (Map p64; ☎ 2249-4977; Rua Visconde de Pirajá 572, Ipanema).

AZUL MARINHO Map p64 Seafood $$

☎ 2513-5014; Av Francisco Bhering, Praia do Arpoador, Ipanema; mains for 2 people R$65-85; ⌚ noon-midnight

Below the Arpoador Inn, Azul Marinho serves an assortment of tasty seafood

COOK IN RIO

At long last, travelers finally have the opportunity to take a locally run cooking course, Cook in Rio (☎ 8761-3653; www.cookinrio.com; Rua Ronald Carvalho 154, Copacabana). Run by Simone Theisen, who was the head chef and creator of the restaurant Fogo Carioca (now a bar), Cook in Rio teaches aspiring chefs how to make some of Brazil's most famous dishes. Each one-day class runs from 11am to 4pm and includes the preparation of either *moqueca* (seafood stew) or *feijoada completa* (multi-dish black bean and pork stew). You'll also learn how to make other sides and drinks including *aipim frito* (fried cassava slices), a perfect pot of rice, dessert and a masterful caipirinha (the secret is in the slicing of the lime). The best part is that you'll get to devour your creations afterwards. Courses cost R$120 per person and include the cost of all food and drinks.

dishes, and the outdoor tables facing the ocean have the best beachside setting you'll find in the Zona Sul (there's no traffic between you and the sea, only sand). Try one of the *moquecas* (seafood stew), the octopus vinaigrette salad or the famous whole fish baked in salt.

ESPAÇO BRASA LEBLON

Map p66 Churrascaria $$

☎ 2111-5700; Av Afrânio de Melo Franco 131, Leblon; all-you-can-eat R$55-65; ⏲ noon-1am
One of Rio's top *churrascarias,* Espaço Brasa features nearly 30 different types of meat as well as sushi, seafood and salads. The beautifully presented all-you-can-eat buffet is set in a dining room with tall ceilings and elegant table settings.

CASA DA FEIJOADA Map p64 Feijoada $$

☎ 2247-2776; Rua Prudente de Morais 10B, Ipanema; feijoada R$55; ⏲ noon-midnight
Admirers of Brazil's iconic *feijoada* (black beans and pork stew) needn't wait until Saturday to experience the meaty meal. The casual Casa da Feijoada serves the rich black-bean and salted-pork dish every day of the week. It comes with the requisite orange slices, *farofa* and grated kale (cabbage), and goes nicely with a caipirinha.

RÁSCAL Map p66 Italian $$

☎ 2259-6437; Shopping Leblon, Av Afrânio de Melo Franco 290, Leblon; all-you-can-eat R$47-52
This popular São Paulo chain arrived in Rio a few years back and quickly earned top marks for its fantastic buffet. The huge spread of Italian cuisine includes salads, bruschetta, pizzas, pastas (six different kinds) and a few juicy grill choices.

ZUKA Map p66 Eclectic $$

☎ 2249-7550; Rua Dias Ferreira 233, Leblon; mains R$45-80; ⏲ 7pm-1am Mon, noon-4pm & 7pm-1am Tue-Fri, 1pm-1am Sat & Sun
One of Rio's best restaurants, Zuka prepares delectable mouthwatering cuisine – zingy ceviche or the confection-like delicacy of Zuka's original foie gras to start, followed by rack of lamb with passion fruit, grilled fish of the day with *mandoquinha* (a kind of sweet root vegetable) purée, seared tuna over heart-of-palm tagliatelle and many other imaginative dishes. All the grilling action happens at the open kitchen to the right (you can sit at the counter and watch the chefs in action), and the cocktails (particularly the lychee saketinis) and desserts are excellent.

top picks

EAT STREETS

- **Rua Barão da Torre, Ipanema** This long, tree-lined street has stylish, time-tested favorites.
- **Rua Dias Ferreira, Leblon** A great street for serious culinary browsing, it is packed with award-winning eateries and ever-daring newcomers.
- **Rua Garcia D'Ávila, Ipanema** One of Ipanema's poshest locales, this is a choice destination for a light meal after window-shopping. Neighboring Rua Aníbal de Mendonça is the runner-up.
- **Rua Almirante Alexandrino, Santa Teresa** Perhaps Rio's most picturesque eat street, this one is lined with colorful restaurants offering sushi, Bahian cuisine, Amazonian cuisine and everything in between.
- **Rua do Rosário, Centro** The eastern end of this old cobblestone street has an enticing selection of sidewalk cafés and bistros.

TEN KAI Map p64 Japanese $$

☎ 2540-5100; Rua Prudente de Morais 1810, Ipanema; mains R$40-80; ⏲ 7pm-1am Mon-Fri, 1pm-midnight Sat & Sun
In the top tier of the city's Japanese restaurants, Ten Kai serves mouthwatering sashimi and sushi, and maintains the strong culinary traditions of the East. The ambience is pure charm, with an interior lit by glowing paper lanterns.

FRONTERA Map p64 Self-Serve $$

☎ 3289-2350; Rua Visconde de Pirajá 128, Ipanema; per kg R$42-46; ⏲ 11:30am-11pm
Run by a Dutch chef, Frontera offers more than 60 plates at its delectable lunch buffet, featuring a mouthwatering assortment of grilled meats, baked casseroles, and seafood pastas, plus salads, fresh fruits, grilled vegetables and desserts. If you're famished, opt for the all-you-can-eat price (R$36 to R$39). Dark woods and vintage prints give the place a cozier feel than most per-kilo places.

SUSHI LEBLON Map p66 Japanese $$

☎ 2512-7830; Rua Dias Ferreira 256, Leblon; mains R$40-50; ⏲ noon-4pm & 7pm-1:30am Mon-Sat, 1pm-midnight Sun
Leblon's top sushi destination boasts a Zen-like ambience with a handsome dark-wood

sushi counter setting the stage for succulent cuisine. In addition to sashimi and sushi, you'll find grilled *namorado* (a type of perch) with passion fruit *farofa*, sea-urchin ceviche and refreshing sake to complement the meal.

CAPRICCIOSA Map p64 Pizzeria $$

☎ 2523-3394; Rua Vinícius de Moraes 134, Ipanema; small/large pizzas from R$36/45; 6pm-1am

Inside this trendy high-end pizzeria, you'll find tasty thin-crust pizzas made with fresh ingredients. The price is high, but the chefs – working in an open kitchen next to the brick oven – are at least generous with the toppings. Among many flavorful combinations is the signature *capricciosa* (ham, bacon, an egg, artichoke hearts and mushrooms).

BENKEI Map p64 Japanese $$

☎ 2540-4829; Av Henrique Dumont 71, Ipanema; all-you-can-eat R$36-48; noon-4pm Tue-Sun, 7pm-midnight daily

This casual Japanese restaurant is a favorite haunt for after-the-beach meals on weekends. Benkei does have a menu, though nearly everyone here comes for the all-you-can-eat sushi buffet, with a wide variety of rolls and sashimi, plus miso soup. You can dine on the small front patio or in the cooler, dining room inside.

NIK SUSHI Map p64 Japanese $$

☎ 2512-6446; Rua Garcia D'Ávila 83, Ipanema; all-you-can-eat lunch R$35, dinner R$45-55; 11:30am-midnight Tue-Sat, 1-11pm Sun

This simple but stylish Japanese restaurant has earned many loyal customers for its all-you-can-eat sushi lunches and dinners. You'll find traditional sushi and sashimi plates as well as creative inventions such as *salmão Ipanema* (lightly grilled salmon with teriyaki and farofa).

FELLINI Map p66 Self-Serve $$

☎ 2511-3600; Rua General Urquiza 104, Leblon; per kg R$46-53; 11:30am-4pm & 7:30pm-midnight

One of Leblon's top buffet restaurants, Fellini has an enticing selection of dishes: salads, pastas, grilled fish and shrimp, a sushi counter and the hallowed roast-meat counter. The modest dining room attracts a mix of hungry patrons – tourists, neighborhood folk and the beautiful crowd included.

PLATAFORMA Map p66 Churrascaria $$

☎ 2274-4022; Rua Adalberto Ferreira 32, Leblon; mains R$35-62; noon-midnight

This well-known *churrascaria* still draws a garrulous mix of politicians, artists and tourists. Dark, mellow woods in the dining room match the tones of the roast meats traveling from table to table. Also in this complex is the Plataforma Show – the over-the-top touristy Carnaval spectacle (headdresses, sequins and lots of skin).

GOURMET PRAIA Map p64 Eclectic $$$

☎ 2267-8790; Av Vieira Souto 234, Ipanema; mains R$35-50; noon-5pm Tue-Sun, 8pm-midnight Tue-Sat

In a converted villa facing the beach, Gourmet Praia spreads a tasty lunch buffet of market-fresh salads and antipasti, plus a daily special (not cheap at R$65 per person). At dinner the a la carte menu includes tilapia filet with heart of palm and pine nuts, risottos and grilled dishes. The dining room overlooks an open kitchen and leads back into a hidden garden, a charming setting for a meal.

ALESSANDRO E FEDERICO Map p64 Pizzeria $$

☎ 2522-5414; Rua Garcia D'Ávila 151, Ipanema; small pizzas R35-40; 6pm-1am

Dominated by the wood-burning oven at center stage, this stylish two-story restaurant serves some of Ipanema's best thin-crust pizzas. A more casual Alessandro e Federico (☎ 2521-0828; Rua Garcia D'Ávila 134; 9am-1am) further south on the same street has a menu of freshly made panini, salads and pastas (but no pizza), with sidewalk seating.

NEW NATURAL Map p64 Vegetarian $$

☎ 2287-0301; Rua Barão da Torre 167, Ipanema; per kg R$36-39; 8am-10pm

Featuring an excellent vegetarian lunch buffet, New Natural was the first health-food restaurant in the neighborhood. Fill up on fresh pots of soup, rice, veggies and beans at the healthy buffet.

NAM THAI Map p66 Thai $$

☎ 2259-2962; Rua Rainha Guilhermina 95B, Leblon; mains R$30-52; 7pm-1am Mon, noon-4pm & 7pm-1am Tue-Fri, noon-1am Sat, to 11pm Sun

Thai cuisine is a rarity in Rio, which makes charming Nam Thai even more of a star.

The French colonial interior is a cozy setting for the eclectic Thai cooking. Favorites are the squid salad and spicy shrimp curry with pineapple. No less intoxicating are Nam Thai's tropical drinks, such as the *caipivodca de lychee* (lychee vodka caipirinha).

ZAZÁ BISTRÔ TROPICAL

Map p64 Contemporary $$

☎ 2247-9101; Rua Joana Angélica 40, Ipanema; mains R$30-50; 🕑 7:30pm-midnight Sun-Wed, to 1:30am Fri & Sat

Inside an art-filled and whimsically decorated converted house, Zazá serves satisfying dishes with Eastern accents, and uses organic ingredients when possible. Two favorites: curry chicken with coconut milk and basmati rice; and semi-raw tuna with vegetables, grilled shrimp and passion fruit sauce. Upstairs, diners lounge on throw pillows, while candles glow along the walls. You can also sit at one of the tables on the front.

GULA GULA

Map p64 Brazilian $$

☎ 2259-3084; Rua Henrique Dumont 87A, Ipanema; mains around R$30; 🕑 noon-midnight

In a cozy villa on Ipanema's western edge, Gula Gula remains one Ipanema's culinary favorites – which means a lot in a neighborhood ever in search of the new. Grilled meats are tops at this casual spot, but those in search of something lighter can opt for quiches and salads. Gula Gula is also in Centro (Map p90; ☎ 3852-1174; Rua Primeiro de Março 23A) and Leblon (Map p66; ☎ 2284-8792; Rua Rita Ludolf 87A) among other places.

GARCIA & RODRIGUES

Map p66 French $$

☎ 3206-4100; Av Ataúlfo de Paiva 1251, Leblon; mains R$28-50; 🕑 8am-midnight Sun-Thu, to 1am Fri & Sat

Garcia & Rodrigues serves changing daily specials (like bouillabaisse or duck breast with figs and pears) to admiring Francophiles. Its two floors provide an elegant if somewhat sedate dining experience, though the café in front attracts a livelier crowd who come for appetizers, sandwiches and desserts. The glass counters surrounding the tiled floor contain breads, cheeses, smoked meats, desserts and Italian-style ice cream.

JUICE CO Map p66 Eclectic $$

☎ 2294-0048; Av General San Martin 889, Leblon; mains R$24-54; 🕑 6pm-midnight Mon-Fri, noon-midnight Sat & Sun

This stylish two-story restaurant serves much more than just tasty, freshly squeezed juices. In an überdesigned loungelike setting, you can sample a wide range of fare – foccacia sandwiches, salads, risottos, grilled fish and roast meats, any of which can be paired nicely with one of 60 juice concoctions.

VIA SETE Map p64 Eclectic $$

☎ 2512-8100; Rua Garcia D'Ávila 125, Ipanema; mains R$26-42; 🕑 noon-midnight

This restaurant on upscale Garcia D'Ávila serves a good selection of salads and grilled vegetable wraps, as well as heartier fare like grilled tuna and a high-end steak burger. Best of all, Via Sete uses 100% organic ingredients (beef included). The pleasant front-side patio is a prime spot for sipping tropical cocktails while practicing the discreet art of people-watching.

GAROTA DE IPANEMA Map p64 Brazilian $$

☎ 2523-3787; Rua Vinícius de Moraes, Ipanema; mains R$25-40 🕑 noon-2am

A mix of tourists and neighborhood regulars pack the tables at the former bar where Tom Jobim and Vinícius de Moraes once held court. Although the food is fairly standard Brazilian fare, one dish stands out – the *picanha Brasileira* (R$65 for two), a scrumptious skillet of sliced sirloin brought sizzling to your table. Wash it down with a few glasses of ice-cold *chope* (draft beer) and you'll realize why Garotas have been springing up all over the city.

DOS & DON'TS

Brazilians are casual about many things. Table manners are not one of them. Where possible, avoid eating with your hands – middle-class Brazilians often eat sandwiches with a knife and fork, and no one eats pizza with their hands. If you dine in someone's home, bring a small gift such as wine or flowers – or win permanent friends with a liter of duty-free whiskey.

Smoking is no longer acceptable in restaurants or bars. But Brazilians love their cell phones – you can make or receive a quick call on any occasion except the most formal.

BRASILEIRINHO Map p64 Brazilian $$

☎ 2513-5184; Rua Jangadeiros 10, Ipanema; mains R$24-42; ⏰ noon-2am

Facing Praça General Osório, this rustically decorated restaurant serves good, traditional Mineiro cuisine. Favorites include *tutu a mineira* (mashed black beans with manioc), *carne seca* and picanha (rump steak). The *feijoada* (black bean and pork) here is tops – not surprising given that Brasileirinho is run by the same owner as the nearby Casa da Feijoada.

ARTIGIANO Map p64 Italian $$

☎ 2512-6107; Av Epitácio Pessoa 204, Ipanema; mains R$22-35; ⏰ 6:30pm-midnight Mon-Sat, noon-midnight Sun

Overlooking the Jardim de Alah, Artigiano is set in a picturesque villa with more than a hint of the old-world about it. Here, you will find an older, well-dressed crowd enjoying classic Italian fare, including some 20 superb varieties of handmade pasta amid the oil paintings and antique furnishings.

DOCE DELÍCIA

Map p66 Brazilian $$

☎ 2249-2970; Rua Dias Ferreira 48, Leblon; mains R$15-30; ⏰ noon-11pm

Doce Delícia has a small but loyal following that is sold on the restaurant's innovative Eastern design concept. Restaurant-goers create their own salads from over 40 ingredients on the menu. Feeling daring? Go for the pumpkin, jerked meat and leeks. The only limit is your imagination, *cara*. There's another branch in Ipanema (Map p64; ☎ 2259-0239; Rua Aníbal de Mendonça 55, Ipanema; ⏰ noon-11pm).

FELICE CAFFÈ & GELATERIA

Map p64 Café $$

☎ 2522-7749; Rua Gomes Carneiro 30, Ipanema; mains R$18-40; ⏰ noon-midnight Mon-Fri, 10am-midnight Sat & Sun

Half a block from the beach, Felice has a small shaded front terrace for taking in the passing people parade. Head inside for air-conditioned splendor, where locals and travelers enjoy gourmet sandwiches (grilled veggies, steak, thick burgers), juicy grilled dishes, bountiful salads, and, most importantly, rich Italian-style ice cream (R$9.25 for two scoops), pulled from the highly enticing display counter in front.

VEGETARIANO SOCIAL CLUB

Map p66 Vegetarian $

☎ 2294-5200; Rua Conde Bernadotte 26L, Leblon; lunch buffet R$20-22; ⏰ noon-midnight Mon-Sat, noon-5:30pm Sun

Vegetarians interested in sampling Brazil's signature dish should visit this small charmer on Sunday when tofu *feijoada* is served. At other times, VSC serves a small (10-dish) lunch buffet, while the more elaborate evening a la carte menu features risottos, yakisoba, heart-of-palm stroganoff and other inventive dishes.

CAFÉ SEVERINO Map p66 Café $

☎ 2239-9398; Rua Dias Ferreira 417, Leblon; mains R$16-26; ⏰ 9am-midnight Mon-Sat, 10am-midnight Sun

In the back of the Argumento bookshop (p111), this charming café is a cozy place to hide away with a book or a new friend. In addition to coffees and lighter fare – sandwiches, salads and desserts – it's justly famed for its tasty crepes (try the salmon with Gruyère).

AMAZÔNIA SOUL Map p64 Amazonian

☎ 2247-1028; Rua Teixeira de Melo 37, Ipanema; light meals R$14-18; ⏰ 9am-9pm

This tiny new café doles out small plates of *caranguejo* (crab meat), *vatapá* (a puree of manioc, dried shrimp, coconut and dendê oil) and *tacacá* a complicated soup made of tapioca, shrimp and manioc root. You can also sample juices and ice creams made from Amazonian fruits. The small shop inside sells handicrafts and edible items from the Amazon.

GALETO DO LEBLON Map p66 Brazilian $

☎ 2294-3997; Rua Dias Ferreira 154, Leblon; mains R$10-24; ⏰ 11am-2am

One of the pioneers on this street, Galeto do Leblon has been around for over 35 years. Although a recent renovation has created an airy, modern feel, with floor-to-ceiling glass windows, Galeto still serves the traditional Brazilian dishes that have made it such a neighborhood favorite over the years. On Saturday, stop in for excellent *feijoada* (R$46 for two).

TALHO CAPIXABA Map p66 Sandwiches $

☎ 2512-8760; Av Ataúlfo de Paiva 1022, Leblon; sandwiches around R$12-24; ⏰ 8am-10pm

This tiny deli and gourmet grocer is one of the city's best spots to put together a takeout meal. In addition to pastas, salads and antipasti, you'll find excellent sandwiches (charged by weight) made from quality ingredients. Dine inside or at the sidewalk tables in front.

BLUE AGAVE Map p64 Tex-Mex $

☎ 3592-9271; Rua Vinícius de Moraes 68, Ipanema; burritos R$12-16; noon-2am

A Tex-Mex place in Rio? A sure sign that times are a-changing, this is a small, well-placed bar and restaurant where you can get good California-style burritos, huge plates of nachos and steaming baked enchiladas. TVs over the bar show the latest football games or perhaps auto-racing on ESPN. Arrive early for a shaded table on the sidewalk.

CAFEÍNA Map p64 Café $

☎ 2521-2194; Rua Farme de Amoedo 43, Ipanema; sandwiches R$12-24; 8am-11:30pm

In the heart of Ipanema, this inviting café (and its sidewalk tables) is a fine spot for having a cup of java while watching the city stroll by. You'll also find freshly made sandwiches, flavorful salads, quiche and some very rich desserts.

DELÍRIO TROPICAL Map p64 Salads $

☎ 3624-8164; Rua Garcia D'Ávila 48, Ipanema; salads R$12-18; 9am-9pm

Famed for its salads, Delírio Tropical serves 16 varieties each day, along with a few soups and hot dishes (veggie burgers, grilled salmon) if you're famished. The open layout has a pleasant, casual feeling and there are two stories with big windows overlooking the street.

BIBI CREPES Map p66 Creperie $

☎ 2259-4948; Rua Cupertino Durão 81, Leblon; crepes R$11-16; noon-1am

This small, open-sided restaurant attracts a young, garrulous crowd who enjoy the more than two dozen sweet and savory crepes available, as well as design-your-own salads (chose from 40 different toppings). Come early to beat the lunch crowds. Bibi Crepes also has a branch in Copacabana (p140).

FONTES Map p64 Vegetarian $

☎ 2512-5900; Rua Visconde de Pirajá 605D, Ipanema; mains R$6-17; 11am-10pm Mon-Sat, noon-8pm Sun

Hidden in a nondescript shopping plaza, this tiny, low-key restaurant is worth seeking out if you're after a decent vegetarian meal. The menu changes daily but features shiitake-filled manioc pastries, green salads, roasted eggplant and the like. On Saturday, the rich, smoked-tofu *feijoada* always draws a crowd.

YALLA Map p66 Middle Eastern $

☎ 2275-4395; Rua Dias Ferreira 45, Leblon; snacks R$8-12; 11:30am until late

One of the few non-fancy options on this culinary street, Yalla is a small, quick-serving restaurant where you can pick up fresh tabouli or couscous salads, sandwiches on lavash bread (Shawarma, falafel, shish kebab) or pasties filled with ricotta, beef or spinach. Don't miss baklava for dessert.

KONI STORE Map p64 Japanese $

☎ 2521-9348; Rua Maria Quitéria 77, Ipanema; hand roll R$7-10; 11am-3am Sun-Wed, to 6am Thu-Sat

With over a dozen branches in Rio, the Koni craze shows no sign of abating. The recipe is simple – *temaki* (a seaweed hand roll) stuffed with salmon, tuna, shrimp, roast beef or a combination – which can then be devoured at one of the tiny bistro tables. It's stylish, tasty and cheap – a few reasons why you'll have to wait in line among club kids for a roll at 4am on a Friday night. Other branches: Ipanema (Map p64; Rua Farme de Amoedo 75); Leblon (Map p66; Av Ataulfo de Paiva 1174); Copacabana (Map p76; Rua Constante Ramos 44).

GALITOS GRILL Map p64 Roast Chicken $

☎ 2287-7864; Rua Farme de Amoedo 62; mains R$10-20; noon-10pm

A handy spot in the neighborhood is this open-sided purveyor of roast chicken. Grab a seat at the counter and enjoy inexpensive nicely seasoned lunch specials (around R$10), whipped up in a hurry.

LAFFA Map p64 Middle Eastern $

☎ 2522-5888; Rua Visconde de Pirajá 175, Ipanema; sandwich small/large R$9/14; 11:30am until late

A new hit on the street food scene, this is a lively little eatery where harried staff whip up satisfying, piping hot grilled lamb or turkey shawarmas, falafel sandwiches or slightly more exotic inventions like strawberry and Nutella wraps – all of which are served on laffa bread, made fresh with each order.

CHAIKA Map p64 Fast Food $

☎ 2267-3838; Rua Visconde de Pirajá 321, Ipanema; mains R$8-27; 9am-1am

One of Ipanema's classics, this bustling restaurant features a stand-up bar in front for quickly devoured hamburgers, pastries and sodas. Tables in back offer a bigger menu (700 items!) – *panini* (bread), salads and pancakes – and the staff will still bring your selection to you in a hurry.

PRIMA BRUSCHETTERIA Map p66 Café $

☎ 2222-2222; Rua Rainha Guilhermina 95, Leblon; bruschetta R$5-8; noon-midnight

There was quite a buzz surrounding this stylish snacking and drinking spot when it opened in 2010. Prima showcases an Italian delicacy not often seen in these parts, with imaginative ingredients like artichokes, gorgonzola, olive tapenade, Prosciutto, smoked salmon and even caviar appearing atop its char-grilled bread. You'll also find fresh salads, antipasto plates and four types of risotto.

UNIVERSO ORGÂNICO Map p66 Vegetarian $

☎ 3874-0186; store 105, Rua Conde Bernadotte 26, Leblon; juices R$7; 8am-7pm Mon, to 9:30pm Tue-Sat, 11am-8pm Sun

In the back of a small shopping center, Universo Orgânico whips up delicious fruit and veggie shakes – like the carrot, ginger, apple and linseed combo – best enjoyed with a veggie burger or savory non-meat *salgados*. The small grocery store sells organic goodies.

MIL FRUTAS Map p64 Ice Cream $

☎ 2521-1384; Rua Garcia D'Ávila 134A, Ipanema; 1/2 scoops R$8/14; 10:30am-1am Mon-Fri, 9:30am-1am Sat & Sun

On chic Rua Garcia D'Ávila, Mil Frutas serves ice cream that showcases fruits from the Amazon and abroad. *Jaca* (jackfruit), lychee and *açaí* are among the several dozen varieties. There's another branch in Jardim Botânico (Map p70; ☎ 2511-2550; Rua JJ Seabra).

ENVÍDIA Map p66 Café $

☎ 2512-1313; Rua Dias Ferreira 45, Leblon; desserts R$6-10; 11am-8pm

Step into this elegant café for heavenly chocolates, ice cream, cakes, teas and coffees. The setting is a cozy escape from the city with its old-fashioned tile floors, dainty chairs and tables, and broad pieces of artwork decorating the walls.

VEZPA PIZZERIA Map p66 Café $

☎ 2540-0800; Av Ataúlfo de Paiva 1063, Leblon; slice R$5-8; noon-4am

Vezpa is a New York-style place, with brick walls and high ceilings, where you can order pizza by the slice. The crusts are thick and crunchy and there are more than a dozen varieties typically on hand (Bufala Vezpa, with sun-dried tomatoes with mozzarella and a spicy sauce is a recent favorite).

ARMAZÉM DO CAFÉ Map p66 Café $

☎ 2259-0170; Rua Rita Ludolf 87B, Leblon; snacks R$4-9; 9am-midnight Sun-Thu to 1am Fri & Sat

Dark-wood furnishings and the fresh-ground coffee aroma lend an authenticity to this Leblon coffeehouse. Connoisseurs rate the aromatic roasts much higher here than neighboring Cafeína. It also serves waffles, snacks and desserts.

SORVETE BRASIL Map p64 Ice Cream $

☎ 2247-8404; Rua Maria Quitéria 74C, Ipanema; ice cream per scoop R$6-6.50; 10am-10pm

A delightful pit stop on a sunny day in Ipanema, Sorvete Brasil scoops up more than 50 different ice-cream flavors including Amazonian *cupuaçu,* lychee, star fruit and guava.

YOGOBERRY Map p64 Frozen Yogurt $

☎ 3281-1512; Rua Visconde de Pirajá 282, Ipanema; small/medium yogurt R$6/8; 10am-10pm

The low-fat frozen yogurt craze officially arrived in Rio with the opening of this place back in 2007. Since then many imitators have come along, though aficionados still say Yogoberry is tops. It comes in just two flavors: *natural* (plain) and *chá verde* (green tea), but the fresh fruit toppings – melon, peach, strawberry – turn it into a delicacy.

BIBI SUCOS Map p66 Juice Bar $

☎ 2259-4298; Av Ataúlfo de Paiva 591, Leblon; juice R$4-6; 8am-2am

Among Rio's countless juice bars, Bibi Sucos is a longstanding favorite. Here you'll find over 40 different varieties, and a never-ending supply of the favorite *açaí*. Sandwiches will quell greater hunger pangs.

EMPÓRIO ARABE

Map p66 Middle Eastern $

☎ 2512-7373; Av Ataúlfo de Paiva 370, Leblon; savory pies R$3-4; ⏲ 9am-8pm Mon-Sat

There are only a few tables inside this tiny restaurant in Leblon, but most people stop by just long enough to down a quick bite from the counter facing the sidewalk. *Esfirras* (triangular pies), filled with chicken, spinach or ricotta, make for a speedy snack on your way back from the beach.

POLIS SUCOS

Map p64 Juice Bar $

☎ 2247-2518; Rua Maria Quitéria 70, Ipanema; juices R$3-6; ⏲ 7am-midnight Sun-Thu, to 2am Fri & Sat

One of Ipanema's favorite spots for a dose of fresh-squeezed vitamins, this juice bar facing the Praça NS de Paz has dozens of flavors, and you can pair those tangy beverages with sandwiches or *pão de queijo*.

LA VERONESE Map p64 Pizzeria $

☎ 2247-3152; Rua Visconde Pirajá 29, Ipanema; mini pizzas R$3; ⏲ 9am-7pm Tue-Fri, 9am-6pm Sat, 9am-2:30pm Sun

You'll have to stand as there's no place to sit, but this charming snack spot is worth the extra trouble: R$3 mini pizzas with crispy crusts are heated on the spot and make a great snack (or have two and make a meal of it). *Palmieres* (palm-shaped cookies) make a nice dessert.

ZONA SUL SUPERMARKET

Map p66 Supermarket

☎ 2259-4699; Rua Dias Ferreira 290, Leblon; ⏲ 24hr Mon-Sat, 7am-midnight Sun

A Rio institution for nearly 50 years, Zona Sul supermarket has branches all over the city. The one in Leblon is the best of the bunch, with fresh-baked breads, imported cheeses and olives, wines, cured meats and other items. The adjoining pizza and lasagna counter serves decent plates. A handy Ipanema branch (Map p64; Rua Prudente de Morais 49) is near Praça General Osório.

HORTIFRUTI Map p66 Supermarket

☎ 2586-7000; Rua Dias Ferreira 57, Leblon; ⏲ 8am-8pm Mon-Sat, to 2pm Sun

This popular grocer and produce market sells a wide variety of fruits and vegetables, plus fresh juices and all the supermarket essentials.

GÁVEA, JARDIM BOTÂNICO & LAGOA

The open-air restaurants around the peaceful Lagoa Rodrigo de Freitas are big draws here. On warm evenings music fills the air as diners eat, drink and enjoy the views across the water. The hot spots for drinking and dining are at the Parque dos Patins on the west side (where some places host live music) and Parque do Cantagalo on the east side.

Gávea has a few dining and drinking spots around Praça Santos Dumont, while Jardim Botânico's thickest concentration of eateries is on Rua JJ Seabra and Rua Pacheco Leão.

OLYMPE Map p70 Eclectic $$$

☎ 2539-4542; Rua Custódio Serrão 62, Lagoa; mains R$53-93; ⏲ 7:30pm-midnight Mon-Sat, noon-4pm Fri

One of Rio's best chefs, Claude Troisgros dazzles guests with unforgettable meals at his award-winning restaurant. Originally from France, Troisgros mixes the old world with the new in dishes like heart-of-palm salad with fresh octopus and red snapper covered with foie gras and asparagus tempura. Set in a lovely house on a quiet tree-lined street.

ESCOLA DO PÃO Map p70 Bistrô $$

☎ 2294-0027; Rua General Garzon 10, Jardim Botânico; brunch R$58; ⏲ 9am-1pm Sat & Sun

In a converted colonial mansion, this beautifully decorated restaurant serves a weekend brunch, the highlights of which are the tasty fresh-baked breads and pastries.

BRÁZ Map p70 Pizzeria $$

☎ 2535-0687; Rua Maria Angélica 129, Jardim Botânico; medium/large pizzas around R$48/53; ⏲ 7pm-midnight Sun-Thu, to 1:30am Fri & Sat

The much-touted pizzeria from São Paulo won a huge Carioca following after it opened in Rio in 2007. Perfect crusts and super-fresh ingredients are two of the components that make Braz the best pizza place in town. This is no secret, so arrive early and plan on having a few quiet *chopes* on the front patio before scoring that table.

GUIMAS Map p70 Eclectic $$

☎ 2259-7996; Rua José Roberto Macedo Soares 5, Gávea; mains R$36-50; ⏲ noon-1am

A classic Carioca *boteco* with a creative flair, Guimas has been going strong for over 20 years. Winning dishes include the *bacalhau à bras* (codfish mixed with potatoes, eggs and onions), shrimp risotto and the juicy *picanha no sal grosso* (grilled rumpsteak). There's outdoor seating in front.

GUY RESTAURANTE
Map p70 Contemporary $$

☎ 3624-8252; Rua Fonte de Saudade 187, Lagoa; mains R$30-40; 🕑 11:30am-11pm Mon-Fri, 9am-midnight Sat, 9am-9pm Sun

In a freestanding house in Lagoa, this restaurant and patisserie has a wrap-around porch (and an attractive upstairs dining room), where patrons enjoy quiches, salads, desserts or heartier pastas, risottos, grilled fish and meat dishes.

00 (ZERO ZERO) Map p70 Contemporary $$

☎ 2540-8041; Planetário da Gávea, Av Padre Leonel Franca 240, Gávea; mains from R$30; 🕑 8:30pm-3:30am Wed-Sun

Housed in Gávea's planetarium, 00 is a sleek restaurant-lounge that serves a wide mix of world cuisine. Poached haddock with Hollandaise sauce, grilled filet mignon, a full sushi counter, gourmet sandwiches and well mixed cocktails are best enjoyed on the open-air veranda. After dinner, have a few cocktails and stick around: some of Rio's best DJs spin at parties here (p166).

ARAB DA LAGOA Map p70 Middle Eastern $$

☎ 2540-0747; Parque dos Patins, Av Borges de Medeiros, Lagoa; platter for 2 R$48; 🕑 10am-1am Sun-Thu, to 2:30am Fri & Sat

One of the lake's most popular outdoor restaurants, serving traditional Middle Eastern specialties such as hummus, baba ghanoush, tabbouleh, kibbe and tasty thin-crust pizzas. The large platters for two or more are good for sampling the tasty varieties. During the day, it's a peaceful refuge from the city, while at night you can hear live samba, *choro* (romantic, intimate samba) or jazz from 9pm (cover charge is R$6).

BRASEIRO DA GÁVEA Map p70 Brazilian $$

☎ 2239-7494; Praça Santos Dumont 116, Gávea; mains R$18-30; 🕑 noon-1am Mon-Thu, to 3am Fri & Sat

This family-style eatery serves large portions of its popular steak with *farofa,* pot roast or fried chicken. On weekends, the open-air spot fills with the din of conversation and the aroma of freshly poured *chope* drifting by. As the evening wanes, a younger crowd takes over, drinking late into the night.

CAFÉ DU LAGE Map p70 Café $

☎ 2226-8125; off Rua Jardim Botânico 414, Jardim Botânico; light lunch R$8-16; 🕑 9am-10:30pm Mon-Fri, 9am-5pm Sat & Sun

Inside the lush Parque Lage, this beautifully sited café serves tasty soups, sandwiches, salads, quiches, desserts and other light fare. On weekends it's a popular gathering spot for young families who come for the brunch (R$17), which features fresh breads and jams, fruits, juices and the like.

COPACABANA & LEME

Rio's most visited neighborhood has an enormous variety of restaurants, from award-winning dining rooms to charming old bistros from the 1950s, as well as creperies, *churrascarias,* sushi bars and other ethnic haunts. In general, you will encounter less experimentation here, but if you're looking for excellent traditional cuisine – both Brazilian and international – you will find plenty of delectable options in Copacabana.

The restaurant strip along Av Atlântica has fine views of the seaside, but generally unexceptional food. The narrow roads crisscrossing Av NS de Copacabana from Leme to Arpoador contain many fine establishments – and many mediocre ones. Do some exploring, trust your instincts and *bom proveito* (happy eating).

SIRI MOLE & CIA Map p76 Brazilian $$$

☎ 2267-0894; Rua Francisco Otaviano 50, Copacabana; mains R$70-95; 🕑 7pm-midnight Mon, noon-midnight Tue-Sun

Rated one of Rio's best Bahian restaurants, Siri Mole & Cia serves outstanding *vatapa, moqueca de camarão* (shrimp stew) and *ensopada de peixe* (fish and coconut milk stew). Stop in on Saturday (before 5pm) for the all-you-can-eat seafood buffet (R$58). Around the corner is Siri Mole's smaller, cheaper and more casual *boteco,* **Toca do Siri** (Map p76; Rua Raul Pompeia 6; 🕑 noon-midnight Tue-Sun), which serves tasty *acarajé* (spicy shrimp-filled croquettes; R$15).

BAR MÔNACO Map p76 Seafood $$

☎ 2521-0195; Rua Miguel Lemos 18, Copacabana; mains for 2 around R$80; 🕑 8am-2am

The fresh fish counter gives it all away: the casual Bar Mônaco is the neighborhood des-

THE KIOSKS OF COPACABANA

The *quiosque* (kiosk) has long been a presence on the beachfront of Rio, doling out cold drinks and snacks to Cariocas on the move, with plastic tables and chairs providing a fine vantage point for contemplating the watery horizon. In recent years Copacabana Beach has seen a new crop of flashy kiosks replacing the old-fashioned wooden ones (angering traditionalists – not to mention a few disenfranchised kiosk owners). Now it's possible to get a decent meal (the kitchens are cleverly concealed underground), an ice-cold draft beer or gourmet snacks without ever leaving the sand.

The new kiosks are sprinkled all along the beach, with the most options between about Rua Siqueira Campos and the Copacabana Palace. Here are a few current favorites:

Bar Luiz (Map p76; near Copacabana Palace; 8am-1am) Famed for its refreshing ice-cold *chope*, Bar Luiz also has good *bolinhos de bacalhau* (codfish balls; R$28 for 10), *salada de batata* (potato salad) and other appetizers.

Champanheria Copacabana (Map p76; near Rua Constante Ramos; 10am-midnight Sun-Thu, to 2am Fri & Sat) An upscale option for those who simply can't gaze across the sea without sipping champagne cocktails (R$12) and eating ciabatta with sardines and capers (R$11).

Nescafé (Map p76; near Copacabana Palace; 8am-1am) Serves nearly 20 varieties of savory or sweet crepes (around R$15), plus breakfast options and, of course, caffeinated drinks.

Recanto do Sol (Map p76; near Praça Julio de Noronha; 24hr) At the northeast end of the beach, this peacefully set kiosk serves small plates of sardines and fresh fish (R$20) as well as strong caipirinhas.

Siri Mole & Cia kiosk (Map p76; near Rua Bolívar; 10am-midnight Tue-Sun, from 3pm Mon) Serves snacks such as *acarajé* (spicy shrimp-filled croquettes; R$10) or heartier Bahian dishes, just like its sit-down restaurant (p136), plus delicious tropical cocktails.

tination for sizzling plates of grilled squid, fresh cherne, shrimp and a mean bowl of Leão Veloso (a rich seafood soup). Sidewalk tables provide a relaxing point for a meal or a drink on a fairly untrafficked street.

FRONTERA

Map p76 Self-Serve $$

☎ 3202-9050; Av NS de Copacabana 1144, Copacabana; per kg R$36-47; 11am-11pm

Much like its Ipanema branch (p129), Frontera spreads an excellent lunch buffet. You'll find dozens of Brazilian dishes plus salads, individual counters for grilled meats, sushi, fried dishes and desserts. At night Frontera serves all-you-can-eat crepes and pizzas for R$15 to R$19 per person.

CARRETÃO

Map p76 Churrascaria $$

☎ 2542-2148; Rua Ronald de Carvalho 55, Copacabana; all-you-can-eat R$36; 11:30am-midnight

It's all about the meat at this decent but inexpensive *churrascaria*. With several branches throughout the city, including an Ipanema Carretão (Map p64; ☎ 2267-3965; Rua Visconde de Pirajá 112), this popular chain serves up consistently good cuts – and heaps of them. There's a small salad bar, and you can order sides from the menu at no added charge.

AZUMI

Map p76 Japanese $$

☎ 2541-4294; Rua Ministro Viveiros de Castro 127, Copacabana; meals R$35-65; 7pm-midnight Tue-Thu & Sun, to 1am Fri & Sat

Some claim Azumi is the bastion of traditional Japanese cuisine in the city. This laid-back sushi bar certainly has its fans – both in the Nisei community and from abroad. Azumi's *sushiman* (sushi chef) masterfully prepares delectable sushi and sashimi, though tempuras and soups are also excellent. Be sure to ask what's in season.

CAPRICCIOSA Map p76 Pizzeria $$

☎ 2255-2598; Rua Domingos Ferreira 187, Copacabana; small/large pizza from R$36/45; 6pm-2am

This stylish spot serves excellent thin-crust pizzas. See the Ipanema review, p130.

FAENZA

Map p66 Self-Serve & Pizzeria $$

☎ 2257-1427; Rua Siqueira Campos 18, Copacabana; lunch per kg R$36-39; noon-midnight

Warmly lit, with exposed brick walls, Faenza offers an extensive lunch buffet of Brazilian dishes and a nightly all-you-can-eat pizza feast (at R$29 per person). Steaming thin-crust pizzas are brought to your table by harried waiters, and there are even dessert options (such as strawberry with Nutella).

COPA CAFÉ

Map p76 Eclectic $$

☎ 2235-2947; Av Atlântica 3056, Copacabana; mains R$26-48; 7pm-1am Mon-Sat

This two-story restaurant facing Copacabana beach brings a dash of style to Av Atlântica. The black-wood floors, white bar stools, trim open layout and ambient electronic music make a nice setting for risottos, seared tuna steaks and gourmet burgers – the house specialty.

SHIRLEY

Map p76 Spanish $$

☎ 2275-1398; Rua Gustavo Sampaio 610, Leme; mains for 2 R$55-74; 11am-1am

The aroma of succulent paella hangs in the air as waiters hurry to and from the kitchen, bearing platefuls of fresh seafood. Shirley, opened in 1954, is one of the few Spanish restaurants in town, and attracts a local following in its small Leme dining room. In addition to paella, the mussel-vinaigrette appetizer and the oven-baked snapper in white wine sauce are also recommended.

DON CAMILLO

Map p76 Italian $$

☎ 2549-9958; Av Atlântica 3056, Copacabana; pastas R$30-45; noon-1am

One of the few decent restaurants on the Copa strip, this handsomely appointed Italian restaurant has flavorful pastas and lasagnas, as well as some excellent seafood dishes. Antique tile floors, distressed wood beams and black-and-white photos make a nice setting to add to your dining pleasure. For pure decadence, try the linguini with lobster, shrimp and cherry tomatoes.

GALERIA 1618

Map p76 Bistrô $$

☎ 2295-1618; Rua Gustavo Sampaio 840, Leme; mains R$30-45; noon-midnight

Opened by two French expats in 2006, the art-filled Galeria 1618 offers a beautifully prepared daily special (R$70 for two), such as *boeuf bourguingnon*, Toulouse-style cassoulet or Tunisian lamb couscous. You can also opt for freshly made pastas, risottos and grilled fish or meat dishes, plus a dozen varieties of crepes. There's live music Friday and Saturday nights (R$15 cover).

SÃO SEBASTIÃO Map p76 Eclectic $$

☎ 2541-5585; Rua Gustavo Sampaio 361, Leme; mains R$30-52; noon-5pm Mon-Sat & 7pm-midnight daily

In an artfully decorated bistro, Chef Pedro Prado prepares beautiful French and Italian dishes that highlight the flavors of the tropics. Salmon with passion fruit, steak tartare, shrimp salad and ceviche are among the eclectic choices. Live jazz some nights adds to the appeal.

AMIR Map p76 Middle Eastern $$

☎ 2275-5596; Rua Ronald de Carvalho 55C, Copacabana; meals R$25-45; noon-midnight Mon-Sat, noon-11pm Sun

Step inside Amir and you'll enter a world of delicate aromas and handsomely dressed waiters in embroidered vests. Daytime crowds come for the buffet (R$33 on weekdays, R$45 weekends), while at night the a la carte menu features all the favorites, including delicious platters of hummus, *kaftas* (spiced meat patty), falafel, kibbe and salads. There's a belly dancer Friday nights (at 9:30pm), while other nights you can smoke from a hookah if you snag a balcony seat.

LE BLÉ NOIR Map p76 Creperie $$

☎ 2287-1272; Rua Xavier da Silveira 15A, Copacabana; crepes R$25-48; 7:30pm-midnight Mon-Thu, to 1am Fri & Sat

Flickering candles and subdued conversation make this restaurant a real date-pleaser. Le Blé Noir offers over 50 different varieties of crepe, pairing rich ingredients like shrimp and artichoke hearts or Brie, honey and toasted almonds.

DEVASSA Map p76 Brazilian $$

☎ 2236-0667; Rua Bolívar 8, Copacabana; mains R$20-35; 11am-2am

The popular Rio chain of upscale *botecos* is well known for its excellent beers. Devassa also serves tasty pub fare, including juicy burgers, veggie quesadillas, seafood pastas and the usual bar food. The open-sided restaurant enjoys a good location on the edge of Ave Atlântica.

LA TRATTORIA Map p76 Italian $$

☎ 2255-3319; Rua Fernando Mendes 7A, Copacabana; mains R$22-44; noon-midnight

Old photos, simple furnishings, hearty dishes and the constant din of conversation have made this trattoria a neighborhood favorite since 1976. Shrimp dishes are the Italian family's specialty – they've won over many diners with their *espaguete com camarão e óleo tartufado* (spaghetti with shrimp and truffle oil).

LA FIORENTINA

Map p76 Italian $$

☎ 2543-8465; Av Atlântica 458A, Leme; mains R$21-36; ⌚ noon-2am Sun-Thu, to 4am Fri & Sat

One of Leme's classic Italian restaurants, La Fiorentina attracted Rio's glitterati in the '60s. Today, its beach-facing outdoor tables draw a loyal, mostly neighborhood crowd, who come to feast on the 15 different flavors of pizza and a well-stocked bar.

ARATACA

Map p76 Amazonian $$

☎ 2548-6624; Rua Domingos Ferreira 41D, Copacabana; mains R$20-38; ⌚ 10am-9pm

The casual, no-nonsense Arataca serves the exotic cuisine of the Amazon. While there's better *tacacá* on offer in Rio (Flamengo's Tacacá do Norte, p142, is the city's best), Arataca is a handy spot to grab a savory bowl of the soup. There's also *pirarucu* (a kind of fish), *pato no tucupi* (roast duck flavored with garlic) or *vatapá,* all of which go nicely with real guarana juice.

RESTAURANTE NATURALEVE

Map p76 Vegetarian $

Travessa Cristiano Lacorte, Copacabana; per kg R$30; ⌚ 11am-4pm Mon-Sat

Set just off Rua Miguel Lemos, this tidy health-conscious restaurant cooks up a reasonably priced lunch buffet, with vegetarian black beans, *moqueca* with salmon, grilled tofu, various baked dishes and fresh salads.

ECLIPSE

Map p76 Brazilian $$

☎ 2287-1788; Av NS de Copacabana 1309, Copacabana; mains R$20-30; ⌚ 24hr

One of the only 24-hour restaurants in town, Eclipse is equal parts juice bar, pizzeria and traditional Brazilian restaurant, with outdoor seating, a stand-up counter and a sit-down air-conditioned restaurant for escaping the heat. It can be a great (and lively!) destination when hunger strikes in the *madrugada* (the wee hours of the night).

CONFEITARIA COLOMBO Map p76 Café $

☎ 3201-4049; Forte de Copacabana, Praça Coronel Eugênio Franco, Copacabana; mains R$15-30; ⌚ 10am-8pm Tue-Sun

Far removed from the hustle and bustle of Av Atlântica, this handsome café offers truly magnificent views of Copacabana Beach. At the outdoor tables, you can sit beneath shady palm trees, enjoying cappuccino, salads, quiche or crepes as young soldiers from the fort file past. To get here, you'll have to pay admission (R$2) to the Forte de Copacabana (Copacabana fort; p75), but it's worth the price. In Centro there's also a Confeitaria Colombo (p144) that is worth a visit.

PORTO VELHO ENOTECA

Map p76 Creperie $

☎ 2522-2836; Rua Francisco Otaviano 20, Copacabana; mains R$14-22; ⌚ 9am-10pm

This tiny French-run café serves tasty crepes, quiches, salads and daily specials – listed on the chalkboard in front. There are a few sidewalk tables, fine for a light meal, coffee or a drink (including wines by the glass and imported beers).

O CRACK DOS GALETOS

Map p76 Roast Chicken $

☎ 2236-7001; Rua Domingos Ferreira 197, Copacabana; mains R$10-20; ⌚ noon-midnight

If you're on a budget, or simply want a break from pricey restaurants, Rio's unfussy roast chicken restaurants are a must. Here, you can sidle up to the wrap-around counter and enjoy juicy plates of chicken fresh off the roaster.

CERVANTES Map p76 Brazilian $

☎ 2275-6147; Av Prado Júnior 335B, Copacabana; sandwiches R$10-18; ⌚ noon-4am Tue-Thu, to 6am Fri & Sat

A Copacabana institution, the late-night Cervantes gathers Cariocas who come to feast on Cervantes' trademark meat and pineapple sandwiches. Its waiters are famed for their fussiness, along with their speed to the tap when your *chope* runneth dry. Around the corner, Cervantes' stand-up boteco (Rua Barato Ribeiro 7) serves up tasty bites in a hurry.

BAKERS Map p76 Patisserie $

☎ 3209-1212; Rua Santa Clara 86B, Copacabana; quiche R$4, sandwiches R$14-20; ⌚ 9am-8pm

The Bakers is one of Copa's best places for flaky croissants, banana Danishes, apple strudels and other fresh-baked treats. There are also salads, gourmet sandwiches (like prosciutto and mozzarella on ciabatta), quiches (ricotta with sun-dried tomatoes), and pecan pie and ice cream for dessert.

BIBI CREPES Map p66 Juice Bar $

☎ 2513-6000; Rua Miguel Lemos 31, Copacabana; juices R$4-6, crepes R$10-16; 🕑 9am-1am

Offering much the same recipe for success as its Leblon branch (p133), Bibi serves dozens of juices, along with savory and sweet crepes, sandwiches, burgers and build-your-own salads. It has outdoor tables and a bustling vibe.

YOFORIA Map p76 Frozen Yogurt $

Rua Constante Ramos 13, Copacabana; small/medium yogurt R$6/8; 🕑 11am-10pm

Cariocas are currently mad for fat-free frozen yogurt, and the sleek, modern Yoforia is a good place as any to get a fix. Yogurt comes in just two varieties (plain and green tea) and you can load it up with toppings – lychee, walnuts, mango, kiwi, blueberries. Small cups are substantial.

O REI DAS EMPANADAS
Map p76 Empanadas $

☎ 3258-3003; Rua Barata Ribeira 48; empanadas R$2.50-3.50; 🕑 9am-11pm

Whether or not you're eating on a budget 'the king of empanadas' certainly deserves a visit. Piping-hot pasties are baked fresh throughout the day and come in a dozen varieties, including *carne picante* (spicy beef), *camarão* (shrimp) or dessert options (banana with chocolate).

BOTAFOGO & URCA

Botafogo generally has a better drinking than dining scene, though there are some top picks hidden in these old streets. Urca, largely untouched by commercial development, has only a few choices.

YORUBÁ Map p80 Bahian $$

☎ 2541-9387; Rua Arnaldo Quintela 94, Botafogo; mains for 2 R$72-95; 🕑 7pm-midnight Wed-Fri, noon-7pm Sat & Sun

Yorubá looks as if it's always prepared for the imminent arrival of an *orixá* (spirit or deity). Leaves lie scattered across the floor as candle flames flicker on the walls. Young waiters in red aprons stand at attention while something mystical transpires in the kitchen. Plates here are simply heavenly: plump shrimp and rich coconut milk blend to perfection in *bobó de camarão*, and the *moqueca* is simply outstanding.

MIAM MIAM
Map p80 Contemporary $$

☎ 2244-0125; Rua General Goés Monteiro 34, Botafogo; mains R$26-42; 🕑 8pm-midnight Tue-Thu, to 1:30am Fri & Sat

Exposed brick walls and a mishmash of retro furnishings set the scene for dining in style at Botafogo's newest culinary darling. Miam Miam, which is French for 'yum yum', is run by chef Roberta Ciasca, who trained at Paris' famous Le Cordon Bleu. Here, she serves up her own brand of 'comfort food', which means bruschetta with pesto and tapenade, endive salad with gorgonzola, pepper-crusted tuna with lentil ragout and many other unique (and yes, yummy) dishes. Don't miss the creative cocktail menu or the desserts.

GAROTA DA URCA Map p80 Brazilian $$

☎ 2541-8585; Rua João Luís Alves 56, Urca; mains R$20-40; 🕑 noon-1am Sun-Thu, to 2:30am Fri & Sat

Overlooking the small Praia da Urca, this neighborhood restaurant serves standard Brazilian fare at decent prices. The weekday lunch specials are good value, and you can enjoy views over the bay from the open-air veranda. By night, a more garrulous crowd meets here for steak and *chope*.

EMPORIUM PAX Map p80 Brazilian $

☎ 3171-9713; 7th fl, Praia de Botafogo 400, Botafogo; mains R$17-32; 🕑 noon-midnight

One of many eateries at Botafogo Praia Shopping, Emporium Pax is a more polished affair than the adjoining food court and offers spectacular views of Pão de Açúcar and Baía de Guanabara. As well as salads, pastas and tasty desserts, the lunch buffet draws in the shoppers and filmgoers.

CAFÉ BOTÂNICA Map p80 Café $

☎ 2535-2465; Rua Capitão Salomão 14B, Botafogo; mains R$15-30; 🕑 9am-7pm Mon-Fri, to 2pm Sat

This letterbox-sized café and bistro serves tasty bites, like goat cheese quiche, pumpkin soup and homemade sandwiches. Don't neglect the tasty pie and cake selection.

FLAMENGO & LARANJEIRAS

The traditional neighborhood of Flamengo has a mix of longtime local favorites and stylish newcomers. Rua Marquês de Abrantes is one of the best streets in which to wander and see old and new vying for attention. Laranjeiras gets few tourists and, although there's not much of a restaurant scene, the neighborhood has several charming options, well worth seeking out for those wanting to get off the beaten path.

PORCÃO RIO'S Map p84 Churrascaria $$$

☎ 3389-8989; Av Infante Dom Henrique, Flamengo; all-you-can-eat R$78; 🕑 11:30am-midnight Sun-Thu, to 1am Fri & Sat

Set in the Parque do Flamengo with a stunning view of Pão de Açúcar, Porcão Rio's is consistently ranked by restaurant critics as the city's best *churrascaria*. Whether you believe the hype – or simply come for the view – you're in for an eating extravaganza. Arrive early, both to score a good table and to see the view before sunset.

RESTAURANTE KIOTO Map p84 Japanese $$

☎ 2556-9880; 3rd fl, Rua Ministerio Tavares Lira 105, Flamengo; all-you-can-eat lunch/dinner R$33/40; 🕑 noon-midnight

Hidden on a street behind Largo do Machado this simple, well-concealed restaurant is worth seeking out when craving a sushi feast that won't break the bank. There's an enormous variety of rolls at the buffet, and you can take pride in dining in a restaurant known to only a handful of Cariocas.

INTIHUASI Map p84 Peruvian $$

☎ 2225-7653; Rua Barão do Flamengo 35D, Flamengo; mains R$28-46; 🕑 noon-3pm & 7-11pm Tue-Sat, noon-5pm Sun

Colorfully decorated with Andean tapestries and artwork, Rio's only Peruvian restaurant serves excellent ceviches, *papas rellenas* (meat-filled potatoes), seafood soups and other classic dishes from the Andes. Wash tamales down with a pisco sour or Inka Cola.

CHURRASCARIA MAJÓRICA Map p84 Churrascaria $$

☎ 2285-6820; Rua Senador Vergueiro 11, Flamengo; mains R$21-63; 🕑 noon-midnight

A true *gaúcho* (person from Rio Grande do Sul) would chuckle at the kitschy cowboy accoutrements inside this restaurant. He'd shut his trap, however, once his plate of steak arrived. Meat is very serious business at Majórica; if you're seeking an authentic *churrascaria* experience, look no further.

LUIGI'S Map p84 Italian $$

☎ 2205-5331; Rua Senador Corrêia 10, Laranjeiras; mains R$22-37; 🕑 lunch & dinner

Well off the beaten path, Luigi's is a casual Italian restaurant set in an old villa in Laranjeiras. Join neighborhood regulars for a drink on the small covered courtyard in front before venturing inside for homemade beet fettuccine with rocket pesto, fresh mushroom and tomato tagliatelle, or green apple and duck risotto.

LAMAS Map p84 Brazilian $$

☎ 2556-0799; Rua Marquês de Abrantes 18A, Flamengo; mains R$20-40; 🕑 8am-2:30am Sun-Thu, to 4am Fri & Sat

This classic Brazilian restaurant opened in 1874 and has fans from all over. In spite of the mileage, dishes here hold up well, and those omniscient waiters in starched white coats will tell you what's hot in the kitchen. You can't go wrong with grilled *lingüiça* (Brazilian sausage) or filet mignon with garlic.

HIDEAWAY Map p84 Pizzeria $$

☎ 2285-0921; Rua das Laranjeiras 308, Laranjeiras; mains R$25-35; 🕑 6pm-midnight Tue-Thu & Sun, 6pm-4am Fri & Sat

Aptly named, Hideaway is secreted inside a converted 19th-century house. The all-glass ceiling (with lush greenery framing the outside) and minimalist design give a contemporary polish to the place. The pizzas, made inside a wood-burning oven, are decent, and the small lounge adjoining the restaurant hosts live jazz and Música Popular Brasileira (MPB) groups.

BELMONTE Map p84 Brazilian $$

☎ 2552-3349; Praia do Flamengo 300, Flamengo; mains R$15-35; 🕑 9am-3am

One of the classic *botecos* in Rio, Belmonte is a vision of Rio from the '50s. Globe lights hang overhead as patrons down ice-cold drafts from the narrow bar. Meanwhile, unhurried waiters make their way across the tile floors, carrying plates of *pasteis de camarão* (shrimp pasties) or steak sandwiches. This hugely successful chain is now widespread across Rio.

ESPAÇO RIO CARIOCA Map p84 Bistrô $

☎ 2225-7332; www.espacoriocarioca.com.br; Rua Leite Leal 45, Laranjeiras; sandwiches R$14-18; 3-10pm Mon-Fri, noon-10pm Sat & Sun

Espaço Rio Carioca, which opened in 2007, is yet another symbol of Laranjeiras' ongoing revitalization. This large multi-level space has a ground-level bookstore, an upstairs bistro with a terrace and a café with wi-fi that hosts live music (see p161) four nights a week. The bistro menu features salads, sandwiches and heartier daily specials (R$15 to R$35): pastas, risotto, grilled steak.

TACACÁ DO NORTE Map p84 Amazonian $

☎ 2205-7545; Rua Barão do Flamengo 35, Flamengo; tacacá R$12; 9am-10pm Mon-Sat, to 7pm Sun

In the Amazonian state of Pará, people order their *tacacá* late in the afternoon from their favorite street vendor. In Rio, you don't have to wait until the sun is setting. The fragrant soup of manioc paste, *jambu* (a Brazilian vegetable) leaves, and fresh and dried shrimp isn't for everyone. But then again, neither is the Amazon. This simple lunch counter also offers excellent *açai* (juice made from an Amazonian berry) and other juices, as well as Amazonian dishes like *pirarucu*.

CATETE & GLÓRIA

Rio's working-class neighborhoods are dotted with inexpensive juice bars and lunch counters – making this a good area for those eating on a dime. Most places are along Rua do Catete, with a couple of standouts hidden along the back streets.

CASA DA SUÍÇA Map p87 Swiss $$

☎ 2252-5182; Rua Cândido Mendes 157, Glória; fondues R$47-58; noon-3pm & 7pm-midnight Mon-Fri, 7pm-1am Sat, noon-4pm & 7-11pm Sun

Tucked inside the Swiss embassy, this cozy restaurant serves top-notch steak tartare, though it specializes in flambés and fondues. The Casa da Suíça creates an almost tangible aura of sensuality – perhaps due to those open fires flaring inside. After dinner, you can hear live music at the St Moritz bar.

NANQUIM Map p87 Self-Serve $$

☎ 2556-5119; Rua do Pinheiro 10, Flamengo; per kg R$52; 11am-3:30pm Mon-Fri

Hidden inside the Instituto dos Arquitetos on a quiet street, this inviting restaurant has a small but excellent self-service lunchtime buffet. Pastas, seafood, risotto, quiches, vegetarian dishes and salads are among the options. The 19th-century building is a mix of rustic and modern, with designs and sketches by Oscar Niemeyer adorning the walls. A second branch in Jardim Botânico (Map p70; ☎ 3874-0015; Rua Jardim Botânico 644) offers the same mix of contemporary design and good food.

ESTAÇÃO REPÚBLICA Map p87 Self-Serve $$

☎ 2225-2650; Rua do Catete 104, Catete; per kg R$35-40; 11am-midnight Mon-Sat, to 11pm Sun

Estação's buffet table is a neighborhood institution, featuring an extensive selection of salads, meats, pastas and vegetables. After 6pm the restaurant offers all-you-can-eat pizzas and crepes (R$14).

TABERNA DA GLÓRIA Map p87 Brazilian $$

☎ 2265-7835; Rua do Russel 32A, Glória; mains R$22-34; 11:30am-1am Sun-Thu, to 2am Fri & Sat

On a small plaza in the heart of Glória, this large outdoor eatery serves decent Brazilian staples, and in abundance – most dishes here serve two. The *feijoada* on Friday and Saturday still draws crowds, and if you're not up for a big meal, appetizers and ice-cold *chope* are a good way to enjoy the open-air ambience.

DINING ON THE BAY

For an alternative take on the local dining scene, Pink Fleet (☎ 2555-4063; www.pinkfleet.com.br) offers lunch or dinner cruises aboard a 180-ft-long vessel that can accommodate (but rarely hosts) up to 400 guests. There are several open-air decks with three bars scattered about, and you can opt for a decent buffet (R$29 per person) of salads, pastas, appetizers and desserts or order Brazilian favorites from the a la carte menu. The ship itself sails around the bay, passing near enough to Santos Dumont airport to hear the roar of embarking jets, with stops near Pão de Açúcar, Oscar Niemeyer's Museu de Arte Moderna, the Niteroi bridge and many other landmarks. Perhaps owing to the price, it's popular with a slightly older Carioca crowd (generally 30 and up). Current sailings depart Marina da Glória (Map p87) on Friday evenings from 9pm to 11pm and on Saturdays from 11:45am to 2:15pm.

CATETE GRILL Map p87 Self-Serve $

☎ 2285-3442; Rua do Catete 239, Catete; per kg R$22-32; 11am-midnight Mon-Sat, to 11pm Sun

The Catete Grill has a good buffet – served all day. This bustling, modern place rolls out pastas, salads, appetizers and baked dishes, though the highlight is the assortment of roast meats. It also offers ice creams – *a quilo* (by the kilo), of course.

CENTRO & CINELÂNDIA

Rio's busiest neighborhood has everything from greasy lunch counters to French bistros. Most restaurants open only for lunch on weekdays. Many pedestrian-only areas throughout Centro (such as Rua do Rosário) are full of restaurants, some spilling onto the sidewalk, others hidden on upstairs floors – restaurant hunting is something of an art. Areas worth exploring include Travessa do Comércio just after work, when the restaurants and cafés fill with chatter; another early-evening gathering spot is Av Marechal Floriano, full of snack bars specializing in fried sardines and beer. Cinelândia, behind Praça Floriano, features a number of open-air cafés and restaurants.

RESTAURANTE ALBAMAR Map p90 Seafood $$$

☎ 2240-8378; Praça Marechal Âncora 186, Centro; mains R$43-68; noon-6pm

With a heralded new chef at the helm, Albamar has reinvented itself as one of Rio's top seafood destinations. Top picks are fresh oysters, grilled seafood with vegetables and *moqueca* dishes. The old-fashioned green gazebo-like structure offers excellent views of the Baía de Guanabara and Niterói.

CAIS DO ORIENTE Map p90 Eclectic $$

☎ 2203-0178; Rua Visconde de Itaboraí 8, Centro; mains R$42-50; noon-4pm Mon, to midnight Tue-Sat

Brick walls lined with tapestries stretch high to the ceiling in this almost-cinematic 1870s mansion. Set on a brick-lined street, hidden from the masses, Cais do Oriente blends West with East in dishes like grilled squid with fish sauce, wild rice and green papaya.

DA SILVA Map p90 Portuguese $$

☎ 2524-1010; 4th fl, Av Graça Aranha 187, Centro; all-you-can-eat R$40, after 2pm R$30; noon-4pm Mon-Fri

Hidden inside the Clube Ginástico Português, this large, simply decorated restaurant spreads one of Rio's best lunch buffets. Portuguese in flavor, like its Leblon sister inside Rio Design Center (Map p66; Av Ataúlfo de Paiva 270, Leblon; lunch & dinner), Da Silva in Centro has delicious salads, steaks and seafood, along with an enormous variety of addictive *bacalhau* dishes and dozens of other dishes.

BAR LUIZ Map p90 German $$

☎ 2262-6900; Rua da Carioca 39, Centro; mains R$20-45; 11am-11pm Mon-Sat

Bar Luiz first opened in 1887, making it one of the city's oldest *cervejarias* (pubs). A festive air fills the old saloon as diners get their fill of traditional German cooking (potato salad and smoked meats), along with ice-cold drafts – including dark beer – on tap.

MANGUE SECO CACHAÇARIA Map p90 Bahian $$

☎ 3852-1947; Rua do Lavradio 23, Lapa; mains for 2 R$40-65; 11am-midnight Mon-Thu, 11am-2am Fri & Sat

Part of the Rio Scenarium empire, Mangue Seco serves a mix of seafood and Bahian fare, with hearty *moquecas* and *bobó de camarão* (shrimp pastries). Upstairs, there's a bar with over 100 types of *cachaça* and live samba Friday and Saturday nights (from 7pm).

RIO BRASA Map p90 Self-Serve $$

☎ 2199-9191; Ave Rio Branco 277, Centro; per kg R$55; 11am-4pm Mon-Sat

Handily located near the Praça Floriana, this shiny new per-kilo restaurant prepares a high-quality lunch buffet with separate counters for salads, sushi, baked dishes and grilled meats (the restaurant's specialty). Prices are lower after 2pm (per kg R$43).

BISTRÔ THE LINE Map p90 French $$

☎ 2233-3571; Casa França-Brasil, Rua Visconde de Itaboraí 78, Centro; mains R$16-30; 10am-8pm

Adjoining the Casa França-Brasil, this charming restaurant with outdoor tables serves bistro fare (mushroom risotto, veal, grilled salmon) at lunchtime as well as snacks (quiche, bruschetta) and desserts from 4pm onwards.

ATELIÊ CULINÂRIO Map p90 Brazilian $

☎ 2240-2573; Praça Floriano, Cinelândia; mains R$18-25; noon-10pm Mon-Fri

Next to the art-house cinema of the same name (the Ateliê Odeon) this place serves up decent Brazilian fare on its open-air terrace to a festive crowd. Ateliê opens onto the Praça Floriano, which is a lively gathering spot on weekday evenings. On weekends, it stays opens during film screenings next door.

CONFEITARIA COLOMBO

Map p90 Patisserie $

☎ **2505-1500; Rua Gonçalves Dias 34, Centro; desserts/mains from R$4/24; 9am-8pm Mon-Fri, 9am-5pm Sat**

Stained-glass windows, brocaded mirrors and marble countertops create a lavish setting for coffee or a meal. Dating from the late 1800s, the Confeitaria Colombo serves desserts –including a good *pastel de nata* (custard tart) – befitting the elegant decor. The restaurant overhead, Cristóvão (buffet R$50; noon-4pm), spreads an extensive buffet of Brazilian dishes for those wanting to further soak up the splendor.

CEDRO DO LÍBANO Map p90 Lebanese $

☎ **2224-0163; Rua Senhor dos Passos 231, Centro; mains R$16-28; 11am-5pm**

White plastic chairs and tables covered by white tablecloths might make you feel like you stumbled into someone's wedding reception at this dining spot in the heart of Saara. But, in fact, the white decorating in this 70-plus-year-old Lebanese institution has more to do with the purity of the Lebanese cooking: kibbe, *kaftas,* lamb – all tender portions of perfection.

RANCHO INN Map p90 Contemporary $

☎ **2263-5197; 2nd fl, Rua do Rosário 74, Centro; mains R$20-32; 11:30am-3pm Mon-Fri**

Exposed brick and tall windows lend a vaguely Parisian air to this charming lunchtime spot. You can opt for the fixed-price buffet (R$24) or order more complicated dishes off the menu: goat cheese and prosciutto salad, risotto with duck and shitake mushrooms, followed by cakes or chocolate mousse for dessert.

TEMPEH Map p90 Vegetarian $

☎ **2232-8007; 2nd fl, Rua Primeiro de Março 24, Centro; per kg R$25; noon-3pm Mon-Sat**

Don't be intimidated by the new-age music. This is one of Centro's best vegetarian restaurants, serving a wide assortment of flavorful dishes, including soups, pastas, veggie burgers, tabouli, fried yucca, soba noodles, vegan sushi and desserts. The old colonial walls add to the charm.

BRASSERIE ROSÁRIO

Map p90 French $

☎ **2518-3033; Rua do Rosário 34, Centro; mains R$20-48; 11am-9pm Mon-Fri, 11am-6pm Sat**

Set in a handsomely restored 1860s building, this atmospheric bistro has a hint of Paris about it. The front counters are full of croissants, *pain au chocolat* (chocolate croissant) and other baked items, while the restaurant menu features roast meats and fish, soups, baguette sandwiches and the like. Old American jazz plays overhead.

BEDUÍNO

Map p90 Middle Eastern $

☎ **2524-5142; Av Presidente Wilson 123, Centro; mains R$18-26; 7am-11pm Mon-Fri, 7am-5pm Sat**

Reliably good food and excellent prices are Beduíno's keys to success, with 30 different traditional Middle Eastern dishes to choose from. Favorites include grilled *kafta,* lamb stew, and rice and lentils.

CAFÉ ARLEQUIM Map p90 Café $

☎ **2220-8471; Paço Imperial, Praça Quinze de Novembro 48, Centro; mains R$14-28; 9am-8pm Mon-Fri, 10am-6pm Sat**

In the middle of a shop selling books and CDs, this small, lively, pleasantly air-conditioned café is a fine spot to refuel, with Italian (Illy) coffee, sandwiches, salads, quiches, lasagna and desserts.

BISTRÔ DO PAÇO Map p90 Self-Serve $

☎ **2262-3613; Paço Imperial, Praça Quinze de Novembro 48, Centro; mains R$12-25; noon-7pm**

On the ground floor of the Paço Imperial, this informal restaurant offers a tasty assortment of quiches, salads, soups and other light fare. Save room for the delicious pies and cakes.

CAFÉ DO BOM CACHAÇA DA BOA

Map p90 Café $

☎ **2509-1018; Rua da Carioca 10, Centro; sandwiches R$9-12; 10am-8pm Mon-Fri, 10am-2pm Sat**

With a vaguely professorial air, this wood-lined café and bookshop doles out sandwiches, coffees and ice cream, but it's best known for its *cachaça* menu – with over 100 varieties available (from R$3.50 to R$29 per shot).

CASA CAVÉ Map p90 Patisserie $

☎ 2222-2358; Rua Sete de Setembro 137, Centro; pastries from R$4; ⏲ 8:30am-7:30pm Mon-Fri, to 1:30pm Sat

Set with attractive tile floors and marble tabletops, this simple, historic coffeehouse (c 1860) lures in passersby with its shop windows full of tempting desserts. Next door is the roomier and elegantly set Manon Gourmet (Rua Sete de Setembro 133; ⏲ noon-7pm Mon-Fri), which serves Casa Cavé's good desserts as well as sandwiches and salads.

SANTA TERESA & LAPA

Great views, a diverse crowd and a scenic atmosphere among late 19th-century buildings all set the stage for a great night out in bohemian Santa Teresa. Most restaurants are within a short stroll of Largo do Guimarães. Although Lapa is known more for its samba than its cuisine, more and more restaurants are opening in the area, catering to the young crowds headed to the dance halls.

TÉRÈZE Map p98 Fusion $$$

☎ 3380-0220; Hotel Santa Teresa, Rua Felicio dos Santos, Santa Teresa; mains R$55; ⏲ noon-5pm daily & 7pm-midnight Mon-Sat

Under the command of French chef Damien Montecer, Térèze provides a memorable dining experience. All the elements are there, from the inventive menu (char-grilled octopus with couscous salad, black risotto with seafood, macadamia-crusted veal tenderloin), to the suggested wine pairings and the superb views over the city. Even the design is green – tables and artwork are made from reclaimed lumber and recycled materials.

APRAZÍVEL Map p98 Brazilian $$

☎ 2508-9174; Rua Aprazível 62, Santa Teresa; mains R$40-60; ⏲ noon-1am Tue & Thu-Sat, noon-7pm Sun

Hidden on a windy road high up in Santa Teresa, Aprazível offers beautiful views and a lush garden setting. Grilled fish and roasted dishes showcase the country's culinary highlights of land and sea (standouts include grilled orange-infused tropical fish with coconut rice and roasted plantains). This place is a bit out of the way, so call ahead (sometimes, the restaurant is booked up by groups) and take a taxi (and have your map handy, as drivers don't always know this place).

SOBRENATURAL Map p98 Seafood $$

☎ 2224-1003; Rua Almirante Alexandrino 432, Santa Teresa; mains for 2 R$70-85; ⏲ noon-midnight Mon-Sat, noon-10pm Sun

The exposed brick and old hardwood ceiling set the stage for feasting on the *frutas do mar* (seafood). Lines gather on weekends for crabmeat appetizers, fresh grilled fish and flavorful platters of *moqueca*. During the week, stop by for tasty lunchtime specials. There's live music Monday, Wednesday, Friday and Saturday nights.

ESPÍRITO SANTA Map p98 Amazonian $$

☎ 2508-7095; Rua Almirante Alexandrino 264, Santa Teresa; mains R$28-39; ⏲ noon-6pm Mon & Wed, to midnight Thu-Sat, 11:30am-10pm Sun

Espírito Santa is set in a beautifully restored mansion in Santa Teresa. Take a seat on the back terrace with its sweeping views or inside the charming, airy dining room, and feast on rich, expertly prepared meat and seafood dishes from the Amazon and the northeast.

NOVA CAPELA Map p98 Portuguese $$

☎ 2252-6228; Av Mem de Sá 96, Lapa; mains R$22-54; ⏲ 11am-5am

This classic, old-time eating and drinking spot opened in 1967 and is a well-known draw for neighborhood bohemians – a noisy mix of artists, musicians and party kids who fill the place till early into the morning. Legendarily bad-tempered waiters serve up big plates of traditional Portuguese cuisine. The *cabrito* (goat) dish (R$60 for two) is their most famous.

SANSUSHI Map p98 Japanese $$

☎ 2224-4658; Rua Almirante Alexandrino 382, Santa Teresa; meals R$20-44; ⏲ 7pm-midnight Tue-Fri, 1pm-midnight Sat, to 10pm Sun

This tiny sushi spot on Santa Teresa's main strip attracts a loyal local following with its delectable sushi and sashimi (36 varieties) as well as teriyaki and other hot dishes.

BAR BRASIL Map p98 German $$

☎ 2509-5943; Av Mem de Sá 90, Lapa; mains R$21-40; ⏲ 11:30am-11pm Mon-Fri, to 6pm Sat

According to legend, this German restaurant went by the name Bar Adolf until WWII. Although the name has been Brazilianized, the cuisine is still prepared in the same tradition as it was back before the war. Sauerkraut, wursts, lentils and an

FEIJOADA

As distinctively Carioca as Pão de Açúcar (Sugarloaf) or Cristo Redentor (Christ the Redeemer), the *feijoada completa* is a dish that constitutes an entire meal, which often begins with a caipirinha aperitif.

A properly prepared *feijoada* is made up of black beans slowly cooked with a great variety of meat – including dried tongue and pork offcuts – seasoned with salt, garlic, onion and oil. The stew is accompanied by white rice and finely shredded kale, then tossed with croutons, fried *farofa* (manioc flour) and pieces of orange.

Feijoada has its origins in Portuguese cooking, which uses a large variety of meats and vegetables; fried *farofa* (inherited from the indigenous inhabitants) and kale are also Portuguese favorites. The African influence comes with the spice and the tradition of using pork offcuts, which were the only part of the pig given to slaves.

Traditionally, Cariocas eat *feijoada* for lunch on Saturday (it's rarely served on other days). Among the top places to sample the signature dish are at Galani (p128), at Hotel Caesar Park, Galeto do Leblon (p132) and Casa da Feijoada (p129), which is one of the few places in Rio that serves *feijoada* daily. Vegetarians can sample tasty meat-free versions of *feijoada* at Vegetariano Social Club (p132) or Fontes (p133).

If you find yourself craving the dish after you return home, try your hand at making it.

Recipe

Ingredients

6 cups dried black beans
500g smoked ham hocks
500g Brazilian *lingüiça* (Brazilian sausage; substitute chorizo or sweet sausage)
500g Brazilian *carne seca* or lean Canadian (loin-cut) bacon
1kg smoked pork ribs
The intrepid can add one each of a pork ear, foot, tail and tongue
2 bay leaves
3 garlic cloves, minced
1 large onion, chopped
3 tablespoons olive oil
4 strips smoked bacon
salt and black pepper
orange slices to garnish
rice, *farofa,* kale or collard greens to serve
hot sauce (optional) to serve

Preparation

After soaking beans overnight, bring them to a boil in 3L of water and then keep them on low to medium heat for several hours, stirring occasionally. Meanwhile, cut up the ham hocks, *lingüiça* and *carne seca* into 3cm or 4cm chunks, separate the pork ribs by twos and place them all in a separate pan full of water and bring to a boil. After the first boil, empty out the water and add the mixture, along with the bay leaves and salt and pepper, to the beans. As the pot simmers, in a separate pan sauté the garlic and onion in olive oil, adding in the smoked bacon. Take two ladles of beans from the pot, mash them and add to the frying pan. Stir around, cook for a few more minutes, then add frying-pan contents to the pot; this will thicken the mixture. Simmer for another two to three hours, until the beans are tender and the stock has a creamy consistency. Remove bay leaves and serve over rice with *farofa* and kale or collard greens. Garnish with fresh orange slices. Add hot sauce if desired, and be sure to enjoy with a cold caipirinha.

ever-flowing tap quench the appetites and thirsts of the sometimes-rowdy Lapa crowd.

MIKE'S HAUS Map p98 German $$

☎ 2509-5248; Rua Almirante Alexandrino 1458A, Santa Teresa; mains R$22-36; noon-midnight Sun-Thu, to 2am Fri & Sat

Mike's Haus has a German pub atmosphere with traditional cooking and cold glasses of imported Weizenbier. Although plates are small here, the place remains a popular gathering spot for expats and Cariocas on Friday and Saturday night.

BAR DO MINEIRO Map p98 Brazilian $$

☎ 2221-9227; Rua Paschoal Carlos Magno 99, Santa Teresa; mains for 2 people R$50-60; 11am-1am Tue-Sun

Black-and-white photographs of legendary singers cover the walls of this old-school *boteco* in the heart of Santa Teresa. Lively crowds have been filling this spot for years to enjoy traditional Minas Gerais dishes. *Feijoada* is tops, and served every day, along with appetizers, including *pasteis* (savory pastries) filled with *abóbora* (pumpkin) or *carne-seca* (dried beef). Strong caipirinhas will help get you in the mood.

CANTINHO DO SENADO

Map p98 Brazilian $$

☎ 2509-0535; Rua do Lavradio 50, Lapa; mains R$17-39; 🕑 11am-11pm Tue-Thu, 11am-2am Fri & Sat

This nondescript restaurant on antique row serves an excellent *feijoada* (R$31), which is enough to feed two. The chalkboard menu in front lists other daily specials, usually grilled plates of steak, trout, chicken or filet of salmon, You can dine in the casual open-sided bar on the ground floor or upstairs amid air-conditioning.

ERNESTO

Map p98 Brazilian $$

☎ 2509-6455; Largo da Lapa 41, Lapa; mains R$17-29; 🕑 11am-midnight Mon-Thu, to 3am Fri & Sat

With high ceilings and exposed brick walls, there's an old-time feel to this restaurant and drinking spot just a short stroll from the samba clubs in Lapa. Ernesto has an extensive menu, though its grilled meats, codfish dishes and German-inspired plates (white sausage with lentils) are standouts. There's live music – MPB or samba – on Wednesday (from 8pm; R$8) and Saturday (from 9:30pm; R$15).

ENCONTROS CARIOCAS

Map p98 Pizza $

☎ 2221-0028; Av Mem de Sá 77, Lapa; pizzas R$16-34; 🕑 7pm-2am Sun & Tue, to 4am Wed-Sat

This late-night pizza parlor is a good place to stop in while exploring Lapa's live music scene. Featuring a wide variety of ingredients (such as shiitake mushrooms, sun-dried tomatoes and jerked beefs), Encontras Cariocas serves tasty pies amid an atmosphere of old-fashioned charm – high wooden ceilings, brick walls and warm lighting.

SANTA SCENARIUM Map p98 Brazilian $

☎ 3147-9007; Rua do Lavradio 36, Lapa; mains R$16-28; 🕑 noon-5pm Mon, to 1am Tue-Sat

Angels, saints and other sacred images adorn the exposed brick walls of this marvelously atmospheric restaurant on Lapa's antique row. Grilled meats and other Brazilian staples are on offer at lunchtime, while at night Cariocas gather for cold beer, appetizers and sandwiches (like the popular filet mignon on ciabatta). There's live music most nights.

LARGO DAS LETRAS

Map p98 Pizza $

☎ 2221-8992; Rua Almirante Alexandrino 501, Santa Teresa; pizzas R$15-25; 🕑 2-10pm Tue-Sat, 2-8pm Sun

Directly above the Largo do Guimarães *bonde* (tram) stop, this bookstore, café and cultural spot (with *capoeira* marshal-art classes four nights a week and a twice-monthly flea market) has shaded outdoor tables that bring out a neighborhood crowd most nights. Pizzas (served from 5pm onwards) are fairly decent, and there's live music from Wednesday to Sunday.

JASMIM MANGA

Map p98 Café $

☎ 2242-2605; Rua Pascoal Carlos Magno 143, Santa Teresa; mains R$13-25; 🕑 10am-11pm

Well-placed beside the *bonde* stop on Largo do Guimarães, Jasmin Mango is a charming spot to linger over sandwiches, quiches, pastas, pizzas and desserts. The airy patio attached to the tiny café is a particularly fine spot for taking in the street scene. A few computers on the 2nd floor are handy for checking email.

CAFECITO Map p98 Café $

Rua Pascoal Carlos Magno 121, Santa Teresa; sandwiches R$10-22; 🕑 10am-10pm Tue-Sun

A few steps above street level, this open-air café attracts a mix of foreigners and neighborhood regulars (the Argentine owner is a longtime Santa Teresa resident). You'll find imported beers, desserts, cocktails (caiprinhas and mojitos), tapas plates and gourmet sandwiches (with ingredients like smoked trout, artichoke hearts and prosciutto).

BARRA DA TIJUCA & WEST OF RIO

Other parts of Rio offer some of the city's more rustic dining experiences. Outside the city limits one can find open-air spots overlooking the coast – beautiful views complemented by fresh seafood. The following places are best reached by private transport.

BIRA

Off Map p107 Seafood $$$

☎ 2410-8304; Estrada da Vendinha 68A, Barra de Guaratiba; mains for 2 R$120-140; ⏰ noon-6pm Thu-Fri, to 8pm Sat & Sun

Splendid views of Baía de Marambaia await diners who make the trek to Bira, about 45 minutes outside the city. On a breezy wooden deck, diners can partake in the flavorful, rich seafood emerging from the kitchen. *Moquecas,* sea bass, shrimp, crabmeat pastries – all are prepared with doting tenderness. It's located about 35km west of Rio in the marvelous seaside setting of Barra da Guaratiba.

TIA PALMIRA Off Map p107 Seafood $$$

☎ 2410-8169; Caminho do Souza 18, Barra de Guaratiba; prix-fixe lunch R$65; ⏰ 11:30am-5pm Tue-Fri, to 6pm Sat & Sun

On weekends Cariocas feast on seafood at this simple open-air eatery overlooking the coast. A venerable destination for 40 years, Tia Palmira keeps its fans coming back for its exquisite seafood *rodízio* (all-you-can-eat barbecue dinner). Plate after plate of *vatapá,* crabmeat, grilled fish, shrimp pastries and other fruits of the sea come to your table until you can eat no more. It's located 40km west of Rio near the coast.

BARREADO

Map p107 Seafood $$

☎ 2442-2023; Estrada dos Bandeirantes 21295, Vargem Grande; mains for 2 R$64-94; ⏰ noon-11pm Thu-Sat, to 8pm Sun

In a lush setting west of Barra, this rustic spot serves fresh Brazilian seafood with a wildly eclectic twist. Meals are prepared in the wood-burning oven, and pumpkin is the serving vehicle of choice. You can order it filled with rich delicacies such as shrimp with *catupiry* (a kind of cheese), scampi, or lobster and mango. *Vatapá* and roast meats are also excellent choices. It's located about 35km west of Rio.

DRINKING

top picks

What's your recommendation? www.lonelyplanet.com/rio-de-janeiro

DRINKING

Blessed with those deliciously warm nights, Rio de Janeiro has some enticing nightspots that make good use of the tropical setting. On nearly any evening of the year (unless it's raining) you'll find Cariocas (residents of Rio) drinking up the views at open-air bars on the lake, enjoying spontaneous gatherings at sidewalk cafés and heading to the corner pub to catch a game. For an insight into Rio's drinking culture, familiarize yourself with one of the great sociocultural icons of the city – the *boteco*. These casual, open-sided bars are scattered all over town, and draw in a broad cross-section of society. You'll find young and old, upper class and working class, men and women, black and white mixing over ice-cold *chope* (draft beer) or caipirinhas (cane-liquor cocktails), swapping the latest gossip as bow-tied waiters move deftly among the crowd. Just as most Cariocas have a favorite team, nearly every local also has a favorite *boteco* to call his or her own. These range from hole-in-the-wall joints where canned beer is handed out to drinkers slouched over plastic tables, to classic, wood-paneled bar rooms, with murals on the walls, expertly mixed drinks and a history dating back several generations. Wherever you go in the city, you'll find food is an important part of the experience, as Cariocas rate bars not just on the drinks and the vibe but on the menu as well.

In addition to *botecos*, there are other options when you're ready to head out for the night. Rio has stylish lounges with electronic music and the usual beautiful crowd. There are also flirty college hangouts, hotel bars with a view and a ragged assortment of bohemian haunts. For those seeking a bit of flash, Leblon and Ipanema are good options – though Leblon boasts classic watering holes, too. You'll find a more youthful bar scene in Gávea and Jardim Botânico, while a good place for a date is at one of the Lagoa kiosks. Copacabana has a mix of brash newcomers and old favorites, while Botafogo is famed for its low-key bars. Centro's colorful, open-air spots are great options on weeknights, when the narrow, colonial streets make a picturesque setting for a few drinks. You'll find similarly atmospheric digs in Santa Teresa. At the opposite end of the spectrum is Barra da Tijuca, home to large entertainment complexes with bars, discos and restaurants all housed in one shopping-mall-like structure.

For a drinking and eating tour through one of Rio's best *boteco*-filled neighborhoods, see p67. For some recommended bars at hotels, see p190.

HOW MUCH?

In *botecos* and most casual places, a draft beer will set you back about R$3.50 to R$4.50, with cocktails running about R$8. The prices rise at fancier spots and can top out at R$20 for a cocktail at Rio's swankiest spots.

Most bars will add a 10% service charge to the bill, as is done for restaurants.

IPANEMA & LEBLON

Ipanema has a mix of stylish and classic bars, with a 20- and 30-something crowd common in most destinations. For drinking al fresco, you will find peacefully set tables along the east side of Praça General Osório.

Leblon has even more bars on offer than Ipanema, with venerable *botecos* and a few lounges as well. A particularly good place to wander in search of a drink is toward the west end of Av General San Martin.

ACADEMIA DA CACHAÇA Map p66 Bar

☎ 2239-1542; Rua Conde de Bernadotte 26G, Leblon; noon-1am Sun-Thu, to 2am Fri & Sat

Although *cachaça* (cane liquor) has a sordid reputation in some parts, here the fiery liquor is given the respect it nearly deserves. Along with traditional Brazilian cooking, this pleasant indoor-outdoor spot serves over 100 varieties of *cachaça,* and you can order it straight, with honey and lime, or disguised in a fruity caipirinha. For a treat (and/or a bad hangover), try the passion-fruit *batida* (*cachaça* and passion-fruit juice).

COBAL DO LEBLON Map p66 Bar

☎ 2239-1549; Rua Gilberto Cardoso, Leblon; closed Mon

Leblon's flower-and-produce market features a number of bars and restaurants, many of which open onto the large terrace in back. A vibrant, youthful air pervades this place, and it's a major meeting spot on weekends and on game days.

EMPÓRIO Map p64 — Bar

☎ 3813-2526; Rua Maria Quitéria 37, Ipanema; ⏲ 8pm-4am

A young mix of Cariocas and gringos stirs things up over cheap cocktails at this battered old favorite in Ipanema. A porch in front overlooks the street – a fine spot to stake out when the air gets too heavy with bad '80s music. From Wednesday to Saturday you can catch live rock shows on the 2nd floor (entrance R$10).

BAR LAGOA Map p64 — Boteco

☎ 2523-1135; Av Epitácio Pessoa 1674, Lagoa; ⏲ 6pm-2am Mon-Fri, noon-2am Sat & Sun

With a view of the lake (but separated by a busy road), Bar Lagoa is one of the neighborhood's classic haunts. Founded in 1935, this open-air spot hasn't changed all that much since then: the bar still has surly waiters serving the excellent beer to over-crowded tables and, in spite of its years, a youthful air pervades.

BAR VELOSO Map p66 — Boteco

☎ 2274-9966; Rua Aristides Espínola, Leblon; ⏲ 11am-3am

Named after the original bar (now Garota de Ipanema, opposite) where Jobim and Vinícius penned the famous song 'Girl from Ipanema', the open-sided Bar Veloso attracts a young, good-looking crowd who spill out onto the sidewalk on busy weekends. Upstairs, is a quieter air-conditioned retreat where men (mostly) can watch the game in peace.

BARTHODOMEU Map p64 — Boteco

☎ 2247-8609; Rua Maria Quitéria 46, Ipanema; ⏲ noon-2am

Barthodomeu is a friendly bar that has *boteco* charm – open-sided, wood tables, minimal decor and waiters bustling about under trays of *chope* and piping hot appetizers, including tasty mini-*moquecas* (seafood stew).

BRACARENSE Map p66 — Boteco

☎ 2294-3549; Rua José Linhares 85B, Leblon; ⏲ 7am-midnight Mon-Sat, 10am-10pm Sun

Opened in 1948, Bracarense is a classic Carioca watering hole, famous for its simple, unpretentious ambience and its heavenly *salgados* (bar snacks). A steady stream of neighborhood regulars enjoys over 20 varieties of the snacks (try the *aipim com camarão* – cassava with shrimp) to the accompaniment of icy-cold *chope*.

CONVERSA FIADA Map p66 — Boteco

☎ 2512-9767; Av Ataúlfo de Paiva 900, Leblon; ⏲ 5pm-midnight Mon-Thu, 5pm-3am Fri, noon-3am Sat, noon-midnight Sun

'Conversa Fiada,' which can mean chit-chat or nonsense depending on the context, is an apt title for this lively Leblon bar. With its deep-red walls, an open-sided entry and a laid-back crowd, it's earned a place among the top neighborhood *botecos*. There's also a location in Ipanema (Map p64; Rua Vinícius de Moraes 75).

DEVASSA Map p64 — Boteco

☎ 2522-0627; Rua Prudente de Moraes 416, Ipanema; ⏲ noon-2am

Serving some of Rio's best beer, Devassa makes its own creamy brews, before offering them up to chatty Cariocas at this bar and restaurant – one of 10 in the Rio chain. The choices: *loura* (pilsner), *sarará* (wheat beer), *ruiva* (pale ale), *negra* (dark ale) and *Índia* (IPA). The food menu features well-prepared pub fare – burgers, steak, pastas, grilled fish and lots of appetizers.

GAROTA DE IPANEMA Map p64 — Boteco

☎ 2523-3787; Rua Vinícius de Moraes 49, Ipanema; ⏲ noon-2am

During its first incarnation, this small, open-sided bar was called the Bar Veloso. Its name and anonymity disappeared once two scruffy young regulars – Tom Jobim and Vinícius de Moraes – penned the famous song here that changed history (and the name of the street, too). Today, you'll find a mix of tourists and Cariocas here, as well as sizzling platters of grilled steak.

JOBI Map p66 — Boteco

☎ 2274-0547; Av Ataúlfo de Paiva 1166, Leblon; ⏲ 9am-4am Sun-Thu, to 5am Fri & Sat

A favorite since 1956, Jobi has served a lot of beer in its day, and its popularity hasn't waned. The unadorned *botequim* (bar with table service) still serves plenty; grab a seat by the sidewalk and let the night unfold. If hunger beckons, try the tasty appetizers – the *carne seca* (jerked beef) and the *bolinhos de bacalhau* (codfish croquettes) are tops.

BAR D'HOTEL Map p66 Lounge

☎ 2172-1100; 2nd fl, Marina All Suites, Av Delfim Moreira 696, Leblon; ⏰ noon-2am

The waves crashing on the shore are just part of the background of this texture-rich bar overlooking Ipanema beach. The narrow bar is like a magnet for the style set, who gather in the intimate space to enjoy tropical drinks to the backdrop of sea and ambient electronic music. The adjoining restaurant serves high-end fusion fare (mains around R$60).

BARETTO-LONDRA Map p64 Lounge

☎ 3202-4000; Av Vieira Souto 80, Ipanema; ⏰ 7pm-2am Mon-Thu, to 4am Fri & Sat

Rio's glammiest bar is inside the Hotel Fasano, and offers a vision of decadence matched by few of the city's nightspots. The intimate space, designed by Philippe Starck, has an enchantingly illuminated bar, leather armchairs and divans, and a DJ spinning a world electronica. The crowd is A-list, the drinks are pricey (beer R$16, martinis R$26), and unless you're a model (or have one draped on your arm), prepare for a long wait at the door.

PIZZARIA GUANABARA Map p66 Pizzeria

☎ 2294-0797; Av Ataulfo de Paiva 1228, Leblon; ⏰ 9am-7am

One of the pillars of Baixo Leblon, this popular drinking spot serves lousy pizza – but that hasn't stopped patrons from packing this place at all hours of the night. Expect simple ambience and a young, flirtatious, beer-drinking crowd.

LORD JIM Map p64 Pub

☎ 2294-4881; Rua Paul Redfern 44, Ipanema; ⏰ 6pm-2am Mon-Thu, 6pm-3am Fri, 1pm-3am Sat & Sun

Something of a novelty for Cariocas, Lord Jim is one of several English-style pubs scattered about the Zona Sul. Darts, English-speaking waiters and a few expat beers – Guinness, Harps, Bass etc – are on hand to complete the ambience. The R$25 all-you-can-drink nights (caipirinhas and Imperial beer) get messy.

SHENANIGAN'S Map p64 Pub

☎ 2267-5860; Rua Visconde de Pirajá 112A, Ipanema; admission after 8pm R$5; ⏰ 6pm-2am Mon-Fri, 2pm-3am Sat, to 2am Sun

Overlooking the Praça General Osorio, Shenanigan's is an English-style pub with a exposed brick walls, imported beers and a couple of tiny balconies perched above the street. Cariocas and sunburnt gringos mix it up over games of pool and darts to the occasional backdrop of live bands.

GÁVEA, JARDIM BOTÂNICO & LAGOA

Gávea has one of Rio's liveliest young drinking spots – an area called Baixo Gávea, near Praça Santos Dumont. The bars here almost always draw in a crowd, with imbibers spilling onto the plaza most nights. Jardim Botânico has a youthful population that comes out en masse to the bars along Rua JJ Seabra. Meanwhile, the lakeside kiosks offer a more sedate experience, with couples gathering for live music to the backdrop of Lagoa and Christ the Redeemer.

DA GRAÇA
Map p70 Bar

☎ 2249-5484; Rua Pacheco Leão 780, Jardim Botânico; ⏰ noon-2am Sun & Tue-Thu, to 3am Fri & Sat

The colorful Da Graça is one of Jardim Botânico's liveliest bars. The decor is festive and kitsch: rising up to the tall ceilings are walls draped with shimmering fabric, and brightly hued lamps decorate the entrance. On weekends, the sidewalk tables and the inside of the bar gather a loud but fun crowd.

DRINK CAFÉ Map p70 Bar

☎ 2239-4136; Parque dos Patins, Av Borges de Medeiros, Lagoa; ⏰ 5pm-1am Mon-Wed, to 2:30am Thu & Fri, noon-2:30am Sat & Sun

One of a handful of lively, open-air restaurants along the lake, the Drink Café makes a fine setting to hear live samba, jazz and bossa nova (live-music charge R$6). Besides the peaceful setting and decent tunes, Drink Café has a small menu featuring German specialties.

BRASEIRO DA GÁVEA Map p70 Boteco

☎ 2239-7494; Praça Santos Dumont 116, Gávea; ⏰ noon-1am Sun-Thu, to 3am Fri & Sat

In an area more commonly referred to as Baixo Gávea, Braeiro da Gávea is one of several bar-restaurants in the area responsible for the local residents' chronic lack of sleep. A mixed crowd celebrates here most nights, with patrons spilling onto the facing Praça Santos Dumont.

CAROLINE CAFÉ Map p70 Lounge

☎ 2540-0705; Rua JJ Seabra 10, Jardim Botânico; noon-2am Sun-Wed, to 4am Thu & Fri, 4pm-4am Sat

Caroline Café has been a major destination for couples (hint: it's a great date spot) for over 15 years. There are a few outdoor tables but inside is where you'll find most of the action – which here means a sizeable drink menu (including 20 different types of beer) and an assortment of dishes (ostrich burgers, sushi and brunch selections).

PALAPHITA KITCH Map p70 Lounge

☎ 2227-0837; Av Epitácio Pessoa, Lagoa; 6pm-3am

A great spot for a sundowner, Palaphita Kitch is an open-air, thatched-roof wonderland with rustic bamboo furniture, flickering tiki torches and a peaceful setting on the edge of the lake. This is a popular spot with couples, who come for the creative (and pricey) cocktails and the fine views.

COPACABANA & LEME

Although overshadowed by younger, hipper Ipanema to the south, Copacabana has seen marked improvement in its nightlife offerings, boosted in part by its ocean-fronting kiosks (p137), which make a great spot for a late afternoon drink. On the other side of the busy road are the open-air restaurants and bars of Av Atlântica, which are generally – with a few exceptions – overpriced tourist traps. More authentic is the emerging nightlife area that some have dubbed 'Baixo Copa' (Lower Copa), with a dozen or so lively bars and restaurants sprinkled along a quiet street just back from Ave Atlântica. To explore this area, head along Rua Aires Saldanha and Rua Domingos Ferreira, between Rua Almirante Gonçalves and Rua Constante Ramos. For something more upscale, the best options are at high-end hotel bars, some of which have million-dollar views.

HORSE'S NECK Map p76 Bar

☎ 2525-1232; Sofitel Rio de Janeiro, Av Atlântica 4240, Copacabana; noon-2am

This bright and airy bar has potted palms, wood furnishings and ocean breezes that give it a tropical vibe. This is the place to come to nurse a Belgian beer, while taking in that magnificent stretch of coastline from one of the tables on the terrace.

PONTO DA BOSSA NOVA Map p76 Bar

☎ 2235-4616; Rua Domingos Ferreira 215, Copacabana; noon-1am Sun & Mon, till 3am Tue-Sat

On a lively street sprinkled with bars, Ponto da Bossa Nova is a cozy wood-lined space with a small outdoor patio that makes a peaceful spot for sampling daily lunch specials (R$13 to R$17), appetizers like *carne seca com aipim* (jerked beef with fried cassava) and well-made caipirinhas. True to its name, there's live bossa nova on Tuesday and Saturday nights.

SINDICATO DO CHOPP Map p76 Bar

☎ 2523-4644; Av Atlântica 3806, Copacabana; 11am-3am

A Copacabana institution, this open-air bar looks out on the wide avenue, with the beach in the background. Owing to its breezy location, it attracts a wide mix of people, all playing a part in Copa's inimitable street theater. The food isn't so hot here, but the beers are icy cold and the ocean is, well, right there. A second Sindicato do Chopp (Map p76; Av Atlântica 514, Leme) is an even more peaceful beach-fronting refuge.

SKYLAB BAR Map p76 Bar

☎ 2106-1500; 30th fl, Rio Othon Palace, Av Atlântica 3264, Copacabana; 7pm-midnight

It's all about the view at this modestly decorated bar in the Rio Othon Palace. From 30 floors up, the coastline unfolds, allowing a glimpse of the *Cidade Maravilhosa* (marvelous city) at its most striking.

BOTEQUIM INFORMAL Map p76 Boteco

☎ 3816-0909; Rua Domingos Ferreira 215, Copacabana; noon-1am

An anchor of the newly emerging nightlife stretch known as Baixo Copa, Botequim Informal is a lively drinking spot with an elevated open-sided deck, frothy drafts and tasty appetizers (including a fried polenta with gorgonzola sauce). There are 10 other branches of Botequim Informal in Rio.

ESPELUNCA CHIC Map p76 Boteco

☎ 2236-4090; Rua Bolívar 17A, Copacabana; 5pm-3am

This inviting drinking spot (whose name means 'chic dump') attracts a 50:50 blend

THE DRINK OF CHOICE

One of the great gifts to the cocktail industry is the caipirinha, which is near universally loved – and/or feared – in Rio.

The ingredients are simple – *cachaça* (cane liquor), muddled lime, sugar and ice – but a well-made caipirinha is a work of art. The key component here is the high-proof (40% or so) cane spirit (also known as *pinga* or *aguardente*), which is produced and consumed throughout the country. The production of *cachaça* is as old as slavery in Brazil, with the first distilleries growing up with the sugar plantations – first to satisfy local consumption and then to export to Africa in exchange for slaves. Popular variations on the lime-based caipirinha include the *caipirinha de maracujá* (passion fruit) and the *caipirinha de abacaxi* (pineapple).

Cachaça can also be mixed with fresh fruit juices to make *batidas* (often served as frothy, half-frozen cocktails) or, if it's a particularly fine label (the best *cachaças* generally come from Minas Gerais), ordered straight up. Those who've had their fill of cane spirits might prefer the *caipirosca* or *caipivodcas*, which replace the *cachaça* with vodka. Some bars and clubs also serve *caipisakes*, a refreshing sake-based version of the classic cocktail.

Despite the widespread love affair with the caipirinha, *chope* (*shoh*-pee; draft beer) is also extremely popular in the city. This pale blond pilsner is lighter than and far superior to canned or bottled beer, and it's served ice cold in most bars, which is perhaps one reason why Cariocas per capita are the largest consumers of *chope* in the country.

Incidentally, one other drink worth mentioning is *agua de coco* (coconut water). Loaded with electrolytes, plus useful minerals such as potassium and sodium, this hydrating drink is one of the best cures for a hangover. Drink two (or three!) if you drank a few too many caipirinhas on the previous night.

of neighborhood locals and tourists who stumble upon it from nearby hotels. The open-air seating in front is a draw.

ALLEGRO BISTRÔ MUSICAL
Map p76 Cafe

☎ 2548-5005; www.modernsound.com.br; Modern Sound records, Rua Barata Ribeiro 502, Copacabana; ⏲ noon-9pm Mon-Fri, to 8pm Sat

This small café and drinking spot in Copacabana features live music most days. See p160 for more details.

BAR DO COPA Map p76 Lounge

☎ 2548-7070; Copacabana Palace hotel, Av Atlântica 1702, Copacabana; admission R$40-80; ⏲ 8pm-2am Wed, 9pm-4am Thu-Sat

Inside Copacabana's most recognizable landmark, this poolside bar received a dramatic R$4million makeover in 2009, raising the stakes in the hotelier design game (for other contenders, see p190). The ceiling, with its 10,000 points of light, aims to mimic the night sky, while crystal chandeliers, glowing column-sized luminaries and gilded mosaics add a vaguely futuristic element to the spacious lounge. There are live bands and DJs; Palace guests get in free.

COPA CAFÉ Map p76 Lounge

☎ 2235-2947; Av Atlântica 3056, Copacabana; ⏲ 7pm-1am Mon-Wed, to 2am Thu-Sun

A notch above most other eateries along Ave Atlântica, this stylish eating and drinking spot has a downstairs lounge that brings a well-dressed cocktail-sipping crowd, with a dining room upstairs that specializes in grilled dishes. See also p138.

BOTAFOGO & URCA

Botafogo is the place to go for lively, authentic Carioca bars, with fun, mixed crowds and little of the pretense you might encounter in bars further south. Rua Visconde de Caravelas is a good place to browse the pub scene. Untouched Urca remains fairly nightlife starved, though it does have several excellent open-air spots, including Praia Vermelha (p162) for live samba.

BAR URCA
Map p80 Bar

☎ 2295-8744; Rua Cândido Gaffré 205, Urca; ⏲ 6:30-11pm Mon-Sat, 8am-7pm Sun

This simple neighborhood bar and restaurant has a marvelous setting near Urca's bayside waterfront. At night, young and old crowd along the seaside wall as waiters bring cold drinks and appetizers.

BOTEQUIM Map p80 Bar

☎ 2286-3391; Rua Visconde de Caravelas 184, Botafogo; ⏲ noon-1am

Another of Botafogo's great neighborhood bars, Botequim is an old-school, down-at-the-heels watering hole serving a friendly crowd. The menu has plenty of appetizers and more substantial dishes if you need something to accompany those *chopes*.

CHAMPANHARIA OVELHA NEGRA
Map p80 Bar

☎ 2226-1064; Rua Bambina 120, Botafogo; ⌚ 5:30-11:30pm Mon-Fri

One of Rio's best happy-hour scenes (and rated the city's best spot for flirting by *Veja Rio*), Ovelha Negra draws a mix of locals who come for the lively conversation and the 40 different varieties of champagne and *prosecco* (Italian sparkling white wine) – the specialties of the house.

COBAL DO HUMAITÁ Map p80 Bar

Rua Voluntafrios da Pátria, Botafogo

A large food market on the western edge of Botafogo (technically in Humaitá), the Cobal transforms into a festive nightspot when the sun goes down, complete with live music and open-air eating and drinking.

ESPÍRITO DO CHOPP Map p80 Bar

☎ 2266-5599; Cobal do Humaitá, Rua Voluntários da Pátria 446, Botafogo; ⌚ 9am-midnight Sun-Thu, to 2am Fri & Sat

One of many open-air venues in the Cobal, Espirito do Chopp fills up its plastic tables most nights with a festive, low-key crowd. The beer flows in abundance and there's always music nearby – either here or at one of the neighboring bars.

GAROTA DA URCA Map p80 Boteco

☎ 2541-8585; Rua João Luís Alves 56, Urca; ⌚ noon-1am Sun-Thu, to 2:30am Fri & Sat

A neighborhood crowd gathers over *chope* and *salgados* in the evening at this low-key spot. See p140.

O PLEBEU Map p80 Boteco

☎ 2286-0699; Rua Capitão Salomão 50, Botafogo; ⌚ 11:30am-4am Mon-Sat, 11:30am-9:30pm Sun

In the liveliest stretch of Botafogo, O Plebeu is a welcoming, open-sided two-story bar with tables spilling onto the sidewalk and a 2nd-floor balcony. Neighborhood regulars pack this place, drawn by ice-cold beer (served in bottles), codfish balls and the unpretentious crowd.

FLAMENGO, LARANJEIRAS & COSME VELHO

Very few tourists find their way to the bars in Flamengo, which are mostly low-key neighborhood hangouts that are popular around happy hour. Rua Marquês de Abrantes is the best street to take in the scene, with bars and restaurants attracting a drinking crowd. Laranjeiras is best known for Rua Alice, which sports a couple of traditional *botecos* as well as the excellent nightspot Casa Rosa (p162). A short taxi ride from there is the pizzeria and nightclub Hideaway (p141).

ARMAZÉM DO CHOPP Map p84 Bar

☎ 2557-4052; Rua Marquês de Abrantes 66, Flamengo; ⌚ 11am-2am

On a bar-sprinkled stretch of Flamengo, Armazém do Chopp looms like a giant over the road. This wooden barnlike structure has outdoor seating on the raised veranda in front and cooler (air-conditioned) seating inside. It's a lively local meeting spot, particularly in the early evening, and there's a good-value selection of dishes (appetizers, grilled meats) to accompany the cold draft beer.

HERR BRAUER Map p84 Bar

☎ 2225-4359; Rua Barão do Flamengo 35; ⌚ noon-midnight Tue-Sun, noon-4pm Mon

Dedicated to the great beers of the world, this cozy new drinking den has already earned many admirers. You'll find Belgian beers (such as Duvel and Deus), German labels (Erdinger, Warsteiner), English brew (Abbot Ale, Newcastle), plus Guinness, Brazilian microbrews and dozens of other offerings (some 80 labels in all). Stop in for happy hour (6pm to 8pm Tuesday to Sunday) when a changing line-up of beers is on special for R$12.

BELMONTE Map p84 Boteco

☎ 2552-3349; Praia do Flamengo 300, Flamengo; ⌚ 9am-3am

One of Flamengo's classic *botecos*, Belmonte serves up well-chilled *chope* until late into the night. When we went there Thursday was the liveliest night. Owing to its popularity, Belmonte branches are now found all over Rio.

DEVASSA Map p84 Boteco

☎ 2556-0618; Rua Senador Vergueiro 2, Flamengo; ⌚ noon-1am

A particularly inviting branch of the growing Devassa network, this bar is set on a shaded square, and serves the usual Devassa hits, including great drafts. See p151 for more details.

CENTRO & CINELÂNDIA

Rio's working stiffs have some fine choices when it comes to joining the happy-hour fray. One of the most magical settings for a sundowner is along the historic Travessa do Comércio. The sidewalk tables on this narrow, cobbled lane are packed on weekday nights, particularly as the weekend nears (Thursday is always a good bet). These places see a bit of action during the day on Saturday (several restaurants along Rua do Rosario serve *feijoada* – black bean and pork stew), but close the rest of the weekend. Another choice after-work spot is Praça Floriano, with its handful of bars.

ATELIÊ CULINÁRIO Map p90 Bar

☎ 2240-2573; Praça Floriano, Cinelândia; 🕑 noon-10pm Mon-Fri

A lunch and after-work crowd gathers at this pleasant open-air bistro on the edge of Praça Floriano. See p143 for more details.

BOTECO CASUAL Map p90 Bar

☎ 2232-0250; Travessa do Comércio 26, Centro; 🕑 noon-midnight Mon-Fri, to 6pm Sat

Hidden in a narrow lane leading off Praça Quinze de Novembro, Boteco Casual is one of several photogenic open-air bars on Travessa do Comércio. The narrow pedestrian lane is a popular meeting spot and a festive air arrives at workday's end as Cariocas fill the tables spilling onto the street.

ESCH CAFÉ Map p90 Bar

☎ 2507-5866; Rua do Rosário 107, Centro; 🕑 noon-10pm Mon-Fri

The smoky twin of the Leblon Esch Café (p161), this Esch offers the same selection of Cuban cigars from its humidor. Its dark-wood interior has stuffed leather chairs and there's a decent food-and-cocktail menu.

AMARELINHO Map p90 Boteco

☎ 2240-8434; Praça Floriano 55, Cinelândia; 🕑 11am-2am

Easy to spot by its bright *amarelo* (yellow) awning, Amarelinho has a splendid setting on the Praça Floriano. Waiters serve plenty of *chope* here, wandering among the crowded tables, with the Teatro Municipal in the background. Amarelinho is a popular lunch spot but packs in even bigger crowds for that ever-important after-work brew.

BAR LUIZ Map p90 Boteco

☎ 2262-6900; Rua da Carioca 39, Centro; 🕑 11am-11:30pm Mon-Sat

Inaugurated in 1887, this saloon and dining spot serves some of the city's best brew. See p143 for more details.

SANTA TERESA & LAPA

Two of Rio's most atmospheric neighborhoods are still rough around the edges, so take care when visiting here. Lapa is at its

BAR BITES

If you're heading home from the beach and can't be bothered with a sit-down meal, go Carioca and grab a meal at a neighborhood bar. While not particularly healthy, these satisfying snacks – known as *petiscos, tira-gostos* or *salgados* – go quite nicely with a *chope*. (For info on local drinks, see p154.) Here are some items you are likely to find at most *botecos*:

Aipim Frito Deep fried slices of cassava.

Bolinhos de aipim Deep-fried cassava balls, sometimes served with shrimp and other treats baked inside.

Bolinhos de bacalhau Deep-fried codfish balls.

Bolinhos de queijo Crispy deep-fried cheese balls.

Carne seca com aipim frito Sundried jerked meat with deep-fried cassava slices.

Coxinha Pear-shaped cornmeal balls filled with fried chicken or beef.

Linguiça acebolada Fried sausage and onions.

Pão de queijo A slightly gooey cheese bread, baked into bite-sized biscuits; the biscuits are so popular in Brazil that a whole franchise was launched on their success (naturally named Pão de Queijo).

Pastel de camarão Crispy deep-fried pastry filled with shrimp. Other fillings include *pastel de carne* (beef) and *pastel de queijo* (cheese – often the mild, stringy catupiry).

Torresmo Deep-fried pork rinds.

wildest during the weekends, with Cariocas from all over the city heading to the neighborhood's samba clubs. Santa Teresa's bar scene is sprinkled along the main street near Largo do Guimarães, though Largo das Neves, with its tiny plaza and open-sided bars, is also a draw. Take a taxi when visiting these neighborhoods at night.

ADEGA FLOR DE COIMBRA Map p98 Bar

☎ 2224-4582; Rua Teotônio Regadas 34, Lapa; 🕒 noon-2am Mon-Sat, noon-6pm Sun

In the same building that was once the home of Brazilian painter Cândido Portinari, the Adega Flor de Coimbra has been a bohemian haunt since it opened in 1938. Back in its early days, leftists, artists and intellectuals drank copiously at the slim old bar looking out on Lapa. Today, it draws a mix of similar types, who drink wine and sangria with Adega's tasty *bolinhos de bacalhau* (codfish croquettes) or *feijoada*.

CHOPERIA BRAZOOKA

Map p98 Bar

☎ 2224-3235; Av Mem de Sá 70, Lapa; 🕒 6pm-2am Tue-Wed, 6pm-5am Thu-Sat

This popular four-story beer house has lots of nooks and crannies where you can while away the night over ice-cold drafts and tasty appetizers. The 20- and 30-something crowd packs this place, so arrive early to score a table.

GOYA-BEIRA

Map p98 Bar

☎ 2232-5751; Largo das Neves 13, Santa Teresa; 🕒 6pm-midnight Sun-Thu, to 2am Fri & Sat

Small but charming Goya-Beira is one of Santa Teresa's gems. This small, intimate bar faces out onto Largo das Neves, with the occasional tram rattling by in the early evening. Owner Rose Guerra prepares intriguing *cachaça* infusions as well as pizzas and appetizers. Things are liveliest on weekends. It's fine to arrive and leave by the tram, but it's unsafe to walk here from Largo do Guimarães – take a taxi instead.

MIKE'S HAUS Map p98 Bar

☎ 2509-5248; Rua Almirante Alexandrino 1458A, Santa Teresa; 🕒 noon-midnight Sun-Thu, to 2am Fri & Sat

This German-style pub attracts a mix of expats and Cariocas on weekend nights. It's a bit off the beaten path, so plan on staying for a while once you get there. Meals are served as well; see p146.

ANTÔNIO'S Map p98 Boteco

☎ 2224-4197; Av Mem de Sá 88, Lapa; 🕒 4pm-3am Sun-Thu, to 5am Fri & Sat

Antônio's in Lapa has lots of old-school charm with its hanging lamps, wrought-iron trimwork and simple wooden tables (with a few seats on the sidewalk for taking in the pulsing street scene). Plenty of other drinking spots are nearby, if you feel like wandering.

ARMAZÉM SÃO THIAGO Map p98 Boteco

☎ 2232-0822; Rua Áurea 26, Santa Teresa; 🕒 noon-midnight Mon-Sat, to 10pm Sun

Still referred to by everyone as the 'Bar do Gomes', this historic, but still hole-in-the-wall drinking establishment, features a few stand-up tables and a counter. It doesn't look like much, and the neighborhood regulars would probably say it isn't – between sips of beer. Regardless, the crowds pack this place on weekends, with punters spilling onto the sidewalks.

BAR DO MINEIRO Map p98 Boteco

☎ 2221-9227; Rua Paschoal Carlos Magno 99, Santa Teresa; 🕒 11am-1am Tue-Sat, to midnight Sun

Famous for its Minas Gerais cuisine, Bar do Mineiro is one of Santa Teresa's most traditional *botecos* – and an excellent place for a drink while catching up on the local gossip. See p146 for more details.

BOTECO DO GOMES

Map p98 Boteco

☎ 2531-9717; Rua do Riachuelo 62, Lapa; 🕒 7am-1am

In Lapa, the Boteco do Gomes has the classical look of an old-time bar with brick walls, art-deco light fixtures, and tile floors. Patrons are a mix of musicians, students and Lapa hangabouts, who gather for a quick drink at stand-up tables in front or at the roomier dining area in back.

TABERNA DO JUCA Map p98 Boteco

☎ 2221-9839; Av Mem de Sá 65, Lapa; 🕒 noon-2am Sun-Thu, noon-5am Fri & Sat

A staple of Lapa's hard-drinking scene, this classic-looking spot attracts a diverse bunch – old artists, shop owners, musicians, prostitutes and the odd ones you can't pin down – and the crowd tends to get more colorful as the night progresses.

BAR DOS DESCASADOS

Map p98 Lounge

☎ 2222-2755; Rua Almirante Alexandrino 660, Santa Teresa; ⏲ noon-midnight

Inside Hotel Santa Teresa (p197), this stylish bar with outdoor seating has lovely views over the city (looking north). You can enjoy decadent cocktails (including a caipirinha made with tangerines grown on the property) and savory snacks (such as salmon tartare), while pondering the A-list crowd and the intriguing history that surrounds you (the building was once a hotel for the recently divorced, and before that the bar functioned as the slave quarters of a working coffee plantation). The bar is fairly empty during the week but becomes a livelier destination, mostly for couples, on weekends.

NIGHTLIFE

top picks

- **Trapiche Gamboa** (p165)
- **Casa Rosa** (p162)
- **Carioca da Gema** (p162)
- **Rio Scenarium** (p164)
- **Democráticus** (p163)
- **Salgueiro** (p163)
- **Baronneti** (p166)
- **Teatro Odisséia** (p165)
- **00** (Zero Zero; p166)
- **Melt** (p168)

What's your recommendation? www.lonelyplanet.com/rio-de-janeiro

NIGHTLIFE

The city that gave the world samba, bossa nova and baile funk offers dozens of ways to spend a sleepless night among the Cariocas (residents of Rio). Music is the lifeblood of Rio, with few places in the world rivaling its dynamism. You'll find samba clubs, jazz bars, dance halls, lounges and nightclubs all churning out that addictive Brazilian sound. In general, Cariocas prefer live bands over DJs, with many places around the city to hear the latest talent (though Lapa is the headquarters of the music scene). While there are fewer nightclubs, these certainly have their supporters and hardcore partiers often end their night on a dance floor after catching live music elsewhere.

As with bar-goers, there are a few different subcultures (models and modelizers, surfers, hipsters and hippies) within the nightlife circuit, though there's plenty of crossover between groups. The well-heeled crowd from the Zona Sul, for instance, tends to favor high-end nightclubs in Gávea and Barra, while an alternative crowd heads to the clubs in Botafogo. Lapa's mix of bars and dance halls attracts a more diverse mix of people from all backgrounds who have little in common aside from a love of samba.

Venues come and go – and the best parties are often one-off events in unique spots – so it helps if you can get the latest from a local source. If you can read a bit of Portuguese, pick up the *Veja Rio* insert in *Veja* magazine, which comes out each Sunday. *Rio Show*, the entertainment insert that comes in the Friday edition of *O Globo*, also has extensive listings. Rio Festa (www.riofesta.com.br) lists the top picks for shows, clubs and happy-hours each week.

MUSIC & DANCE

Rio has a world-class music scene. Samba, jazz, bossa nova, Música Popular Brasileira (MPB), rock, hip-hop, reggae, electronic music and the fusions among them are a big part of the picture. Brazil's many regional styles – *forró* (traditional Brazilian music from the northeast), *chorinho* (romantic, intimate samba) and *pagode* (relaxed and rhythmic samba) – are also a part of the music scene.

Venues range from megamodern concert halls seating thousands to intimate samba clubs in edgy neighborhoods. Antiquated colonial mansions, outdoor parks overlooking the city, old-school bars, crumbling buildings on the edge of town and hypermodern lounges facing the ocean are all part of the mix.

CONSUMPTION CARD

At many clubs in Rio, you'll be handed a control card when you walk in the door. Rather than paying for individual drinks with cash, each time you place an order it will be marked on your card. At the end of the night, you'll head to the cashier and pay for your food and drinks, the 10% service fee, plus the admission charge. Whatever you do, hang on to that card! If you lose it, most places will charge you a fee of R$100.

LIVE MUSIC

Although straight-up bossa nova isn't much in fashion today in Rio, jazz has been growing in popularity, and there's even a dedicated newsstand where you can catch live blues once or twice a week. Those looking to dance should check out samba clubs (p162). For more information on Brazilian music, see p34.

ALLEGRO BISTRÔ MUSICAL Map p76

☎ 2548-5005; www.modernsound.com.br; Modern Sound, Rua Barata Ribeiro 502, Copacabana; admission free; 🕐 store 9am-9pm Mon-Fri, to 8pm Sat

This ever-expanding café in Copacabana's music store Modern Sound (p118) features live music most nights of the week. Jazz, samba and MPB groups play to a slightly older Carioca crowd from 5pm to 9pm, though Allegro also hosts afternoon piano recitals (1pm to 5pm). Reservations are recommended – though you can always mill about in the store if you can't get a table. No cover, but sometimes there's a minimum consumption requirement (R$10 to R$40 per person for well-known singers).

ASA BRANCA Map p98

☎ 2224-9358; Av Mem de Sá 17, Lapa; admission R$10-20; 🕐 8pm-3am Wed-Sat

Near the Arcos da Lapa, Asa Branca attracts lovers of *forró* to its large, smoky dance floor. Recently renovated, this is one of the mainstays of Lapa, with a slightly older crowd packing in on weekends. In addition to some of the best *forró* in the city, the club also hosts samba and MPB.

BECO DO RATO Map p98

☎ 2508-9574; Rua Joaquim Silva 11, Lapa; admission free; 🕑 8pm-3am Tue-Fri

One of Lapa's classic samba spots, this tiny bar has excellent live groups playing to a cheerful crowd. The outdoor seating and informal setting are an unbeatable mix. Marcio, the friendly owner, hails from Minas Gerais; to get the night started, ask him for a tasty *cachaça* (cane liquor) from his home state. Friday night is particularly good to catch live samba; it's closed on Saturdays.

BIP BIP Map p76

☎ 2267-9696; Rua Almirante Gonçalves 50, Copacabana; admission free; 🕑 6:30pm-1am

For years, Bip Bip has been one of the city's favorite spots to catch a live *roda de samba* (informal samba played around a table). Although it's just a storefront with a few battered tables, as the evening progresses the tree-lined neighborhood becomes the backdrop to serious jam sessions, with music and revelers spilling into the street. The schedule at the time of writing was samba on Thursday and Sunday at 8pm, *choro* (short for *chorinho* – romantic, intimate samba) on Tuesday and Wednesday at 8:30pm and bossa nova on Monday at 9pm.

DRINKERIA MALDITA Map p76

☎ 3439-1978; Rua Aires Saldanha 98, Copacabana; admission R$5-20; 🕑 8pm-3am Tue-Sat, 4pm-1am Sun

Brought to you by the folks of Casa da Matriz (p166) this loud, dark, rock-loving bar moved from Botafogo to this open space in 2009 and presents a line-up of indie rock bands, DJs and karaoke nights, which are currently Wednesday and Sunday – arrive early if you're itching to sing.

ESCH CAFÉ Map p66

☎ 2512-5651; Rua Dias Ferreira 78, Leblon; 🕑 noon-1:30am Mon-Sat, noon-midnight Sun

Billing itself as the House of Havana, Esch offers a blend of Cuban cigars and jazz. The dark-wood interior combined with the well-dressed over-30 crowd will probably make you feel like you're stepping into a Johnnie Walker photo shoot. Groups perform on Friday and Saturday nights (admission R$25 to R$50).

CARIOCA NIGHTS

One of Rio's best summer-long parties is the annual Noites Cariocas, featuring a mix of Brazilian and international stars playing before a festive, dance-loving crowd. In recent years performers like Jorge Benjor, Gilberto Gil and Marcelo D2 have all played. The event kicks off in mid-November and runs through early February, with concerts held on Friday and Saturday night from about 10pm to 4am. Locations change from year to year, with past *noites* taking place atop Pão de Açúcar and more recently at the Pier Mauá, just north of Centro. Admission is typically around R$80. See the website of Noites Cariocas (www.noitescariocas.com.br in Portuguese) for more details.

ESPAÇO RIO CARIOCA Map p84 Bistrô $

☎ 2225-7332; www.espacoriocarioca.com.br; Rua Leite Leal 45, Laranjeiras; admission R$10-20; 🕑 3-10pm Mon-Fri, noon-10pm Sat & Sun

This creative space, equal parts bookstore, café and bistro (p142), hosts live music from Wednesday to Saturday nights in the intimate café, beginning around 8:30pm. A mix of MPB and jazz groups play here.

FAR UP Map p80

☎ 2266-5599; Cobal do Humaitá, Rua Voluntários da Pátria 446, Botafogo; admission R$5-25; 🕑 9pm-2am Tue-Thu, to 5am Fri & Sat

Featuring live music most nights of the week, Far Up is a good destination if you're hanging out in Botafogo. The program leans toward rock and MPB, although the Tuesday night karaoke session mixes things up.

HIDEAWAY Map p84

☎ 2285-0921; Rua das Laranjeiras 308, Laranjeiras; admission R$15-25; 🕑 6pm-2am Mon-Thu, to 4am Fri & Sat

In a small club hidden inside a popular pizzeria (p141), Hideaway hosts live jazz and MPB concerts. Call for the latest schedule.

MAZE INN Map p87

☎ 2558-5547; www.jazzrio.info; Casa 66, Rua Tavares Bastos 414, Catete; admission before/after 10pm R$10/20; 🕑 10pm-3am 1st Fri of month

Also known as the 'Casa do Bob' after owner Bob Nadkarni, this once-a-month event is well worth attending if you're in town. It's set in the guesthouse (p196) of the same name high up in Tavares Bastos (Rio's safest favela). There's a fun mix of Cariocas and expats, with good live jazz and fantastic views over the city.

PARADA DA LAPA Map p98

☎ 2524-2950; www.paradadalapa.com.br, in Portuguese; Rua dos Arcos 10, Lapa; admission R$10-20; ⏰ 6pm-1am Tue-Thu, 6pm-4am Fri, 8pm-4am Sat

In an annex next to Fundição Progresso, this multi-level bar and live-music venue has an upstairs open-air terrace with magical views of the Lapa arches. The stage inside hosts an eclectic line-up of live samba, MPB, jazz, rock and cabaret performances, plus football (soccer) matches broadcast on the big screen on Wednesday nights.

PRAIA VERMELHA Map p80

☎ 2275-7292; Praça General Tibúrcio, Urca; cover R$6-12; ⏰ noon-midnight Mon-Wed, to 2am Thu-Sat

Perched over the beach of the same name, Praia Vermelha has gorgeous views of Pão de Açúcar looming overhead. By night, jazzy MPB bands play from 6pm onward, making for an enviable open-air setting. The food is less spectacular, though the pizzas are fairly decent.

SEVERYNA DE LARANJEIRAS Map p84

☎ 2556-9398; Rua Ipiranga 54, Laranjeiras; admission R$10; ⏰ 11:30am-2am

At night this broad, rustically decorated dining hall forms the backdrop to Brazilian rhythms, and there's a broad menu of northeastern fare. Large percussive groups perform *samba, forró* and MPB, among other styles, to a sometimes packed house. Shows begin around 9pm.

TEATRO RIVAL PETROBRAS Map p90

☎ 2524-1666; www.rivalpetrobras.com.br, in Portuguese; Rua Álvaro Alvim 33, Cinelândia; admission R$30-60; ⏰ box office noon-8pm Mon-Fri, 3:30-8pm Sat

Near Praça Floriano, this modern 450-seat hall has become a popular spot for some of the city's up-and-coming groups as well as veteran musicians well known in Brazil (Tania Alves, Mart'nalia). Four or five nights a week, Teatro Rival hosts MPB, *pagode,* samba, *chorinho* and *forró* groups.

VINÍCIUS PIANO BAR Map p64

☎ 2523-4757; Rua Prudente de Morais 34, Ipanema; admission R$30-40

Billing itself as the 'temple of bossa nova,' Vinícius Piano Bar has been an icon in the neighborhood since 1989. The indoor/outdoor tables make a fine setting to listen to decent bossa nova and a few samba and MPB singers. Opening singers start at 9:30pm; the featured artist plays at 11pm.

Samba Clubs

Gafieiras (dancehalls) have risen from the ashes of a once-bombed-out neighborhood and reinvigorated it with an air of youth and song. The neighborhood in question is Lapa, and after years of neglect it has reclaimed its place as Rio's nightlife center. In the '20s and '30s Lapa was a major destination for the bohemian crowd, who were attracted to its decadent cabaret joints, brothels and *gafieiras.* Today its vintage buildings hide beautifully restored interiors set with wide dance floors. Although not all the places mentioned here are in Lapa – and not all of them can be technically classed as *gafieiras* either – they all reconnect with that great samba sound.

BAR DA LADEIRA Map p98

☎ 2224-9828; Rua Evaristo da Veiga 149, Lapa, Santa Teresa; admission R$10-20; ⏰ 8pm-2am Thu-Sat

Just around the corner from the Arcos da Lapa, this early 1900s house throws down a fair bit of live samba. The large space has a small dance floor, a pool table, and plenty of little nooks and crannies. The samba bands get going around 10pm.

CARIOCA DA GEMA Map p98

☎ 2221-0043; Av Mem de Sá 79, Lapa; admission R$20-25; ⏰ 6pm-1:30am Mon-Thu, to 3:30am Fri & Sat

Although it's now surrounded by clubs, Carioca da Gema was one of Lapa's pioneers when it opened in 2000. This small, warmly lit club still attracts some of the city's best samba bands, and you'll find a festive, mixed crowd filling the dance floor most nights. Catch free live music here from Monday to Friday around 8pm.

CASA ROSA Map p84

☎ 2557-2562; Rua Alice 550, Laranjeiras; admission R$15-25; ⏰ 11pm-5am Fri & Sat, 7pm-2am Sun

In the first few decades of the 20th century Casa Rosa was one of the city's most

SAMBA SCHOOLS & SHOWS

Starting in September (in preparation for Carnaval) – or sometimes as early as July – most big samba schools open their weekly rehearsals to the public. An *escola de samba* (samba school) is a professional troupe that performs in the grand samba parade during Carnaval. They typically charge between R$5 and R$30 at the door (prices are higher the closer you are to Carnaval), and you'll be able to buy drinks. These are large dance parties, not specific lessons in samba, that are fun to watch, although you may learn to samba at some of them. Many samba schools are in the favelas (shanty towns), so use common sense and consider going with a Carioca for safety. It's best to take a taxi – and afterwards, there are usually plenty of taxis in front. Mangueira and Salgueiro are among the easiest schools to get to.

Following is a list of samba schools, contact information and rehearsal days – they all get incredibly packed as Carnaval approaches. The schools that are most popular with tourists are generally Salgueiro and Mangueira. It's always best to confirm if there is going to be a rehearsal. A decent website for checking times and reading up on other Carnaval-related activities is www.rio-carnival.net.

Beija-Flor (☎ 2791-2866; www.beija-flor.com.br; Praçinha Wallace Paes Leme 1025, Nilópolis; 🕑 9pm Thu)

Grande Rio (☎ 2671-3585; www.granderio.org.br; Rua Almirante Barroso 5-6, Duque de Caixas; 🕑 10pm Fri)

Imperatriz Leopoldinense (☎ 2560-8037; www.imperatrizleopoldinense.com.br; Rua Professor Lacê 235, Ramos; 🕑 8pm Sun)

Mangueira (Map p60; ☎ 2567-4637; www.mangueira.com.br; Rua Visconde de Niterói 1072, Mangueira; 🕑 10pm Sat)

Mocidade Independente de Padre Miguel (☎ 3332-5823; www.mocidadeindependente.com.br; Rua Coronel Tamarindo 38, Padre Miguel; 🕑 10pm Sat)

Porta da Pedra (☎ 3707-1518; www.unidosdoportodapedra.com.br; Av Lúcio Tomé Feteiro 290, Vila Lage, São Gonçalo; 🕑 8pm Wed)

Portela (☎ 2489-6440; Rua Clara Nunes 81, Madureira; 🕑 10pm Fri)

Rocinha (Map p60; ☎ 3205-3318; www.academicosdarocinha.com.br; Rua Bertha Lutz 80, São Conrado; 🕑 10pm Sat)

Salgueiro (Map p60; ☎ 2238-0389; www.salgueiro.com.br; Rua Silva Teles 104, Andaraí; 🕑 10pm Sat)

Unidos da Tijuca (☎ 2518-3957; www.unidosdatijuca.com.br; Clube dos Portuários, Rua Francisco Bicalho 47, Cidade Nova; 🕑 10pm Sat)

Vila Isabel (☎ 2578-0077; www.gresunidosdevilaisabel.com.br; Av Blvd 28 de Setembro 382, Vila Isabel; 🕑 10pm Sat)

Viradouro (☎ 2628-7840; www.unidosdoviradouro.com.br; Av do Contorno 16, Barreto, Niterói; 🕑 10pm Sat)

famous brothels in Rio's red-light area. Times have changed somewhat and today the demure Pink House is one of Rio's best nightspots. It has a large outdoor patio between several dance floors, where different bands play throughout the night. Saturday is the best night to go, though Casa Rosa's Sunday *roda de samba* party also draws its fans.

CENTRO CULTURAL CARIOCA

Map p90

☎ 2252-6468; www.centroculturalcarioca.com.br, in Portuguese; Rua do Teatro 37, Centro; admission R$20-30; 🕑 7pm-1am Mon-Thu, 8:30pm-2am Fri & Sat

This carefully restored 19th-century building hosts an excellent musical line-up throughout the week, and it is a good option for those wanting to escape the Lapa crowds. The scene here is slightly more staid, which makes it a good choice for couples.

DEMOCRÁTICUS

Map p98

☎ 2252-4611; Rua do Riachuelo 93, Lapa; admission R$20-40; 🕑 10pm-3am Wed-Sat

Murals line the foyer of this 1867 mansion. The rhythms filter down from above. Follow the sound up the marble staircase and out into a large hall filled with tables, an enormous dance floor and a long stage covered with musicians. A wide mix of Cariocas gathers here to dance, revel in the music and soak up the splendor of the samba-infused setting. If you come to just one *gafieira* in Lapa, Democráticus is a good choice.

ESTRELA DA LAPA

Map p98

☎ 2507-6686; Av Mem de Sá 69, Lapa; admission R$15-30; ⏰ 9pm-1am Wed & Thu, to 3am Fri & Sat

On Lapa's liveliest street, this multilevel space has an eclectic music scene and hosts bands playing *choro*, blues and hip-hop. Shows begin at 10pm, followed by a DJ (Thursday to Saturday) who keeps the dance floor going until late.

ESTUDANTINA MUSICAL Map p90

☎ 2507-5131; Praça Tiradentes 79, Centro; admission R$10-20; ⏰ 10pm-3:30am Thu-Sat

This old dance hall packs large, older crowds on the weekend, there to enjoy the excellent samba bands. Occasional big-name artists perform here (like Maria Bethânia in 2010). The open-air veranda provides a nice spot to cool off if you've danced yourself into a sweat.

LAPA 40 GRAUS Map p98

☎ 3970-1338; Rua Riachuelo 97, Lapa; admission R$5; ⏰ 6pm-4am

This impressive multistory music venue and pool hall has tables for lounging on the 1st floor, over a dozen pool tables on the 2nd floor, and a small stage and dancing couples on the top floor. Pop, rock, samba and *choro* kick off nightly around 7pm and 11pm (admission to shows is R$5 to R$30).

MANGUE SECO CACHAÇARIA

Map p90

☎ 3852-1947; Rua do Lavradio 23, Lapa; admission R$10; ⏰ 11am-midnight Mon-Thu, to 2am Fri & Sat

Set in a street lined with a mix of antique shops and bars, the two-story Mangue Seco has a casual bar and restaurant on the 1st floor and a *cachaçaria* (*cachaça* bar) on the 2nd floor. Sample over 100 different brands of the fiery stuff while listening to live *choro*, bossa nova or samba bands (starting at 6pm Monday to Thursday, and 9pm or 10pm Friday and Saturday).

MAS SERÁ O BENEDITO Map p98

☎ 2232-9000; www.seraobenedito.com; Av Gomes Freire 599, Lapa; admission R$10-20; ⏰ noon-4pm & 5pm-3am Mon-Sat

This beautifully restored space (occupying a 19th-century mansion) opened in 2009 and immediately attracted a following. There's a restaurant on the ground floor, two pool tables on the 2nd floor and a concert space with live samba on the 3rd floor, where bands play nightly.

MISTURA CARIOCA Map p98

☎ 7830-6098; Av Gomes Freire 791, Lapa; admission R$12-18; ⏰ 8pm-3am Wed-Sat

A classic but less popular samba club in Lapa, Mistura Carioca has two levels, with the band playing on the 1st floor, and a quiet upper level, where you can look down on the scene below. Big glass chandeliers add to the old-time charm.

RIO SCENARIUM

Map p98

☎ 3147-9000; www.rioscenarium.com.br, in Portuguese; Rua do Lavradio 20, Lapa; admission R$20-30; ⏰ 7pm-2am Tue-Thu, 8pm-5am Fri & Sat

One of the city's most photogenic nightspots, Rio Scenarium has three floors, each lavishly decorated with antiques. Balconies overlook the stage on the 1st floor, with dancers keeping time to the jazz-infused samba, *choro* or *pagode* filling the air. Rio Scenarium receives much press outside of Brazil, and attracts at least as many foreigners as locals.

SACRILÉGIO Map p98

☎ 2222-7345; Av Mem de Sá 81, Lapa; admission R$16-25; ⏰ 7pm-1am Tue, to 3am Wed-Fri, 9pm-3am Sat

Next door to Carioca da Gema (p162), Sacrilégio is another major spot for catching live bands in an intimate setting. The outdoor garden makes a fine spot for imbibing a few cold *chopes* while the music filters through the windows. In addition to samba, Sacrilégio hosts *choro*, *forró* and MPB bands.

SEMENTE Map p98

☎ 9781-2451; Rua Joaquim Silva 138, Lapa; admission R$15-25; ⏰ 8pm-2am Sat-Thu

One of the few venues in Lapa that holds court on Sunday and Monday nights, Semente has longevity. Although it has closed and reopened a few times, it was one of the first places in Lapa to bring samba back to the city. Its current incarnation is small and intimate, with good bands and a crowd that comes for the music rather than the Lapa mayhem (note that it's closed Friday night).

SAMBA DA MESA *Carmen Michael*

On Friday night Rio's samba community congregates in front of the faded colonial facades of Rua do Mercado under a canopy of tropical foliage to play *samba da mesa* (literally, samba of the table). On the worn cobblestones a long table stands, altar-like. Around it the musicians sit and the crowd gyrates, paying homage to their favorite religion. *Samba da mesa* in Rio today is a grassroots movement of musicians and appreciators passionately committed to keeping their music on the street and in an improvised form.

It typically involves a table, at least one *cavaquinho* (small, ukulele-like instrument) player, an assortment of *tambores* (drums) and any number of makeshift instruments like Coke cans, knives and forks that will make a rattle. The standard of the music can be outstanding, and it is not uncommon to catch sight of a samba *bamba* (big-name samba performer) keeping the beat for the group or belting out one of its tunes. Depending on which bohemians have blown through for the night, you might even catch a duel, in which two singers will pit their wits against each other in a battle of rhymes. It is a challenge of the intellect, and the topics include everything from love to poverty to the opponent's mother. Even if you speak some Portuguese, you probably won't understand the slang and local references, but the delight of the crowd is infectious.

Street samba has taken a battering from the commercialization of music and space, the rising popularity of funk in the favelas and the police clampdown on 'noise pollution' in public spaces. However, for those still interested in a little piece of bohemian Rio, there are several established places that support free, improvised street music. On Friday night Rua do Mercado and Travessa do Comércio near Praça Quinze in Centro attract the younger radical chic set. On Sunday and Thursday night Bip Bip (p161), a tiny bar in Copacabana, caters for hard-core *sambistas* (samba singers). If you're around on December 2, Dia de Samba (Samba Day), then you can join the samba train bound for Oswaldo Cruz with the rest of Rio's samba community. The musicians disembark in the dusty backstreets of this working-class suburb, which is transformed every year into a labyrinth of makeshift bars and stages that host a 24-hour marathon of *samba da mesa*.

Impromptu street gatherings in Rio are more elusive at other times and finding them can sometimes be challenging. But it's an unforgettable experience if you find one. There are few fixed places for these parties, and they move from one week to the next. The *bairro* (neighborhood) of Lapa, in particular Rua Joaquim Silva, generally has something going on, but if not, keep your ears open for the unmistakable sound of the *samba bateria* (percussive-style samba) – follow that sound and you will find a party. Pay heed to the local etiquette: ensure you do not talk over the music, don't use cameras with a flash and don't sit down unless you are a contributing musician.

TEATRO ODISSÉIA

Map p98

☎ 2224-6367; Av Mem de Sá 66, Lapa; admission R$10-20; ⌚ 10pm-5am Tue-Sun

This spacious three-story Lapa club features live music shows and DJs, with a relaxed area upstairs if you need a break from the sounds. There's also a terrace with views of the Lapa arches. You'll find plenty of samba, and MPB and rock make an occasional appearance at the club.

TRAPICHE GAMBOA

Map p90

☎ 2516-0868; www.trapichegamboa.com.br, in Portuguese; Rua Sacadura Cabral 155, Gamboa; admission R$12-20; ⌚ 7pm-2am Tue-Thu, to 3am Fri, 9pm-4am Sat

Another charming live samba joint, Trapiche Gamboa is set in a multistory colonial edifice in Gamboa (just north of Centro) and has a friendly mixed crowd and decent appetizers. It's a casual affair, with samba musicians gathering around a table on the ground floor, and dancers spilling out in front of them. It's best reached by taxi (R$25 or so from the Zona Sul).

CONCERT VENUES

In addition to small bars and clubs, Rio has a few large concert halls that attract Brazilian stars such as Gilberto Gil and Milton Nascimento, as well as well-known international bands visiting Rio on world tours. Citywide music festivals include Noites Cariocas (p22), held on summer weekends (December to February). In addition to the venues listed here, during the warmer months concerts sometimes take place on the beaches of Copacabana, Botafogo, Barra da Tijuca and, more often, the Marina da Glória.

CANECÃO Map p80

☎ 2105-2000; www.canecao.com.br, in Portuguese; Av Venceslau Brás 215, Botafogo

Near the Rio Sul Shopping, Canecão holds big-venue music concerts – rock, MPB, hip-hop – throughout the year. Tickets are available at Ticketronics outlets (p170) or at the Canecão box office (cash only).

PARTY ON THE BAY

The newest fest to hit Rio is the Boat Party (☎ 3798-5772; www.rioboatparty.com.br; per person R$60), a five-hour schooner cruise around the bay, with DJs, free caipirinhas (pace yourselves, people), great views and a young, dance-loving (and mostly foreign) crowd. Departures from the Marina da Glória (Map p87), which are dependent on the weather, typically happen on Saturdays at 2pm and glide past the city's iconic landmarks, making stops for a swim near the peaceful beach of Praia Itaipu, and return to a marvelous sunset. Call for the latest schedule or stop by Stone of a Beach hostel (p194) for details.

CIRCO VOADOR
Map p98

☎ 2533-0354; www.circovoador.com.br, in Portuguese; Rua dos Arcos, Lapa; admission R$40-50
In a curvilinear building behind the Arcos da Lapa, Circo Voador hosts big-name Brazilian and international artists. The acoustics here are excellent, and after a show you'll find plenty of other musical options in the area. Check the website to see what's on. You can also take classes in *capoeira* (Afro-Brazilian martial arts), dance, percussion and yoga.

CITIBANK HALL
Map p107

☎ 0300-789-6846; Av Ayrton Senna 3000, Barra da Tijuca
Rio's largest concert house tends to change names every few years, but continues to host top international and Brazilian bands. As well as music shows, Citibank Hall stages ballet, opera and an occasional circus. The hall, which seats around 6000, is in the Via Parque Shopping Center in Barra. Purchase tickets through Ticketmaster (p170).

FUNDIÇÃO PROGRESSO
Map p98

☎ 2220-5070; www.fundicao.org; Rua dos Arcos 24, Lapa; admission R$20-30
This former foundry in Lapa hides one of Rio's top music and theater spaces. A diverse range of shows is staged here, which include big-name acts like Manu Chao and Caetano Veloso, as well as theater, video arts and ballet. The foundation is one of Lapa's premier arts institutions, and you can study dance, *capoeira* and circus arts here.

NIGHTCLUBS

Rio has some great places to shake your *bunda* (booty). DJs pull from the latest house, drum 'n' bass and hip-hop favorites as well as more uniquely Brazilian combinations like electro-samba and bossa-jazz. In addition to local DJs, Rio attracts a handful of vinyl gurus from São Paulo, New York and London to spin at bigger affairs. Flyers advertising dance parties and raves (pronounced *hah*-vees) can be found in some boutiques in Ipanema and Leblon, and in the surf shops in Galeria River (p118) by Praia Arpoador. Most clubs give a discount if you've got a flyer. You'll also save money if you're female. Men pay about 50% more than women for club entrance.

00 (ZERO ZERO) Map p70

☎ 2540-8041; Planetário da Gávea, Av Padre Leonel Franca 240, Gávea; admission R$20-45; ⏲ 10pm-4am Fri & Sat, 7pm-2am Sun
Housed in Gávea's planetarium, 00 is a restaurant by day, sleek lounge by night. A mix of Cariocas joins the fray here, though it mostly tends to be a fashion-literate, Zona Sul crowd. In addition to rotating parties, the club also hosts CD-release parties.

BAR BUKOWSKI Map p80

☎ 2244-7303; Rua Álvaro Ramos 270, Botafogo; admission R$20-35; ⏲ 11:30pm-5am Fri & Sat
Paying homage to the bohemian American writer, this club has a downstairs dance floor and bar, and an upstairs level for live bands playing rock, pop and blues. There's also a pool table, darts and you can have a go at one of the water pipes.

BARONNETI Map p64

☎ 2522-1460; Rua Barão da Torre 354, Ipanema; admission R$20-35; ⏲ 11pm-5am Tue-Sun
One of Ipanema's few nightclubs, Baronneti has a sleek and trim interior with a choice of two dance floors. Given its prime Zona Sul location, you'll find a young, well-heeled crowd here. Eclectic DJs and fruity cocktails keep the fans returning again and again.

CASA DA MATRIZ Map p80

☎ 2266-1014; www.casadamatriz.com.br; Rua Henrique de Novaes 107, Botafogo; admission R$10-25; ⏲ 11:30pm-5am Mon & Thu-Sat
Artwork lines this space in Botafogo. With numerous rooms to explore (lounge, screening room, dance floors), this old mansion

embodies the creative side of the Carioca spirit. Check the website for party listings.

CINE LAPA Map p98

☎ 2509-5166; Av Mem de Sá 23, Lapa; admission R$10-20

In the heart of Lapa, this newly revamped space serves up a steady diet of rock, with punk, psychedelic, Brit pop and straight-up classic rock; live bands sometimes take the stage. The two-floor space also has a small cinema (seating 40), and plans for club events and art events throughout the year.

CLANDESTINO Map p76

☎ 3209-0348; Rua Barata Ribeiro 111, Copacabana; entrance R$10-30; 11pm-5am Wed-Sat

Next door to Stone of a Beach hostel, Clandestino brings together an eclectic mix

GAY RIO

Rio has been a major destination for gay travelers since the 1950s. Back then the action was near the Copacabana Palace – and remnants of this distant past are still there, popular with a slightly older crowd (look for the rainbow-hued flag). Today, however, the party has mostly moved on, with the focal point of the GLBT (gay, lesbian, bisexual, transgender) scene, especially for visitors, in Ipanema. The gay beach at the end of Rua Farme de Amoedo (again, look for the rainbow flag) is the stomping ground of some of Rio's buffest men, sometimes known as 'barbies' in Carioca slang. The bars and cafés of nearby streets – Rua Teixeira de Melo and Rua Farme – attract a mixed crowd – a good spot to explore if you're not quite ready to jump into the beach scene.

Rio also hosts an enormously popular Gay Pride Rio festival (p22). For more info on the gay scene in Rio, including recommendations on nightclubs, bars, cafés and guesthouses, visit Rio Gay Guide (www.riogayguide.com).

Nightlife

For the following listings, most places kick off around 11pm or midnight and close around 4am.

Cabaret Casanova (☎ 2221-6555; Av Mem de Sá 25, Lapa; Fri & Sat) This is one of Rio's oldest clubs, featuring a good mixed crowd, drag queens and slightly trashy music.

Cafeína (Map p64; ☎ 2521-2194; Rua Farme de Amoedo 43, Ipanema; 8am-11:30pm) A popular Ipanema café that attracts a mix of gays and straights.

Cine Ideal (Map p90; ☎ 2252-3460; www.cineideal.com.br, in Portuguese; Rua da Carioca 62, Centro; Fri & Sat) An old movie theater, and now an electronic music club, Ideal has an outdoor terrace with views of old Rio.

Copa (☎ 2256-7412; Rua Aires Saldanha 13A, Copacabana; Fri & Sat) The Copa, a restaurant, bar and dance club, is a relaxed hangout, attracting an 'intellectual' crowd of guys and girls aged 30 and up.

Dama de Ferro (Map p64; ☎ 2247-2330; www.damadeferro.com.br, in Portuguese; Rua Vinícius de Moraes 288, Ipanema; Tue-Sat) This club boasts one of the best electronic-music scenes in town but no one goes until very late.

Fosfobox (Map p76; ☎ 2548-9478; Basement, loja 22A, Rua Siqueira Campos 143, Copacabana; Tue-Sun) This small underground club has live alternative bands, a mixed crowd and easygoing ambience.

Galeria Café (Map p64; ☎ 2523-8250; www.galeriacafe.com.br; Rua Teixeira de Mello 31, Ipanema; Thu-Sat) This bar with a very mixed crowd has lovely decor.

La Cueva (☎ 2267-1364; www.boatelacueva.com; Basement, Rua Miguel Lemos 51, Copacabana; Tue-Sun) This small club caters mostly for bear crowds and the more mature on weekends, but throws great parties on weekdays, especially Tuesday.

La Girl (Map p76; ☎ 2247-8342; www.lagirl.com.br, in Portuguese; Rua Raul Pompéia 102, Copacabana; Mon, Fri & Sat) This lesbian club has a great atmosphere.

Le Boy (Map p76; ☎ 2513-4993; www.leboy.com.br, in Portuguese; Rua Raul Pompéia 102, Copacabana; Tue-Sun) Open since 1992, Le Boy is Rio's gay temple. There are theme nights with drag shows and go-go boys.

Tô Nem Aí (Map p64; ☎ 2247-8403; Rua Farme de Amoedo 57, Ipanema; noon-3am) On Ipanema's gayest street, this popular bar is a great after-beach spot.

The Week (Map p90; ☎ 2253-1020; Rua Sacadura Cabral 154, Centro; Sat) Rio's newest and (currently) best gay dance club has a spacious dance floor, excellent DJs and lots of go-go dancers.

of Cariocas and backpackers, with an urban underground vibe, courtesy of DJs spinning hip-hop, and funk and art films playing on a screen in the background.

CLUB SIX Map p90

☎ 2510-3230; Rua das Marrecas 38, Lapa; admission R$10-40; ⏰ 11pm-6am Fri & Sat
Near the Arcos da Lapa, Club Six is a huge industrial space housing three dance floors, five bars and a number of spots for lounging, scattered about the building. It's a top pick for dancing, with DJs spinning house, hip-hop, trance and MPB till daybreak.

FOSFOBOX
Map p76

☎ 2548-7498; Rua Siqueira Campos 143, Copacabana; admission R$10-25; ⏰ 11pm-4am Thu-Sat
This subterranean club is hidden under a shopping center near the metro station. Good DJs spin everything from funk to glam rock, and the crowd here is one of the more eclectic in the club scene.

MARIUZINN Map p76

☎ 2545-7672; Av NS de Copacabana, Copacabana; admission R$20-40; ⏰ 10pm-4am Thu-Sat
Mariuzinn has been around for ages (more than 30 years) and still brings in the dance-loving crowds. DJs on its two floors spin a wide mix – hip-hop, drum 'n' bass, funk, pop-rock and straight-up techno. Look for flyers around town to save R$10 on admission.

MELT Map p66

☎ 2249-9309; www.meltbar.com.br; Rua Rita Ludolf 47, Leblon; admission R$20-40; ⏰ 10pm-4am Mon & Thu-Sat, 11pm-4am Tue & Wed
The Melt club gathers a young, attractive crowd in its candlelit main-floor lounge, sipping brightly colored elixirs. Upstairs, DJs break beats over the dance floor, with the occasional band making an appearance.

NUTH LOUNGE Map p107

☎ 3575-6850; www.nuth.com.br, in Portuguese; Av Armando Lombardi 999, Barra da Tijuca; admission men R$40-70, women R$20-30; ⏰ 9pm-4am
This club (pronounced 'Nooch') is one of the city's favorite dance spots, despite its location in Barra. Expect a friendly, well-dressed crowd grooving to DJs spinning electro-samba, house and hip-hop. If you don't like the venue, or the price tag, there are other bars and restaurants nearby. There's also a newly opened Nuth Club (Map p64; Av Epitácio Pessoa 1244) that attracts much the same beauty crowd in Lagoa.

PISTA 3 Map p80

☎ 2266-9691; Rua São João Batista 14, Botafogo; admission R$12-30; ⏰ midnight-4am Wed-Sat
Brought to you by the same owners of nearby Casa da Matriz (p166), Pista 3 is another good dance spot, with notable DJs spinning a wide mix of rock, electronica and funk. It has two floors: one for dancing, one for lounging (complete with pool table and an area for drinking and snacking).

THE ARTS

top picks

THE ARTS

Although most visitors don't come to Rio for the ballet, the city does have some attractions for lovers of the arts. Dance, theater, classical music, performance art and opera have their small but loyal Carioca (residents to Rio) following. Cinema, on the other hand, is a bigger deal, with Rio being one of the leading film centers in Latin America.

Rio has produced a number of successful dance troupes, including the contemporary Companhia de Dança Deborah Colker, which spends much of its time touring abroad. A home-grown talent you might catch in town is the Cia de Dança Dani Lima, an avant-garde troupe that weaves provocative pieces together through dance and aerial gymnastics. Also keep an eye out for the Lapa-based Intrépida Trupe, whose talented acrobat/dancers bring surreal works to the stage. There aren't any spaces dedicated solely to dance, and performances can take place at many of the venues listed in this chapter. Rio's biggest dance festival, Festival Panorama de Dança (p22), is held in November. For classical dance, try to see a production by the Ballet do Theatro Municipal, which puts on highly professional performances at Rio's most venerable theater.

There's a long history of theater in Brazil, with literary greats from the 19th century, including the highly imaginative Carioca Machado de Assis, giving vision to the stage. Talents from the 20th century, like the great Nelson Rodrigues and more recently Gerald Thomas, have kept the flame alive, and you can still see some of their work on Rio's stages. There are more than two dozen theaters in town. Unfortunately, if you don't speak Portuguese you won't get a lot out of an evening at the theater.

In the classical music scene, Rio has several symphony orchestras and irregular appearances by chamber groups and soloists. The best venues are the Sala Cecília Meireles, with its excellent acoustics, and the magnificent Theatro Municipal. You might also attend a performance at the Centro Cultural Banco do Brasil or the Fundação Eva Klabin (p72), both of which host orchestral works periodically.

The biggest classical music festival is Música no Museu (Music in the Museum; www.musicanomuseu.com.br), held in museums, churches and cultural centers around town. See p171 for details.

For other festivals in Rio, see p20. See p160 for the top places to hear samba, bossa nova, rock and many other musical styles – and for background on the city's burgeoning music scene, see p34.

Tickets & Reservations

TICKETMASTER

☎ 0300-789-6846; www.ticketmaster.com.br, in Portuguese; 9am-8pm Mon-Sat

This international company sells tickets to shows at Citibank Hall (p166) in Barra da Tijuca and the Theatro Municipal (p94) in Centro. Tickets can be purchased over the phone or online (you'll need Portuguese) and at Modern Sound (p118).

TICKETRONICS

Map p76

☎ 3344-5500; www.ticketronic.com.br, in Portuguese; Modern Sound, Rua Barata Ribeiro 502, Copacabana; 9am-8pm Mon-Sat

Tickets for a wide range of shows, concerts and dance performances can be purchased through Ticketronics either over the phone (Portuguese only) or through a distributor like Modern Sound (p118).

PERFORMING ARTS

The city's theaters and concert halls generally stage many event types, with classical concerts, plays, dance performances, recitals, author readings and the odd samba concert filling up the calendar at the same venue.

ARTE SESC CULTURAL CENTER Map p84

☎ 3138-1020; www.sescrio.org.br, in Portuguese; Rua Marquês de Abrantes 99, Flamengo

Housed in one of Flamengo's old mansions, Arte SESC has occasional classical recitals throughout the year. It also hosts panel discussions on various art and cultural topics.

CENTRO CULTURAL OI FUTURO

Map p87

☎ 3131-3060; www.oifuturo.org.br; Rua Dois de Dezembro 63, Catete

This hyper-modern cultural center and gallery space also stages dance performances and concerts. The fare here generally steers well clear of the mainstream. In 2009 Oi Futuro opened a smaller Ipanema branch (3rd fl, Rua Visconde de Pirajá 54) and it also stages concerts and exhibitions. See also p86.

ESPAÇO BNDES Map p90

☎ 2277-7757; Av República do Chile 100, Centro

Weekly concerts are held at this Centro venue throughout the year. Featuring a mix of popular and classical music, BNDES in the past has featured musicians exploring symphonic pop, and experimental groups playing samba-jazz.

ESPAÇO SESC Map p76

☎ 2547-0156; www.sescrj.org.br, in Portuguese; Rua Domingos Ferreira 160, Copacabana

Hosting an excellent assortment of theater and dance performances, Espaço SESC is a bulwark of the Copacabana arts scene. The repertoire tends toward the experimental and avant-garde, particularly during annual dance and theater festivals.

SALA CECÍLIA MEIRELES Map p98

☎ 2332-9176; www.salaceciliameireles.com.br, in Portuguese; Largo da Lapa 47, Lapa; ticket office 1-6pm

Lapa's splendid early-20th-century gem hosts orchestral concerts throughout the year. Lately, the repertoire has included contemporary groups, playing both *choro* (romantic, intimate samba) and classical music. Concerts start at 7:30pm.

SALA MUNICIPAL BADEN POWELL Map p76

☎ 2548-0421; Av NS de Copacabana 360, Copa-cabana

One of the few music halls in the Zona Sul, the 500-seat Sala Baden Powell hosts a broad range of concerts throughout the year, with MPB and jazz figuring prominently (the hall even hosts a 10-day jazz fest in January). Most tickets are around R$20, with shows taking place Thursday through Sunday nights starting around 9pm.

TEATRO CARLOS GOMES Map p90

☎ 2232-8701; Rua Pedro I, 22, Centro

Facing the Praça Tiradentes, the large Teatro Gomes stages avant-garde dance shows and experimental theater. The theater seats 600; tickets for events here can be purchased through Ticketronics (p170).

MUSIC IN THE MUSEUM

Classical music lovers should try to attend a concert held during the four-month-long event Música No Museu (www.musicanomuseu.com.br). Held from January to April each year, this event has been growing in popularity, and now features dozens of concerts (all free) held at museums and cultural spaces around the city, including inside the Museu de Arte Moderna (p89), Museu da República (p86), Centro Cultural Banco do Brasil (p89) and Parque das Ruinas (p99). Most concerts are held during the daytime (typically starting sometime between noon and 3pm), making it an alternative to the beach if you need a break. Visit the website or pick up a brochure from the tourist office (p228) for the current schedule.

TEATRO DO CENTRO CULTURAL BANCO DO BRASIL Map p90

☎ 3808-2020; www.bb.com.br; Rua Primeiro de Março 66, Centro

In addition to its exhibitions, this large cultural center in downtown Rio has two stages and a cinema. Film, dance and musical events are often coordinated with current exhibits.

TEATRO DO LEBLON Map p66

☎ 2529-7700; Rua Conde Bernadotte 26, Leblon

This nicely located theater shows a mix of drama, cutting-edge and children's performances on three different stages. In the same complex is a bookstore, and a range of eating/drinking spots.

TEATRO LAURA ALVIM Map p64

☎ 2267-4307; Av Vieira Souto 176, Ipanema

Across from the beach in Ipanema, this small center stages plays and hosts classical and other live-music styles. It also has art exhibition openings, a cinema and an atrium café.

TEATRO NELSON RODRIGUES Map p98

☎ 2262-0942; Av República do Chile 230, Centro

Inside the wildly modernist 1970s-era Caixa Cultural complex, you'll find one of Brazil's best stages for dance and theater. Also on-site are several art galleries, a lunchtime bistro, gardens and a koi pond.

THEATRO MUNICIPAL Map p90

☎ 2332-9195; www.theatromunicipal.rj.gov.br; Praça Floriano, Cinelândia

This gorgeous art-nouveau theater provides the setting for Rio's best opera, ballet and symphonic concerts. Tickets are available at the box office or at Ticketronics (p170). The theater seats 2400, and sight lines are generally quite good. At research time the theater was closed for renovations and due to reopen in 2012.

CINEMA

There's plenty of variety at Rio's many cinemas. The market here is remarkably open to foreign and independent films, documentaries and avant-garde cinema. This isn't to say that mainstream Hollywood films are in short supply. The latest American blockbusters get ample airtime at movie megaplexes, while cultural centers, museums and old one-screen theaters offer a more diverse repertoire. Films are shown in the original language with Portuguese subtitles. On weekends, popular shows often sell out, so buy your ticket early. Prices range from R$14 to R$24 per ticket, with cheaper matinee prices Monday through Thursday and the highest prices (and longest lines) on Friday to Sunday. For extensive listings and times pick up a copy of *O Globo*, *Jornal do Brasil* or *Veja Rio*.

CASA DA CULTURA LAURA ALVIM

Map p64

☎ 2267-1647; Av Vieira Souto 176, Ipanema

Facing the beach, the charming Laura Alvim cultural center screens foreign (of the non-Hollywood variety) and independent flicks. Its small screening room seats 72.

CINE SANTA TERESA

Map p98

☎ 2222-0203; www.cinesanta.com.br; Rua Paschoal Carlos Magno 136, Santa Teresa

This small, single-screen theater is well located on Largo do Guimarães. Befitting the art-loving 'hood, the cinema screens a selection of independent and Brazilian films.

ESPAÇO MUSEU DA REPÚBLICA

Map p87

☎ 3826-7984; Museu da República, Rua do Catete 153, Catete

The screening room located behind the dramatic Museu da República shows films you aren't likely to encounter elsewhere. The focus is world cinema – both contemporary and classic films. Entrance is via the Parque do Catete.

ESPAÇO DE CINEMA Map p80

☎ 2226-1986; Rua Voluntários da Pátria 35, Botafogo

This two-screen cinema in Botafogo shows a range of films – Brazilian, foreign, independent and the occasional Hollywood film. It has a lovely café inside, as well as a shop selling used records and books with a number of works focusing on the film arts.

ESTAÇÃO BOTAFOGO Map p80

☎ 2226-1988; Rua Voluntários da Pátria 88, Botafogo

One block from Espaço de Cinema, this small three-screen theater shows a mix of Brazilian and foreign films. The small café in front is a good place to grab a quick *cafézinho* (small black coffee) before the movie.

ESTAÇÃO IPANEMA Map p64

☎ 2279-4603; Rua Visconde de Pirajá 605, Ipanema

On the 1st floor of a small shopping complex in Ipanema, Estação Ipanema screens popular contemporary films from Brazil and abroad. Its single theater seats 140.

ODEON PETROBRAS Map p90

☎ 2240-1093; Praça Floriano 7, Cinelândia

Rio de Janeiro's landmark cinema is a remnant of the once flourishing moviehouse scene that gave rise to the name Cinelândia. The restored 1920s film palace shows independent films, documentaries

RIO DE JANEIRO INTERNATIONAL FILM FESTIVAL

The Rio film fest is one of the biggest in Latin America, with more than 300 films representing 60 countries shown at theaters all across Rio, and occasional screenings at the Marina da Glória and other open-air spots around town. In past years, the two-week festival has attracted over 300,000 viewers. It runs from the last week of September to the first week of October, with top prizes handed out in the form of iconic Troféus Redentores (Redeemer Prizes): small, slightly abstract, gold statues shaped like Christ the Redeemer. Although there's a wide variety of international fare screened here, the festival often sets the stage for the success of Brazilian films aimed at wide release. For more on the festival, including films, locations and where to buy tickets, check the multilingual www.festivaldorio.com.br.

and foreign films, and sometimes hosts the gala for prominent film festivals. It also shows worthwhile monthly events like the Maratona Odeon, a three-film movie marathon that runs from 11pm to 6am on the first Friday of the month (admission R$20). Next door, the restaurant and café of Ateliê Culinário (p143) opens around weekend screenings and makes a great spot for a bite before or after weekend screenings.

ROXY Map p76

☎ 2461-2461; Av Nossa Senhora de Copacabana 945, Copacabana

Copacabana's only cinema is a good retreat when the weather sours. The Roxy shows the usual films on wide release.

TEATRO LEBLON

Map p66

☎ 2461-2461; Av Ataúlfo de Paiva 391, Leblon

Leblon's popular theater has two screens showing the latest Hollywood releases.

UCI – NEW YORK CITY CENTER

Map p107

☎ 2461-1818; New York City Center, Av das Americas 5000, Barra da Tijuca

UCI – New York City Center is Brazil's largest megaplex, featuring 18 different screening rooms complete with large, comfortable chairs and stadium seating. Films are screened constantly (every 10 minutes on weekends).

SPORTS & ACTIVITIES

top picks

- **Jogging or cycling along the beach** (p181)
- **Hang gliding** (p179)
- **Rock climbing the face of Pão de Açúcar** (p177)
- **Hiking through tropical rain forest** (p179)
- **Surfing waves off Prainha** (p180)
- **Learning to samba** (p181)
- **Playing *capoeira*** (p182)

What's your recommendation? www.lonelyplanet.com/rio-de-janeiro

SPORTS & ACTIVITIES

When it comes to the pursuit of sport, Cariocas (residents of Rio) seem to be ruled by the sun, spilling out of doors on lovely days for pick-up games of football (soccer), volleyball and *futevôlei* (volleyball played without using the hands). Runners, cyclists and power-walkers take to the streets, as hikers and rockclimbers head for the hills and surfers make for the beach.

Those who'd rather sit than spin can head to the stadium (or the pub) for the big game. Like other Brazilians, Cariocas are addicted to football, with every man, woman and child expected to profess their undying devotion to one team or another by about the age of five. *Futebol* games are an intense spectacle – as much because of the crazed fans as the teams out on the field. The rivalries are particularly intense when Rio's club teams – Botafogo (black-and-white-striped jerseys), Flamengo (red jerseys with black hoops), Fluminense (red, green and white stripes) and Vasco da Gama (white with a black sash) – play each other. An excellent book on Brazil's great sport, and its relationship to culture, religion and politics, is *Futebol: The Brazilian Way of Life* (2002) by Alex Bellos. For results, schedules and league tables visit Samba Foot (http://en.sambafoot.com/).

On the national level, Brazilians have proven that they are among the world's best footballers, having produced scores of brilliants players and winning the World Cup five times.

While the nation has a fairly one-track mind when it comes to professional sports, Brazilians have distinguished themselves in other arenas. They dominate in auto racing, for instance. Brazilian drivers have won more Formula One world championships than any other nationality, a fact that probably won't surprise anyone who rents a car for the weekend. The greatest racer, three-time world champion Ayrton Senna, was almost canonized after his death.

Tennis also has its following, helped along by Gustavo 'Guga' Kuerten who was once ranked number one in the world and won the French Open three times between 1997 and 2001. He retired in 2008. Before him came Hall-of-Famer Maria Esther Bueno, winner of 19 Grand Slam titles in the 1950s and '60s.

Basketball (with three Brazilian players in the NBA), volleyball (both men's and women's teams were ranked number one in 2010 according to the Federation Internationale de Volleyball's world ranking) and even professional bull riding have their Brazilian stars.

Amid such a sporting nation, there are plenty of ways to join the fray. Rio's lush mountains and glimmering coastline cry out for action, and you can hone your game – whether it be volleyball, soccer or *frescobal* (played with wooden racquets and a rubber ball) – without ever leaving that sparkling shoreline. Nearby, palm-lined paths set the stage for jogging, hiking, walking and cycling. While the mountain backdrops are fine to gaze at, they are also the setting for some of the city's unique adventures: you can climb up them, hangglide down from them or go hiking in the forests that surround them. For something a little different, sign up for a dance class, learn some *capoeira* (martial art) or Brazilian jiujutsu, go scuba diving off the islands near Rio, book a surfing lesson or stretch those sunburned gams at a yoga class. And for those who'd rather take their sport sitting down, there's always Maracanã (p176), the world's largest football stadium.

SPECTATOR SPORTS

FOOTBALL

MARACANÃ FOOTBALL STADIUM

Map p60

☎ 2334-1705; Av Maracanã, São Cristóvão; admission R$15-100; Ⓜ Maracanã

As Rio prepares for the 2014 World Cup, the famed Rio stadium will be closed indefinitely from August 2010 as the stadium undergoes extensive renovations.

Once it reopens (probably not until 2012 or 2013), a game at Maracanã is a must-see for visitors. Matches here rate among the most exciting in the world, and the behavior of the fans is no less colorful. The devoted pound huge samba drums, letting out a roar as their team takes the field, and if things are going badly – or very well – fans are sometimes driven to sheer madness. Some detonate smoke bombs in team colors, while others rip out the seats or launch objects into the seats below.

(Things have calmed slightly since alcohol was banned inside the stadium some years back.) Enormous flags spread across large sections of the bleachers as people dance in the aisles and taunt their opponents.

Games take place year-round and generally happen on Saturday or Sunday (starting at 4pm or 6pm) or on Wednesday and Thursday (around 8:30pm). Although buses run to and from the stadium, on game days the metro is generally faster and less crowded. The stadium has color-coded seating, with tourists and more sedate folk generally sitting in the somewhat isolated white section, and rowdier flans flocking to the green and yellow sections or the wildest blue section on the lowest level. Those who want the best views at any price opt for the *especial* seats, which run R$100 a seat. The ticket price is R$15 to R$30 for most games. For more information on the stadium, see p103.

If you prefer to go in a group – which is, of course, more fun – several English-speaking tour operators organize game-day outings, including round-trip transportation. Leading big-group tours are Brazil Expedition (☎ 9998-2907, 7894-7523; www.brazilexpedition.com; per person R$70) and Be A Local (☎ 9643-0366; www.bealocal.com; per person R$80-90). For something more small-scale, independent guide Sergio Manhães (☎ 9210-0119; futebolnomaracana.blogspot.com; ssm10@hotmail.com; per person R$110-120) takes up to four guests with him on game day. All have been recommended by readers.

HORSE RACING

JOQUEI CLUBE Map p70

☎ 3534-9000; www.jcb.com.br, in Portuguese; Jardim Botânico 1003, Gávea; ⌚ 6pm-midnight Mon, 4-11pm Fri, 2-8pm Sat & Sun

One of the country's loveliest racetracks, with a great view of the mountains and Corcovado, the Joquei Clube (Jockey Club) seats 35,000 and lies on the Gávea side of the Lagoa Rodrigo de Freitas opposite Praça Santos Dumont. Local race fans are part of the attraction – it's a different slice of Rio life.

Tourists are welcome in the members' area, which has a bar overlooking the track. Races are held on Monday, Friday, Saturday and Sunday. The big event is the Brazilian Grand Prix (the first Sunday in August).

OUTDOOR ACTIVITIES

Climb, hike, surf or hang glide your way across Rio's enticing landscapes and seascapes. For those seeking more than just a taste of the outdoors, take a class and become an expert in your sport of choice. For other organized activities – walking tours, boat trips, fishing excursions, helicopter rides and favela (shanty town) tours – see p224.

CLIMBING

Rio is the center of rock climbing in Brazil, with 350 documented climbs within 40 minutes of the city center. Climbing in Rio is best during the cooler months of the year (April to October); during the summer, the tropical sun heats up the rock to oven-like temperatures and turns the forests into saunas. People do climb during the summer, but usually only in the early morning or late afternoon when it's not so hot.

A number of agencies offer climbing and hiking tours. Rio also has several well-organized climbing clubs, which have weekly meetings. The clubs, which welcome outsiders (though you'll need some Portuguese), also have a social component for those interested in meeting like-minded Cariocas. Safety-conscious outfitters typically charge R$150 for a full-day climbing excursion.

In addition to organized outings, you can also try your hand at the rock-climbing wall in Parque da Catacumba (p72). Avid climbers who want to keep fit might want to stay in Tupiniquim hostel (p195), which also has a climbing wall.

CRUX ECOADVENTURE

☎ 3474-1726, 9392-9203; www.cruxecoaventura.com.br

This highly reputable outfit offers a range of climbing excursions and other outdoor adventures. The most popular is the ascent up Pão de Açúcar, which isn't as impossible as it looks. Guides are very safety conscious and have years of experience. Other possibilities include rappelling down waterfalls, full-day hikes through Floresta da Tijuca, and biking and kayaking trips.

CLIMB IN RIO

☎ 2245-1108; www.climbinrio.com

This respected agency (around since 1990) offers climbing trips led by experienced guides. Navigating more than 400 routes around Rio (50 up Pão de Açúcar alone) and the state, this is a good pick for climbing junkies. There are half- and full-day climbs as well as multiday mountain ascents. The agency also offers climbing courses.

CENTRO EXCURSIONISTA BRASILEIRA Map p90

CEB; ☎ 2252-9844; www.ceb.org.br, in Portuguese; 8th fl, Av Almirante Barroso 2, Centro; office 2-6pm Mon-Fri, meetings 7pm Thu

Founded in 1919, CEB sponsors day hikes and weekend treks (with camping). The club plans activities at its weekly meeting, a good spot to have a chat with the laid-back enthusiasts. The office is open during the week and provides info on upcoming excursions.

CLUBE EXCURSIONISTA CARIOCA Map p76

CEC; ☎ 2255-1348; www.carioca.org.br, in Portuguese; Ste 206, Rua Hilário de Gouveia 71, Copacabana; meetings 8:30pm Thu

Although CEC has been around since 1946, it's still going strong. Typically, CEC arranges hikes and technical climbs, as well as periodic rappelling and rafting outings.

DIVING

SUBCENTER Map p90

☎ 2242-7799; www.subcenter.com.br; 3rd fl, Rua da Alfândega 108, Centro

This aquatic supplier offers basic and advanced diving courses (around R$900) in waters near Rio as well as excursions for certified divers to Arraial do Cabo and further afield to the dive Mecca of Fernando Noronha, a lovely island in the northeast. Some instructors speak English.

DIVE POINT Map p66

☎ 2239-5105; www.divepoint.com.br; Shop 04, Av Ataúlfo de Paiva 1174, Leblon

Scuba divers can rent equipment or take classes from Dive Point. It also offers diving courses, and dive tours around Rio's main beaches and Ilha Cagarras (the island in front of Ipanema), as well as the premier dive spots in Arraial do Cabo, west of Rio.

MAR DO RIO Map p87

☎ 2225-7508; www.mardorio.com.br, in Portuguese; Shop 16, Marina da Glória, Av Infante Dom Henrique, Glória

One of several dive operators in the Marina da Glória, Mar do Rio offers two-tank dives

WORLD CAPITAL OF BRAZILIAN JIUJUTSU

In the martial arts community, Brazilian jiujutsu has a loyal following, with practitioners traveling from all corners of the globe to learn the grappling art at its world headquarters in Rio de Janeiro. The fighting style (known for its joint-locks and chokeholds) was created by a family known as the Gracies, who adapted the art from Japanese judo and perfected it over the course of the 20th century.

Why study here? As one jiujutsu black belt explained to us, 'The benefits of learning martial arts, most specifically jiujutsu, in Brazil are that there are always plenty of advanced people to practice with, but also that practice times are much more lax, meaning you can basically train as much as you want without getting hurried off the mats when the official class time is over.'

Popular international jiujutsu schools typically charge a flat fee (around R$150 to R$200) to take unlimited classes, plus the use of free weights and other facilities. All of the following gyms are laid-back and welcoming to foreigners and visitors.

De La Riva Jiu-Jitsu (Map p76; Academia Equipe 1; ☎ 2255-2554; www.academiaequipe1.com.br; Av NS de Copacabana 702B, Copacabana) Popular among foreigners, the Equipe 1 gym where the school is located also offers classes in other styles, including boxing, judo and kick boxing.

Gracie Barra (Map p107; ☎ 7824-3295; www.graciebarra.com; Ave Comandante Júlio de Moura 300, Barra da Tijuca) Gracie Barra is the world's biggest jiujutsu affiliation and focuses exclusively on jiujutsu, teaching no other martial arts.

Nova União Team (Map p84; Academia Upper; ☎ 2553-3485; Rua Marquês de Abrantes 88, Flamengo) Owned by one of the greatest Mixed Martial Arts (MMA) and jiujutsu coaches in the world, Andre Pederneiras, this place offers three-to-four jiujutsu classes a day, plus muay thai, boxing and MMA classes taught by some of the best MMA fighters in the world.

For Mixed Martial Arts events in Rio, check the bilingual www.graciemag.com website.

(R$120) on Saturday and Sunday, departing at 8:30am and returning at 2:30pm. It also offers night dives twice a month. Less-experienced divers can opt for one of the courses, including a five-day PADI-certified basic course.

FISHING

MARLIN YACHT TOURS

Map p87

☎ 2225-7434; www.marlinyacht.com.br; Marina da Glória, Av Infante Dom Henrique, Glória

The Marina da Glória has a number of boating outfits, although Marlin Yacht Tours has the largest fleet – including schooners, sailboats and motorboats. Here you can hire a vessel for a sailing, fishing or diving adventure, creating your own itinerary. Prices aren't cheap, so it's best to gather a group.

UNIVERSIDADE DA PESCA

☎ 2234-1119; www.upesca.com.br, in Portuguese

Universidade da Pesca offers a wide range of fishing tours – from day trips around Baía de Guanabara and Ilha Cagarras to week-long adventures in the Amazon. Trips include instructors and multilingual guides.

HANG GLIDING

If you weigh less than 100kg (about 220lb) and have a spare R$250 to spend, you can do the fantastic hang glide off 510m Pedra Bonita – one of the giant granite slabs that tower above Rio – onto Pepino beach in São Conrado. No experience is necessary. We've been assured that the winds are very safe here and the pilots know what they are doing. Guest riders are secured in a kind of pouch that is attached to the hang glider.

Naturally, hang gliding is one of those activities that is at the mercy of weather and wind conditions. During summer you can usually fly on all but three or four days a month, and conditions during winter are even better. If you fly early in the day, you will have more flexibility to accommodate unforeseen weather delays. You should also ensure that your flight lasts as long as possible; try to get a guarantee of at least seven to 10 minutes; 15 minutes is ideal.

The price of the flight includes pick-up and drop-off from your hotel. Travel agents can book tandem flights, but they add their own fee; to cut out the middle-men, call direct.

DELTA FLIGHT IN RIO

☎ 9693-8800; www.deltaflight.com.br

With more than 20 years experience, Ricardo Hamond has earned a solid reputation as a safety-conscious and extremely professional pilot; he has flown more than 12,000 tandem flights.

JUST FLY

☎ 2268-0565, 9985-7540; www.justfly.com.br

Paulo Celani is a friendly and highly experienced tandem flyer with over 6000 flights to his credit and over 20 years of experience.

SUPERFLY

☎ 3322-2286, 9982-5703; www.riosuperfly.com.br

Founder Ruy Marra has more than 27 years of flying experience (and 19,000 tandem flights!) and is an excellent pilot. Regarded as one of the best in Rio, Ruy is also the person to see if you want to paraglide (gliding with a special parachute).

TANDEM FLY

☎ 2422-6371, 2422-0941; www.riotandemfly.com.br

Two experienced pilots (and brothers) run this flight outfit, and they'll also give lessons for those wanting to learn how to fly solo.

HIKING

Rio is good for hiking and offers some outstanding nature walks. Visitors can hike one of the many trails through Floresta da Tijuca (p105) or head to one of the three national parks within a few hours of the city.

In recent years there's been a boom in organized hikes around the city, including hikes through wilderness areas around Corcovado, Morro da Urca and Pão de Açúcar, and of course Tijuca. It's advisable to go with a guide for a number of obvious reasons – getting lost and getting robbed being at the top of the list. Group outings can also be a great way to meet Cariocas.

RIO ADVENTURES

☎ 2705-5747; www.rioadventures.com; full-day hiking/climbing/rafting tours from R$150/250/250

Offering a range of outdoor activities, Rio Adventures leads hikes through Tijuca National Park, including short treks up Pico Tijuca – an easy one-hour hike to a rocky summit that affords fantastic views over

SURFING RIO

Rio has some fine options when it comes to surfing, with some great breaks just outside the city. If you're not ready to leave the Zona Sul, there are a few options, including fairly consistent breaks in front of Posto 10 in Ipanema and Posto 11 in Leblon. Copacabana gets an OK break between Posto 4 and 5. You'll find better waves near the spit of land dividing Copacabana from Ipanema. On the west side, off Praia do Diabo (Map p64), you get right and left breaks, which can reach up to 2m high, but it's not a good spot for beginners. On the other side of the rocks is Arpoador, which is generally more consistent with fast, hollow breaks to the left ranging from 0.5m to 3m. The big drawback here is that the place gets crowded, making maneuvering extremely difficult. To beat the crowds, go early on weekday mornings.

If you're serious about surfing, you'll want to head down to the beaches west of Rio. Just past Barra and Recreio is Macumba beach, with left and right breaks, which draws both long-boarders and beginners. After Macumba is lovely Prainha, which is widely considered the best surf spot in the area, with waves reaching 3m on good days. If it's too packed, you can continue on to Grumari, where the swell isn't as good but the crowds are thinner.

Further afield, you'll find good waves at Saquarema, a low-key town and surf destination 100km east of Rio, with decent waves from Itauna to Vila beach (3km from town). To the west, Ilha Grande (p207) is a gorgeous island known for some powerful surf – particularly off Lopes Mendes beach.

You'll find more detailed information on all the breaks around Rio on www.wannasurf.com. If you can read Portuguese, check out www.riosurfpage.com.

Boards, Transport, Surf Camps

For boards and other gear, visit Galeria River (p118). Some hostels, like Stone of a Beach (p194) and Tupiniquim (p195), also rent boards.

To get to the great surf spots outside of Rio, catch a ride on the Surfbus (☎ 8702-2837; www.surfbus.com.br; one way R$4), which will take passengers and their boards down to Prainha, with stops along the way. It departs at 7am, 10am, 1pm and 4pm from Largo do Machado (and picks up passengers in the Zona Sul en route).

Beginners who want to learn to surf can take classes through informal *escolinhas* (schools) off Ipanema beach and off Barra. Rio Surf 'N Stay (p199) offers lessons (in English) and overnight accommodation.

the Tijuca forest and the beaches of São Conrado and Barra. For something more challenging, the company offers ascents up Pedra Bonito.

Rio Adventures also offers sightseeing tours, rock climbs (Pão de Açúcar, Corcovado and Pico da Tijuca), rafting excursions (to Paraibuna River, 175km northwest of Rio) and parachuting and paragliding trips. It employs experienced guides, who speak Portuguese, English and Spanish, among other languages.

RIO HIKING

☎ 2552-9204; www.riohiking.com.br; full-day tour from R$150

Founded by a mother-son team back in 1999, this popular outfit offers hiking trips ranging from easy to strenuous and covering a variety of terrains around Rio. Favorite treks include going up Pedra da Gávea – a challenging climb up a steep and rugged trail (three hours up to the summit), with great views over the coast from the top, and Pão de Açúcar. You can also arrange kayaking, diving, river rafting and numerous other adventure sports here.

PADDLE BOATING

Those who've always dreamed of paddling a swan boat around the Zona Sul's largest lake can do just that on the Lagoa Rodrigo de Freitas. Paddle-boat hire (Map p70; per 30min R$20; 9am-9pm Sat & Sun summer) is available on summer weekends, on the east shore near the Parque do Cantagalo.

VOLLEYBALL & OTHER BEACH SPORTS

Volleyball is Brazil's second-most popular sport (after football). A natural activity for the beach, it's also a popular spectator sport on TV. A local variation of volleyball you'll see on Rio's beaches is *futevôlei* – played without using hands. Good luck!

Usually played on the firm sand at the shoreline, *frescobal* involves two players, each with a wooden racquet, hitting a small rubber ball back and forth as hard as possible. Playing was recently banned on crowded beaches; one of the last places to join in is on Praia do Diabo (Map p64), near Ponto do Arpoador.

ESCOLINHA DE VÔLEI Map p64

☎ 9702-5794; www.peledapraia.com, in Portuguese, near Garcia D'Avila, Ipanema beach

Those interested in improving their volleyball game, or just meeting some Cariocas, should pay a visit to Pelé de Ipanema. Pelé, who speaks English, has been hosting volleyball classes for over 10 years. Lessons range from one to two hours. Look for his large Brazilian flag on the beach near Rua Garcia D'Ávila. Pelé's students are a mix of Cariocas and expats, who then meet for games after honing the fundamentals.

WALKING, JOGGING & CYCLING

Splendid views and the sounds of the ever-present ocean are just two of the features of the many good walking and jogging paths of the Zona Sul. The Parque do Flamengo (p83) has plenty of paths stretching between city and bay. Further south the Lagoa Rodrigo de Freitas (p71) has a 7.5km track for cyclists, joggers and inline skaters. At the lakeside Parque do Cantagalo you can rent bicycles (R$10 per hour), tricycles or quadricycles (around R$20 per hour). The favorite option is the seaside path (p72) from Leme to Barra da Tijuca. Sunday is the best day to go, as the road is closed to traffic but open to the city's many outdoor enthusiasts.

Closed to bicycles but open to walkers and joggers is the short Pista Cláudio Coutinho (Map p80), between the mountains and the sea at Praia Vermelha in Urca. It's open 7am to 6pm daily. See p216 for bike-rental information.

HEALTH & FITNESS

DANCING

Given samba's resurgence throughout the city, it's not surprising that there are several places where you can learn the moves. You can also find places to study *forró* (dance accompanied by the traditional, fast-paced music from the northeast), salsa and the tango. A dance class is a good setting to meet other people while getting those two left feet to step in time.

CASA DE DANÇA CARLINHOS DE JESUS Map p80

☎ 2541-6186; www.carlinhosdejesus.com.br; Rua Álvaro Ramos 11, Botafogo

At this respected dance academy in Botafogo, Carlinhos and his instructors offer evening classes in samba, *forró,* salsa and tango. On some Friday nights, open dance parties for students and guests are held. One of Botafogo's colorful *bloco* parties, Dois Pra Lá, Dois Pra Cá (see p52) begins from here during Carnaval.

CENTRO CULTURAL CARIOCA

Map p90

☎ 2252-5751; www.centroculturalcarioca.com.br, in Portuguese; Rua Sete de Setembro 237, Centro; 🕑 11am-8pm Mon-Fri

The cultural center offers one-hour classes in samba, ballroom dancing and the sensual lambada. Most classes meet twice a week and cost around R$70 for a month-long course. The large dance hall hosts parties on Friday at which samba bands perform.

FUNDIÇÃO PROGRESSO

Map p98

☎ 2220-5070; www.fundicaoprogresso.org, in Portuguese; Rua dos Arcos 24, Lapa

This cultural center offers a wide range of courses, including classes in dancing (African styles, as well as salsa, tango and samba). Those seeking something different can sign up for classes in percussion, acrobatics (run by the respected dance-theater-circus outfit Intrépida Trupe) or *capoeira* (Afro-Brazilian martial arts). Courses are typically around R$150 for the month.

NÚCLEO DE DANÇA RENATA PEÇANHA

Map p90

☎ 2221-1011; www.renatapecanha.com.br, in Portuguese; Rua da Carioca 14, Centro

A large upstairs studio on the edge of Lapa, this dance academy offers classes in *forró,* salsa, zouk (a slow and sensual dance derived from the lambada) and samba. Twice-weekly classes cost about R$75 per month.

RIO SAMBA DANCER

☎ 8229-2843; riosambadancer.com; 90min private lesson per person R$30-40

English-speaking dance instructor Hélio Ricardo offers private one-on-one dance classes (in samba or *forró*), and he'll even provide a partner for you if you're a male. He also will take you out to dance places around town where you can practice your new moves (R$80 per person including dance lesson, R$100 for couples).

DAY SPAS

Surprisingly, for a city that is totally devoted to looking good, Rio does not have many spa options for visitors. You will find two of the best and newest spas in Rio inside Hotel Santa Teresa (p197) and the Copacabana Palace (p191).

SPA MARIA BONITA

Map p64

☎ 2513-4050; www.spamariabonita.com.br, in Portuguese; Level P, Rua Prudente de Morais 729, Ipanema

Although better known for its lush spa resort in Friburgo, Maria Bonita does offer a full range of treatments for those who'd rather not trek out to the countryside. Options at the Ipanema branch include aromatherapy baths, deep tissue massage, shiatsu and acupuncture. There is also a new organic and raw food restaurant on-site.

EMPÓRIO ZEN

Map p64

☎ 2239-3567; Store 108, Rua Visconde de Pirajá 595, Ipanema; 🕒 9am-7pm Mon-Sat

Hidden in the back of a small shopping center, Empório Zen offers shiatsu, acupuncture, aromatherapy, Ayurvedic massage, Reiki and other treatments. A one-hour massage costs R$80.

GYMS

Many hotels in Rio feature small workout centers with, perhaps, an adjoining sauna, but for those looking for a more intensive workout there are other options.

BODY TECH Map p66

☎ 2529-8898; Rua General Urquiza 102, Leblon; day/month pass R$100/410; 🕒 6am-11pm Mon-Fri, 9am-8pm Sat, 9am-2pm Sun

Body Tech has gyms all over the Zona Sul, which offer a full range of services:

CAPOEIRA

The only surviving martial art native to the new world, *capoeira* was invented by Afro-Brazilian slaves about 400 years ago. In its original form, the grappling martial art developed as a means of self-defense against the slave owners. Once the fighting art was discovered, it was quickly banned and *capoeira* went underground. The slaves, however, continued to hone their fighting skills; they merely did it out of sight, practicing secretly in the forest. Later the sport was disguised as a kind of dance, allowing them to practice in the open. This is the form that exists today.

Capoeira, which is referred to as a *jogo* (game), is accompanied by hand clapping and the plucking of the *berimbau* (a long, single-stringed instrument). Initially the music was used to warn fighters of the boss' approach; today it guides the rhythm of the game. Fast tempos dictate the players' exchange of fast, powerful kicks and blows, while slower tempos bring the pace down to a quasi-dance. The *berimbau* is accompanied by the *atabaque* (floor drum) and a *pandeiro* (Brazilian tambourine).

The movements combine elements of fighting and dancing, and are executed (at least by the highly skilled) as fluid and circular, playful and respectful. *Capoeira's* popularity has spread far beyond Brazil's borders (there's even a *capoeira* club in Serbia). You can see musicians and spectators arranged in the *roda de capoeira* (*capoeira* circle) at the weekly Feira Nordestina (p102) in São Cristóvão.

Those interested in taking classes can try one of the following. Note that all classes are in Portuguese.

Angola N'Golo (Map p98; ☎ 3770-7256; www.angolangolo.com; Rua Almirante Alexandrino, Santa Teresa; per class/month R$20/80; 🕒 7-10pm Mon & Wed, 10am-1pm Sat) This welcoming place to study *capoeira* in Santa Teresa is run by Mestre José Carlos. Classes are held in the open-sided space next to the Largo das Letras bookshop and restaurant above Largo do Guimarães.

Associação Centro de Capoeira Angola (Map p87; ☎ 9954-3659; www.ccarj.com; Rua do Catete 164, Catete; per class/month R$25/100) A *capoeira* center in Catete with two-hour classes on weekdays (running from 4pm to 10pm Monday through Thursday and 6pm to 10pm on Friday).

Casa Rosa (Map p84; ☎ 8874-8804; www.casarosa.com.br; Rua Alice 550, Laranjeiras; classes per month R$60) The popular music space in Laranjeiras offers classes on Tuesday and Thursday from 7pm to 9pm taught by Senhor Caroço (☎ 9540-2786).

Fundição Progresso (Map p98; ☎ 2220-5070; www.fundicao.org; Rua dos Arcos 24, Lapa) This major arts and music center offers classes in a wide range of fields, including *capoeira,* with classes currently on Monday and Wednesday (8pm to 10pm).

swimming pool, free weights and cardio machines, and classes such as dance, gymnastics and spinning. The best of the bunch is the three-story Leblon branch, but there are also a couple of Body Techs in Ipanema on Rua Barão de Torre 577 (Map p64) and Rua Gomes Carneiro 90 (Map p64), and one in Copacabana (Map p76) on Av NS de Copacabana 801.

YOGA

Yoga's popularity is on the rise in Rio, with a growing number of places where you can hone your sun salutations. Those around on Sunday can take a free class at 10am in Parque da Catacumba (Map p72) in front of Lagoa Rodrigo de Freitas. At most places, your first class is free.

BLYSS YÔGA Map p64

☎ 3627-0108; www.blyss.com.br; Ste 211, Rua Visconde de Pirajá 318, Ipanema; per class R$30
Near Praça Nossa Senhora da Paz, this peaceful center offers a full schedule of morning, afternoon and evening classes Monday to Saturday in Vinyasa, Iyengar and Hatha yoga. Some instructors speak English.

SIVANANDA CENTER
Map p80

☎ 2266-4896; www.yogasivananda.com.br; Rua das Palmeiras 13, Botafogo; per month R$90-150
A branch of the respected international organization, this Sivananda Center has a good mix of beginner and advanced classes, as well as a free meditation class on Friday evening.

SLEEPING

top picks

- **Hotel Santa Teresa** (p197)
- **Maze Inn** (p196)
- **Ipanema Plaza** (p187)
- **Ritz Plaza Hotel** (p188)
- **Porto Bay Rio Internacional** (p191)
- **Design Hotel Portinari** (p192)
- **Ouro Verde Hotel** (p192)
- **Castelinho 38** (p197)
- **Cama e Café** (p197)
- **Hotel Fasano** (p186)

SLEEPING

Rio has some excellent lodging options, including newly opened boutique hotels along the beach, trendy hostels and cozy B&Bs. The majority of hotel rooms are in high-rises in the Zona Sul (Copacabana has scores of options), though you'll also find elegant hotels, bohemian guesthouses and budget favorites in offbeat neighborhoods. Many guestrooms have received a makeover in recent years, particularly since Rio won the right to host both the 2014 FIFA World Cup (shared with other cities in Brazil) and the 2016 Olympics.

For those unfamiliar with Rio, here's the lowdown on where to stay. If you want to be in the heart of the action and don't mind paying for it, stay in Ipanema or Leblon, with beautiful beaches, and excellent restaurants, shopping and nightlife. If you don't want to pay a premium for those neighborhoods, opt for busier Copacabana. Here you'll find more (including some less expensive) lodging options, and you'll still be near the beach, and a short taxi ride or possibly a walk to Ipanema; you'll also have better access to the metro, which is handy for zipping to other neighborhoods. If you're not in Rio for the beaches or simply want an alternative view, take a peak at Santa Teresa's colonial guesthouses. This historic 'hood has culture, some unique overnight options, and good restaurants and cafés. It's also close to the unrivaled music scene of Lapa. Neighborhoods along the metro line (Botafogo, Flamengo and Catete) generally have cheaper options than the beachside southern neighborhoods; and for those who want the beach, and nothing but the beach, there's Barra, which is laid back but far from the rest of Rio (meaning you'll need a car or boatloads of patience to endure those long bus or pricey taxi rides). Use the airport hotels (p215) only if necessary.

The best way to save money on lodging is by booking online. You can save anywhere from 30% to over 50% off the rack rates by booking through reliable Rio booking agencies such as www.ipanema.com and www.riocharm.com.br.

Wherever you stay, try to reserve ahead. Hotel rates are about 30% higher during the summer months (December through mid-March) and many places book up. Prices double or triple for New Year's Eve and Carnaval, and most accommodations, including hostels, will only book in four-day blocks around these holidays.

Keep in mind that many hotels add between 5% and 15% in taxes and service charges. The cheaper places don't generally bother with this. Another caveat: in recent years some midrange and high-end hotels have begun charging extra for breakfast (anywhere from R$15 to R$30 per person); some also charge for wi-fi, so be sure to read the fine print before booking.

Accommodations are listed in each neighborhood by price, from most to least expensive.

IPANEMA & LEBLON

These elegant neighborhoods have much allure: stay here and you'll be a short stroll from lovely beaches, top restaurants and vibrant nightlife. Although many more hotels litter the beaches of Leme and Copacabana, there are abundant lodging options here (more so in Ipanema than Leblon), including boutique hotels, serviced apartments, hostels and plenty of cookie-cutter high-rises. Prices here are generally much higher than elsewhere, though it's still possible to find affordable – if rather modest – lodging.

HOTEL FASANO Map p64 Hotel $$$

☎ 3202-4000; www.fasano.com.br; Av Vieira Souto 80, Ipanema; d from R$1250;

With stylish rooms, a great location and a much-touted seafood restaurant and bar, this is the top destination for the style set and celebutantes (Beyoncé and Madonna both stayed here in 2010). Designed by Philippe Starck, the Fasano has 91 sleek rooms set with Egyptian cotton sheets, goose-down pillows and high-tech fittings. The best rooms have balconies overlooking the crashing waves of Ipanema beach, which lies just across the road. Rooms without a view simply don't justify the price. The lovely rooftop pool (open to guests only) is truly breathtaking – as are the room rates.

MARINA ALL SUITES Map p66 Boutique Hotel $$$

☎ 2172-1100; www.marinaallsuites.com.br; Av Delfim Moreira 696, Leblon; ste from R$777;

Here you'll find beautifully decorated rooms, doting service and all the creature comforts. As per the name, it's all suites here, meaning that, between the comfy bedroom and living room, you'll have 39 to 75 sq meters in which to stretch out. The best rooms in the oceanfront hotel have splendid views of the shoreline; other attractions are the trendy Bar D'Hotel (p152), the lovely top-floor pool and the spa with a full range of treatments.

CAESAR PARK
Map p64 Hotel $$$

☎ 2525-2525; www.caesar-park.com; Av Vieira Souto 460, Ipanema; d from R$610;

This place breathes opulence from the moment you catch sight of a classical pianist playing in the foyer. The rooms are sizable, with a warm, cozy feel and have artwork on the walls, flat-screen TVs and high-speed internet connections. The best rooms have ocean views.

IPANEMA PLAZA
Map p64 Hotel $$$

☎ 3687-2000; www.goldentulipipanemaplaza.com; Rua Farme de Amoedo 34, Ipanema; d from R$530;

A top choice in Ipanema, the 18-story Plaza features nicely decorated rooms with tile floors, a muted color scheme and sizable windows to let in the tropical rays. You'll also find broad, comfortable beds, spacious bathrooms (all with bathtubs) and a lovely rooftop pool. Some rooms overlook the ocean, while others face the outstretched arms of Cristo Redentor.

IPANEMA TOWER
Map p64 Hotel $$$

☎ 2247-7033; www.ipanematower.com; Rua Prudente de Morais 1008, Ipanema; ste from R$450;

Along one of Ipanema's main thoroughfares, the all-suites Ipanema Tower has large, fully furnished apartments with pressed-wood floors, a balcony (some with ocean views), small kitchen, living room and bedroom. While the furnishings are far from opulent, they're cozy enough, with a decent kitchen table and a few pieces of modern artwork on the walls.

SHERATON
Map p66 Hotel $$$

☎ 2274-1122; www.sheraton-rio.com; Av Niemeyer 121, Vidigal; d from R$450;

The Sheraton is a true resort hotel, with large, peaceful grounds. Every room has a balcony, facing either Leblon and Ipanema or verdant greenery. The rooms are nicely furnished in a cozy, contemporary style, and if you stay out here you'll enjoy a nearly private beach in front, tennis courts, swimming pools and a good health club. The main drawback is that it's a bit far from the action.

PRICE GUIDE

Most prices are for double rooms, except for hostels with only dorm beds, in which case the price is for one person in a dorm bed.

$$$	more than R$350
$$	R$150 to R$350
$	less than R$150

VISCONTI
Map p64 Serviced Apartments $$$

☎ 2111-8600; www.promenade.com.br; Rua Prudente de Morais 1050, Ipanema; ste from R$440;

The Visconti has stylish modern suites (wood floors, stuffed leather furniture, modular lamps) with living-dining rooms, balconies and bedrooms. It's on a residential, tree-lined street a block from the beach.

MARINA PALACE
Map p66 Hotel $$$

☎ 2172-1000; www.hotelmarina.com.br; Av Delfim Moreira 696, Leblon; d standard/deluxe/ste from R$424/454/578;

Occupying a privileged position overlooking Praia do Leblon, this 26-story hotel has contemporary rooms with artwork, sizable beds, flat-screen TVs, and DVD and CD players. Deluxe rooms face the ocean and add more space to the equation. The Marina has top-notch service and a top-floor bar and restaurant with 360-degree views.

HOTEL PRAIA IPANEMA
Map p64 Hotel $$$

☎ 2141-4949; www.praiaipanema.com; Av Vieira Souto 706, Ipanema; d from R$420;

With a view of Ipanema beach, this popular 16-story hotel offers trim, comfortable rooms, each with a balcony. The design is sleek and modern, with off-white tile floors, recessed lighting and artwork on the walls. Stretch out on the molded white lounge chairs next to the rooftop pool. The bar has a view, and there's a small fitness center.

RITZ PLAZA HOTEL

Map p66 Serviced Apartments $$$

☎ 2540-4940; www.ritzhotel.com.br; Av Ataúlfo de Paiva 1280, Leblon; s/d from R$380/420;

This newly renovated, stylish hotel with spa is in one of Rio's most desirable areas. Here you'll find handsome, uniquely designed rooms and common areas that give the place a boutique feel. The one- or two-bedroom suites all have kitchen units, balconies – some with partial ocean views – art on the walls, good lighting and spotless bedrooms.

SOL IPANEMA

Map p64 Hotel $$$

☎ 2525-2020; www.solipanema.com.br; Av Vieira Souto 320, Ipanema; s/d R$375/415, with ocean view R$465/520;

Occupying prime real estate facing Ipanema beach, the tall, slender Sol Ipanema features rooms decorated in warm hues, with dark-wood furnishings and good lighting. Standard rooms are roughly the same size as the deluxe rooms, though the latter face the ocean, meaning you can hear the waves crashing on the shore as you drift off to sleep.

EVEREST RIO

Map p64 Hotel $$$

☎ 2525-2200; www.everest.com.br; Rua Prudente de Morais 1117, Ipanema; s/d from R$380/409;

Another of Ipanema's elegant high-rise hotels, the Everest Rio features nicely decorated rooms (ranging from small to spacious), professional service and an enviable location. All the rooms have large windows and modern bathrooms with bathtubs. Deluxe here means more space (the view is the same) and a queen-size bed. The best rooms – Luxo Superior – have a view of the lake.

MERCURE RIO DE JANEIRO

Map p64 Hotel $$$

☎ 2114-8100; www.accorhotels.com.br; Av Rainha Elizabeth 440, Ipanema; d from R$390;

Not to be confused with the slightly fancier Mercure Arpoador (p192), this hotel offers trim and tidy suites, with pressed-wood floors, big windows and light, muted colors. Some rooms have balconies, and the upper two floors (eight and nine) have slightly better views (though you still won't see the ocean). There's also a pool, which is surrounded by tall buildings.

LONG-TERM RENTALS

If you're planning to stay in Rio for longer than a few nights, you might consider renting an apartment. There are a number of agencies dedicated to tracking down short-term hires for foreigners, and it's a fairly straightforward affair. Typically, you'll typically need to pay 30% to 50% up front (some agencies accept credit cards, others work with Paypal). Make sure you inquire whether utilities and/or cleaning fees are included in the price. As is the case with hotels and hostels, prices double or triple during Carnaval and New Year's, with places booking up far in advance. Nightly rates start around R$120 for a studio apartment.

Aurélio Rio Guide (☎ 7828-6382; www.aurelioriog uide.com) Aurélio rents Ipanema and Copacabana apartments, as well as a house in Búzios.

Blame it on Rio 4 Travel (Map p76; ☎ 3813-5510; www.blameitonrio4travel.com; Rua Xavier da Silveira 15B, Copacabana) Created by a kind, helpful expat from New York, this professional agency rents many types of apartments and also runs a full-service travel agency.

Candida Botafogo (☎ 2247-7079; candidabotafogo@hotmail.com) Candida rents several lovely apartments located in a villa in Ipanema.

Copacabana Holiday (Map p76; ☎ 2542-1525; www.copacabanaholiday.com.br; Rua Barata Ribeiro 90A, Copacabana) Specializing in Copacabana, this agency rents apartments in Copacabana and Ipanema starting at R$120 for a studio, R$150 for a one-bedroom.

Fantastic Rio (Map p76; ☎ 2543-2667; http://fantasticrio.br.tripod.com; Apt 501, Av Atlântica 974, Leme) Multilingual Peter Corr of Fantastic Rio rents modest one-bedrooms to spacious four-bedrooms with beach views.

Rio Apartments (Map p76; ☎ 2247-6221; www.rioapartments.com; Rua Rainha Elizabeth 85, Copacabana) A Swedish-run outfit with many apartment rentals in the Zona Sul.

MAR IPANEMA Map p64 Hotel $$$

☎ 3875-9190; www.maripanema.com.br; Rua Visconde de Pirajá 539, Ipanema; d R$359-449;

This reliable hotel in Ipanema has trim, modern rooms with decent beds, good lighting and an inviting color scheme. It's also in a great location, on Ipanema's lively shopping strip, just two blocks from the beach. The downside is the lack of a view, which is a small loss if you plan to spend your day out enjoying the city.

MONSIEUR LE BLOND

Map p66 Serviced Apartments $$$

☎ 3722-5000; www.redeprotel.com.br, in Portuguese; Av Bartolomeu Mitre 325, Leblon; ste from R$356;

A five-minute walk from Praia de Leblon, this spot combines the service of a hotel with the convenience of an apartment. The colorful accommodations are all comfortably furnished with small kitchens, combined living-dining areas and balconies – some with fine views. The pool, which gets direct sunlight only part of the day, makes a fine place for sunbathing and mingling.

IPANEMA HOTEL RESIDÊNCIA

Map p64 Serviced Apartments $$

☎ 3125-5000; www.ipanemahotel.com.br; angelicaihr@ig.com.br; Rua Barão da Torre 192, Ipanema; d from R$330;

Set on one of Ipanema's lovely tree-lined streets, this high-rise has large apartments, with kitchen units, lounge areas and pleasant bedrooms. Each apartment is furnished differently, so look at a few before committing.

LEBLON OCEAN HOTEL RESIDÊNCIA

Map p66 Serviced Apartments $$

☎ 2158-8282; Rua Rainha Guilhermina 117, Leblon; apt from R$330;

This all-suites hotel has a range of spacious, simply furnished suites, all with kitchen units and small balconies. There's also a small indoor pool and sauna, and Rio's best restaurants (and a handful of bars) are just outside the door. The only catch is that you have to book a minimum of five days.

ARPOADOR INN Map p64 Hotel $$

☎ 2523-0060; www.arpoadorinn.com.br; Rua Francisco Otaviano 177, Ipanema; s/d R$219/244, with view R$455/506;

Overlooking Praia do Arpoador (Arpoador beach), this six-story hotel is the only one in Ipanema or Copacabana that doesn't have a busy street between it and the beach. The rooms are small and basic, but the brighter, prettier 'deluxe' rooms have glorious ocean views.

HOTEL VERMONT Map p64 Hotel $$

☎ 3202-5500; www.hotelvermont.com.br; Rua Visconde de Pirajá 254, Ipanema; s/d/tr from R$210/230/300;

One of the few second-rate hotels in Ipanema, the Hotel Vermont offers guests no-frills accommodations. Although the place received a slight makeover in recent years, the rooms are nothing fancy – clean but not spotless, with tile floors and elderly bathrooms.

IPANEMA PALACE

Map p64 Serviced Apartments $$

☎ 3505-1904; Rua Visconde de Pirajá 161, Ipanema; apt from R$220;

Modern furnished apartments with kitchen, lounge and balcony (no view) are good value here. All are different, but the best have cozy touches like an Oriental carpet, artwork or stylish furniture. Guests also have access to two outdoor pools, a sauna and a laundry. The only problem is booking this place. You'll need some Portuguese to work things out with the manager, Senhor Soares.

IPANEMA INN Map p64 Hotel $$

☎ 2523-6092; www.ipanemainn.com.br; Rua Maria Quitéria 27, Ipanema; d R$212-330;

This is a simple hotel with nice touches. Rooms have woodblock prints on the walls, off-white tile floors and modern bathrooms with big bathtubs. *Superiores* (front-facing rooms) don't have ocean views but, if you lean far enough out the window, you get a glimpse of the glistening sea.

HOTEL SAN MARCO

Map p64 Hotel $

☎ 2540-5032; www.sanmarcohotel.net; Rua Visconde de Pirajá 524, Ipanema; s/d from R$212/229;

Like the Vermont up the road, it's all about location here. A tiny elevator carries you up to the rooms, which are small, dark and cramped, with faded green duvets and tile floors. There are even a couple of coffin-sized 'economy' rooms that run R$173/193 for a single/double. The beach, however, is just two blocks away.

top picks

HOTEL BARS

- Bar dos Descasados (Hotel Santa Teresa; p157) A beautifully designed open-air lounge in Santa Teresa set in the former slave quarters of a coffee plantation.
- Baretto-Londra (Hotel Fasano; p152) Attracts a pure A-list crowd, mingling over cocktails in the lovely Philippe Starck–designed lounge.
- Bar do Copa (Copacabana Palace; p154) The elegant, old-world setting at the bar is among the best features of this grand dame.
- Azul Marinho (Arpoador Inn; p128) Boasting unobstructed views of Ipanema beach, this restaurant-café is a fine spot for a sundowner.
- Bar D'Hotel (Marina All Suites; p152) A trendy Zona Sul crowd gathers over cocktails to the backdrop of waves crashing on Ipanema beach.
- Horse's Neck (Sofitel; p153) Nurse a cocktail on the relaxing terrace and enjoy the splendid views over Copacabana beach.

MARGARIDA'S POUSADA Map p64 Hotel $

☎ 2239-1840; margaridacarneiro@hotmail.com; Rua Barão da Torre 600, Ipanema; s/d/tr from R$130/200/220;

For those seeking a smaller, cozier atmosphere than the high-rise hotels can provide, this excellently located Ipanema guesthouse *(pousada)* is a good option. You'll find 11 pleasant, simply furnished rooms scattered about the low-rise building. Margarida also operates a secluded guesthouse in Jardim Botânico; contact her in Ipanema for details.

YAYA HOTEL Map p64 Hotel $$

☎ 3813-3912; www.yayario.com; Rua Farme de Amoedo 135, Ipanema; s/d/tr R$130/180/240;

A good alternative to high-rise hotels, Yaya (opened in 2007) has eight private rooms set in a converted house on a quiet street. You'll find wood floors, artwork on the walls and a clean, bright appearance. The downside: the rooms share four bathrooms. There's a small lounge for relaxing.

BONITA Map p64 Hostel $

☎ 2227-1703; www.bonitaipanema.com; Rua Barão da Torre 107, Ipanema; dm R$40-50, d with/without bathroom R$180/160;

This peacefully set converted house has history – it's where bossa nova legend Tom Jobim lived from 1962 to 1965 writing some of his most famous songs. Rooms are clean but simply furnished and open onto a shared deck overlooking a small pool and outdoor lounge.

MANGO TREE

Map p64 Hostel $

☎ 2287-9255; www.mangotreehostel.com; Rua Prudente de Morais 594, Ipanema; dm with/without air-con R$50/40, d R$140-170;

In a handsome villa in Ipanema, this popular hostel offers rooms with two-toned wood floors and a welcoming atmosphere. The front porch provides open-air space for unwinding, and there's also a lounge/TV room and a small backyard.

IPANEMA BEACH HOUSE

Map p64 Hostel $

☎ 3202-2693; www.ipanemahouse.com; Rua Barão da Torre 485, Ipanema; dm/d/tr R$45/140/180;

This is one of Rio's best-looking hostels. It's set in a converted two-story house with six- and nine-bed dorms (in the form of three-tiered bunk beds). There are private rooms, indoor and outdoor lounge spaces, a small bar and an attractive pool.

LIGHTHOUSE HOSTEL

Map p64 Hostel $

☎ 2522-1353; www.thelighthouse.com.br; No 20, Rua Barão da Torre 175, Ipanema; dm/d without bathroom R$50/140;

Along with a handful of other budget spots on this quiet lane, the Lighthouse has an easygoing vibe and clean, simple rooms that attract a good mix of backpackers. Accommodations consist of eight-bed dorm rooms and one private double (with a fold-out sofa to sleep three).

LEMON SPIRIT HOSTEL

Map p66 Hostel $$

☎ 2294-1853; www.lemonspirit.com; Rua Cupertino Durão 56, Leblon; dm/d/tr R$45/160/195;

Leblon's first hostel boasts an excellent location one block from the beach. The dorm rooms (nine beds in three-tier bunks) are clean and simple without much decor. There's also a tiny courtyard in front, and the attractive bar in the lobby is a good spot for meeting other travelers over caipirinhas (cane-liquor cocktails).

TERRASSE HOSTEL Map p64 Hostel $

☎ 2247-6130; www.terrassehostel.com.br; Rua Farme de Amoedo 35, Ipanema; dm/s/tw/d R$40/80/120/140;

This small, narrow hostel has basic rooms and not much in the way of atmosphere. It is, however, brilliantly located on one of Ipanema's best streets, with good cafés, bars and of course the beach just steps from the door.

CHE LAGARTO IPANEMA

Map p64 Hostel $

☎ 2512-8076; www.chelagarto.com; Rua Paul Redfern 48, Ipanema; dm R$40-55, d R$120-135;

Part of a small empire of hostels in South America, Che Lagarto's Ipanema branch is a popular budget spot for those young travelers who want to be close to the beach. It's a five-story hostel, with basic rooms and not much common space – aside from a pricey bar on the 1st floor.

HOSTEL HARMONIA

Map p64 Hostel $

☎ 2523-4905; www.hostelharmonia.com; Casa 18, Rua Barão da Torre 175, Ipanema; dm R$50;

Run by three Swedes, Hostel Harmonia is one of the best choices on Ipanema's hostel row, with a good traveler vibe. The lounge and rooms have two-toned wood floors, and quarters are clean and nicely maintained with six beds in each room.

RIO HOSTEL – IPANEMA

Map p64 Hostel $

☎ 2287-2928; www.riohostelipanema.com; Casa 1, Rua Canning 18, Copacabana; dm/d R$40/130;

This friendly hostel is set in a small villa on a peaceful stretch of Ipanema. A good mix of travelers stay here, enjoying the clean rooms, the airy top-floor deck with hammocks and the small front veranda. The same owners operate the respected Santa Teresa hostel (p198) of the same name.

COPACABANA & LEME

Rio's unofficial tourist district has more hotels than any other neighborhood in town. Av Atlântica is lined with high-rise lodging, while backstreets offer similar options at slightly lower prices. Copacabana caters to all styles and budgets: backpackers, business travelers and families all find their way here.

COPACABANA PALACE

Map p76 Hotel $$$

☎ 2548-7070; www.copacabanapalace.com.br; Av Atlântica 1702, Copacabana; d from R$785;

Rio's most famous hotel has hosted heads of state, rock stars and other prominent personalities (Queen Elizabeth once stayed here, as did the Rolling Stones). The dazzling white facade dates from the 1920s, when it became a symbol of the city. Today accommodations range from deluxe rooms to spacious suites with balconies. Despite the price tag, some rooms could do with better upkeep. But there's a lovely pool, excellent restaurants and fine service.

SOFITEL RIO DE JANEIRO

Map p76 Hotel $$$

☎ 2525-1232; www.sofitel.com; Av Atlântica 4240, Copacabana; d from R$720;

One of Rio's priciest hotels, the French-owned Sofitel does its best to impress. The excellent service, comfortable rooms, two lovely pools and beachfront location have earned many fans. All rooms have balconies and are tastefully furnished. Deluxe rooms and suites have ocean views.

PORTO BAY RIO INTERNACIONAL

Map p76 Hotel $$$

☎ 2546-8000; www.portobay.com.br; Av Atlântica 1500, Copacabana; d/ste from R$480/850;

The Rio Internacional had a total overhaul in 2004, which transformed it into one of Copacabana's top beachfront hotels. The rooms have a light and airy feel and are painted in cool, elegant tones (mint is a favorite). Large white duvets, light hardwoods, stylish furnishings and simple artwork all complement each other nicely. Big windows let in lots of light, and most rooms have balconies.

PESTANA RIO ATLÂNTICA

Map p76 Hotel $$$

☎ 2548-6332; www.pestana.com; Av Atlântica 2230, Copacabana; s/d from R$480/510;

Beautifully located along Copacabana beach, the Pestana has excellent amenities, decent service and a wide range of rooms. The best have wood floors, balconies and a bright, modern design scheme. Rooms at the lower end are carpeted, rather bland and too small to recommend.

MERCURE ARPOADOR

Map p76 Hotel $$$

☎ 3222-9600; www.accorhotels.com.br; Rua Francisco Otaviano 61, Copacabana; s/d R$367/397;

This dapper all-suites hotel is nicely located in Arpoador, giving easy access to both Ipanema and Copacabana. The suites have sleek white leather sofas that open into beds, modern kitchenettes, TVs with a stereo and a DVD player, ambient lighting and comfortable bedrooms. All of the rooms have balconies, although there is no view to look at. Rates are lower on weekends.

COPACABANA HOTEL RESIDÊNCIA

Map p76 Serviced Apartments $$

☎ 3622-5200; www.atlanticahotels.com.br, in Portuguese; Rua Barata Ribeiro 222, Copacabana; s/d from R$266/306;

This is a fine choice for those seeking a bit more space. The clean, well-maintained suites all have small kitchen units and lounge rooms with good natural lighting. Keep in mind that busy Barata Ribeiro is awfully noisy; try to snag a top-floor apartment.

RIO GUESTHOUSE

Map p76 Hotel $$

☎ 2521-8568; www.rioguesthouse.com; Rua Francisco Sá 5, Copacabana; d R$300-450;

This small guesthouse is a split-level penthouse on the top floors of a high-rise overlooking Copacabana beach. It offers excellent rooms in a cozy setting, topped only by the warm welcome you'll receive throughout your stay among the antique furnishings and colorful artwork. The outdoor patio has gorgeous views over Copacabana.

DESIGN HOTEL PORTINARI

Map p76 Hotel $$

☎ 3222-8800; www.hotelportinari.com.br; Rua Francisco Sá 17, Copacabana; s/d from R$300/320;

This stylish 13-story hotel demonstrates real design smarts. The rooms have tile floors, artful lighting and big windows, and each floor is decorated in a different style. The top-floor restaurant is set with tropical plants and boasts fine views through the floor-to-ceiling windows.

ASTORIA PALACE Map p76 Hotel $$

☎ 2545-9550; www.astoriapalacehotel.com; Av Atlântica 1886, Copacabana; s/d R$290/310, with ocean view R$330/350;

Beautifully set overlooking the beach (and a stone's throw from the Copacabana Palace), the Astoria has rooms with a clean, modern design – though it's probably not worth the cost unless you get a room with a view.

OLINDA OTHON CLASSIC Map p76 Hotel $$

☎ 2159-9000; www.othon.com.br; Av Atlântica 2230, Copacabana; d with/without ocean view from R$342/270;

Set in a handsome, white building overlooking Copacabana beach, the Olinda Othon is indeed a classic. Its marble lobby, complete with chandeliers, Oriental carpets and grand piano, has an old-world charm, although its rooms are modern. The best of the bunch face the ocean and are worth the extra *reais*.

ROYAL RIO PALACE Map p76 Hotel $$

☎ 2122-9292; www.royalrio.com; Rua Duvivier 82, Copacabana; s/d/tr R$240/270/340;

Not far from the beach, this shiny glass-and-steel high-rise offers comfortable, modern lodging and decent amenities. The rooms are well maintained, and boast wood floors, a nice design aesthetic and sizable windows. There's a pleasant top-floor pool and two rarely used saunas.

WINDSOR MARTINIQUE HOTEL

Map p76 Hotel $$

☎ 2195-5200; www.windsorhoteis.com.br; Rua Sá Ferreira 30, Copacabana; d from R$260;

Near the Ipanema end of Copacabana, this is an all-glass high-rise with clean, comfortable, somewhat small rooms with good beds that are a midrange option for the neighborhood. It's just 30m to the beach, and the hotel spreads a fine breakfast buffet.

OURO VERDE HOTEL Map p76 Hotel $$

☎ 2543-4123; www.dayrell.com.br; Av Atlântica 1456, Copacabana; s R$200-260, d R$230-280;

One of the most reasonably priced hotels on the beachfront, Ouro Verde is set in an attractive 1950s building overlooking Copacabana beach. Rooms here are a little old-fashioned and the carpets and bathrooms are certainly showing their age. On the plus side, the quarters are spacious and, once you pull up those metal window grates, you'll enjoy that incredible view (at least in the *luxo* rooms).

RIO ROISS HOTEL Map p76 Hotel $$

☎ 3222-9950; www.rioroiss.com.br; Rua Aires Saldanha 48, Copacabana; s/d from R$220/270;
This friendly low-key place has fairly new carpets and flat-screen TVs, but otherwise rather dated rooms. For added space and bigger windows, opt for a corner room (any room ending in 2).

ORLA COPACABANA

Map p76 Boutique Hotel $$

☎ 2525-2425; www.orlahotel.com.br; Av Atlântica 4122, Copacabana; d R$248-313;
The Spanish-owned Orla Copacabana has attractive, understated rooms, but the beach-facing location is the real draw. The standard rooms are too dark and cramped to recommend, so it's not worth staying here unless you book one of the deluxe rooms with that desirable ocean view.

ACAPULCO Map p76 Hotel $$

☎ 3077-2000; www.acapulcohotel.com.br; Rua Gustavo Sampaio 854, Leme; s/d from R$215/240;
The Acapulco hotel lies just a short stroll (one block) from the immortalized Copacabana beach. Recent renovations have made it an attractive and fairly priced option. Most rooms have a neat look about them with pressed-wood floors and colorful duvets and curtains.

SOUTH AMERICAN COPACABANA HOTEL Map p76 Hotel $$

☎ 2227-9161; www.southamericanhotel.com.br; Rua Francisco Sá 90, Copacabana; s/d from R$216/238;
Solid value for its trim, modern rooms, this 13-story hotel is nicely located a short stroll from both Copacabana and Ipanema beaches. Rooms are set with pressed-wood floors, colorful bedspreads and a touch of artwork on the walls.

HOTEL VILAMAR Map p76 Hotel $$

☎ 3461-5601; www.hotelvilamarcopacabana.com.br; Rua Bolívar 75, Copacabana; s/d weekdays R$230/250, weekends R$175/200;
This 15-story hotel, set on a quiet street in Copacabana, is a fair-priced place that has inviting rooms with pressed-wood floors, cheery yellow bedspreads and big windows affording decent natural light. Weekend rates are slightly lower.

AUGUSTO'S COPACABANA

Map p76 Hotel $$

☎ 2547-1800; www.augustoshotel.com.br; Rua Bolívar 119, Copacabana; s/d/tw R$205/228/250;
Augusto's plays off the kitschy ancient Rome theme with murals of charioteers and lyre-playing toga-wearers. The rooms, however, are fairly straightforward with a light and airy feel, and modern bathrooms. Some rooms have balconies (but no views). The biggest rooms end in 1 or 8.

REAL PALACE HOTEL

Map p76 Hotel $$

☎ 2101-9292; www.realpalacehotelrj.com.br; Rua Duvivier 70, Copacabana; s/d R$204/220;
Set on a quiet street a few blocks from Copacabana's famous beach, this simple 13-story hotel has small, sparsely furnished rooms. Tiles (of the faux-wood variety) cover the clean-swept floors, and the rooms all get decent light. There's a small rooftop pool, though it lies in shadows for most of the day.

RESIDENCIAL APARTT

Map p76 Serviced Apartments $$

☎ 2522-1722; www.apartt.com.br; Rua Francisco Otaviano 42, Copacabana; s/d R$138/217;
This old-fashioned all-suites hotel doesn't have much charm about it, but the price and location are excellent. Basic one-bedroom suites have small kitchen units, a gloomy lounge room (with cable TV) and a bedroom with adequate natural lighting. Breakfast is included in the price (served until 1pm).

MAR PALACE Map p76 Hotel $$

☎ 2132-1500; www.hotelmarpalace.com.br; Av NS de Copacabana 552, Copacabana; s/d R$200/215;
On Copacabana's busiest road, this sleek glass-and-steel high-rise building hides modest-sized rooms with faux-wood floors and large windows overlooking the street. There's a tiny pool and a sauna on the top floor, as well as a workout room with views of Cristo Redentor.

ATLANTIS COPACABANA HOTEL

Map p76 Hotel $$

☎ 2521-1142; www.atlantishotel.com.br, in Portuguese; Rua Bulhões de Carvalho 61, Copacabana; d R$210-260;

Atlantis' rooms are clean and perfectly serviceable, but the whole place could use an update. The location, however – a short walk to either Ipanema or Copacabana beach – is excellent. The rooms above the 9th floor generally have fine views, and there is a modest pool and a sauna on the roof.

APA HOTEL

Map p76 Hotel $$

☎ 2548-8112; www.apahotel.com.br; Rua República do Peru 305, Copacabana; s/d R$150/200;

The midrange Apa is a seven-story, 52-room hotel with bright sparsely furnished rooms with tile or wood floors, balconies (in most rooms) and fairly reasonable prices.

HOTEL SANTA CLARA

Map p76 Hotel $

☎ 2256-2650; www.hotelsantaclara.com.br; Rua Décio Vilares 316, Copacabana; s/d in back R$155/175, in front R$170/190

Along one of Copacabana's most peaceful streets, this simple three-story hotel has some charming, old-fashioned features, and it's a nice alternative to the high-rises found elsewhere in the neighborhood. The rooms in back are a little gloomy; upstairs rooms are best (and well worth the extra R$15), with wood floors, antique bed frames, a writing desk and a balcony.

EDIFICIO JUCATI

Map p76 Hostel & Serviced Apartments $$

☎ 2547-5422; www.edificiojucati.com.br; Rua Tenente Marones de Gusmão 85, Copacabana; s/d/tr/q R$130/160/190/220;

A few steps away from a small park, on a tranquil street, Jucati doesn't offer much in the way of atmosphere (there are no common areas), though it does have large, simply furnished apartments trimmed with artwork, with slate floors and small, but serviceable kitchens. Have a look at the layout before committing. Most apartments have just one bedroom with a double bed and a living room with a bunk bed.

BAMBOO RIO Map p76 Hostel $

☎ 2236-1117; www.bamboorio.com; Rua Lacerda Coutinho 45, Copacabana; dm R$32-39, d R$120-140;

Yet another hostel set in a former villa, Bamboo Rio is a friendly, comfortable hostel with tidy air-conditioned dorm rooms (sleeping from five to 12), ample lounge space, a tiny pool and an inviting bar area. Overall, it's a nice choice for Copacabana, with a good traveler vibe.

CHE LAGARTO Map p76 Hostel $

☎ 2256-2776; www.chelagarto.com; Rua Anita Garibaldi 87, Copacabana; dm R$32-40, d with/without bathroom R$134/116;

A favorite among young backpackers, Argentine-owned Che Lagarto attracts a festive crowd that gathers over the pool table or at the patio bar for beer and caipirinhas most nights. It's a good place for meeting fellow partiers. Dorms are air-conditioned.

CASTELO Map p76 Hostel $

☎ 2521-5130; www.castelohostel.com.br; Rua Saint Roman 20, Copacabana; dm/d R$35/100;

The aptly named Castelo occupies a beautifully converted castle-like mansion (built in the 1920s) on a quiet stretch of Copacabana. Here you'll find huge dorm rooms with single beds (no bunks) and polished wood floors, plus spacious common areas (including an outdoor veranda and a lounge with a pool table). FYI: Rua Saint Roman leads up into Pavão-Pavãozinho, a once-dicey favela that is now considered safe (there's a permanent police presence on the street).

WALK ON THE BEACH HOSTEL

Map p76 Hostel $

☎ 2545-7500; www.walk-on-the-beach.com; Rua Dias da Rocha 85, Copacabana; dm R$35-45;

Set in an unsigned two-story villa on one of Copacabana's rare quiet streets, this nicely designed hostel offers good-value fan-cooled dorm rooms (each with three to 12 beds). It has a lounge room and a small bar, and maintains a welcoming, low-key vibe.

STONE OF A BEACH HOSTEL

Map p76 Hostel $

☎ 3209-0348; www.stoneofabeach.com.br; Rua Barata Ribeira 111, Copacabana; dm R$30-39, d R$90-120;

This popular full-service hostel offers good-value dorm rooms (with six to 18 beds) amid a friendly, party atmosphere. The small rooftop pool with adjoining bar and restaurant (serving inexpensive meals nightly) is a good place to meet other travelers, and the hostel has loads of activities for solo backpackers – boat parties, nights out in Lapa, BBQs and more.

BOTAFOGO

Botafogo, with its growing number of hostels, has some of the best budget options in the city. Though lacking beach access, the neighborhood, with its mix of high-rises and colonial villas, has its appeal, including the chance to experience the authentic side of Rio – tree-lined streets, old-school *botecos* (neighborhood bars) and restaurants that attract a festive, mostly local crowd.

EL MISTI

Map p80 Hostel $

☎ 2226-0991; www.elmistihostel.com; Praia do Botafogo 462, Casa 9; dm R$29-40, s R$40, d R$110-130;

Located along Botafogo's hostel row, El Misti is a popular budget spot among Brazilian and foreign travelers for its cheap dorm rooms (with triple bunk beds) and lively atmosphere. It's a short walk to the Botafogo metro station.

VILA CARIOCA

Map p80 Hostel $

☎ 2535-3224; www.vilacarioca.com.br; Rua Estácio Coimbra 84; dm/d from R$32/110;

On a peaceful tree-lined street, this low-key and welcoming hostel has six- to 15-bed dorms in an attractively decorated house. The common areas are a fine spot to mingle with other travelers.

TUPINIQUIM Map p80 Hostel $

☎ 2244-1286; www.tupiniquimhostel.com.br; Rua São Manoel 19; dm R$30-35, d with/without bathroom R$100/80;

Tupiniquim offers plenty of amusement and activities for those seeking something beyond just a cheap bed for the night. There's a rock-climbing wall, ping-pong, pool table, foosball, record player, book and DVD library, and an enclosed patio, with barbecues several nights a week. The facilities are comfortable (plenty of hot showers, good mattresses and double rather than triple bunk beds).

ACE HOSTEL Map p80 Hostel $

☎ 2527-7452; www.acehostels.com.br; Rua São Clemente 23; dm R$25-40, s/d R$109/129;

One block from the metro, this small well-run hostel has a range of rooms (the cheapest lack air-conditioning) and a roomy lounge/TV room. Ace also has a hostel in Petrópolis.

FLAMENGO

One of Rio's oldest neighborhoods, Flamengo attracts visitors who are seeking a more authentically Carioca experience – its neighborhood feel, traditional bars and youthful inhabitants add to the charm. Prices here are lower than in Copacabana or Ipanema. Keep in mind that although Flamengo is near a sandy shoreline, the bay is too polluted for swimming. Although there aren't many options in Flamengo proper, nearby Catete (p195) offers decent accommodation giving speedy access to this neighborhood.

AUGUSTO'S PAYSANDU HOTEL

Map p84 Hotel $$

☎ 2558-7270; www.paysanduhotel.com.br; Rua Paissandu 23, Flamengo; s/d R$149/165;

Set on a quiet street lined with imperial palm trees, the Paysandu is an affordable and decent option in Flamengo. The best rooms feature high ceilings, good natural light and space to stretch out.

BROTHERS HOSTEL Map p84 Hostel $

☎ 2551-0997; www.brothershostel.com; Rua Farani 18; dm/d without HI card from R$47/140, with HI card from R$37/120;

In a handsomely converted house, Brothers Hostel has airy, meticulously clean rooms and common areas, with polished wood floors and tall ceilings – with eight beds maximum to a room. It was started by four Brazilian brothers who have traveled the world (one is a photographer whose travel photos decorate the lounge room). The rock-loving bar brings together both Cariocas (residents of Rio) and international visitors.

CATETE & GLÓRIA

Aside from the historic Glória hotel – which is currently closed as it receives a massive makeover – this area is largely a budget destination, with battered guesthouses within a short walk of the Catete metro station. If you don't mind roughing it, you'll be able to take advantage of the city's cheapest accommodations, but don't expect much in the way of ambience.

FLAMENGO PALACE Map p87 Hotel $$

☎ 2557-7552; hotelflamengopalace.com.br; Praia do Flamengo 6, Flamengo; s/d from R$170/190;

Trapped in the '70s, the Flamengo Palace has bare rooms with simple furnishings and an odd touch here and there – like wooden-framed oval mirrors and wild curtain patterns. *Luxo* rooms have excellent views of the bay but are noisier.

HOTEL REGINA Map p87 Hotel $$

☎ 3289-9999; www.hotelregina.com.br; Rua Ferreira Viana 29, Flamengo; s/d R$172/190, with balcony R$188/210;

On a quiet street just off the main avenue through Flamengo, the handsomely renovated Regina boasts 117 rooms, each with a bright modern appearance, with wood or tile floors and sparkling bathrooms. Front-facing rooms *(luxos)* have sizable balconies for catching a breeze off the bay. There's also a full-service spa.

IMPERIAL HOTEL Map p87 Hotel $$

☎ 2558-5815; www.imperialhotel.com.br; Rua do Catete 186, Catete; s/d R$150/170;

The Imperial Hotel wins the award for longest hallway. The attractive white building has only three stories but goes back endlessly to reveal a crop of recently renovated rooms and suites. Some rooms are too dark for our taste, while others have better natural lighting and that all-important Jacuzzi tub.

HOTEL INGLÊS Map p87 Hotel $$

☎ 2558-3052; www.hotelingles.com.br; Rua Silveira Martins 20, Flamengo; s/d R$120/150;

Boasting a colonial facade, Hotel Inglês has a range of simple rooms, the best with high ceilings and windows overlooking the leafy Parque do Catete. Rooms in back are too cramped to recommend.

BEIJA FLOR HOTEL Map p87 Hotel $

☎ 2285-2492; Rua Ferreira Viana 20, Flamengo; s/d R$135/145;

This remodeled hotel has clean rooms with tile floors, firm mattresses and modern bathrooms. On the downside, some rooms lack decent ventilation (opening onto an air shaft). It's on a quiet street within walking distance of the metro.

MAZE INN Map p87 B&B $

☎ 2558-5547; www.jazzrio.info; Casa 66, Rua Tavares Bastos 414, Favela Tavares Bastos; s/d from R$80/100

Set in Tavares Bastos, one of Rio's safest favelas, the Maze Inn is a fantastic place to overnight – for those looking for an alternative view of Rio. The rooms are uniquely decorated with original artworks (for sale) by English owner and Renaissance man Bob Nadkarni, while the veranda offers stunning views of the bay and Pão de Açúcar. Don't miss the monthly jazz parties (first Friday of the month).

HOTEL FERREIRA VIANA Map p87 Hotel $

☎ 2205-7396; Rua Ferreira Viana 58, Flamengo; s/d R$75/95;

Not the nicest place in the area, but Ferreira Viana is at least cheap. Your *reais* will buy you a small, dark room with tile floors and thin mattresses. Some rooms are better than others so take a peek before committing.

HOTEL RIAZOR Map p87 Hotel $

☎ 2225-0121; www.hotelriazor.com.br; Rua do Catete 160, Catete; s/d R$75/90;

The lovely colonial facade of the Riazor hides worn quarters short on style. The equation here is simple: bed, bathroom, TV, air-conditioning, and a door by which to exit the room and explore the city. You'll find a mix of travelers and lost souls here.

ART HOSTEL Map p87 Hostel $

☎ 2205-1983; www.arthostelrio.com; Rua Silveira Martins 135, Catete; dm R$29-45, s/d from R$50/90;

On a quiet street off busy Rua do Catete, this long, narrow three-story hostel attracts an alternative, somewhat bohemian crowd. Dorm rooms pack anywhere from four to 14 beds. The main art-filled lounge overlooking the street becomes an exhibition and performance space (poetry readings, art shows) twice a month.

SANTA TERESA & LAPA

In the last few years, Santa Teresa has enjoyed something of a renaissance, with a growing number of handsome new guesthouses opening their doors. Travelers who stay here will be far from the beaches, but the trade-off is that you're in the heart of Rio's Montmartre. More than a few travelers who've passed through here have fallen for the atmospheric 'hood and ended up staying far longer than they originally intended.

HOTEL SANTA TERESA

Map p98 Hotel $$$

☎ 2221-1406; www.santateresahotel.com; Rua Almirante Alexandrino 660, Santa Teresa; d from R$750;

Probably the finest boutique hotel in Rio, it's set in a lavishly restored building (part of a coffee plantation in the 19th century) with artfully designed rooms, an award-winning restaurant, a full-service spa, a stylish bar and a pool with fine views over the city. The design incorporates a certain tropical elegance with art and artifacts from across Brazil on display in common areas – and even in some rooms.

MAMA RUISA Map p98 Hotel $$$

☎ 2242-1281; www.mamaruisa.com; Rua Santa Cristina 132, Santa Teresa; d from R$560;

Mama Ruisa aims for bohemian chic in its seven spacious, uniquely designed guestrooms. Every whim is catered for in this inspiring converted colonial mansion, and guests can opt for massages and private tours or just enjoy the spectacular view over the bay from the swimming pool.

SOLAR DE SANTA Map p98 Hotel $$$

☎ 2221-2117; www.solardesanta.com; Ladeira do Meireles 32, Santa Teresa; r with/without bathroom from R$480/255;

This marvelous colonial mansion has just four rooms and one private bungalow, each with polished wood floors and colorful artwork. Rooms open onto a veranda with splendid views through the lush foliage out front to the downtown. The downside: only three rooms come with a bathroom. The whole mansion plus staff is also available for rent (R$2600 per night), and can accommodate up to 13 guests.

CASTELINHO 38 Map p98 Hotel $$

☎ 2252-2549; www.castelinho38.com; Rua Triunfo 38, Santa Teresa; s/d from R$170/220;

Another Santa charmer, Castelinho offers a range of spacious rooms with high ceilings, wood floors and a light, airy design. It's set in a mid-19th-century mansion and has an outdoor terrace with a garden and lounge space.

CASA ÁUREA Map p98 B&B $

☎ 2242-5830; www.casaaurea.com.br; Rua Áurea 80, Santa Teresa; dm R$65, s/d with bathroom R$160/190, without bathroom R$110/140;

Set on a quiet street, this handsome two-story house has been converted into a simple guesthouse with cozy rooms. It's within a short walking distance of the *bonde* (tram) as well as the neighborhood's best restaurants and bars. Casa Áurea's best feature is the large private garden beside the house.

CAMA E CAFÉ Map p98 B&B $

☎ 2225-4366; www.camaecafe.com; Rua Progresso 67, Santa Teresa; s/d with bathroom from R$110/140, without bathroom R$75/95;

Run by several young entrepreneurs dedicated to rejuvenating the area, Cama e Café is a bed-and-breakfast network that links travelers with local residents. There are several dozen colonial houses to choose from, with accommodations ranging from modest to lavish – indeed the best rooms are antique-filled suites set inside castlelike mansions with verandas and lush gardens.

CASA MANGO MANGO Map p98 Hotel $

☎ 2508-6440; www.casa-mangomango.com; Rua Joaquim Murtinho 587, Santa Teresa; dm R$40, d with/without bathroom from R$140/130;

In an atmospheric 19th-century mansion, this friendly guesthouse has a mix of uniquely designed rooms, including a 10-bed dormitory, several spacious but windowless rooms with separate sleeping lofts and two bright, beautifully designed rooms filled with artwork (R$220 per double). The grounds have a small patio and pool, plus enormous 200-year-old mango trees.

TERRA BRASILIS Map p98 Hostel $

☎ 2224-0952; www.terrabrasilishostel.com; Rua Murtinho Nobre 156, Santa Teresa; dm R$35-40, d R$130-150;

Near the Parque das Ruinas, this peacefully set guesthouse has a mix of dorm rooms (sleeping six to 12) and private doubles, all with wood floors and French doors that open onto a veranda overlooking the city. The breezy patio with bar is a fine place to nurse a drink in the afternoon.

LOVE AMONG THE CARIOCAS

Living in such a crowded city, Cariocas (residents of Rio) sometimes have a terrible time snatching a few moments of privacy. For those living with their parents or sharing a tiny apartment with roommates, an empty stretch of beach, a park bench or a seat in the back of a café are all fine spots to steal a few kisses, but for more...progressive action, Cariocas take things elsewhere – to the motel, aka the *love* motel.

Love motels aren't so much a Carioca oddity as they are a Brazilian institution. They are found in every part of the country, usually sprouting along the outskirts of cities and towns. Some are designed with lavish facades – decked out to resemble medieval castles, Roman temples or ancient pyramids – while others blend more discreetly into the surrounding landscape. Regardless of the exteriors, the interiors are far removed from the 'less is more' design philosophy. Mirrors cover the ceiling while heart-shaped, vibrating beds stretch beneath them. Rose-tinted mood lights, Jacuzzis, televisions loaded with porn channels, dual-headed showers and a menu on the bedside table featuring sex toys that guests can order to the room – all these come standard in most love motels. Such places scream seediness in the West. In Brazil, however, they're not viewed as anything out of the ordinary. People need a place for their liaisons – they might as well have a laugh and a bit of fun while they're at it. The motels are used by young lovers who want to get away from their parents, parents who want to get away from their kids and couples who want to get away from their spouses. They are an integral part of the nation's social fabric, and it's not uncommon for Cariocas to host parties in them.

Most motels rent rooms by the hour, though some give discounted prices for four-hour blocks or offer lunchtime specials. In Rio many of them are out on the roads that lead to the city, such as Av Brasil in the Zona Norte and Av Niemeyer between Leblon and São Conrado. There are a few, however, scattered about Centro, Flamengo and Botafogo.

The quality of the motels varies, reflecting their popularity across social classes. The most lavish are three-story suites with a hot tub beneath a skylight on the top floor, a sauna and bathroom on the 2nd floor, and the garage underneath (allowing anonymity). They come standard with all the other mood-enhancement features mentioned earlier. For the best suites, expect to pay upwards of R$400 for eight hours, and more on weekends. Standard rooms cost quite a bit less, and Cariocas claim that an equally fine time can be had there.

If you're interested in checking out this cultural institution, here are some accessible options:

Shalimar (Map p60; ☎ 3322-3392; www.hotelshalimar.com.br; Av Niemeyer 218, Vidigal; r for 6hr R$48-195)

Sinless (Map p60; ☎ 2512-9913; www.sinless.com.br; Av Niemeyer 214, Vidigal; r for 6hr R$48-195)

Viña del Mar (Map p98; ☎ 2509-1857; www.vinadelmar.com.br; Rua Joaquim Silva 57, Lapa; r for 6hr R$51-190)

Vips (Map p60; ☎ 3322-1662; www.vipsmotel.com.br; Av Niemeyer 418, Vidigal; ste for 8hr R$100-500).

RIO HOSTEL Map p98 Hostel $

☎ 3852-0827; www.riohostel.com; Rua Joaquim Murtinho 361, Santa Teresa; dm R$37, d R$120-140;

This Santa favorite provides travelers with a home away from home. The spacious lounge, backyard patio with pool, ping-pong room and kitchen for guests all add to the charm. The rooms are clean, and there are attractive double rooms, including a private suite behind the pool. The hostel overlooks downtown Rio and lies along the *bonde* line. It can be a bit tricky to find – if you reach Curvelo Sq (the first major *bonde* stop), you've gone too far. Disembark and walk 200m back down the hill.

POUSADA FAVELINHA Map p98 Hostel $

www.favelinha.com; Rua Antonio Joaquim 13, Morro do Pereirão da Silva; dm/d R$35/75;

Located in the favela of Pereirão da Silva, Pousada Favelinha has four double rooms and a five-bed dorm, all with balconies that have stunning views over the city to Pão de Açúcar. There's also a terrace, a lounge and lots of insider info from the welcoming Brazilian-German owners. While this is one of Rio's more peaceful favelas, it isn't for everyone – some love it, some don't. To get there, take the *bonde* to Colegio Asunção (Rua Almirante Alexandrino 2024) and enter the favela through the school grounds.

HOTEL MARAJÓ

Map p98 Hotel $

☎ 2224-4134; Rua Joaquim Silva 99, Lapa; s/d/tw R$55/60/80;

A few paces from the Selarón steps (p100), this basic hotel rents simple, fairly clean rooms, all with air-conditioning. The best rooms are quite sunny, the worst are rather gloomy.

BARRA DA TIJUCA & WEST OF RIO

Few foreign travelers stay in the neighborhoods west of Leblon, as it's a hassle getting around without a car. The advantage, however, is being close to some of Rio's best beaches – which get wilder the further west you go.

LE RELAIS MARAMBAIA

off Map p107 Hotel $$

☎ 2394-2544; www.lerelaisdemarambaia.com.br; Estrada Roberto Burle Marx 9346, Barra da Guaratiba; d from R$250;

Perched on the edge of the ocean in the peaceful community of Barra da Guaratiba, this boutique hotel (which opened in 2008) has five attractive rooms, each with wood floors, balconies and high-end fittings. Some rooms also have private Jacuzzis. There's a restaurant and small outdoor terrace with pool that makes a great spot at sunset.

RIO SURF 'N STAY

Map p107 Hostel $

☎ 3418-1133; www.riosurfnstay.com; Rua Raimundo Veras 1140, Recreio dos Bandeirantes; dm/d R$40/110;

Just a short stroll to the fine surf off Macumba Beach, this converted house, which is owned by a New Zealander and a Brazilian, is the go-to spot for anyone who has come to Rio to learn to surf. The two dorm rooms (sleeping four or five people) and three private doubles are comfortably furnished, and the hosts do their best to make everyone feel at home. There is a kitchen for guest use and a grassy lawn with palm trees that is fine for lazing about. Surf packages – that include lessons and accommodation – are available. Rio Surf 'N Stay is about a 40-minute bus ride from the Zona Sul; take bus 175 – Recreio from the coastal road along Copacabana, Ipanema or Leblon beaches.

EXCURSIONS

contents

EXCURSIONS

Although most travelers have a hard time tearing themselves away from Rio, fabulous beaches, mountain getaways and rain-forest-covered islands are just a short drive from town. Whether you seek adventure or an idyllic retreat, you'll find countless options in the relatively small state of Rio de Janeiro.

On sunny weekends, Cariocas (residents of Rio) craving a relaxing beach holiday head east to Búzios (p209). Once a remote fishing village, the town lies on a peninsula with pretty beaches and scores of elegant *pousadas* (guesthouses), top-notch restaurants and a lively bar scene. Surfers and those wanting a more sedate experience might detour to Saquarema or the sleepy beach town of Arraial do Cabo.

West of Rio lies the beautiful coastline of the Costa Verde (Green Coast), where lush mountains meet the sea, with hundreds of islands and beaches in the area. The star attraction here is peaceful Paraty (p204), an old gold-mining town with handsomely preserved cobblestone streets and jewel-box churches. Antique-filled *pousadas* now occupy some of the colonial buildings, with an assortment of spots for fine dining. It's particularly popular with couples seeking a romantic getaway.

This coastline is also home to Ilha Grande (p207), a hilly car-free island, with dozens of beaches and more than 100km of hiking trails amid Mata Atlântica (Atlantic rain forest). The seaside town of Vila do Abraão, with its mellow vibe, is an excellent intro to island life.

Cariocas with a yearning for the mountains have a few options. Just north of Rio stands the imperial city of Petrópolis (p211). Its palaces, cathedral, and European-style gardens and boulevards lie beneath the jagged mountains of Serra dos Órgãos, one of the great climbing meccas of Rio. In addition to rock climbing, visitors can raft in mountain streams and hike through the nearby national park.

Further out, in the northwest corner of the state, is Brazil's oldest national park, the Parque Nacional de Itatiaia, where stark high-country plateaus and rocky spires intermingle with lush, low-country jungle. Bordering the park, the towns of Visconde de Mauá (p213) welcome visitors with rustic cabins, rushing streams and fresh-grilled trout.

BEACHES & ISLANDS

Though no longer the 'undiscovered' paradise that it was in the 1960s, Búzios (p209) still has gorgeous beaches. Some are easy to reach, while others require a hike. By night, the bayside promenade offers plenty of nightlife diversions with its outdoor restaurants and bars. Scenic beaches also lie near Paraty (p204), while Arraial do Cabo (p210) and surfer-favorite Saquarema (p210) draw their share of visitors. Ilha Grande (p207) also has striking beaches, several of which rank among Brazil's prettiest.

NATIONAL PARKS

Breathe in the fresh mountain air and hike the trails of Rio state's untamed national parks. North of Rio, the peaks of the Parque Nacional da Serra dos Órgãos (p213) make an impressive backdrop to treks in the area. Four hours northwest of Rio, the Parque Nacional de Itatiaia (p214) is packed with waterfalls, clear blue lakes and dramatic peaks.

TOWNS

In a cool mountain climate, Petrópolis (p211), with its canals, landscaped parks and city squares, has a European air. Its palaces and museums are good places to discover Brazil's imperial epoch. For a window into Brazil's early settlement days, strike out for Paraty (p204), a perfectly preserved colonial town, with much history hidden inside its churches and 18th-century townhouses. Northwest of Rio, the villages of Visconde de Mauá (p213) and its surroundings are set in a lush alpine area, with idyllic streams, waterfalls, and cozy chalets scattered along country lanes.

DRIVES

The Costa Verde (accessible via BR 101 west) provides the setting for one of the country's most spectacular drives. The panoramic road hugs the coast's edge as it winds its way past lush peaks, beaches and colonial settlements. The prettiest stretches run some 150km from

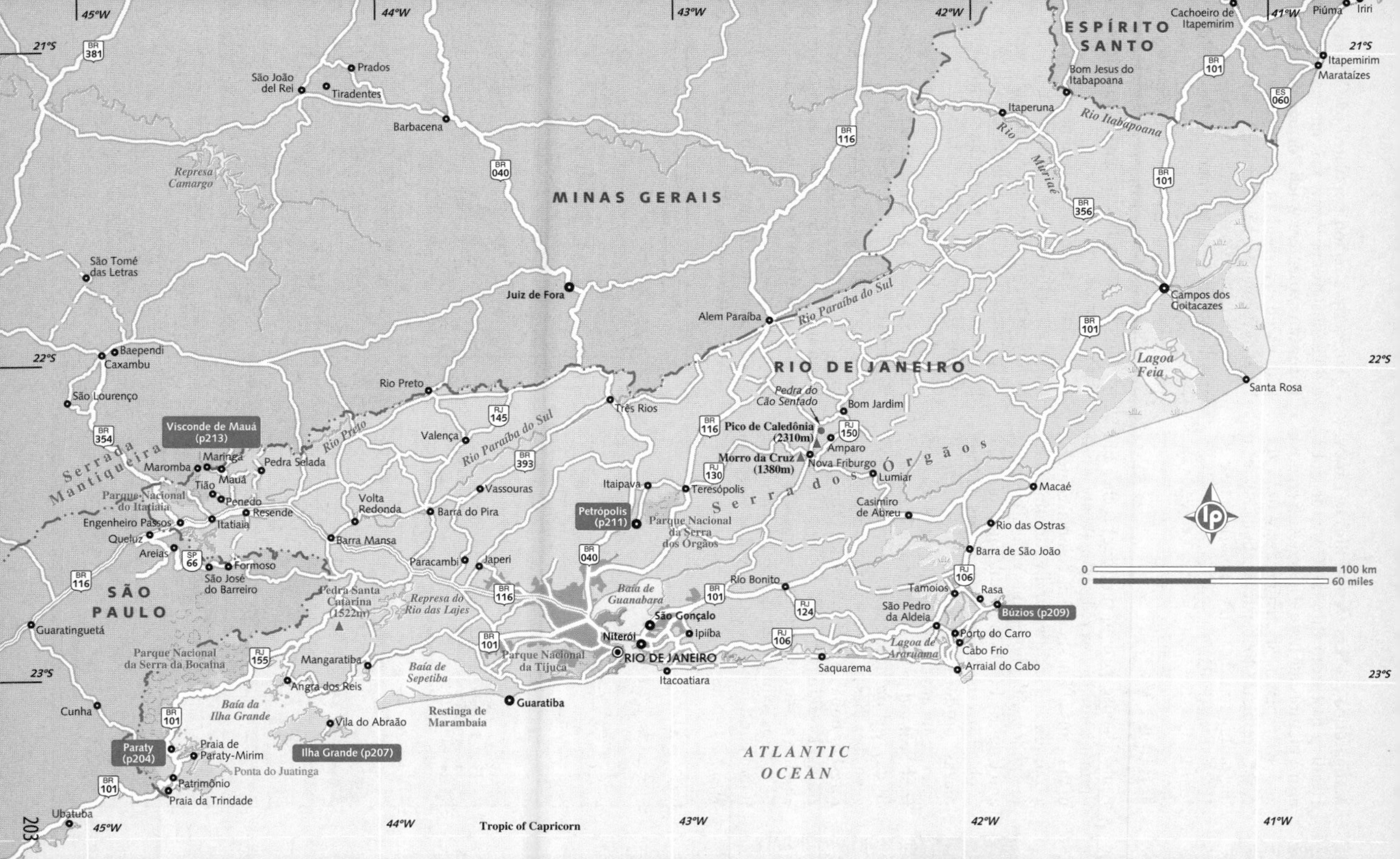
MINAS GERAIS
ESPÍRITO SANTO
RIO DE JANEIRO
SÃO PAULO
ATLANTIC OCEAN
Tropic of Capricorn
21°S
22°S
23°S
45°W
44°W
43°W
42°W
41°W
Cachoeiro de Itapemirim
Piúma
Iriri
Itapemirim
Marataízes
Bom Jesus do Itabapoana
Itaperuna
Rio Itabapoana
Rio Muriaé
Campos dos Goitacazes
Lagoa Feia
Santa Rosa
Prados
São João del Rei
Tiradentes
Barbacena
Represa Camargo
São Tomé das Letras
Juiz de Fora
Alem Paraíba
Rio Paraíba do Sul
Baependi
Caxambu
São Lourenço
Rio Preto
Três Rios
Pedra do Cão Sentado
Bom Jardim
Pico de Caledônia (2310m)
Amparo
Morro da Cruz (1380m)
Nova Friburgo
Lumiar
Serra dos Órgãos
Visconde de Mauá (p213)
Serra da Mantiqueira
Maromba
Maringá
Mauá
Pedra Selada
Tião
Penedo
Resende
Parque Nacional do Itatiaia
Engenheiro Passos
Itatiaia
Queluz
Areias
Formoso
São José do Barreiro
Valença
Vassouras
Volta Redonda
Barra do Pira
Barra Mansa
Itaipava
Teresópolis
Petrópolis (p211)
Parque Nacional da Serra dos Órgãos
Casimiro de Abreu
Macaé
Rio das Ostras
Barra de São João
Paracambi
Japeri
Pedra Santa Catarina (1522m)
Represa do Rio das Lajes
Baía de Guanabara
São Gonçalo
Niterói
Ipiíba
Rio Bonito
Tamoios
Rasa
Búzios (p209)
São Pedro da Aldeia
Porto do Carro
Cabo Frio
Arraial do Cabo
Lagoa de Araruama
Saquarema
Guaratinguetá
Parque Nacional da Serra da Bocaina
Mangaratiba
Baía de Sepetiba
Parque Nacional da Tijuca
RIO DE JANEIRO
Itacoatiara
Angra dos Reis
Guaratiba
Restinga de Marambaia
Cunha
Baía da Ilha Grande
Vila do Abraão
Ilha Grande (p207)
Paraty (p204)
Praia de Paraty-Mirim
Ponta do Juatinga
Patrimônio
Praia da Trindade
Ubatuba
BR 381
BR 040
BR 116
BR 101
BR 356
ES 060
BR 354
RJ 145
BR 393
RJ 150
RJ 130
SP 66
RJ 155
RJ 124
RJ 106
0 100 km
0 60 miles

Mangaratiba (111km west of Rio) to Paraty. Heading east from Rio, the Costa do Sol is also a picturesque littoral, filled with lagoons and swampland. Stretching away from the coast are plains that extend about 30km to the mountains. For DIY exploring, take RJ 106 east to RJ 102.

PARATY

Amid a landscape of picturesque beaches and dramatic jungle-covered peaks, Paraty is one of the gems of Rio state. The colonial center is a tranquil and architecturally stunning place to wander, with photogenic colonial churches and brightly hued stone buildings lining the cobbled streets. On summer nights its leafy plazas, outdoor restaurants and open-air cafés come alive as visiting crowds feast on fresh seafood to the backdrop of live music. By day, visitors head out to the dozens of gorgeous beaches in the area, hike through rain forest or book an adventure tour (horseback riding, kayaking or scuba diving). The town also has a colorful art gallery scene and some fine shops selling high-quality *cachaça* (cane liquor) and handicrafts, as well as works of art.

Formerly a region populated by Guianás indigenous group, Paraty first emerged as a European settlement when Portuguese from São Vicente arrived in the 16th century. Paraty's boom time began in the 17th century when gold was discovered in Minas Gerais, and the port became an important link as the riches were shipped back to Portugal. Until 1954 the only access to Paraty was by sea. You can still find a few old-timers around town who fondly remember the days when Paraty was so remote.

In addition to the town's culinary and historical attractions, you'll find striking natural beauty in the surrounding countryside, with steep, forested mountains plunging right down into the sea, and a varied coastline replete with dozens of pristine beaches and islands.

A good introduction to Paraty is the excellent **Casa da Cultura** (☎ 3371-2325; Rua Dona Geralda 177; admission R$8; 🕒 11am-7:30pm Wed-Mon), which has a fascinating permanent exhibition that includes interviews with local residents (in audio and video format), as well as relics from the past. All exhibits are in both English and Portuguese.

A 20-minute walk north of town, **Forte Defensor Perpétuo** (admission free; 🕒 9am-noon & 2-5pm Wed-

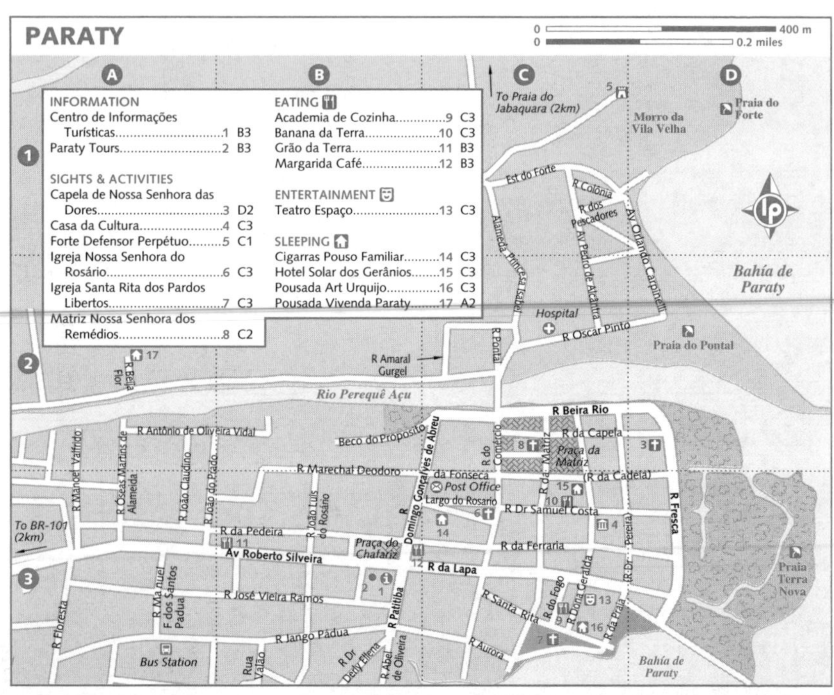

PARTYING IN PARATY

The city by the sea has a calendar packed full with colorful festivals. Among the biggest events is Paraty's Festa do Divino Espírito Santo, which features all sorts of merrymaking that revolves around the *fólios* (musical groups that go door to door, singing and joking). The vibrant festival begins nine days before Pentecostal Sunday (the seventh Sunday after Easter).

Festas Juninas are held throughout June, when the town becomes the stage for music, street parties and folk dancing such as the *xiba* (a circle clog dance) and the *ciranda* (a *xiba* with guitar accompaniment). The final festival is on June 29 with a maritime procession to Ilha do Araújo, one of the islands near Paraty. From Friday to Sunday on the third weekend in August, Paraty hosts its popular Festa da Pinga (*pinga* is a more polite term for *cachaça*, the fiery sugarcane spirit). Local distilleries are on hand to dazzle (or at least intoxicate) festival-goers with their rare spirits.

The Festival Literária Internacional de Parati (www.flip.org.br), launched in 2003, brings authors from around the world to Paraty for five days each August. The opening concert often features big names in Brazilian music.

The Festa de Nossa Senhora (NS) dos Remédios culminates on September 8, with street processions and religious celebrations on the preceding week.

The city also attracts a crowd to its Carnaval, when revelers cover themselves in mud and dance wildly through the streets.

New festivals keep springing up each year, including festivals of photography and video art, gastronomy and seafood. See www.paraty.com.br/eventos.asp, in Portuguese, for a full list.

Sun) commands a fine view over the bay. It was built in 1703 (and rebuilt in 1822) to defend against pirate raids on the gold pipeline that ran to Minas Gerais. The fort, located on the Morro da Vila Velha (the hill past Praia do Pontal) also houses an arts center.

A visit to the town's old churches provides a glimpse of the complexities of 18th-century life: two were built for whites, one for blacks and a fourth for freed mulattos (persons of mixed black and white ancestry).

Built by slaves in 1725, the Igreja Nossa Senhora do Rosário (cnr Rua Dr Samuel Costa & Rua do Comércio; admission R$2; 9am-noon & 2-5pm Tue-Sun) served as the city's black parish. Its two wooden, gilt-trimmed side altars showcase the talents of early 19th-century wood-carvers. Note also the black St Benedict holding the Christ child to the left of the altar, the stone pulpit carved into the wall, and the pineapple-like chandelier base in the roof – a symbol of prosperity. An old burial ground lies beneath the church floorboards.

Overlooking the lush Praça da Matriz, the Matriz Nossa Senhora dos Remédios (cnr Rua da Matriz & Rua da Capela; admission R$2; 9am-noon & 2-5pm Tue-Sun) is a fine stone church with handsome tiled floors, wedding cake–style alcoves and a row of glass-encased saint figures peering down at would-be worshippers. Paraty's settlement began around the time builders first erected the church. In 1646, the benefactor Maria Jácome de Melo donated the land between the rivers on two conditions: that a chapel dedicated to Our Lady be built and that no harm come to the indigenous people residing there. Sadly, the second demand was ignored.

Freed mulattos worshipped in the Igreja Santa Rita dos Pardos Libertos (Rua Santa Rita; admission R$2; 9am-noon & 2-5pm Wed-Sun). It houses a tiny museum of sacred art and some fine woodwork on the doorways and altars.

Facing the sea, the small, white Capela de Nossa Senhora das Dores (cnr Rua Fresca & Rua da Caplea; 9am-noon & 2-5pm Tue-Sun) gathered the colonial white elite. Dating from 1800 but renovated in 1901, the church hides a fascinating cemetery in the inner courtyard. It opens only sporadically.

Paraty has 65 islands and 300 beaches in its vicinity. The first beach you'll reach walking north of town (just across the canal) is Praia do Pontal, which can get a little murky at times. A handful of open-air restaurants line its shore. The cleaner and relatively secluded Praia do Forte

TRANSPORTATION: PARATY

Distance from Rio 261km

Direction West

Travel Time 4½ hours

Car From the Zona Sul, head north on Av D Infante Henrique, which follows the curve of the bay as it eventually links up with Av Presidente Kubitschek. Look for signs to merge onto Av Brasil; this turns into BR 101, which leads all the way out to Paraty.

Bus Costa Verde buses (R$52) depart eight times daily between 6am and 9pm from Novo Rio bus station in Rio.

DETOUR: COASTAL BEAUTY

Paraty's resplendent natural setting makes for some fine exploring. Gorgeous beaches lie within a 30-minute drive and a one-hour boat ride, and most are surrounded by green mountains with deep blue seas lapping at the shore. Two of the best beaches are Praia de Paraty-Mirim, 27km east of Paraty, where there are a few *barracas* (food stalls) on the beach, and Praia da Trindade, with calm seas that reflect the lush vegetation surrounding it. If you'd prefer to hike into the forest, visit a waterfall and take a dip in a natural swimming hole, there's the nearby Parque Nacional da Serra da Bocaina. This national park has rich plant and animal life, but with the park's limited infrastructure it's hard to see much of this. For a short visit, head west out of Paraty about 15km along the Paraty–Cunha road (Estrada Paraty Cunha), which winds its way uphill. Stop at the Cachoeira do Tobogã (look for signs: it's a brief hike off the Paraty–Cunha road) where you can go for a swim.

On your way back to Paraty, at the 7km marker on the road, stop at the lovely Vila Verde (☎ 3371-7808; Paraty–Cunha road; mains R$22-36; 11am-6pm Tue-Sun), which serves homemade pastas, risottos and smoked salmon as well as good desserts and coffee. The restaurant is beautifully landscaped – a small brook trickles through the property, surrounded by lots of greenery.

lies a quick walk north from there. Another 2km further north is Praia do Jabaquara, a spacious beach with great views, shallow waters and a small restaurant overlooking the sand.

For visits to the less accessible sands, schooner tours depart daily, making stops at several beaches; book through Paraty Tours (p206). An alternative is to hire one of the small motorboats at the port. Local boatmen know some great spots in the region and will happily take you for the right price (plan on R$40 per hour).

INFORMATION

Centro de Informações Turísticas (☎ 3371-1222; www.paraty.com.br; Av Roberto Silveira 1; 9am-9pm) Distributes good maps of the area (as does Paraty Tours, next door) and maintains updated information on hotels and restaurants in the area.

Paraty Tours (☎ 3371-1327; www.paratytours.com.br; Av Roberto Silveira 11; 9am-8pm) One of several tour companies in town, Paraty Tours is a good source of information and offers a range of tours (including schooner tours), and kayaking, cycling, horseback riding and diving trips. It's at the colonial end of town. It also rents bikes.

EATING

Academia de Cozinha (☎ 3371-6468; Rua Dona Geralda 288; dinner R$180; dinner) Mixing theater and haute cuisine, the Academia de Cozinha stages cooking shows in Portuguese and English. Guests learn about the regional cuisines, watch chef Yara Castro Roberts in action, then enjoy the fruits of her labor. The price of dinner includes cocktails, wine, desserts and a wide variety of other fare. Book ahead.

Banana da Terra (☎ 3371-1725; Rua Dr Samuel Costa 198; mains R$40-60) One of Paraty's most elegant options, Banana da Terra serves delectable oven-baked fish dishes. Try the seafood, vegetables and saffron rice served in banana leaves, and follow it with banana pastry with ginger ice cream.

Margarida Café (☎ 3371-2441; Praça do Chafariz; mains R$24-38; noon-midnight) This charming restaurant serves tasty seafood dishes and wood-fired pizzas, which you can enjoy in the spacious lounge area or inner courtyard. Live music most nights.

Grão da Terra (☎ 3371-8627; Av Roberto Silveira 328; mains R$14-28; 11am-9pm) This all-vegetarian restaurant serves a delicious assortment of baked dishes, quiche, salads and juices – including all the great Brazilian fruits you won't find at home.

SLEEPING

Pousada Arte Urquijo (☎ 3371-1362; www.urquijo.com.br; Rua Dona Geralda 79; d from R$370;) Artist-owner Luz Urquijo rents out six beautiful, uniquely designed guest rooms in this boutique guesthouse. All rooms are set in a handsomely restored 18th-century mansion, and some of the rooms have balconies and sea views. There is also a stylish bar and a swimming pool.

Pousada Vivenda Paraty (☎ 3371-4272; www.vivendaparaty.com; Rua Beija Flor 9; d/bungalow incl breakfast R$200/285;) A 10-minute walk from the historic center, Vivenda offers stylish, comfortably furnished bungalows set amid lush gardens surrounding a pool. The fine breakfast is brought to your veranda.

Cigarras Pouso Familiar (☎ 3371-1497; www.paraty.com.br/cigarras; Largo do Rosario 7; d from R$150) Decorated with colorful lamps and run by a retired professor, this elegant colonial building retains the feel of a family home. Some rooms have kitchenettes, and there's a veranda with views of the facing square.

Hotel Solar dos Gerânios (☎ 3371-1550; www.paraty.com.br/geranio, in Portuguese; Praça da Matriz 2; s/d from R$70/90) This colonial hotel overlooking the Praça da Matriz features wood and ceramic sculptures, heavy rustic furniture and *azulejos* (Portuguese tiles). Some rooms have balconies, so check a few before committing.

ENTERTAINMENT

Teatro Espaço (☎ 3371-1575; Rua Dona Geralda 327; puppet-show admission R$50; performances 9pm Wed & Sat) For years the Teatro Espaço has been garnering praise for its famous puppet theater. The performances are staged by the Grupo Contadores de Estórias, who present powerful, wordless theater (with musical accompaniment) with their lifelike puppets.

ILHA GRANDE

The fabulous Ilha Grande is a pristine island of tropical scenery and gorgeous beaches among sheltered bays, brooks and waterfalls. Virgin Atlantic rain forest still blankets the hillsides and the guttural cry of howler monkeys can be heard on parts of the island.

Ilha Grande owes its pristine condition to its unusual history. Before the Portuguese arrival, the island was home to the Tupinambá Indians whose trails around the island are still in use. Once Europeans reached Brazil, Ilha Grande became a shelter for pirates and smugglers from the 16th to the 18th centuries. The island was also the site of a prison (Lazareto), first built at Abraão Bay and later moved to Dois Rios, a tiny settlement on the south side. The latter was demolished in 1994 (you can still see the ruins), and since then tourism has fast become the island's chief source of income. In 2010 the island suffered from heavy rainfalls, which caused landslides that left a trail of devastation along the coast, including the deaths of some tourists.

Vila do Abraão is the principal village, and the starting point for many adventures. From here, you can take schooner tours to gorgeous beaches such as Praia Lopes Mendes (which often tops charts listing the world's most beautiful beaches), Saco do Céu, Lagoa Azul and Lagoa Verde. Schooner companies organize regular trips to points around the island, with daily

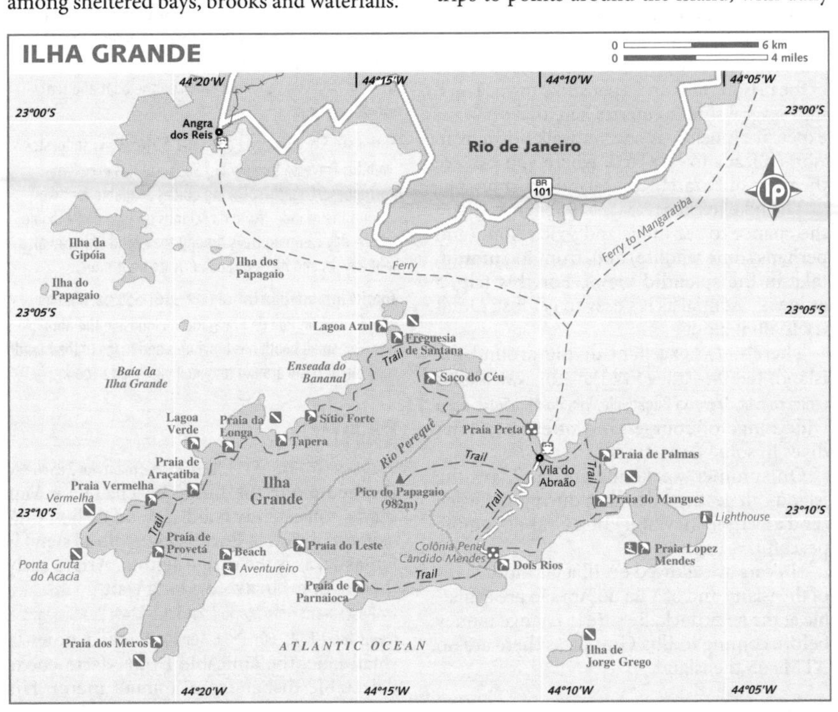

TRANSPORTATION: ILHA GRANDE

Distance from Rio 150km

Direction West

Travel Time Two hours to Mangaratiba, 2¼ hours to Conceição do Jacarei or 2½ hours to Angra dos Reis, and then a 90-minute ferry ride.

Car From the Zona Sul, head north on Av D Infante Henrique, which follows the curve of the bay as it goes north to Centro and eventually links up with Av Presidente Kubitschek. Look for signs to merge onto Av Brasil. This turns into BR 101, which leads all the way out to Mangaratiba, Conceição do Jacarei or Angra. Both places offer long-term parking near the dock for around R$15 per day.

Ferry Once you reach either Mangaratiba, Conceição do Jacarei or Angra, catch the ferry to Vila do Abraão. Boats from Mangaratiba depart at 8am and return at 5:30pm daily. More frequent boats depart from Conceição do Jacarei, which is the closest point to the island, departing to Abraão currently at 9am, 11:30am, 3pm and 6:15pm daily (50 minutes, one way R$15). From Angra, boats depart at 3:30pm Monday to Friday and 1:30pm Saturday, Sunday and bank holidays. A one-way ferry ride costs around R$7 Monday to Friday and R$14 Saturday and Sunday. Ferry schedules fluctuate, so it's wise to confirm the times when making a reservation at your hotel.

Bus Costa Verde buses depart every 45 minutes between 5am and 9pm from the main Novo Rio bus station (Map p60) to either Mangaratiba (R$22), Conceição do Jacarei (R$25) or Angra (R$36). Make sure you verify ferry connections to avoid getting stuck overnight on the mainland.

departures to Lopes Mendes. You can also reach the beach via a forest trail by heading east of Vila do Abraão.

There are numerous hikes you can do from Vila do Abraão. One excellent day hike (13km, or about six hours return trip) takes you over the top of the island to a gorgeous beach (Dois Rios) framed by two rivers. This is also the site of the prison ruins and a ghostlike town. You'll find several simple eateries here that serve inexpensive lunches. A shorter walk north from Abraão leads to Praia Preta, where you can see the ruins of Lazareto, the island's first prison.

The hike to Pico do Papagaio (982m) gives you the chance to see the island's rich flora (and perhaps some wildlife) and, from its summit, take in the splendid views. For this trip, a guide is essential as it's easy to get lost. Don't try to do it alone.

There's also excellent diving around the island. Elite Dive Center (☎ 3361-5501; www.elitedivecenter.com.br; Travessa Buganville, Vila do Abraão) has a wide range of courses and offers two-tank dives in some fantastic spots.

On summer weekends and holidays the island can get crowded, but during the week (and any time in winter) Ilha Grande is quite peaceful.

No cars are allowed on Ilha Grande. Maps of the island and of Vila do Abraão are available at the ferry dock. Be sure to change money before coming to Ilha Grande as there are no ATMs on the island.

INFORMATION

Phoenix Turismo (☎ 3361-5822; www.phoenixturismo.com.br; Rua da Praia 703; excursions R$25-55) A few doors down from O Pescador hotel, Phoenix is one of many outfits offering schooner tours of the island. The most popular destinations are Praia Lopes Mendes, Lagoa Azul and Lagoa Verde. Boat trips last anywhere from a half to a full day; you can order lunch on the boat and rent snorkeling gear.

Sudoeste SW Turismo (☎ 3361-5516; www.sudoestesw.com.br; Travessa Buganville) Sudoeste has excellent Portuguese/English-speaking guides available for hikes around the island – from day climbs up Pico do Papagaio to five-day camping treks around the island. You can also rent kayaks and bikes or book private boat tours.

Tourist Information Office (☎ 3361-5508; www.ilhagrande.com.br; Rua da Praia) Right alongside the Abraão pier, this small booth has brochures and maps of the island; staff can also call around for you if you need a room.

EATING

Lua e Mar (☎ 3361-5113; Rua da Praia; mains for 2 R$40-66) Perched along the sandy beach, Lua e Mar serves consistently good seafood dishes. *Caldeirado* (a kind of Portuguese seafood stew) is fantastic, as is the casual setting. Arrive early (before 8pm) to avoid a long wait.

Restaurant Dom Mario (☎ 3361-5349; Rua Buganville; mains for 2 R$45-60; 6-10pm) Tucked down a small lane, the amicable Dom Mario cooks delectable dishes from a small menu. His best dish is fish filet with passion-fruit sauce, though he also cooks up a juicy filet mignon.

Sagu (☎ 3361-5660; www.saguresort.com; Praia Brava; mains for 2 R$45-60; 6-10pm) A 20-minute walk west along the beach, this Italian-owned resort serves traditional old-world fare and fresh seafood on an elevated deck overlooking the sea.

O Pescador (☎ 3361-5114; www.opescadordailha.com.br; Rua da Praia; mains R$24-38) This place near the dock serves tasty seafood dishes best enjoyed on the front veranda. It also has cozily furnished rooms (double R$200 to R$230) – though it can get noisy in the high season.

SLEEPING

Asalem (☎ 3361-5602; www.asalem.com.br; s/d R$294/350) A 25-minute walk east of Abraão, this idyllic *pousada* is surrounded by lush scenery. All of the rooms face the sea, with a sleeping loft upstairs and a lounge with hammock on the first level.

Naturalia (☎ 3361-9583; www.pousadanaturalia.net; Praia do Abraão 149; s/d from R$190/230) A 10-minute walk east of the dock, this beautifully landscaped *pousada* has handsome rooms, each with wood floors, lovely sea views and a hammock in which to while away the afternoon.

Pousada Manaca (☎ 3361-5404; www.manaca.ilhagrande.org; Praia do Abraão; d from R$180) Nicely located facing the beach, this cozy guesthouse has just seven rooms (three with beach views and balconies). Rooms are small but nicely designed. Like Naturalia, Manaca uses solar energy panels.

Pousada Ancoradouro (☎ 3361-5153; www.pousadancoradouro.com.br; Praia do Abraão; d from R$160) Another beach-fronting guesthouse, this eight-room place receives warm reviews for the friendly service and the simple but good-value rooms (four with sea views).

BÚZIOS

Búzios is a lovely beach resort on a jutting peninsula scalloped by 17 beaches. It was a simple fishing village until the early 1960s, when it was 'discovered' by Brigitte Bardot and her Brazilian boyfriend. Today, Búzios has much more to offer than just its spectacular natural setting. The village has boutiques, elegant restaurants, open-air bars and lavishly decorated B&Bs. Many foreign-owned (especially Argentinean) *pousadas* and restaurants have sprouted along the peninsula's shores, and a mix of international travelers adds to the jumble of languages you'll hear on the streets.

Búzios is not a single town but rather three settlements on the peninsula: Ossos, Manguinhos and Armação de Búzios.

The main village of Armação de Búzios has two main streets running through it. The posh Rua das Pedras hugs the shoreline, with waterfront *pousadas*, bars and restaurants lining the stone-paved street. Rua das Pedras turns into Orla Bardot as it heads north. Rua Turibe Farias, just behind Rua das Pedras, has a number of good boutiques, ice-cream parlors and a pleasant square (Praça Santos Dumont) that becomes a scenic gathering spot at night.

Sparkling white-sand beaches are the daytime attraction in Búzios, with over a dozen within a short drive from the center. To get an overview of the area, take a schooner tour, or rent a buggy and explore the area on your own. In general, the southern beaches are

TRANSPORTATION: BÚZIOS

Distance from Rio 176km

Direction East

Travel Time 2½ hours

Car From the Zona Sul, head north to the Rio–Niterói bridge (toll R$4). After passing the toll, take BR 101 in the direction of Rio Bonita. After reaching Rio Bonito, take RJ 124 (Via Lagos Hwy; toll weekday/weekend R$10/15) west. Stay on this highway until it ends, then continue east another 7km until you reach an Ipiranga gas station at the entrance of São Pedro da Aldeia. Take a left at the gas station and then a right onto RJ 106 in the direction of Macaé–Búzios. After another 14km you will reach the Atéque Enfim gas station. Turn right and stay on this road until you reach Búzios. For those who'd rather take the slower, scenic route, a coastal road runs from Itacoatiara out to Cabo Frio then north.

Bus From Novo Rio bus station, Viação 1001 buses depart seven times daily (R$32 to R$35, three hours) – phone ☎ 4004-5001 for details. Alternatively, take an hourly bus to Cabo Frio and transfer to Búzios.

DETOUR: COASTAL SPOTS

Along the way from Rio to Búzios, there are a number of scenic beaches, surfing spots and fishing villages.

Follow the directions for getting to Búzios (ie take the Rio–Niterói bridge and turn off at Rio Bonito). Turn onto RJ 124 at Rio Bonito (the Via Lagos Hwy) and continue for 23km until you reach the turnoff for Saquarema. This small community lies about 100km east of Rio de Janeiro, and enjoys long stretches of open beach, bordered by lagoons and mountains. The town still has a somnolent air to it, though on weekends it attracts a large surfer crowd, thanks to waves of up to 3m. A number of beaches lie near the town, including the popular Barra Nova and Praia da Vila. About 3km north of Saquarema is Praia Itaúna, a good spot that hosts an annual surfing contest during the first two weeks of October.

From Saquarema continue east along the coastal road for another 60km and you'll reach Arraial do Cabo, a moderate-sized village with beaches that compare to the finest in Búzios. Unlike Búzios, however, Arraial is a sleepy, somewhat blue-collar town. Discovered a few centuries ago by Amerigo Vespucci, Praia dos Anjos has beautiful turquoise water, but a little too much boat traffic for safe swimming. It also has a Museum of Oceanography (Praia dos Anjos; 9am-noon & 1-4:30pm Tue-Sun). Aside from Praia dos Anjos, the most popular beaches in Arraial do Cabo are Praia do Forno, Praia Brava and Praia Grande.

The Gruta Azul (Blue Cavern), on the southwestern side of Ilha de Cabo Frio, is another beautiful spot. Be alert to the tides: the entrance to the underwater cavern isn't always open. There are lots of dive operators running tours here, including Sandmar (2622-5703; www.sandmar.com.br).

Ten kilometers north of Arraial do Cabo lies Cabo Frio, which sits between the Canal do Itajuru on one side and the ocean on the other. It's a bit overdeveloped by tourism, but there is some lovely landscape nearby. East of town, along a scenic road, is the Praia do Forte with bleached white sand and a backdrop of low scrub, cacti and grasses. At the northern end of Praia do Forte is a stone fortress, Forte São Mateus (10am-4pm Tue-Sun), which was built in 1616 and served as a stronghold against pirates.

The sand dunes around Cabo Frio are one of the region's most interesting features. The dunes facing the excellent surfing spot of Praia do Peró lie 6km north of town in the direction of Búzios. Praia do Peró is near Ogivas and after Praia Brava and Praia das Conchas. The Pontal dunes of Praia do Forte stretch from the Forte São Mateus to Morro de Miranda (Miranda Hill), while the Dama Branca (White Lady) sand dunes are on the road to Arraial do Cabo. The dunes can be dangerous due to robberies, so talk to locals before heading out.

trickier to get to, but they're prettier and have better surf. The northern beaches are closer to the towns and more sheltered.

Boasting a long stretch of sand and good surf, Geribá remains one of the most popular beaches. Lively restaurants and bars lie scattered along the shore and sun-seekers pack the sands. A bit calmer and less developed is the small Ferradurinha (Little Horseshoe), just east of Geribá. Continuing counterclockwise you'll find Ferradura, another horseshoe-shaped beach that's popular with windsurfers. Next are Lagoinha, a rocky beach with rough water, and Praia da Foca and Praia do Forno, both of which have colder water than the other beaches. Praia Olho de Boi (Bull's Eye) has the unique distinction of being named after Brazil's first postage stamp. It's a pocket-sized beach reached by a little trail from the long, clean beach of Praia Brava, which lies to the west.

João Fernandinho and João Fernandes are good locations for snorkeling, as are the topless beaches of Azedinha and Azeda. The Praia dos Ossos, Praia da Armação, Praia do Caboclo and Praia dos Amores are pretty to look at, but are not ideal for sunbathing as they can get crowded with boats just offshore, which won't leave you with much privacy. Praia da Tartaruga is quiet and pretty. Praia do Gaucho and Manguinhos are town beaches further along the coastal strip.

Although the best choice of restaurants and nightlife is in Armação de Búzios, some travelers prefer to stay at the beach (Geribá is a top choice), while others opt for Ossos. At the northernmost tip of the peninsula, this is the oldest and most attractive village, with a harbor and yacht club, and a few hotels and bars. Manguinhos, at the isthmus, is the busiest and most commercial village, and is probably the least enticing option. There's also Rasa, northwest along the coast, where Brazil's political dignitaries and CEOs come to relax.

Owing to Búzios' charm and popularity with Cariocas, prices rise substantially on holidays (especially New Year's Eve and Carnaval).

INFORMATION

Queen Lory (2623-1179; www.queenlorytours.com.br; Rua João Fernandes 89, Ossos) This outfit offers daily 2½-hour and five-hour schooner tours (from R$50) to Ilha Feia, Tartaruga and João Fernandinho. It also rents buggies (around R$120 per day) and arranges fishing and diving trips.

Secretaria de Turismo (2623-6200; www.buziosturismo.com; Praça Santos Dumont, Búzios; 9am-9pm) Pick up a map of the beaches in the area at this tourist-information office, which is one block from Rua das Pedras. Another branch is at the entrance to Búzios.

Tour Shop (2623-4733; www.tourshop.com.br; Orla Bardot 550, Armação de Búzios) This outfit runs a variety of excursions (from R$40), including a daily two-hour open-sided bus tour that visits 12 of the peninsula's beaches. You can also book schooner and rafting tours, and trips by glass-bottomed catamaran.

EATING & DRINKING

Sawasdee (2623-4644; Orla Bardot 422, Armação de Búzios; mains from R$45) One of the best Thai restaurants in the state, Sawasdee showcases fresh seafood in its mouthwatering dishes. Start off with a *kaipilychia* (lychee and cane-liquor cocktail).

Cigalon (2623-0932; Rua das Pedras 199, Armação de Búzios; mains R$34-60) You'll find decadent French cuisine and lovely views at this romantic beachside spot in the center of town.

Restaurante David (2623-2981; Rua Turíbio de Farias 260, Armação de Búzios; mains R$35-55) Still going strong after three decades, David's serves enjoyable seafood dishes at little wooden tables with checkered tablecloths.

Chez Michou (2623-2169; Av José Bento Ribeiro Dantas 90, Armação de Búzios; mains R$12-17) This well-known spot near Rua das Pedras serves decent crepes (some 36 varieties), but it's better known as a lively drinking and dance destination, with a fun crowd, DJs and various TV screens adding to the stimulation overload.

SLEEPING

Pousada Terra do Mar (2623-2640; www.buziosterradomar.com.br; Ave do Atlântico 467-589, Praia da Ferradura; bungalow R$270;) A five-minute walk to Ferradura beach, this charming French-owned place offers excellent value in its attractively designed bungalows with thatched roofs. There's also an inviting pool and a lounge. The owners speak French, Spanish and English.

Pousada Saint Germain (2623-3206; Alto do Humaitá, Armação de Búzios; d from R$200;) Although there's no ocean view, this Brazilian-American-run guesthouse receives high marks for its friendly welcome, bright spacious rooms and good location (100m to Orla Bardot, 400m to Rua das Pedras).

Ilha Formosa (2623-2759; www.buziosilhaformosa.com.br; Rua Maria Joaquina 26; Armação de Búzios; d R$120-180) A few steps from the cobblestones of Rua das Pedras, Ilha Formosa has clean, simply furnished rooms, the best of which have excellent ocean views.

PETRÓPOLIS

An attractive mountain retreat with a decidedly European air, Petrópolis is a favorite weekend getaway for Cariocas. Horse-drawn carriages still clatter through the streets, and the city's small bridges and canals, manicured

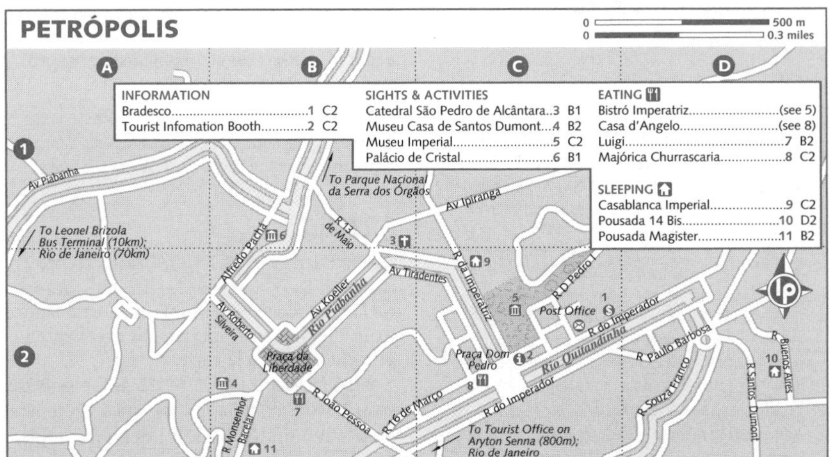

parks and old-fashioned lampposts add to its charm. The city makes a fine place for strolls and taking in the museums, and is an excellent starting point for exploring the picturesque countryside of this region.

Emperor Dom Pedro I first came across the lovely setting on a journey from Rio to Minas Gerais. It was little more than farmland in the 1830s, but Dom Pedro liked the scenery so much that he decided to buy some land. Although he abdicated the throne and returned to Portugal, the land passed to his son, Dom Pedro II, who built a summer retreat here. By the 1840s, the whole court had jumped on the bandwagon, and a palace rose against the mountains. With mansions and a looming cathedral, Petrópolis earned the nickname 'Imperial City.'

Downtown Petrópolis is a living museum that provides a window into the past. One of the city's gems is the neoclassical Museu Imperial (☎ 2237-8000; Rua da Imperatriz 220; adult/child R$8/4; 11am-5:30pm Tue-Sun), which served as the home away from home for Dom Pedro II and his wife, Dona Teresa, when the humidity (and mosquitoes) in Rio became unbearable. The lavish, faithfully preserved building features exhibits from the royal collection, including a 1.7kg crown covered with 639 diamonds and 77 pearls.

North of the Museu Imperial, the Catedral São Pedro de Alcântara (☎ 2242-4300; Rua São Pedro de Alcântara 60; admission free; 8am-noon & 2-6pm) houses the tombs of Dom Pedro II, Dona Teresa and their daughter Princesa Isabel. From the steps of the cathedral you'll have fine views of most of the region, with the spires of the town set against the mountains.

Another eye-catching sight in Petrópolis is the Palácio de Cristal (☎ 2247-3721; Rua Alfredo Pachá; admission free; 9am-5:30pm Tue-Sun), which was built for Princesa Isabel in France and brought to the country in 1884. It houses a greenhouse, just as it did back then, and features fountains and lush greenery in front.

Following the imperial era, in the late 19th century Petrópolis became a center for intellectuals and artists, nurturing the talents of Austrian writer Stefan Zweig, composer Rui Barbosa and Santos Dumont – the inventor, architect and writer often dubbed the 'father of Brazilian aviation' for his early flights (he also invented the wristwatch). You can learn more about Dumont by touring the small, fascinating home that he designed himself at the Museu Casa de Santos Dumont (☎ 2247-3158; Rua do Encanto 22; admission R$5; 9:30am-5pm Tue-Sun).

Some uncommonly charming château-like restaurants lie near Petrópolis, but you'll need a car to visit them as the best places are outside the city center. If you're just around for the day, you can easily explore the historic center on foot, though with its crisp, calm nights and surplus of cozy cottages and B&Bs, Petrópolis makes a great overnight trip. If you visit, keep in mind that most museums close on Monday.

TRANSPORTATION: PETRÓPOLIS

Distance from Rio 68km

Direction North

Travel Time 1½ hours

Car Take the Linha Vermelha Hwy from Rio. After passing signs for the international airport, be on the lookout for BR 040; you'll merge onto this highway (also called Rodovia Washington Luís) and follow the signs to Petrópolis.

Bus Única Fácil (☎ 0800-886-1000) buses departs from Novo Rio bus station approximately every 30 minutes between 5am and 8:30pm (one way R$16). For the best views be sure to leave well before sundown. Buses arrive at Leonel Brizola bus station in Bingen, some 10km from downtown, where you'll have to change to a local Esperança bus (bus 10 or 100) or taxi to reach the Centro Histórico.

INFORMATION

Bradesco (Rua do Imperador 268; 10am-5pm Mon-Fri) It has an ATM.

Tourist Information Booth (☎ 2246-9377; Praça dos Expedicionários; 9am-5pm) Stocks brochures and maps, and can recommend hotels in the area. There's also a good information office at the obelisk on the way into town from Rio.

Trekking Petrópolis (☎ 2235-7607; www.rioserra.com.br/trekking) Organizes hikes, mountain-biking, rafting and bird-watching trips through Mata Atlântica rain forest.

EATING

Majórica Churrascaria (☎ 2242-2498; Rua do Imperador 754; mains R$26-42; noon-10pm Tue-Sun) This *churrascaria* (barbecue restaurant), a short distance from the Museu Imperial, has excellent cuts of meat, served à la carte.

Bistrô Imperatriz (☎ 2231-1188; Av Imperatriz 220; mains R$24-38; 10am-7pm Tue, Wed & Sun, to 10pm Thu-Sat) Within the Museu Imperial complex,

DETOUR: MOUNTAIN TOWNS

The lush greenery of the mountains makes a lovely setting for a scenic drive, but if you'd like to see the greenery from the inside, head to Parque Nacional Da Serra Dos Órgãos (☎ 2152-1100; admission R$20; main entrance 8am-5pm). The national park has extensive trails through Mata Atlântica rain forest and has a variety of rich plant and animal life. Dedo de Deus (God's Finger), Cabeça de Peixe (Fish Head) and Verruga do Frade (Friar's Wart) are among the more imaginative trail names. This is a major rock-climbing destination – best arranged through one of the outfits in Rio (p177).

Those wanting a short hike (and a picnic) can take the 3.5km walking trail, visiting the waterfalls, natural swimming pools, tended lawns and gardens. There are two entrances to the park, both on BR 116. The one closer to Teresópolis offers more facilities.

Another village in the mountains is Nova Friburgo, which has good hotels and restaurants, as well as many lovely natural attractions: woods, waterfalls, trails, sunny mountain mornings and cool evenings. Do be aware that it gets chilly and rainy during the winter months, from June to August.

The area around Nova Friburgo was first settled by families from the Swiss canton of Friburg. During the Napoleonic wars, Dom João encouraged immigration to Brazil. At the time, people were starving in Switzerland, so in 1818 around 300 families packed up and headed for Brazil. The passage overseas was grueling and many families died en route. Those who survived settled in the mountains and established the small village of Nova Friburgo in the New World.

A tourist information office (☎ 2543-6307; Praça Dr Demervel B Moreira; 8am-8pm) is in the center of town. Scout out the surrounding area from Morro da Cruz (1380m), which is accessible by chairlift (9am-6pm Sat, Sun & holidays); the chairlift station is in the center at Praça Teleférico. Alternatively, there's Pico da Caledônia (2310m), offering fantastic views and launching sites for hang gliders. It's a 6km uphill hike, but the view is worth it.

From Nova Friburgo you can hike to Pedra do Cão Sentado, explore the Furnas do Catete or visit the mountain towns of Bom Jardim (23km northeast on BR 116) or Lumiar (25km east of the turnoff at Muri, which is 9km south of Nova Friburgo). In Lumiar, hippies, cheap pensions, waterfalls, walking trails and white-water canoe trips abound.

this charming bistro serves up a tasty assortment of light fare at lunch, as well as afternoon tea, and gourmet Brazilian dishes for dinner.

Luigi (☎ 2244-4444; Praça da Liberdade 185; mains R$18-38; 11am-10pm) A charming Italian restaurant set in an old house with high ceilings, creaky floors and candlelit ambience. Lunch specials are particularly good value.

Casa d'Angelo (☎ 2242-0888; Rua do Imperador 700; mains R$13-26; 8am-1am) Opened in 1914, this low-key restaurant, café and bar is a Petrópolis institution, where regulars amble in for a *cafezinho* (coffee – short, black, strong and usually quite sweet) or a beer at all hours. It's especially worth visiting on Saturday, when a tasty and inexpensive *feijoada* (black bean and pork stew) is served.

SLEEPING

Pousada Magister (☎ 2242-1054; www.pousadamagister.com.br; Rua Monsenhor Bacelar 71; d R$180-225) Near the Casa de Santos Dumont, this century-old mansion offers attractive, bright rooms with wood floors and trim furnishings.

Pousada 14 Bis (☎ 2231-0946; www.pousada14bis.com.br; Rua Buenos Aires 192; s/d from R$100/160) One of Petrópolis' most charming hotels, the Pousada 14 Bis has handsome rooms with wooden floors and large windows overlooking the street or onto the pleasant garden out the back.

Casablanca Imperial (☎ 2242-6662; www.casablancahotel.com.br, in Portuguese; Rua do Imperatriz 286; s/d from R$160/198) The Casablanca Imperial is a grand old dame near the Museu Imperial. Its 50 rooms are a mixed bag, but the best feature high ceilings, old shutters, long bathrooms with tubs, and antique furnishings.

VISCONDE DE MAUÁ

Set in the Itatiaia, a region of charming country towns, wandering streams and lush forests, Visconde de Mauá is actually made up of three small villages (Mauá, Maringá and Maromba) scattered a few kilometers apart along the Rio Preto. The chief reason for coming is to soak up the lovely, peaceful setting, best enjoyed from one of the cozy chalets in the region. It's a perfect spot to unwind. Picturesque walks along quiet lanes lie just outside your door.

Although the scenery is undoubtedly New World tropics, there's an element of the Old World in Itatiaia. It was first settled by Swiss and German immigrants in the early 20th century. (Nearby Penedo, with its saunas, was settled by the Finns.) Visconde de Mauá lies roughly halfway between Rio and São Paulo, in the alpine Serra da Mantiqueira.

DETOUR: PARQUE NACIONAL DE ITATIAIA

One of Brazil's loveliest national parks is a short drive from Visconde de Mauá. The Parque Nacional do Itatiaia contains virgin rain forest, breathtaking mountain trails and plenty of idyllic rivers, lakes and waterfalls in which to splash about. It's also packed with wildlife, including some 400 bird species, as well as monkeys, sloths and many other rain-forest creatures. There are numerous trails in the park ranging from hour-long hikes to multiday treks. A recommended day hike (six hours) is the Tres Picos hike, an uphill route that leads past the refreshing Rio Bonito before continuing on to a fantastic lookout point. At the main park entrance, 7km north of the BR 116, you can pick up trail maps at the visitors centre (park entry R$10; 8am-5pm). To get there from Visconde de Mauá head back to BR 116, take a right and look for the signed turnoff to the right another 6km further on.

Hikes in the area include walks to waterfalls. The Santa Clara Cachoeira, the nicest in the area, is a 6km walk north of Maringá on the Ribeirão Santa Clara. Trails on either side of the falls pass through bamboo groves. You'll find a natural pool in the Rio Preto between Visconde de Mauá and Maringá. Reach it by turning left just before the bridge. Beyond Maromba, you can take a 2.5km walk out of town (follow the signs) to Cachoeira do Escorrega, where a naturally formed water slide slants into a chilly swimming hole. If you continue along the same road and take the first left at the fork, you'll reach Cachoeira Veu de Noiva, another beautiful waterfall.

INFORMATION

Tourist Information Hut (3387-1283; 9am-noon & 1-8pm Tue-Sun) At the entrance to the village of Mauá, this small booth can provide information in Portuguese.

www.viscondedemaua.info A good website with information about the region.

TRANSPORTATION: VISCONDE DE MAUÁ

Distance from Rio 152km

Direction Northwest

Travel Time 3½ hours

Car Take Av Brasil north to BR 116. Take BR 116 west to Resende, where you'll see signs pointing north to Visconde de Mauá. The last 10km is unpaved.

Bus From Novo Rio bus station, Cidade do Aço buses (2253-8471) depart Friday at 7.35pm for Maromba (R$48, 4½ hours). They return on Sunday at 4pm. Another option is to catch a more frequent Cidade do Aço bus to the transport-hub town of Resende (2¼ hours, R$28 to R$38), and an onward bus (R$7, two hours, three to four daily) to Visconde de Mauá.

EATING

Paladar da Montanha (3387-1594; Estrada Maringá/Moromba 7km; mains R$24-36; 11am-10pm Fri-Wed) In the village of Maringá, Paladar da Montanha serves regional specialties (including trout) as well as steaks, wood-oven-baked pizzas, and chocolate fondue for dessert. The fireplace adds a cozy touch.

Filho da Truta (3387-1527; www.ofilhodatruta.com.br; Vale do Pavão; mains R$24-40; 11am-11pm) Run by an enterprising couple of Lebanese-French descent, this restaurant – also in Maringá – has won national acclaim for its 37 different trout recipes. The attached guesthouse has three small freestanding wood cabins starting at R$110 (or R$160 with three meals a day).

SLEEPING

Olho d'Agua (3387-1386; www.olhodaguamaua.com.br, in Portuguese; Maringá; chalet R$150-240) In the center of Maringá, Olho d'Agua has seven free-standing chalets, set amid peaceful gardens. Each is handsomely decorated in bright colors, and most have little decks strung with hammocks; several also have huge spa bathtubs and fireplaces.

Pousada Moriá (3387-1505; www.pousadamoria.com.br in Portuguese; Estrada da Maromba; d R$150-260;) This idyllic hideaway is opposite the Cachoeira do Escorrega. The stone- and wood-lined chalets all have fireplaces, and most have Jacuzzis; the on-site restaurant serves trout and fondue. Breakfast is served in a glass-walled cabin or out on the deck overlooking the waterfall.

TRANSPORTATION

CLIMATE CHANGE & TRAVEL

Every form of transport that relies on carbon-based fuel generates CO_2, the main cause of human-induced climate change. Modern travel is dependent on aeroplanes and while they might use less fuel per kilometre per person than most cars, they travel much greater distances. It's not just CO_2 emissions from aircraft that are the problem. The altitude at which aircraft emit gases (including CO_2) and particles contributes significantly to their total climate change impact. The Intergovernmental Panel on Climate Change believes aviation is responsible for 4.9% of climate change – double the effect of its CO_2 emissions alone.

Lonely Planet regards travel as a global benefit. We encourage the use of more climate-friendly travel modes where possible and, together with other concerned partners across many industries, we support the carbon offset scheme run by ClimateCare. Websites such as climatecare.org use 'carbon calculators' that allow people to offset the greenhouse gases they are responsible for with contributions to portfolios of climate-friendly initiatives throughout the developing world. Lonely Planet offsets the carbon footprint of all staff and author travel.

AIR

Many international flights pass through São Paolo before arriving in Rio at the Aeroporto Internacional Antonio Carlos (Tom) Jobim (commonly called Galeão) on Ilha do Governador (Governor's Island; Map p60). TAM (www.tam.com.br) is Brazil's biggest international carrier. Gol Airlines (www.voegol.com.br) is the country's biggest domestic carrier and also connects Brazil to other South American cities.

Flights, tours and rail tickets can be booked online at www.lonelyplanet.com/travel_services.

Airlines

Aerolineas Argentinas (AR; ☎ 0800-707-3313; www.aerolineas.com.ar)

Air Canada (AC; ☎ 0xx11-3254-6600; www.aircanada.ca)

Air France (AF; ☎ 4003-9955; www.airfrance.com)

Alitalia (AZ; ☎ 0800-704-0206; www.alitalia.com)

American Airlines (AA; ☎ 4502-4000; www.aa.com)

Avianca (AV; ☎ 2240-4413; www.avianca.com)

Azul (AD; ☎ 3296-2850; www.voeazul.com.br)

British Airways (BA; ☎ 4004-4440; www.britishairways.com)

Continental Airlines (CO; ☎ 0800-702-7500; www.continental.com)

COPA (CM; ☎ 0800-771-2672; www.copaair.com)

Delta Airlines (DL; ☎ 4003-2121; www.delta.com)

Gol (G3; ☎ 0300-115-2121; www.voegol.com.br)

Iberia (IB; ☎ 0xx11-3218-7130; www.Iberia.com)

Japan Airlines (JL; ☎ 0xx11-3175-2270; www.jal.com)

KLM (KL; ☎ 0800-891-5024; www.klm.com)

Lan Chile (LA; ☎ 0800-761-0056; www.lan.com)

Lufthansa (LH; ☎ 0xx11-3048-5800; www.lufthansa.com)

Ocean Air (06; ☎ 4004-4040; www.oceanair.com.br)

South African (SA; ☎ 0xx11-3065-5115; www.flysaa.com)

Swissair (LX; ☎ 0xx11-3049-2720; www.swiss.com)

TAM (KK; ☎ 4002-5700; www.tam.com.br)

TAP Air Portugal (TP; ☎ 2131-7771; www.flytap.com)

Trip (8R; ☎ 0300-789-8747; www.voetrip.com.br)

United Airlines (UA; ☎ 2217-1951; www.united.com)

THINGS CHANGE...

The information in this chapter is particularly vulnerable to change. Check directly with the airline or a travel agent to make sure you understand how a fare (and ticket you may buy) works and be aware of the security requirements for international travel. Shop carefully. The details given in this chapter should be regarded as pointers and are not a substitute for your own careful, up-to-date research.

Airports

Rio's Galeão international airport (Aeroporto Internacional António Carlos (Tom) Jobim; Map p60) is 15km north of the city center on Ilha do Governador. It has left-luggage facilities, an internet café, ATMs and currency-exchange desks, pharmacies as well as a few shops and restaurants. Aeroporto Santos Dumont (Map p90), used by some domestic flights, is by the bay, in the city center, 1km east of Cinelândia metro station. It has fewer facilities, with ATMs, a few shops and an internet café. See p217 for information on getting into town.

There are two hotels at the international airport. They're not pleasant places to stay: rooms are basic, with no windows.

Hotel Pousada Galeão (☎/fax 3398-3848; d from R$195) On the 1st floor of international arrivals. Rooms are small and clean but gloomy.

Rio Luxor Aeroporto (☎ 2468-8998; www.luxor-hotels.com.br; s/d R$340/378) On the 3rd floor of the airport, it's the marginally better of the two hotels. The 64 rooms have basic furnishings, with cable TV, modern bathrooms and 24-hour room service.

Departure Tax

The international departure tax from Brazil is US$36. This has probably been included in the price of your ticket: if it's not, you'll have to pay it in cash (either in US dollars or *reais*) at the airport before departure.

BICYCLE

Although traffic can be intimidating on Rio's roads, the city has many kilometers of bike paths along the beach, around Lagoa and along Parque do Flamengo. You can rent bikes from stands along the east side of Lagoa Rodrigo de Freitas for around R$10 per hour. Other places to rent bikes include the following:

Ciclovia (Map p76; ☎ 2275-5299; Av Prado Júnior 330, Copacabana & Rua Francisco Otaviano 55A; per hr/day R$9/50; 9am-7pm Mon-Fri, 9am-4pm Sat) Free delivery to hotels in the Zona Sul.

Special Bike (Map p64; ☎ 2513-3951; Rua Visconde de Pirajá 135B, Ipanema; per hr/day R$15/45; 9am-7pm Mon-Fri, 9am-3pm Sat)

BOAT

Rio has several islands in the bay that you can visit by ferry; another way to see the city is by taking the commuter ferry to Niterói. Niterói's main attraction is the Museu do Arte Contemporânea (p104), but many visitors board the ferry just for the fine views of downtown and the surrounding landscape. The ferry (☎ 0800-704-4113; www.barcas-sa.com.br) costs R$5.60 return and departs every 20 minutes from Praça Quinze de Novembro (Map p90) in Centro.

See p104 for more information on the following trips.

Ilha de Paquetá (Map p90; ☎ ferry 0800-704-4113; www.barcas-sa.com.br) The ferry takes 70 minutes and costs R$9 return, leaving every two to three hours between 5:30am and 11pm. The most useful departure times for travelers are currently 7:10am, 10:30am and 1:30pm.

Ilha Fiscal (Map p90; ☎ 2104-6992) Boats depart from the Espaço Cultural da Marinha three times a day (1pm, 2:30pm and 4pm) from Thursday to Sunday and include a guided tour of the Palácio da Ilha Fiscal (p104). It's a short ride (15 minutes) and costs R$9.

BUS

City Bus

By far the most widespread form of transport is the city bus. You'll see them traveling at breakneck speeds around hairpin curves or clogged in stifling traffic jams at rush hour. There are hundreds of lines crisscrossing the city, with the most useful for visitors coursing along the corridors between Leblon and Copacabana. Every bus has its destination written on the front and on the side. If you see the bus for you, hail it by sticking your arm straight out (drivers won't stop unless flagged down).

Board the bus from the front, and pay the collector (who can make change) sitting at the turnstile. You'll exit through the rear. Most buses cost around R$2.20 to R$2.80.

In addition to long-distance bus stations listed next (p216), the Terminal Alvorada (Map p107; cnr Av das Américas & Av Ayrton Senna) is Barra da Tijuca's main bus station, with connections to the Zona Sul, both airports, Novo Rio Rodoviária and other districts of Rio.

Rio buses have a bad reputation in the international media as the setting for robberies, bombings and indiscriminate violence (the 2002 documentary film *Bus 174* didn't help matters much). In truth, such acts are rare and usually limited to outer-suburban areas where tourists are unlikely to travel. Do keep an eye on your belongings while riding, and don't travel by bus at night; taxis are generally a safer option.

Long-Distance Bus

Buses connect Rio with cities and towns all over the country. Most arrive and depart from the loud Novo Rio Rodoviária (Novo Rio bus station; Map p60; ☎ 3213-1800; Av Francisco Bicalho 1, São

GETTING INTO TOWN

The most economical way of reaching the international airport is to take the Real Auto Bus (☎ 0800-240-850), known locally as the *frescão*. These relatively safe, air-conditioned buses go from the international airport (outside the arrivals floor of terminal 1 or the ground floor of terminal 2) to Novo Rio bus station (Map p60), Aeroporto Santos Dumont, southward through Glória, Flamengo and Botafogo, and along the beaches of Copacabana, Ipanema and Leblon to Barra da Tijuca (and vice versa). The buses run every 20 to 30 minutes, 5:20am to 12:10am, and will stop wherever you ask. One-way fare is currently R$7. You can transfer to the metro at Carioca station.

Heading to the airports, you can catch the Real Auto Bus in front of the major hotels along the main beaches, but you have to look alive and flag it down.

Comun (standard) taxis from the international airport are generally safe, though robberies are occasionally reported. Radio taxis are safer, but more expensive. You pay a set fare at the airport. A yellow-and-blue *comun* taxi should cost around R$40 to R$50 to Ipanema if the meter is working (see p218). Radio taxis all charge the same rate (R$80 to Ipanema or Copacabana). It's payable by credit card (or cash) at the counters just before leaving the international arrivals area.

Many hotels and hostels also arrange airport transport, typically charging around R$60 to R$80.

Cristóvão), which lies about five minutes by bus northwest of the city center. The people at the Riotur desk on the bus station's ground floor can provide information on transportation and lodging.

The other Rio bus station is the Menezes Cortes Rodoviária (Menezes Cortes bus station; Map p90; ☎ 2533-9881; Rua São José 35, Centro), which handles services to some destinations in Rio de Janeiro state, such as Petrópolis and Teresópolis. You can catch buses to these two destinations from Novo Rio as well.

If you arrive in Rio by bus, it's a good idea to take a taxi to your hotel, or at least to the general area where you want to stay. Traveling on local buses with all your belongings is a little risky. A small booth near the exit at Novo Rio bus station organizes the yellow taxis out the front. Excellent buses leave every 15 minutes or so for São Paulo (six hours). Most major destinations are serviced by very comfortable *leito* (executive) buses leaving late at night.

It's a good idea to buy a ticket a couple of days in advance if you can, especially if you want to travel on a weekend or during a Brazilian holiday period.

CAR

Driving & Parking

In the city itself, driving can be a frustrating experience even if you know your way around. Traffic snarls and parking problems do not make for an enjoyable holiday. If the bus and metro aren't your style, there are plenty of taxis. However, if you do drive in the city, it's good to know a couple of things: At night, Cariocas (residents of Rio) don't always stop at red lights, because of the small risk of robberies at deserted intersections. Between 10pm and 6am, cars slow at red lights and then proceed if no one is around. Another thing to know is that if you park your car on the street, it's common to pay the *flanelinha* (parking attendant) a few *reais* (usually R$2) to look after it. Some of the *flanelinhas* work for the city, others are 'freelance,' but regardless, it's a common practice throughout Brazil.

Rental

Renting a car is relatively cheap, but gasoline is expensive. If you don't mind the expense, it's a great way to explore some of the remote beaches, mountain towns and national parks near Rio. Getting a car is fairly simple as long as you have a driver's license, a credit card and a passport. Most agencies require renters to be at least 25 years old, though some will rent (with an added fee) to younger drivers. Ideally, you should have an International Driving Permit, which you'll need to pick up from your home country. In reality, rental-car companies accept any driver's license – it's the cops who will want to see an International Driving Permit.

Prices start around R$100 per day for a car without air-conditioning, but they go down a bit in the low season. There is some competition between the major agencies, so it's worth shopping around. If you are quoted prices on the phone, make sure they include insurance, which is compulsory.

Car-rental agencies can be found at either airport or scattered along Av Princesa Isabel in Copacabana. At the international airport, Hertz (☎ 0800-701-7300), Localiza (☎ 0800-979-2000) and Unidas (☎ 2295-3628) provide rentals. In

Copacabana, among the many are Hertz (Map p76; ☎ 2275-7440; Av Princesa Isabel 500) and Localiza (Map p76; ☎ 2275-3340; Av Princesa Isabel 150).

METRO

Rio's subway system (www.metrorio.com.br) is an excellent way to get around. It's open from 5am to midnight Monday through Saturday, and 7am to 11pm on Sunday and holidays. During Carnaval the metro operates nonstop from 5am Saturday morning until at least 11pm on Tuesday (in 2010 it ran nonstop until the weekend after Carnaval). Both lines are air-conditioned, clean, fast and safe. The main line goes from Ipanema-General Osório (a station that opened in 2009) to Saens Peña, connecting with the secondary line to Estácio (which provides service to São Cristóvão, Maracanã and beyond). The main stops in Centro are Cinelândia and Carioca. More stations are planned in the coming years, and the city plans to integrate the rest of Ipanema and Leblon into the transport system.

A single ride ticket is called a *unitário* and costs R$2.80. To avoid waiting in lines, you can purchase a *cartão pré-pago* (prepaid card) with a minimum of R$10 or more; you can then recharge it (cash only, no change given) at kiosks inside some metro stations. If you're going somewhere outside of the metro's range (Cosme Velho or Barra for example), you can purchase metro-bus tickets. For details, see p218. Free subway maps are available from most ticket booths.

MINIVAN

Minivans (Cariocas call them *vans*) are an alternative form of transportation in Rio and usually much faster than buses. They run along Av Rio Branco to the Zona Sul as far as Barra da Tijuca. On the return trip, they run along the coast almost all the way into the city center. They run frequently, and cost between R$2 and R$4.50. They do get crowded, and are not a good idea if you have luggage. Call out your stop (*'para!'*) when you want to disembark.

TAXI

Rio's yellow taxis are prevalent throughout the city. They're generally a speedy way to zip around and are usually safe. Drivers are mostly honest, though you may occasionally encounter fare inflation or tinkered-with taxi meters. Many of the drivers who hang around the hotels are sharks, so it's worth walking a block or so to avoid them.

Always opt for the meter. 'Set fares' to Pão de Açúcar or Corcovado are a sure sign you're being had. Also, make sure the meter works. If it doesn't, ask to be let out of the taxi. Meters

METRO-BUS TICKETS

If you're not staying near a metro station or are traveling somewhere off the metro map, integrated metro-bus tickets can be a cheap and speedy way to get to a destination. Metrô-Ônibuses (metro buses; www.metrorio.com.br) are modern, silver buses that make limited stops as they shuttle passengers to and from metro stations. For most destinations, a one-way *metrô na superficie* (surface metro) ticket costs the same as a single metro ride (R$2.80) but includes both the bus and the metro ride (hold onto your ticket). Although there are growing numbers of these buses on Rio's streets, the most useful one for travelers staying in Leblon and western Ipanema is the metro bus marked 'Ipanema-Gávea'. This will take you to and from the metro station at Praça General Osório. If you're entering the metro and plan on connecting to a bus, be sure to request *metrô + metrô na superficie* tickets at the booth; otherwise, you'll just receive single-use metro tickets.

If you're going from the metro to Gávea or Jardim Botânico, disembark at Botafogo station and catch the integrated metro bus from there. Stops are at Cobal do Humaitá, Rua Maria Angélica (near Rua Jardim Botânico 164), the Hospital da Lagoa (Rua Jardim Botânico 518), the edge of the botanical gardens (Rua Jardim Botânico 728), Praça Santos Dumont, Gávea Trade Center (Marquês de São Vicente 124) and PUC (Av Rubens Berardo 175).

Other useful buses are the following Integração Expresso (R$3.70) lines:

Bus 511A connects Botafogo with Urca

Bus 584A connects Largo do Machado with Cosme Velho (via Laranjeiras).

You can also go to Barra by metro bus (the *Barra Expresso*). The integrated metro-bus ticket costs R$3.80 and departs from Praça General Osório station, with stops at Posto 9 (Ipanema beach), Posto 12 (Leblon beach), São Conrado Fashion Mall, Praia do Pepino (São Conrado), Shopping Downtown, Barra Shopping and Casa Shopping, among others.

have a flag that switches the tariff; this should be in the number-one position (80% fare), except on Sunday, holidays, between 9pm and 6am, when driving outside the Zona Sul and during December.

The flat rate is around R$4.35, plus around R$1 per kilometer. Radio taxis are 30% more expensive than regular taxis.

Most people don't tip taxi drivers, but it's common to round up the fare.

A few radio-taxi companies:

Coopatur (☎ 2573-1009)

Coopertramo (☎ 2209-9292)

Cootramo (☎ 3976-9944)

Transcoopass (☎ 2590-6891)

In Rocinha and some other favelas, moto-taxis (basically a lift on the back of a motorcycle) are a handy way to get around, with short rides (usually from the bottom of the favela to the top or vice versa) costing R$2.

TRAIN

The suburban train station, Estação Dom Pedro II (Central do Brasil; Map p90; ☎ 2111-9494; Praça Cristiano Ottoni, Av Presidente Vargas, Centro), is one of Brazil's busiest commuter stations, but it's definitely not the safest area to walk around. To get there, take the metro to Central station and head upstairs. This is the train station that was featured in the Academy Award–nominated film *Central do Brasil* (Central Station).

TRAM

Rio was once serviced by a multitude of *bondes* (trams), with routes throughout the city. The only one still running is the Santa Teresa tram, known locally as the *bondinho*. It's still the best way to get to this neighborhood from downtown.

The bonde station (Map p90; Rua Lélio Gama 65) in Centro is best reached by traveling via Rua Senador Dantas and taking a turn west into Rua Lélio Gama. At the top of the small hill, you'll find the station. *Bondes* (R$0.60) depart every 30 minutes. The two routes currently open have been in operation since the 19th century. Both travel over the Arcos da Lapa (p100) and along Rua Joaquim Murtinho before reaching Largo do Guimarães (p100) on Rua Almirante Alexandrino, in the heart of boho Santa Teresa. From there, one line (Paula Matos) takes a northwestern route, terminating at Largo das Neves (p100). The longer route (Dois Irmãos) continues from Largo do Guimarães uphill and southwest before terminating near the water reservoir at Dois Irmãos.

The favelas (shanty towns) down the hillsides still make this a high-crime area. Go, by all means, but it's best to stick to the populated areas – around Largo do Guimarães. See p97 for more details.

ACCOMMODATIONS

Accommodation listings in the Sleeping chapter (p186) are organized by neighborhood, and arranged by price, from most expensive to cheapest within each neighborhood. In Rio, the average double room with bathroom costs about R$220, with seasonal variations (highest in summer, from December to February). Over New Year's Eve and during Carnaval, every place in town will double or triple their prices, and most will require minimum stays of four days.

See our price guide, p187, for an indication of the standard price range for top-end, midrange and budget accommodations.

We've quoted standard rates, but booking online may save you cash. Numerous websites allow you to peruse listings and make reservations online, including www.lonelyplanet.com, www.ipanema.com and www.riocharm.com.br.

BUSINESS HOURS

Office hours in Rio are from 9am to 6pm, Monday to Friday. Most shops and government services (such as the post offices) are open from 9am to 6pm Monday to Friday, and from 9am to 1pm on Saturday.

Because many Cariocas (residents of Rio) have little free time during the week, Saturday mornings are often spent shopping. Shops are usually open weekdays from 9am to 6pm and on Saturday from 9am to 1pm. Stores in the large shopping malls are open from 10am to 10pm Monday through Saturday and on Sundays from 3pm to 10pm.

Banks, always in their own little world, generally open from 9am or 10am to 3pm or 4pm Monday to Friday. Currency-exchange places often open an hour after that, when the daily dollar rates become available.

CHILDREN

Brazilians are very family-oriented, and many hotels let children stay free, although the age limit varies. Baby-sitters are readily available and most restaurants have high chairs.

Don't forget Lonely Planet's *Travel with Children*, by Brigitte Barta et al, gives a lot of good tips and advice on traveling with kids in the tropics.

See p79 for more details on sights and activities for children.

CLIMATE

Rio lies only a few dozen kilometers north of the Tropic of Capricorn, so it has a classic tropical climate. In summer (December to February), it is hot and humid; temperatures around 28°C (82°F) are common, but days sometimes go above 40°C (104°F). Frequent, short rains cool things off a bit, but the summer humidity makes things uncomfortable for people from cooler climates. At other times of the year, temperatures are generally in the mid-20s °C (low 70s °F), sometimes rising to 31°C (88°F).

COURSES

Rio makes a fine setting for soaking up an exhilarating dose of the tropics, but if action is what you're after, there's a wealth of opportunities for visitors, from diving to surfing to honing one's volleyball game on the sands. See Sports & Activities (p176) for more information on surfing, hang gliding, volleyball, dance classes and more.

Cooking

There aren't many cooking classes available in English in Rio de Janeiro. One notable exception is the one-day Cook in Rio (www.cookinrio.com) course, which teaches folks how to make a rich *moqueca* (seafood stew cooked in coconut milk) or a decadent pot of *feijoada* (black beans and pork stew). For complete details, see p128.

Language

Most language institutes charge high prices for group courses. You can often find a private tutor for less. Hostels are a good place to troll for instructors, with ads on bulletin boards posted by native-speaking language teachers available for hire. One organization that offers competitively priced classes is Casa do Caminho Language Centre (Map p64; ☎ 2267-6552;

www.casadocaminho-languagecentre.org; Ste 403, Rua Farme de Amoedo 75, Ipanema), which has intensive group classes – three hours a day for five days for R$320, or 60 hours of class time over a month for R$820. Profits go toward the Casa do Caminho (www.casadocaminhobrasil.org) orphanages in Brazil.

Instituto Brasil-Estados Unidos (IBEU; Map p76; ☎ 2548-8430; www.ibeu.org.br; 5th fl, Av NS de Copacabana 690, Copacabana) is one of the oldest, more respected language institutions in the city. It currently has three different levels of classes, which meet two hours a day, four days a week for four weeks. Each course costs R$1220. For information, stop by or visit the website. IBEU also has a decent English library.

Music

Maracatu Brasil (Map p84; ☎ 2557 4754; www.maracatubrasil.com.br; 2nd fl, Rua Ipiranga 49; 10am-6pm Mon-Sat) is one of the best places in Rio to study percussion. It's very active in music events throughout the city. Instructors here offer courses in a number of different drumming styles: zabumba, pandeiro and symphonic percussion, as well as guitar and other instruments. If you plan to stick around a while, you can arrange private lessons (R$250 for four one-hour classes) or sign up for group classes (from R$100 a month). On the 1st floor of the lime-green building, Maracatu sells instruments (p120).

CUSTOMS REGULATIONS

Travelers entering Brazil can bring in 2L of alcohol, 400 cigarettes and one personal computer, video and still camera. Newly purchased goods worth up to US$500 are permitted duty-free. Meat and cheese products are not allowed.

ELECTRICITY

The current is almost exclusively 110V or 120V, 60 Hz, AC. Some hotels also have 220-volt current. The most common power points have two sockets, and most will take both round and flat prongs. If you're packing a laptop – or any electronic device – be sure to use a surge protector.

Electrical current is not standardized in Brazil, so if you're traveling around the country it's a good idea to carry an adapter. For more information on electricity, plugs and other curious tidbits, visit www.kropla.com.

EMBASSIES

Many foreign countries have consulates or embassies in Rio. If they're not listed here, you'll find consulates listed in the back of Riotur's quarterly *Rio Guide.*

Argentina (Map p84; ☎ 2553-1646; consar.rio@openlink.com.br; Sobreloja/1st fl 201, Praia de Botafogo 228, Botafogo)

Australia (Map p90; ☎ 3824-4624; honcon au@terra.com.br; 23rd fl, Av Presidente Wilson 231, Centro)

Canada (Map p76; ☎ 2543-3004; www.brasil.gc.ca; 5th fl, Av Atlântica 1130, Copacabana)

France (Map p90; ☎ 3974-6699; www.ambafrance-br.org; 6th fl, Av Presidente Antônio Carlos 58, Centro)

UK (Map p84; ☎ 2555-9600; www.reinounido.org.br; 2nd fl, Praia do Flamengo 284, Flamengo)

USA (Map p90; ☎ 3823-2000; www.embaixadaamericana.org.br; Av Presidente Wilson 147, Centro)

EMERGENCY

If you have the misfortune of being robbed, you should report it to the Tourist Police (Delegacia Especial de Apoio ao Turismo; Map p66; ☎ 2332-2924; Rua Humberto de Campos 315, Leblon; 24hr). No major investigation is going to occur, but you will get a police form to give to your insurance company.

To call emergency telephone numbers in Rio you don't need a phone card. Useful numbers include the following:

Ambulance ☎ 192

Fire ☎ 193

Police ☎ 190

GAY & LESBIAN TRAVELERS

Rio is the gay capital of Latin America. There is no law against homosexuality in Brazil. During Carnaval, thousands of expatriate Brazilian and gringo gays fly in for the festivities. Transvestites steal the show at all Carnaval balls, especially the gay ones. Outside Carnaval, the gay scene is active, but less visible than in cities like San Francisco and Sydney.

You may hear or read the abbreviation GLS, particularly in the entertainment section of newspapers and magazines. It stands for Gays, Lesbians and Sympathizers, and when used in connection with venues or events basically indicates that anyone with an open mind is welcome. In general, the scene is much more integrated than elsewhere; and the majority of parties involve a pretty mixed crowd.

The Rio gay guide (www.riogayguide.com) is an excellent website full of information for gay and lesbian tourists in Rio, including sections entitled 'Bars & Cafés,' 'Carnival in Rio' and 'Rio for Beginners.' It's available in German, English and Portuguese versions.

For more details on gay life in Rio de Janeiro, see p167.

HOLIDAYS

On public holidays banks, offices, post offices and most stores close. Public holidays include the following:

New Year's Day January 1

Epiphany January 6

Dia de São Sebastião January 20 (St Sebastian Day; p20)

Carnaval February or March (to plan your dates for Carnaval, see p51)

Easter March or April

Tiradentes Day April 21

Dia de São Jorge April 23 (St George Day; p21)

Labor Day May 1

Corpus Christi May or June

Dia de Independência do Brasil September 7 (Independence Day; p22)

Our Lady of Aparecida Day October 12

All Souls' Day November 2

Proclamation Day November 15

Black Consciousness Day November 20

Christmas Day December 25

School break coincides with Rio's summer, running from mid-December to mid-February. It's when the city gets overrun with both Brazilian vacationers and travelers from abroad. Another break occurs in July, when Brazilian vacationers come to Rio.

INTERNET ACCESS

About the only places that don't provide internet access for guests packing laptops are budget hotels. Most other places – including hostels and midrange and top-end hotels – provide high-speed internet access from your room, and wi-fi is increasingly common. The city has also implemented free wi-fi on the beach, running from Leblon up to Copacabana – though carrying your laptop out to the sands isn't the brightest idea (that said, when the network is working, you can usually get service without crossing Av Atlântica).

Internet cafés are prevalent throughout Rio, with Copacabana having the highest concentration of them. Most places charge between R$4 and R$8 an hour.

@Onze (Map p84; Rua Marquês de Abrantes 11; 9am-11pm)

Central Fone (Map p90; Basement, Av Rio Branco 156, Centro; 9am-9pm Mon-Fri, 10am-4pm Sat)

Cyber Café (Map p90; Av Rio Branco 43, Centro; 9am-7pm Mon-Fri)

Fone Rio (Map p76; Rua Constante Ramos 22, Copacabana; 8am-midnight)

Jasmim Manga (Map p98; Rua Pascoal Carlos Magno 143, Santa Teresa; 10am-10pm Wed-Mon)

Letras e Expressões Ipanema (Map p64; Rua Visconde de Pirajá 276; 8am-midnight); Leblon (Map p66; Av Ataúlfo de Paiva 1292; 24hr)

Locutório (Map p76; Av NS Copacabana 1171, Copacabana; 8am-2am)

Telerede (Map p76; Av NS de Copacabana 209A, Copacabana; 8am-2am)

LEGAL MATTERS

In Brazil, 18 is the legal drinking age; it's also the legal age of consent and the minimum driving age.

You are required by law to carry some form of identification. For travelers, this generally means a passport, but a certified copy of the relevant ID page will usually be acceptable.

The police in Rio are very poorly paid, with the honest ones needing two or three other jobs to make ends meet. Corruption and bribery are not uncommon.

In the last few years, Rio has gotten serious about drunk driving, and the penalties of driving under the influence are severe. Marijuana and cocaine are plentiful in Rio, and both are very illegal. An allegation of drug trafficking or possession provides the police with the perfect excuse to extract a not-insignificant amount of money from you – and Brazilian prisons are brutal places. If you are arrested, know that you have the right to remain silent, and that you are innocent until proven guilty. You also have a right to visitation by your lawyer or a family member.

MAPS

The company Quatro Rodas produces the best maps of Rio and of Brazil. Its guide *Ruas Rio de Janeiro* has detailed maps of city streets published in book format. It's updated annually and is available at newsstands and bookstores (priced around R$30).

Riotur (p228) provides a useful free map of Rio de Janeiro with a detailed street layout. It's available from Riotur information booths.

MEDICAL SERVICES

Some private medical facilities in Rio de Janeiro are on a par with US hospitals. The UK and US consulates (p221) have lists of English-speaking physicians.

Brazilian blood banks don't always screen carefully. If you need an injection, ask to have the syringe unwrapped in front of you, or use your own.

Hospitals

The best hospital for foreigners is the Clinica Galdino Campos (Map p76; ☎ 2548-9966; www.galdinocampos.com.br; Av NS de Copacabana 492, Copacabana; 24hr). Here you'll find high-quality care and multilingual doctors (who even make outpatient calls). The clinic works with most international health plans and travel insurance policies.

Pharmacies

Pharmacies stock all kinds of drugs and sell them much more cheaply than in the West. However, when buying drugs anywhere in South America, be sure to check the expiration dates and specific storage conditions. Some drugs that are available in Brazil may no longer be recommended, or may even be banned, in other countries. Common names of prescription medicines in South America are likely to be different from the ones you're used to, so ask a pharmacist before taking anything you're not sure about.

There are scores of pharmacies in town, a number of which stay open 24 hours. In Copacabana try Drogaria Pacheco (Map p76; Av NS de Copacabana 115 & 534; 24hr). In Ipanema, visit Drogaria Pacheco (Map p64; ☎ 2239-5397; Av Visconde de Pirajá 592).

MONEY

Since 1994 the monetary unit of Brazil has been the *real* (R$, pronounced hay-*ow*); the plural is *reais* (pronounced hay-*ice*). The *real* is made up of 100 *centavos.* Most prices in this guide are quoted in *reais,* though some hoteliers prefer to list their rates in less-stable currencies like US dollars and euros.

Coins come in the usual denominations, and there is both a R$1 coin and a R$1 note.

Brazilian bank notes are printed in different colors with different animals on each, so there's no mistaking one denomination for another. In addition to the green R$1 note (hummingbird), there's a blue R$2 (hawksbill turtle), a violet R$5 (egret), a scarlet R$10 (macaw), a yellow R$20 (lion-faced monkey), a golden-brown R$50 (jaguar) and a blue R$100 (the not terribly romantic grouper fish).

Over the last six years the *real* has proven to be a strong, stable currency. For exchange rates, see inside the front cover of this book; for details of costs in Brazil, see p23.

ATMs

ATMs are the handiest way to access money in Rio. Unfortunately, there has been an alarming rise in card cloning, with travelers returning home to find unauthorized withdrawals on their cards. Always cover your hands when inputting your PIN and don't leave ATM receipts inside the bank.

Banco do Brasil, Bradesco and HSBC are the best banks to try when using a debit or credit card – also these ATMs don't currently charge a whopping R$10 transaction fee for foreign card ATM use (Citibank and Banco 24 Horas do charge this fee). Look for the sticker of your card's network (Visa, MasterCard, Cirrus or Plus) on the ATM, and you may have to try a few machines before finding one that accepts your card. Even though many ATMs advertise 24-hour service, these 24 hours usually fall between 6am and 10pm. This is really for the best, since it's unwise to withdraw money after dark. On holidays, ATM access ends at 3pm.

Most banks have a maximum withdraw limit of R$600, though with HSBC it's R$800.

You can find ATMs in the following locations:

Banco do Brasil Centro (Map p90; Rua Senador Dantas 105); Copacabana (Map p76; Av NS de Copacabana 1292); Galeão international airport (3rd fl, Terminal 1)

Citibank Centro (Map p90; Rua da Assembléia 100); Ipanema (Map p64; Rua Visconde de Pirajá 459A); Leblon (Map p66; Av Ataúlfo de Paiva 1260)

HSBC Centro (Map p90; Av Rio Branco 108); Copacabana (Map p76; Av NS de Copacabana 583); Ipanema (Map p64; Rua Vinícius de Moraes 71); Leblon (Map p66; Rua Cupertino Durão 219)

Changing Money

Easier than dealing with banks is going to money exchanges (*casas de câmbio*, usually shortened to *câmbios*). Recommended *câmbios* include Casa Aliança (Map p90; Rua Miguel Couto 35C, Centro; 9am-5:30pm) and Casa Universal (Map p76; Av NS de Copacabana 371, Copacabana).

Credit Cards

Visa is the most widely accepted credit card in Rio; MasterCard, American Express and Diners Club are also accepted by many hotels, restaurants and shops.

Credit-card fraud is rife in Rio, so be very careful. When making purchases keep your credit card in sight at all times. Have staff bring the machine to your table – don't give them your card.

To report lost or stolen credit cards, ring the following emergency numbers:

American Express ☎ 04134-3233-6266

Diners Club ☎ 0800-784-480

MasterCard ☎ 0800-891-3294

Visa ☎ 0800-891-3680

Tipping

Most service workers get tipped 10%, and as the people in these services make the minimum wage – which is not nearly enough to live on – you can be sure they need the money. In restaurants the service charge is usually included in the bill and is mandatory; when it is not included in the bill, it's customary to leave a 10% tip. If a waiter is friendly and helpful, you can give more.

There are many other places where tipping is not customary but is a welcome gesture. The workers at local juice stands, bars and coffee corners, and street and beach vendors, are all tipped on occasion. Parking assistants receive no wages and are dependent on tips, usually about R$2. Gas-station attendants, shoe shiners and barbers are also frequently tipped. Taxi drivers are not usually tipped, but it is common to round up the fare.

NEWSPAPERS & MAGAZINES

Ownership of Brazil's media industry is concentrated in the hands of a few organizations. O Globo, based in Rio, controls one of the nation's leading newspapers and TV networks.

Foreign-Language Press

In Rio you will find three daily newspapers in English: the *Miami Herald, USA Today* and the *International Herald Tribune*. They are usually on the newsstands by noon.

Imported newspapers and magazines are available, but are quite expensive. Several bookstores in Ipanema and Leblon offer foreign-language publications. See Shopping (p110) for details.

Portuguese-Language Press

The *Jornal do Brasil* and *O Globo* are Rio's main daily papers. Both have entertainment listings.

The country's best-selling weekly magazine is *Veja*. In Rio, it comes with the *Veja Rio* insert, which details the weekly entertainment options (the insert comes out on Sunday). It's a colorful, well-produced magazine, and it's not difficult reading if you're learning Portuguese. *Isto É* has the best political and economic analysis, and reproduces international articles from the British *Economist*, but it's not light reading. It also provides good coverage of current events.

For something a little more lowbrow, check out *O Dia*, which keeps Cariocas up-to-date with all the latest scandals. Environmental issues (both national and international) are covered in the glossy monthly magazine *Terra*.

ORGANIZED TOURS

There are many ways to experience Rio, whether by boat, helicopter, jeep or good old-fashioned walking. Joining an organized tour is also a good way to meet other travelers. For hiking and climbing tours, see p177.

Bay Cruises

With its magnificent coastline, Rio makes a fine backdrop for a cruise. Tours depart from the Marina de Glória (Map p87), and you can purchase tickets in advance from 8am to 4pm Monday to Friday. In addition to the new party boat (p166) and a dining cruise offered by Pink Fleet (p142), you can see the bay on the following boat trips:

Macuco Rio (Map p87; ☎ 3286-8130; www.macucorio.com.br; Marina de Glória, Glória; boat tours R$50-100) Offers daily tours in a high-velocity speed boat, which can carry 28 people. The first trip heads south to the pristine Cagarras Archipelago all the way to Redondo Island, where you can spot migratory birds and perhaps dolphins, turtles and even whales at certain times of the year. The other route heads to the north passing beside the Museu do Arte Contemporânea (MAC) and historic sites along the bay. Both tours last just under two hours, with a choice of morning or afternoon cruises.

Marlin Yacht Tours (Map p87; ☎ 2225-7434; www.marlinyacht.com.br; Marina de Glória, Glória; cruise R$50-80) Offers several daily tours aboard its large 30-person schooners to Cagarras Island, stopping for a beach swim along the way. It also offers sunset cruises, sailing and diving trips, and is known for its fishing tours.

Saveiros tours (Map p87; ☎ 2225-6064; www.saveiros.com.br; Marina de Glória, Glória; cruise R$50-80) Saveiros leads daily two-hour cruises out over Baía de Guanabara in large schooners. The route follows the coastline of Rio and Niterói with excellent views of Pão de Açúcar (Sugarloaf), the MAC, Ilha Fiscal and the old fort of Urca. You'll sail under the Niterói bridge.

City Tours

A number of private guides lead customized tours around the city, taking in the major daytime sights, leading nightlife tours and organizing just about anything Rio has to offer. Recommended guides include the following:

Aurélio Rio Guide (☎ 3592-0445, 7828-6382; www.aurelioriog uide.com) Offers low-key tours around the city, including a unique favela tour; also rents apartments.

Brazil Expedition (☎ 9998-2907; www.brazilexpedition.com; city tours R$85) The friendly English-speaking guides from Brazil Expedition run a variety of traditional tours around Rio, including trips to Cristo Redentor, nightlife tours in Lapa, game-day outings at Maracanã and favela tours.

Lisa Rio Tours (☎ 9894-6867; www.lisariotours.com) This outfit leads recommended tours around the city.

Madson Araújo (☎ 9395-3537; www.tourguiderio.com) Professional English- and French-speaking guide offering custom-made day or night tours around Rio.

Marcelo Esteves (☎ 9984-7654; marcelo.esteves@hotmail.com) A highly experienced multilingual Rio expert offering private tours around the city.

Favela Tours

The pioneer of favela tourism, Marcelo Armstrong (☎ 3322-2727, 9989-0074; www.favelatour.com.br; per person R$65), takes small groups on half-day tours to the favelas of Rocinha and Vila Canoas near São Conrado. The itinerary includes an explanation of the architecture and social infrastructure of the favela – particularly in relation to greater Rio de Janeiro. The trip also includes a walk through the streets, and a stop at both a community center and a handicraft center where visitors can purchase colorful artwork made by locals. A portion of Marcelo's profits goes toward social causes in the favela. To avoid paying a commission, call him directly.

Alternatively, you could try Be A Local (☎ 9643-0366; www.bealocal.com.br), a popular outfit that offers daily trips into Rocinha (you'll ride up by moto-taxi, and walk back down), with stops along the way (R$65 per person). Be a Local also organizes a night out at a *baile* funk party in Castelo das Pedras on Sunday night (R$60), and organizes trips to Maracanã on game days (R$80 to R$90).

Run by a longtime resident of Rocinha, Aurélio Rio Guide (☎ 3592-0445, 7828-6382; www.aurelioriog uide.com) shows an authentic side of life in Rocinha, going up by moto-taxi then descending through the narrow lanes and alleys, stopping en route to meet local residents (Aurélio is well known here). Tours are R$60 per person, or R$100 with the optional barbecue lunch at the end of the tour.

SHOULD I STAY OR SHOULD I GO?

Favela tours are now among the most popular day tours you can book in the city, but many visitors wonder if it's little more than voyeurism to take a trip into the Rocinha 'slums.' In fact, there can be some positive things that come out of the experience. Local residents, who feel marginalized by their own government, are often flattered that foreigners take such an interest in them. Projects focused on the arts are growing in the favelas; and one of the best ways to support the community directly is to purchase locally made paintings and handicrafts.

Choosing a guide is also essential. Try to get the lowdown before you sign up. Does he or she give time or money to the community? If so, how much and where does it go? Does the guide live in the favela? While the majority of agencies operating in Rocinha are simply opportunists, there are a few who are bringing more than just tourists to the neighborhood. Ask around, as for those who are interested in seeing Rocinha from the inside – as a volunteer – there are numerous ways to get involved.

Helicopter Tours

In business since 1991, Helisight (☎ 2511-2141; www.helisight.com.br; per person 6-/30-min flight R$150/520) offers eight different tours, lasting from six to 60 minutes. From one of its four helipads, helicopters travel around Cristo Redentor, from where you can get a bird's-eye view of Rio's most famous monument. Helisight also has flights over the Parque Nacional da Tijuca and above the mountains and beaches. Helipad locations are in Parque Nacional da Tijuca facing Corcovado; on Morro da Urca, the first cable-car stop up Pão de Açúcar (p80); on the edge of Lagoa (Map p70); and Pier Mauá downtown at the docks.

Jeep Tours

Excursions led by Jeep Tour (☎ 2108 5800; www.jeeptour.com.br) travel to the lush Parque Nacional da Tijuca in a large convertible jeep. Four-hour tours, which cost around R$85 per person, consist of a stop at the Vista Chinesa, then on to the forest for an easy hike, and a stop for a swim beneath a waterfall, before making the return journey. On the way back, you'll stop at Praia do Pepino, the landing strip for hang gliders from nearby Pedra Bonita. Other excursions offered by Jeep Tour include trips around the beaches of Búzios. The price of all tours includes pick up and drop off at your hotel.

Another reputable jeep tour operator is Rio by Jeep (☎ 9693-8800; www.riobyjeep.com) created by trusted hang-gliding pilot Ricardo Hamond. He offers two different jeep tours (in French, Spanish and English): one that provides a good overview of the city (following the waterfront from the Zona Sul to Centro, through Lapa up to Santa Teresa, on to Cristo Redentor then into Floresta da Tijuca, R$135 to R$170). The second focuses on Floresta da Tijuca, taking in views, a waterfall and a short hike (R$95 to R$110).

Walking Tours

Run by art historian Professor Carlos Roquette, who speaks English and French as well as Portuguese, Cultural Rio (☎ 9911-3829; www.culturalrio.com.br; tours from R$110) offers visitors an in-depth look at social and historical aspects of Rio de Janeiro. Roquette has a wealth of Carioca knowledge (and a quirky sense of humor) and he feels as comfortable discussing Jobim and the bossa nova scene as he does the sexual indiscretions of the early Portuguese rulers. Itineraries include a night at the Theatro Municipal, colonial Rio, baroque Rio, imperial Rio and a walking tour of Centro. He's been in business for over 20 years, and has led thousands of private walking tours.

POST

Postal services are decent in Brazil, and most mail gets through. Airmail letters to the USA and Europe usually arrive in a week or two. For Australia and Asia, allow three weeks.

There are yellow mailboxes on the street, but it's safer to go to a post office *(corréió)*. Most post offices are open 8am to 6pm Monday to Friday, and until noon on Saturday.

Branches include Botafogo (Map p80; Praia do Botafogo 324), Copacabana (Map p76; Av NS de Copacabana 540) and Ipanema (Map p64; Rua Prudente de Morais 147).

Any mail addressed to Poste Restante, Rio de Janeiro, Brazil, ends up at the post office in Centro (Map p90; Rua Primeiro de Março 64). The post office will hold mail for 30 days and is reasonably efficient.

SAFETY

Rio gets a lot of bad international press about violence, and unfortunately it's not all hype. The crime rate is high, and tourists are sometimes targeted. To minimize your risk of becoming a victim, you should take some basic precautions. First off: dress down and leave expensive (or even expensive-*looking*) jewelry, watches and sunglasses at home.

Copacabana and Ipanema beaches have a police presence, but robberies still occur on the sands, even in broad daylight. Don't ever take anything of value with you to the beach. Late at night, don't walk on any of the beaches.

Buses are well-known targets for thieves. Avoid taking them after dark, and keep an eye out while you're on them. Take taxis at night to avoid walking along empty streets and beaches. That holds especially true for Centro, which becomes deserted in the evening and on weekends, and is better explored during the week.

Get in the habit of carrying only the money you'll need for the day, so you don't have to flash a wad of *reais* when you pay for things. Cameras and backpacks attract a lot of attention. Consider using disposable cameras while you're in town; plastic shopping bags also nicely disguise whatever you're carrying. Maracanã football stadium is worth a visit, but take only your spending money for the day and avoid the crowded sections. Don't wander into the favelas at any time, unless you go with a knowledgeable guide.

If you have the misfortune of being robbed, slowly hand over the goods. Thieves in the city are only too willing to use their weapons if given provocation.

TELEPHONE

Rio is not known for its efficient telephone service, which hasn't improved much after privatization. Lines cross and fail frequently. The only solution is to keep trying.

Public phones are nicknamed *orelhões* (floppy ears). They take a phone card *(cartão telefônico)*, which are available from newsstands and street vendors. The cheapest cards start at R$5 for 20 units. All calls in Brazil, including local ones, are timed. Generally, one unit is enough for a brief local call (but calls to cell phones will quickly burn through your phone card). The phone will display how many units your card has left. Unless you're very lucky, you will have to try at least two or three phones before you find one that works.

Wait for a dial tone and then insert your phone card and dial your number. For information, call ☎ 102. The Portuguese-speaking operator can usually transfer you to an English-speaking operator.

To phone Rio from outside Brazil, dial your international access code, then 55 (Brazil's country code), 21 (Rio's area code) and the number.

Cell Phones

The cell phone is ubiquitous in Rio and goes by the name *celular* (this is also the nickname given to hip flasks of liquor).

Cell phones have eight-digit numbers, which usually begin with '9' or '8'. If you have an unlocked GSM phone (using the 900MHz and 1800MHz wavelengths, the same as used in Europe), you can simply buy a SIM card (called a *chip*) for around R$10 to R$16. To buy the card, you'll need your passport or at least a copy of it. Among the major carriers, TIM, Vivo, Oi and Claro, TIM generally has the best, most hassle-free service. You can then add minutes by purchasing pre-paid cards *(cartões pre-pago)* from any newspaper stand. Cards come in denominations of R$20, R$40, R$60, which you'll burn through at the rate of around R$1.90 per minute for a local call.

If you'd rather rent a phone, ConnectCom (☎ 2215-0002; www.connectcomrj.com.br) has the goods, and will even deliver to your door. With advance notice, it will also give you a number before you arrive. Phone rental is R$10 a day plus call charges.

Long-Distance & International Calls

International calls aren't cheap in Brazil. Skype (www.skype.com) is the best way to make free or inexpensive international calls from many internet cafés, hostels and guesthouses.

If you'd rather call from a landline, your best bet is buying an Embratel phone card from a newsstand (sold in denominations of R$20 to R$80). These have a bar on the back that you scratch off to reveal a code to enter along with the number you are calling (instructions are printed on the cards in English and Portuguese). You can make calls through some pay phones. Rates run about R$2 a minute for calls to the US, R$3 a minute to Europe, and about twice that to Asia and Australia.

Many internet cafés in Copacabana also have private phone booths for making calls. Rates, which fluctuate quite a bit, generally run at about R$1 to R$2 per minute for calls to the US and Europe, and much more to Australia and Asia. In Copacabana, try Telenet (Map p76; Rua Domingos Ferreira 59; 9am-10pm Mon-Sat, 11am-9pm Sun), Telerede (Map p76; Av NS de Copacabana 209A; 8am-2am) or Locutório (Map p76; Av NS Copacabana 1171; 8am-2am). In the center of town there is Central Fone (Map p90; Basement, Av Rio Branco 156, Centro; 9am-9pm Mon-Fri, 10am-4pm Sat).

To make a call to other parts of Brazil, you need to select the telephone company you want to use. To do this, you must insert a two-digit number between the 0 and the area code of the place you're calling. For example, to call Búzios from Rio, you need to dial ☎ 0 + xx + 22 (0 + phone company code + Búzios city code) + the eight-digit number. Embratel (code 21), Intelig (code 23) and TIM (code 41) are several big carriers.

Unfortunately, you cannot make collect calls from telephone offices. Public phones and those in hotels are your best bet. For calling collect within Rio, dial ☎ 9090 + phone number; to call collect within Brazil, dial ☎ 90 + phone company code + area code + phone number. A recorded message (in Portuguese) will ask you to say your name and where you're calling from after the beep. For international collect calls, try dialing ☎ 0800-703-2111.

TIME

Brazil has four official time zones. Rio, in the southeastern region, is three hours behind Greenwich Mean Time (GMT) and four hours behind during the northern-hemisphere summer. Rio also observes daylight-saving time, pushing the clocks one hour forward from late November to late February.

TOURIST INFORMATION

Riotur is the generally useful Rio city tourism agency. It operates a tourist information hot line called Alô Rio (☎ 0800-285-0555, 2542-8080; 9am-6pm Mon-Fri). The receptionists speak English and are very helpful. Riotur's flashy new multilingual website, www.rioguiaoficial.com.br/en, is also a good source of information.

All of the Riotur offices distribute maps and the quarterly *Rio Guide*, which is packed with information and major seasonal events. You'll find information kiosks at the following locations:

Copacabana (Map p76; ☎ 2541-7522; Av Princesa Isabel 183; 9am-6pm Mon-Fri) Has the most helpful staff.

Copacabana Beach Kiosk (Map p76; Av Atlântica near Rua Hilário de Gouveia; 8am-10pm)

Galeão international airport Terminal 1 (Domestic Arrival Hall; ☎ 3398-3034; 7am-11pm); Terminal 2 (International Arrival Hall; ☎ 3398-2245; 6am-11pm)

TRAVELERS WITH DISABILITIES

Rio is probably the most accessible city in Brazil for disabled travelers to get around, but that doesn't mean it's always easy. It's convenient to hire cars with driver-guides, but for only one person the expense is quite high compared to the cost of the average bus tour. If there are several people to share the cost, it's definitely worth it. For transport around the city, contact Coop Taxi (☎ 3295-9606).

The metro system has electronic wheelchair lifts, but it's difficult to know whether they're actually functional. Major sites are only partially accessible – there are about 10 steps to the gondola base of Pão de Açúcar, for instance; and although there is access to the base of Cristo Redentor, there are about two dozen steps to reach the statue itself. Jeep Tour (p226) recently began offering excursions to mobility-impaired travelers.

The streets and sidewalks along the main beaches have curb cuts and are wheelchair accessible, but most other areas do not have cuts. Most of the newer hotels have accessible rooms, but many restaurants have entrance steps.

The Centro de Vida Independente (Map p70; ☎ 2512-1088; www.cvi-rio.org.br, in Portuguese; Rua Marquês de São Vicente 225, Gávea) can provide advice for travelers with disabilities visiting Brazil.

Those in the USA might like to contact the Society for Accessible Travel & Hospitality (SATH; ☎ 212-447-7284; www.sath.org). SATH's website is a good resource for disabled travelers. Another excellent website to check is www.access-able.com.

VISAS

Brazil has a reciprocal visa system, so if your home country requires Brazilian nationals to secure a visa, then you will need one to enter Brazil. US, Canadian and Australian citizens need visas, but UK, New Zealand, French and German citizens do not. You can check your status with the Brazilian embassy or consulate in your home country.

Tourist visas are issued by Brazilian diplomatic offices. They are valid upon arrival in Brazil for a 90-day stay and are renewable in Brazil for an additional 90 days. In most Brazilian embassies and consulates, visas can be processed within 24 hours. You will need to present one passport photograph, a round-trip or onward ticket (or a photocopy of it) and a valid passport. If you decide to return to Brazil, your visa is valid for five years.

The fee for visas is also reciprocal. It's usually between US$20 and US$60, though for US citizens visas cost US$130.

Applicants under 18 years of age wanting to travel to Brazil must also submit a notarized letter of authorization from a parent or legal guardian.

Business travelers may need a business visa. These are also valid for 90 days and have the same requirements as a tourist visa. You'll need a letter on your company letterhead addressed to the Brazilian embassy or consulate, stating your business in Brazil, your arrival and departure dates, and your contacts. The letter from your employer must also assume full financial and moral(!) responsibility for you during your stay.

For up-to-the-minute advice on visa requirements for Brazil, check the Lonely Planet website at www.lonelyplanet.com.

Entry/Exit Card

On entering Brazil, all tourists must fill out an entry/exit card *(cartão de entrada/saida)*; immigration officials will keep half, you keep the other. They will also stamp your passport and, if for some reason they are not granting you the usual 90-day stay in Brazil, the number of days will be written beneath the word *Prazo* (Period) on the stamp in your passport.

When you leave Brazil, the second half of the entry/exit card will be taken by immigration officials. Don't lose your card while in Brazil, as it could cause hassles and needless delays when you leave.

WOMEN TRAVELERS

In Rio, foreign women traveling alone will scarcely be given a sideways glance. Although machismo is an undeniable element in the Brazilian social structure, it is less overt here than in many other parts of Latin America. Flirtation (often exaggerated) is a prominent element in Brazilian male-female relations. It goes both ways and is nearly always regarded as amusingly innocent banter. You should be able to stop unwelcome attention by merely expressing displeasure.

WORK

Brazil has high unemployment, and visitors who enter the country as tourists are not legally allowed to take jobs. It's not unusual for foreigners to find work teaching English in language schools, though. The pay isn't great (if you hustle you can make around R$1500 a month), but you can still live on it. For this kind of work it's always helpful to speak some Portuguese, although some schools insist that only English be spoken in class. Private language tutoring may pay a little more, but you'll have to do some legwork to find students.

To find out about this type of work, log on to a Brazilian web server such as terra (www.terra.com.br, in Portuguese) or uol (www.uol.com.br, in Portuguese) and search for English academies. You could also ask around at the English-language schools.

Volunteering

Río Voluntário (☎ 2262-1110; www.riovoluntario.org.br, in Portuguese), headquartered in Rio de Janeiro, supports several hundred volunteer organizations, from those involved in social work and the environment to health care. It's an excellent resource for finding volunteer work.

One notable volunteer organization is the Rio-based Iko Poran (☎ 3852-2916; www.ikoporan.org), which links the diverse talents of volunteers with those required by needy organizations. Previous volunteers have worked as dance, music, art and language instructors, among other things. Iko Poran also provides housing options for volunteers.

The UK-based Task Brasil (www.taskbrasil.org.uk) is another laudable organization that places volunteers in Rio. Here, you'll have to make arrangements in advance and pay a fee that will go toward Task Brasil projects and your expenses as a volunteer.

See Action Without Borders (www.idealist.org) for the best volunteer opportunities.

LANGUAGE

Portuguese is one of the most commonly spoken languages in the world, with over 200 million speakers globally. The majority of them hail from Brazil, the only Portuguese-speaking country in South America. Brazilian Portuguese differs from European Portuguese, owing in part to New World influences: Portuguese colonists first arrived in the 16th century, and as they came into contact with the Tupi tribes living along the Atlantic coast, they adopted the Tupi language to such an extent that Tupi, along with Portuguese, became the lingua franca of the colony. The Jesuits had a great deal to do with this, since they translated prayers and songs into Tupi, and in so doing recorded and promoted the language. However, Tupi was banned when the crown expelled the Jesuits in 1759, and Portuguese remained the country's official language.

In the 19th century, the Bantu and Yoruba languages arrived in Brazil with African slaves. At the same time, European Portuguese went through linguistic changes as it came in contact with French, while Brazilian Portuguese retained some of its earlier features. Today the differences between the two variaties are similar to those between American English and British English.

Although Portuguese shares many lexical similarities with its Romance-language cousin Spanish, the two are quite different. Spanish speakers will be able to read many things in Portuguese, but will have difficulty understanding Brazilians. English is not commonly taught in Brazil, except in the more exclusive private schools. Fortunately Brazilians are quite patient, and appreciate any effort to speak their language. If you want to learn more of the lingo than we've included here, pick up a copy of Lonely Planet's comprehensive and user-friendly *Brazilian Portuguese* phrasebook.

PRONUNCIATION

Vowels

Vowel sounds are quite similar to those found in English, so you should be able to get talking with confidence.

A characteristic of Brazilian Portuguese is the use of nasal vowels. Nasalization is represented by n or m after a vowel, or by a tilde over it (eg ã). The nasal i exists only approximately in English, with the 'ing' in 'sing', for example. Nasal vowels are pronounced as if you're trying to force the sound out your nose rather than your mouth, creating a similar sound to when you hold your nose.

Consonants

The consonant sounds in Brazilian Portuguese are very similar to those of English, and even the rolled r will be familiar to most people (it's similar to the 'r' in Spanish). Also note:

ç	as the 's' as in 'sleep'
ch	as the 'sh' as in 'ship'
lh	as the 'lli' in 'million'
nh	as the 'ny' in 'canyon'

SOCIAL

Meeting People

Hello.
Olá.
Hi.
Oi.
Goodbye.
Tchau.
Please.
Por favor.
Thank you (very much).
(Muito) obrigado/obrigada. (m/f)
Yes./No.
Sim./Não.
Excuse me.
Com licença.
Sorry.
Desculpa.
Do you speak (English)?
Você fala (inglês)?
Do you understand?
Você entende?
I (don't) understand.
Eu (não) entendo.
What does … mean?
O que quer dizer …?

OI, CARA! (HEY, GUY/GAL)

Making an effort with the language is something Brazilians will greatly appreciate. *Diria* (slang) is a big part of the Carioca dialect spoken by the residents of Rio. Here are a few words and phrases :

babaca (ba·*ba*·ka) – jerk
bunda (*boon*·da) – bottom/arse
Eu gosto de você. (*e*·oo *gosh*·too zhi vo·*se*) – I like you.
Falou! (fa·*low*) – Absolutely!/You said it!.
Fique à vontade. (feek a van·*tazh*) – Make yourself at home.
fio dental (*fee*·oo den·*tow*) – dental floss, aka bikini
gata/gato (*ga*·ta/*ga*·too) – good-looking woman/man
Nossa! (*no*·sa; lit, 'Our Lady') – Gosh!/You don't say!
sunga (*soong*·ga) – tiny Speedo-type swim shorts favored by Carioca men
Ta ótimo/Ta legal! (ta *a*·che·moo/ta lee·*gow*) – Great/Cool/OK!
Tudo bem? (*too*·doo beng) – Everything OK?
Tudo bem. (*too*·doo beng) – Everything's OK.
Valeu. (va·*le*·o) – Thanks.
Vamu nessa! (va·moo·*ne*·sa) – Let's go!

Could you please …?
Você poderia por favor …?

repeat that	repetir isto
speak more slowly	falar mais devagar
write it down	escrever num papel

Going Out

What's on …?
O que está acontecendo …?

locally	aqui perto
this weekend	neste final de semana
today/tonight	hoje/á noite

Where can I find …?
Onde posso encontrar …?

clubs	um lugar para dançar
gay venues	lugares gays
places to eat	lugares para comer
pubs	bares

PRACTICAL

Question Words

Who?	Quem?
What?	(o) que?
When?	Quando?
Where?	Onde?
How?	Como é que?
Why?	Por que?
Which?	Qual/Quais? (sg/pl)

Numbers & Amounts

0	zero
1	um
2	dois
3	três
4	quatro
5	cinco
6	seis
7	sete
8	oito
9	nove
10	dez
11	onze
12	doze
13	treze
14	quatorze
15	quinze
16	dezesseis
17	dezesete
18	dezoito
19	dezenove
20	vinte
21	vinte e um
22	vinte e dois
30	trinta
40	quarenta
50	cinquenta
60	sessenta
70	setenta
80	oitenta
90	noventa
100	cem
200	duzentos
1000	mil

Days

Monday	segunda-feira
Tuesday	terça-feira
Wednesday	quarta-feira
Thursday	quinta-feira
Friday	sexta-feira
Saturday	sábado
Sunday	domingo

Banking

Where's …?
Onde tem …?

an ATM	um caixa automático
a foreign exchange office	uma loja de câmbio

I'd like to …
Gostaria de …

cash a check	descontar um cheque
change money	trocar dinheiro
change travelers checks	trocar traveller cheques

Post

Where is the post office?
Onde fica o correio?

I want to send a …
Quero enviar …

fax	um fax
letter	uma carta
parcel	uma encomenda
postcard	um cartão-postal

I want to buy …
Quero comprar …

an aerogram	um aerograma
an envelope	um envelope
stamps	selos

Phones & Cell Phones/Mobiles

I want to make …
Quero …

a call (to …)	telefonar (para …)
a reverse-charge/ collect call	fazer uma chamada a cobrar

I'd like a/an …
Eu gostaria de …

adaptor plug	comprar um adaptador
battery for my phone	comprar uma bateria para o meu telephone
cell/mobile phone for hire	alugar um cellular
phone card	comprar um cartão telefônico
prepaid cell/ mobile phone	comprar um cellular pré-pago
SIM card for your network	comprar um chip para sua rede

Internet

Where's the local internet cafe?
Onde tem um internet café na redondeza?

I'd like to …
Gostaria de …

check my email	checar meu e-mail
get online	ter acesso à internet

Transport

When's the … (bus)?
Quando sai o … (ônibus)?

first	primeiro
last	último
next	próximo

What time does it leave?
Que horas sai?
What time does it get to (Parati)?
Que horas chega em (Parati)?

Which … goes to (Niterói)?
Qual o … que vai para (Niterói)?

boat	barco
bus	ônibus
plane	avião
train	trem

Is this taxi available?
Este táxi está livre?
Please put the meter on.
Por favor ligue o taxímetro.
How much is it to …?
Quanto custa até …?
Please take me to (this address).
Me leve para (este endereço) por favor.

FOOD

breakfast	café da manhã
lunch	almoço
dinner	jantar
snack	lanche

Can you recommend a …?
Você pode recomendar um …?

bar/pub	bar
cafe	café
restaurant	restaurante

Is service/cover charge included?
O serviço está incluído na conta?
What's in that dish?
O que tem neste prato?
I'll have that.
Eu quero isto.
I'm a vegetarian.
Eu sou vegetariano/vegetariana. (m/f)
I don't eat fish/meat/poultry.
Eu não como peixe/carne/frango.
I'm allergic to (peanuts).
Eu sou alérgico/alérgica à (amendoims). (m/f)

Common Brazilian Dishes

acarajé – specialty of Bahia made from peeled brown beans mashed with salt and onions, and then fried in *dendê*; inside these croquettes is dried shrimp, pepper and tomato sauce
angú – a kind of savory cake made with very fine corn flour called *fubá,* mixed with water and salt
bobó de camarão – manioc paste cooked and flavored with dried shrimp, coconut milk and cashew nuts
camarão á paulista – unshelled fresh prawns (shrimp) fried in olive oil with lots of garlic and salt
canja – hearty soup made with chicken broth
caranguejjada – crab cooked whole in seasoned water
carne de sol – tasty salt-cured meat, grilled and served with beans, rice and vegetables
caruru – dish of African origin, made with boiled okra or other vegetables mixed with grated onion, salt, shrimp, chili peppers and *dendê*; traditionally, a saltwater fish such as *garoupa* (grouper) is added
casquinha de caranguejo or siri – stuffed crab prepared with manioc flour
cozido – any kind of stew, usually with vegetables (such as potatoes, sweet potatoes, carrots and manioc)
dendê – palm oil
dourado – a scrumptious freshwater fish found throughout Brazil
farofa – otherwise known as cassava or manioc flour, it is a legacy of the Indians; it remains a Brazilian staple
feijoada – the Carioca answer to cassoulet; see p146
frango ao molho pardo – chicken pieces stewed with vegetables and covered with a sauce made from the blood of the bird
moqueca – a kind of sauce or stew, as well as a style of cooking from Bahia, properly prepared in a clay pot; fish, shrimp, oyster, crab or a combination of those are served with a *moqueca* sauce, which is defined by its heavy use of *dendê* and coconut milk, and often contains peppers and onions
moqueca capixaba – a *moqueca* from Espírito Santo that uses lighter *urucum* (from the seeds of the berrylike fruit of the annatto tree) oil from the Indians instead of *dendê*
pato no tucupi – roast duck with garlic, cooked in *tucupi* sauce, which is made from the juice of the manioc plant and *jambu,* a local vegetable
peixada – fish cooked in broth with vegetables and eggs
peixe a delícia – broiled fish usually served in a sauce made with bananas and coconut milk
petiscos – appetizers
picanha – thin cut of rump steak
prato de verão – literally, a 'summer plate,' which is served at many juice stands in Rio; basically a fruit salad
prato feito – literally a 'made plate,' usually a serving of rice, beans and salad, with chicken, fish or beef; sometimes abbreviated to 'PF'
pirarucu ao forno – *Pirarucu,* the most famous fish from the rivers of Amazônia, baked with lemon and other seasonings
tacacá – an Indian dish of dried shrimp cooked with pepper, *jambu,* manioc and much more
tutu á mineira – bean paste with toasted bacon and manioc flour, often served with cooked cabbage
vatapá – a seafood dish with a thick sauce made from manioc paste, coconut and *dendê*; perhaps the most famous Brazilian dish of African origin
xinxim de galinha – pieces of chicken flavored with garlic, salt and lemon; shrimp and *dendê* are often added

EMERGENCIES

Help!
Socorro!
It's an emergency.
É uma emergência.
Could you please help?
Você pode ajudar, por favor?
Call a doctor/an ambulance!
Chame um médico/uma ambulância!
Call the police!
Chame a polícia!
Where's the police station?
Onde é a delegacia de polícia?

HEALTH

Where's the nearest ...?
Onde fica ... mais perto?

(night) chemist	a farmácia (noturna)
dentist	o dentista
doctor	o médico
hospital	o hospital
medical centre	a clínica médica

I'm ill.
Estou doente.
I need a doctor (who speaks English).
Eu preciso de um médico (que fale inglês).

I have (a) ...
Tenho ...

diarrhoea	diarréia
fever	febre
nausea	náusea
pain	dor
sore throat	dor de garganta

GLOSSARY

See p54 for more Carnaval terms.

açaí – juice made from an Amazonian berry
agouti – small rodent; looks like a large guinea pig
a quilo – per kilo

baía – bay
baile – dance party in the favelas
baile funk – dance, ball
bairro – neighborhood
baixo – popular area with lots of restaurants and bars
banda – street party
barraca – food stall
batida – mixes of *cachaça*, sugar and assorted fruit juices
berimbau – stringed instrument used to accompany *capoeira*
bloco – see *banda*
bonde – tram
bondinho – little tram
boteco – small neighborhood bar
botequim – bar with table service

cachaça – potent cane spirit
caipirinha – *cachaça* cocktail
câmbios – money exchange
Candomblé – religion of African origin
capoeira – Afro-Brazilian martial art
capela – chapel
cara – guy, dude (slang term used for male or female)
Carioca – resident of Rio
carro – car
cartão telefônico – phone card
celular – cellular (mobile) phone
cerveja – beer
cervejaria – pub
chocante – cool, excellent
chope – draft beer
chorinho or choro – romantic, intimate samba
churrascaria – traditional barbecue restaurant
cidade maravilhosa – nickname for Rio de Janeiro (literally 'marvelous city')
convento – convent
corréio – post office

escola de samba – samba school
estação do metro – metro (subway) station
estrada – road

farmácia – pharmacy (chemist)
favela – shanty town
fazenda – ranch, plantation, large farm
feijoada – black beans and pork stew
feira – open-air market
festa – party
forró – traditional fast-paced music from the northeast of Brazil
frescão – air-conditioned bus
frescobol – game played on the beach with two wooden racquets and a rubber ball
futebol – football (soccer)

gafieira – dance club/dance hall
gente – people

igreja – church
ilha – island

jardim – garden

lagoa – lake
largo – plaza
legal – cool, excellent
livraria – bookshop

malandros – con men
mar – sea
Mata Atlântica – Atlantic rainforest
mirante – lookout
morro – mountain
mulatto – person of mixed black and white ancestry
museu – museum

novela – TV soap opera

onibus – bus
orelhôes – public telephones
orixá – spirit or deity of the Candomblé religion

pagode – relaxed and rhythmic form of samba; first popularized in Rio in the 1970s
parque – park
ponte – bridge
posto – lifeguard station
pousada – guest house
praça – square
praia – beach

reais – plural of *real*
real – Brazil's unit of currency
refrigerante – soft drink
rio – river
rodoviária – bus terminal
rua – street

salgados – bar snacks
sobreloja – above the store; first floor up
suco – juice bar
supermercado – supermarket

trem – train

Zona Norte – Northern Zone
Zona Sul – Southern Zone

BEHIND THE SCENES

THIS BOOK

This 7th edition of Rio de Janeiro was written by Regis St Louis, with contributions from Carmen Michael (The Dance Halls of Old, Samba da Mesa), Tom Phillips (Brazil's Favorite Voice) and Marcos Silviano do Prado (Carnaval Party Planner). Regis also wrote the 4th, 5th and 6th editions, while editions one to three were written by Andrew Draffen, with contributions from Heather Schlegel on the 3rd edition.

This guidebook was commissioned in Lonely Planet's Oakland office and produced by the following:

Commissioning Editors Kathleen Munnelly, Suki Gear

Coordinating Editor Evan Jones

Coordinating Cartographer Amanda Sierp

Coordinating Layout Designer Kerrianne Southway

Managing Editors Bruce Evans, Brigitte Ellemor

Managing Cartographers Adrian Persoglia, Alison Lyall

Managing Layout Designer Indra Kilfoyle

Assisting Editors Janice Bird, Kristin Odijk, Anna Metcalfe, Jocelyn Harewood

Assisting Cartographer Andrew Smith

Cover Research Pepi Bluck

Internal Image Research Sabrina Dalbesio

Language Content Laura Crawford

Thanks to Heather Dickson, Averil Robertson, John Taufa, Rebecca Lalor, John Mazzocchi, Juan Winata, Lisa Knights, Raphael Richards, Paul Iacona

Cover photographs Cristo Redentor statue on Corcovado, Kevin O'Hara/Photolibrary (top); Woman doing a somersault on the beach, Ricardo Gomes/Lonely Planet Images (bottom)

Internal photographs All images are copyright of the photographer unless otherwise indicated. Many of the images in this guide are available for licensing from Lonely Planet Images: www.lonelyplanetimages.com.

THANKS

REGIS ST LOUIS

I owe a big thanks to many Cariocas and expats who helped along the way. Special thanks to Cristiano Nogueira, Cândida Botafogo, Marcelo Esteves, Marta & John Miller, Madson Araujo, Aurélio Curtim, Simone Theisen, Nelly Pager, Ricardo Hamond, John Tabor, Laurent Tran, Marcos Silviano do Prado, Kevin Raub and the many travelers who wrote in with tips. I'd also like to thank the folks at Riotur, the Caprichosos de Pilares friends who paraded with me during Carnaval and the Rocinha gang for fun during the technical rehearsal. At Lonely Planet, I'd like to thank Kathleen Munnelly, Craig Kilburn, Alison Lyall and the other talented editors working behind the scenes to make the book a success.

OUR READERS

Many thanks to the travelers who used the last edition and wrote to us with helpful hints, useful advice and interesting anecdotes:

Paulina Achurra, Moreau Alexandra, Rob B, Leanne Bird, Stanley Burg, Ines Cormier, Ingrid Cozma, Bianka Cypriano,

THE LONELY PLANET STORY

Fresh from an epic journey across Europe, Asia and Australia in 1972, Tony and Maureen Wheeler sat at their kitchen table stapling together notes. The first Lonely Planet guidebook, *Across Asia on the Cheap*, was born.

Travelers snapped up the guides. Inspired by their success, the Wheelers began publishing books to Southeast Asia, India and beyond. Demand was prodigious, and the Wheelers expanded the business rapidly to keep up. Over the years, Lonely Planet extended its coverage to every country and into the virtual world via lonelyplanet.com and the Thorn Tree message board.

As Lonely Planet became a globally loved brand, Tony and Maureen received several offers for the company. But it wasn't until 2007 that they found a partner whom they trusted to remain true to the company's principles of traveling widely, treading lightly and giving sustainably. In October of that year, BBC Worldwide acquired a 75% share in the company, pledging to uphold Lonely Planet's commitment to independent travel, trustworthy advice and editorial independence.

Today, Lonely Planet has offices in Melbourne, London and Oakland, with over 500 staff members and 300 authors. Tony and Maureen are still actively involved with Lonely Planet. They're traveling more often than ever, and they're devoting their spare time to charitable projects. And the company is still driven by the philosophy of *Across Asia on the Cheap*: 'All you've got to do is decide to go and the hardest part is over. So go!'

Ellyn Freed, Anne Gbiorczyk-Morel, Pat Glionna, Darren Halford, Steven Hibbert, Hotel Novo Mundo, Hotel Santa Teresa, Jonas Jacobsen, Vicente Jatahy, Bernd Kleinmaier, Anna Korbut, John Landstreet, Alexandra Malsoute, Alexey Marina, Zach Marks, Eduardo Marques, James Masi, Julie Mitchell, Laure Modesti, Vincent Muraire, Daniel Musikant, Anneleen Nauwelaerts, Chia-Yih Phung, Sean Riordan, Alexandre Rocca-Serra, Greg Rutland, Victor Santiago, Scott True, Colin Turner, Karin Vavatzanidis, Joris Verboomen, Constance Wong.

SEND US YOUR FEEDBACK

We love to hear from travelers – your comments keep us on our toes and help make our books better. Our well-traveled team reads every word on what you loved or loathed about this book. Although we cannot reply individually to postal submissions, we always guarantee that your feedback goes straight to the appropriate authors, in time for the next edition. Each person who sends us information is thanked in the next edition and the most useful submissions are rewarded with a free book.

To send us your updates – and find out about Lonely Planet events, newsletters and travel news – visit our award-winning website: lonelyplanet.com/contact.

Note: We may edit, reproduce and incorporate your comments in Lonely Planet products such as guidebooks, websites and digital products, so let us know if you don't want your comments reproduced or your name acknowledged. For a copy of our privacy policy visit lonelyplanet.com/privacy.

Notes

Notes

INDEX

See also separate indexes for:

ARTS

CINEMAS

PERFORMING ARTS

DRINKING

BARS

ELECTRONICS

FOOD MARKETS

FOOTWEAR

HANDICRAFTS

HEALTH FOOD

HOME DECO

JEWELRY

MARKETS & FAIRS

000 map pages
000 photographs

MUSIC

MUSICAL INSTRUMENTS

OUTDOOR GEAR

PHOTOGRAPHY

SHOPPING CENTERS

WINE & SPIRITS

SIGHTS

ARTS CENTERS

BEACHES

CHURCHES & CATHEDRALS

CULTURAL CENTERS

FOOD MARKETS

FOOTBALL

FORESTS

FORTS

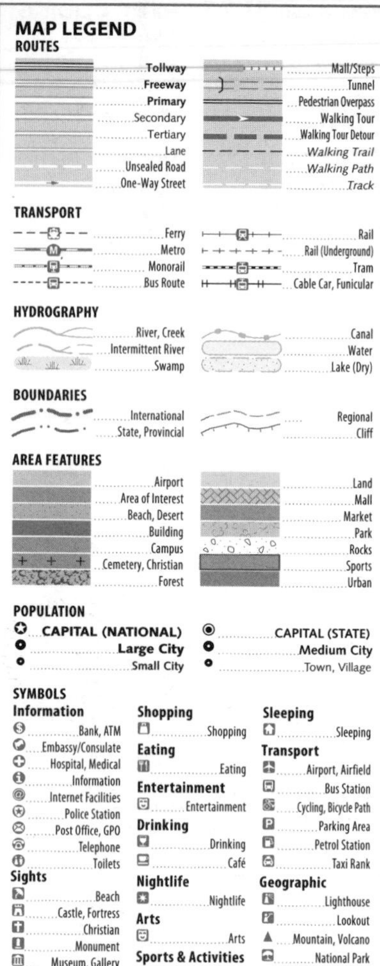

Published by Lonely Planet Publications Pty Ltd
ABN 36 005 607 983

Australia (Head Office)
Locked Bag 1, Footscray, Victoria 3011,
☎03 8379 8000, fax 03 8379 8111

USA 150 Linden St, Oakland, CA 94607,
☎510 250 6400, toll free 800 275 8555,
fax 510 893 8572

UK 2nd fl, 186 City Rd, London, EC1V 2NT,
☎020 7106 2100, fax 020 7106 2101

Contact talk2us@lonelyplanet.com
lonelyplanet.com/contact

Printed by Toppan Security Printing Pte. Ltd.
Printed in Singapore.